Take a Look

Observation and Portfolio Assessment in Early Childhood

THIRD EDITION

SUE MARTIN

Centennial College

PEARSON

Addison Wesley

Toronto

To
Pauline Brown
Nursery Class
Wanstead Church School
London E.11
England

because she practices what I preach

National Library of Canada Cataloguing in Publication

Martin, Sue, 1951-
    Take a look : observation and portfolio assessment in early childhood / Sue Martin. — 3rd ed.

Includes bibliographical references and index.
ISBN 0-201-76005-3

    1. Child development—Evaluation—Textbooks. 2. Observation
(Psychology)—Methodology—Textbooks. 3. Behavioral assessment of
children—Textbooks. I. Title.

BF722.M37 2003   305.231   C2003-900278-0

ISBN 0-201-76005-3

Vice-President, Editorial Director: Michael J. Young
Acquisitions Editor: Christine Cozens
Marketing Manager: Ryan St. Peters
Associate Editor: Paula Druzga
Production Editor: Charlotte Morrison-Reed
Production Coordinator: Patricia Ciardullo
Page Layout: Heidi Palfrey
Art Director: Mary Opper
Interior and Cover Design: Gail Ferreira Ng-A-Kien
Cover Image: Bananastock Royalty Free/First Light

 3 4 5   08 07 06 05 04

Printed and bound in Canada.

PEARSON
Addison
Wesley

Contents

Preface

Take a Look: Observation and Portfolio Assessment in Early Childhood is intended for people who seek a deep and reflective approach to working and living with young children. The majority of these readers will fall into one or more of the following categories:

- early childhood educators
- student teachers
- kindergarten and elementary school teachers (K–3)
- parents of young children
- resource teachers
- educational psychologists
- child and youth workers
- social workers

The book provides a focused approach to authentic assessment in early childhood. Its detailed coverage of observation methods leads the reader to develop skills in seeing, recording, and understanding the development of young children. While offered as the basis of authentic assessment processes, it also reflects a sympathetic understanding of childhood and encourages adults to be responsive to the individual needs of each child.

Infants, toddlers, preschoolers, and school-age children can be observed in numerous settings. This book guides readers to take note of the context of children as they observe and record their behaviour. In philosophy *Take a Look* emphasizes the importance of our taking the time to gather pertinent information about individual children so that we can understand them holistically. Armed with this knowledge, the adults in the children's lives can learn to respond more fully to those children. A child's family background and culture specially influence each child's life, and these factors are important parts of the diversity that enriches our society. Professionals in early childhood education must acquire skills in working with parents as partners in the lives of their children and familiarize themselves with the children's characteristics, gaining insight into the children's backgrounds. This can be challenging as there is a fine line between open inquiry and being intrusive. Making decisions about children's needs should be made in consultation with their parents and other caregivers. When we understand why the partnership exists, both educators and parents find that information important about that child is more likely to surface. *Take a Look* helps readers understand why this context is important and how to work collaboratively while sharing information appropriately.

Children spend much of their time in family environments, child-care centres, play groups, early learning settings, nursery schools, and the early grades in school. The child's development takes place in all of these settings. Readers of *Take a Look* will learn to observe and record what is happening in ways that benefit both the children and the observer. Observing children may be part of an adult's own learning process—it is the best way to understand the principles and theories of child development. However, in practice, observing, recording, and analyzing observational information are undertaken to improve the child's environment, to help make decisions appropriate to those children and for sharing information with families.

This book focuses on why naturalistic observation can give us better information about who a child is and what he needs than any standardized testing can provide. While some standardized measures of performance are needed in limited situations, the emphasis here is on the significance of a contextualized understanding of each child's competence. In *Take a Look* I explain why observation and portfolio documentation provide full, meaningful, and authentic ways of assessing children's development. I believe this approach also gives educators a clear idea of how to support a child's emerging skills, deliver a curriculum according to his or her individual styles, and when to plan to introduce meaningful learning experiences.

The more the adult observes, the better she can understand the patterns of children's growth and development. The educator's skills in documenting that development will improve with practice. With a range of techniques in her professional toolkit the educator will learn to employ the methods that meet her needs. As observer she will fine-tune what she is looking for and be able to interpret what she has recorded. As the reader increases her knowledge of the principles of child development she will gradually be able to apply them to the children she observes.

Making hasty decisions about children can affect them negatively in the long term. Similarly, judging children's behaviour based on too little evidence can also damage them, and assessing children in a way that leads to planning that is not responsive to the individual needs or developmental stage can be avoided by using the *Take a Look* approach. I deal with many issues throughout the book. I encourage you to be thoughtful and reflective as an observer while honouring both your own objectivity and your intuitive responses to children.

Take a Look also takes advantage of recent research in neuroscience, as well as up-to-date perspectives on children's development. You will find that the contents follow current trends in curriculum development and guidance strategies. Many educators are struggling to maintain what they know to be good developmentally appropriate practice with young children while having to deliver a content-driven curriculum at the same time. *Take a Look* shows how the authentic assessment process can be used as either the central approach to assessment or to complement and round out system-wide formal assessments.

Parents reading this book will learn to look at their children more closely, record what they see, and appreciate the significance of the child's behaviour. In learning about authentic assessment, parents will also be able to support that approach being used in a school or other setting. This will benefit everyone.

An Outline of the Book

Chapter 1 explores why, what, when, and how to observe young children. It outlines the principles of observation and portfolio assessment. It also clearly explains why observation is central to professional practice and refers to key early-childhood professional organizations. Chapter 2 focuses on the mechanics of children's development. It outlines developmental domains, patterns, principles, and some theories. Up-to-date perspectives on human development and individuality are discussed.

Chapters 3 through 7 each explore a different method, style, or means of observational recording and demonstrate how each of them can be used. New technologies and their use are highlighted. Chapter 8 addresses the philosophy and uses of portfolios in early childhood. This chapter draws from the preceding chapters in demonstrating how different observational methods can be incorporated into the process. I define approaches to data collection in detail. The processes of handling, sorting, selecting, and analyzing the data are also discussed at length.

Chapter 9 deals with measuring educational outcomes and discusses the philosophy and challenges of this kind of documentation. Chapter 10 then offers an overview of the uses and limitations of standardized screening and various assessment tools. Chapter 11, the final chapter, encourages the reader to take a fresh look at the child's environment and consider how it might influence her behaviour. I identify indicators of quality environments based on the most current research. I urge readers to be more aware of the impact of the child's environment on both her immediate surroundings and wider circle, and I recommend tools you can use to focus on those environmental factors and record significant data for the child's benefit.

Learning Outcomes

In addition to the specific learning outcomes that each chapter aims to fulfil, the book as a whole helps readers achieve the following five general outcomes:

- Develop a philosophy of assessment of children in their early years.
- Compare and contrast a variety of different observation and recording methods, and select and use those that best meet their needs.
- Create a comprehensive portfolio record-keeping system suited to the needs of an early childhood agency and its stakeholders.
- Analyze observational and contextual data in order to create holistic and sympathetic assessments of individual children.
- Demonstrate the use of observation and portfolio documentation as a measure of program accountability.

Features of the third edition

After the book's success in its previous editions it was exciting to update and polish the material for this new edition. I very much appreciate the feedback I've received from readers, which has resulted in the following changes:

- several changes in format to make the book more reader-friendly
- a wider group of stakeholders are addressed who influence the lives of children (as noted at the beginning of this preface)
- the focus and the content of *Take a Look* have been proved valid—and manageable through its widespread use in both education and child-care settings
- a broader review of perspectives on children's development
- inclusion of a section on children's sexual development—and its indicators in children's behaviour
- updated ideas about using newer technologies for recording
- the assessment cycle and its authenticity are explained more clearly

- a wider perspective on what constitutes the child's environment and how to observe aspects of it
- summaries at the end of the chapters provide a quick overview of those chapters
- useful web sites are added

General features of *Take a Look*

Focus Questions   Each chapter begins with a series of questions that enable readers to review their current understanding and skill level. The focus questions start the process of learning with reflection and provide an overview of the content. Answers are provided in the *Instructor's Manual* for review.

Learning Outcomes   Chapters have their own learning outcomes that summarize the knowledge readers will gain.

Definitions   Clear explanations of the methods of observation and information-gathering are essential to understanding, choosing, and using each. The definitions help readers find basic information quickly and efficiently.

Features   The characteristics of each observational method are fully described. "Key Features" boxes provide quick summaries of important points to help students choose an appropriate method for each situation.

Using the Methods Advantages and **Disadvantages**   All data-collection techniques have positive and negative aspects; concise lists clearly indicate the strengths and weaknesses of each observation method. These lists will help students select appropriate methods and avoid common pitfalls.

Child Development Focus   Each standard method of observing and recording data is reviewed, clearly indicating which developmental domains are addressed or likely to be highlighted.

Taking a Special Look   Students and practitioners alike may encounter children with a wide variety of special needs, whether developmental, linguistic, or cultural. Notes give information on how to observe children with special needs and what to keep in mind when analyzing these observations.

Key Terms/Glossary   Key terms are shown in boldface the first time they are defined in each chapter and are defined in the glossary at the end of the book as well. Refer to the glossary as a quick aid to understanding the text. Use the lists of key terms at the end of each chapter to review and test your knowledge.

Summaries   These quickly pull together and highlight the major points of each chapter.

Observation Samples   Samples that demonstrate good practice for the core observational and recording methods are included at the end of each chapter (except Chapter 10, "Screening and Assessment"). As every observation is unique to the child, situation, observer, and chosen methodology, an "ideal" is difficult to supply, but all the samples have identifiable strengths. Learners are asked pertinent questions to help them appreciate the strengths and challenges of each sample.

Bibliography   This includes all the references cited in the text as well as other books and articles that offer particularly useful information on topics covered in *Take a Look*.

Web sites   Useful Internet sites are offered at the end of each chapter. They will reinforce and extend your understanding of that chapter.

Instructor's Manual

The *Instructor's Manual* offers a variety of discussion points, activity ideas, and expanded resources, including the following:

History Notes   To help the learner appreciate the background and development of the ideas presented in each chapter, a set of history notes was provided at the beginning of the chapters of the first two editions and now have been moved to the *Instructor's Manual*. These notes help us understand the changes in the ways children are perceived and in how records are kept to monitor their progress.

Assignment Options   The assignments are designed to build your skills in the use of observation methods as well as to aid your appreciation of the philosophy of observation as developmentally appropriate evaluation. Individual and group exercises will help you improve your perceptions, make recordings that are more objective, and analyze data more successfully. They also support your development of critical thinking skills.

The assignments include examples to critique, along with criteria for assessing them. This evaluation process is an essential learning tool. Instructors will find the evaluation criteria helpful in teaching and in assessing students' work.

Chapter 10, "Screening and Assessment," does not include assignments because most readers will not normally administer standardized tests. Such tests may form part of a portfolio, however, so educators must know their place, be prepared to consult with other professionals about their use, and be able to interpret the results, comparing them with other data from observational sources. Some commonly used screening and assessment tools are described briefly in the *Instructor's Manual*.

Test Bank   The test bank includes matching, true/false, multiple-choice, and short-answer questions for each chapter.

Observation Samples   Blank charts for the various observation methods are provided in full-page format. These can be reproduced for student practice or made into overhead transparencies for classroom use.

Answer Key   Suggested answers are given for the Focus Questions that begin each chapter. Complete answers for the test bank are also provided.

Acknowledgements

Much has changed since the first edition. Jacob has gone where all good dogs end up—to dog heaven, son Simon is saving lives in Thunder Bay, and daughter Cas is studying Criminology at the University of Toronto—so the house is much quieter these days. Andrew, my husband, who has supported me through more than 30 years in education, has continued to provide administrative expertise and attention to detail with research and bibliographies. Thank you for all your help; there is little reward! My dad always supports my work even if he disagrees with my opinions: thanks, I appreciate you so much!

Last year brought some mammoth challenges to my life, but my family and friends helped me through them and we all became closer; thanks to all of you for your patience. These are the times when you find out who your real friends are. Mine are connected mostly to the world of early childhood. They function in different corners of education: university professors, government employees, students, and other folks starting out on their teaching careers. Some of the very best have been Dr. Patricia Corson, Esther Keys, Michael Pimento, Sara Slater, Cathy Coulthard, and Marlene Watson. I wish I could do more than acknowledge their contributions here. I have been fortunate to have been inspired by some special people involved in the lives of children who have come from several countries—Hungary, Finland, Canada, the United States, the United Kingdom, and India: James Hoot, Isabel Doxey, Tunde Szecsi, Beth Etopio, Vidya Thiramurthy, Shirley Raines, Eeva Hujala, and James Ernest have been particularly important. Thank you for sharing some of your wisdom and insight.

There have been changes at the publishing house and a new set of terrific people to work with. Adrienne has been very focused on details and timelines. Many thanks to her for keeping me on track, and keeping me smiling! The reviewers of *Take a Look* supplied useful ideas for improvement, for which I am most grateful. Thanks also to Winnie the Pooh who offered the insight "It's best to know what you are looking for before you look for it." The greatest wisdom can come from where you least expect it.

Credits

The publishers acknowledge the following sources of material reprinted in this book and would gladly receive information enabling them to rectify any errors in references or credits.

Laura E. Berk, *Infants, Children, and Adolescents*. Published by Allyn and Bacon, Boston, MA. Copyright © 1993 by Pearson Education. Reprinted by permission of the publisher.

From *Exceptional Children: Inclusion in Early Childhood Programs, 2nd edition,* by K. E. Allen, C. Paasche, and A. Cornell © 1998. Reprinted with permission of Nelson Thomson Learning: a division of Thomson Learing. Fax 800 730-2215.

Department of Health, Great Britain (HMSO). *Protecting Children: A Guide for Social Workers Undertaking Comprehensive Assessment* (p. 85).

Urie Bronfenbrenner, *The Ecology of Human Development Experiments by Nature and Design* (Harvard University Press, 1979).

GENOGRAMS IN FAMILY ASSESSMENT by Monica McGoldrick and Randy Gerson. Copyright © 1985 by Monica McGoldrick and Randy Gerson. Used by permission of W. W. Norton & Company, Inc.

Ontario Ministry of Education and Training (*The Arts: The Ontario Curriculum, Grades 1-8, 1998*) © Queen's Printer for Ontario, 1998. Reproduced with permission.

Ontario Ministry of Education and Training (*The Common Curriculum, Grades 1-9, 1993*) © Queen's Printer for Ontario, 1993. Reproduced with permission.

Early Childhood Resource Teacher Network of Ontario (*Checklinst for Quality Inclusive Education: A Self-Assessment Tool and Manual for Early Childhood Settings, 1997*).

Carol H. Schlank and Barbara Metzger, *A Room Full of Children* (1989). RAEYC (Rochester Association for the Education of Young Children).

Centennial College Early Childhood Education Programs and Child Care Centres (*Philosophy Check-in*, 1998).

Canadian Childcare Federation.

"From Lesley's Journal." *YMCA Playing to Learn*. YMCA of Greater Toronto.

Prentice-Hall (Janice Beaty, *Observing Development of the Young Child*, 2nd Edition).

From *The Mindful School: The Portfolio Connection* by Kay Burke, Robin Fogarty, and Susan Belgrad. © 1994 IRI/SkyLight Training and Publishing, Inc. Reprinted by permission of SkyLight Professional Development www.skylightedu.com, or (800) 348-4474.

Allyn & Backon (Harrington/Meisels, *Thinking Like a Teacher*, 2002) From Samuel L. Meisels, Et al. *Thining Like a Teacher: Using Observational Assessment to Improve Teaching and Learning*. Published by Allyn and Bacon, Boston, MA. Copyright © 2002 by Pearson Education. Reprinted by permission of the publisher.

NAEYC (Bredekamp/Copple, eds., *Developmentally Appropriate Practice in Early Childhood Programs, Rev. Ed.*, Washington, 1997) Reprinted with permission from the National Association for the Education of Young Children

Observation: An Introduction

chapter 1

You well know that the teacher in our method is more of an observer than a teacher; therefore this is what the teacher must know, how to observe.

Maria Montessori (1913)

Observation can lead to the collection of valid, reliable information without intruding on or transforming the daily classroom life and without constraining the children's behaviour so as to limit their demonstration of competence.

Tynette W. Hills (1992)

We don't see things as they are. We see them as we are.

Anaïs Nin

Observing this little boy as he plays with clay presents little difficulty, but recording his actions and interpreting them can be more challenging.

People Watching

A mother gazes at her newborn infant. The baby looks at her. At first the baby's sight is unfocused, yet she is attracted by the configuration of her mother's face. The infant is, perhaps, "programmed" to have this interest. It encourages social interaction and leads to emotional bonding. Drawn to faces and signs of movement, the infant learns through watching as well as through her other senses. All babies are born to be people watchers. Mother and baby look at each other!

"Don't stare," says a mother to her young child, in the expectation that she can shape the child's instinctive **behaviour**. Socially acceptable behaviour requires that observation be subtle. Required behaviour is learned more by example than by verbal reinforcement; watching others is integral to the process of social learning.

Have you ever watched the hellos and goodbyes being said at an airport? If you were not too caught up in your own emotions, you might have wondered about the demonstrations of feeling, the honesty of expressions, or the social or cultural determination of particular behaviours. What are the stories behind all those faces? If you have ever done this kind of thing, then you too are an observer.

"I did not expect her to do that," "She must be frustrated to react that way," and "He is a very quiet person" are all informal observations. We all observe, deduce, and respond in all our communications with other people. Most adults go through this process without really considering what is happening.

The same process occurs when we are more conscious of making observations. The significant difference is that, when we use observation as a method for collecting information, we must do it carefully, systematically, and accurately.

Why Observe?

We observe children because we are drawn to them; we want to protect, nurture, and teach them. Every adult involved with young children in any role or capacity will observe the children for somewhat different reasons. The adults may be parents or other relatives, babysitters, caregivers, teachers, early childhood educators, psychologists, doctors, social workers, play therapists, students, child life workers (who work with children in hospitals), recreation leaders, camp counsellors, or any other interested parties. All of these have some duty of care to the children, though the kind of responsibility varies. The following list gives, in no particular order, some of the reasons that adults may observe children:

- to gaze with love
- to ensure safety
- to see if the child is healthy
- to note changes in behaviour
- to see what the child consumes
- to learn about the child's interests
- to see how long a child's attention span is
- to determine the child's physical skills and needs
- to tune in to the child's rhythms
- to assess a program's effectiveness
- to make inferences about a child's cognitive activity
- to note social relationships
- to deduce how the child is feeling
- to help design a program plan for an individual child or the group
- to evaluate the use of space
- to make written records of the child's development
- to assess the child for particular sensory disabilities
- to help appreciate the child's learning style
- to learn about the ages and stages of child development
- to help build one's skill in objective observation
- to determine the child's progression through stages of development
- to assess the child's behaviour in reference to "norms"
- to report information to other professionals
- to let a parent know how the child is developing
- to enable parents to seek professional opinions about the child's progress or perceived concerns
- to gain written documentation for legal purposes
- to record any regression in the child's behaviour
- to confirm or contradict a formal assessment
- to help change routines to be more effective
- to determine appropriate guidance strategies
- to determine when and how to "**scaffold**" (to extend the child's learning)
- to establish the frequency of a particular behaviour

- to acknowledge the complexity of the child's play
- to determine the quality of the child's interaction with an adult
- to record activities the child undertakes
- to note the child's response to a new situation
- to evaluate the effectiveness of play as therapy
- to help determine the interaction among various aspects of a child's development
- to gain insight into the child's personality and individuality
- to evaluate the appropriateness of the learning environment
- to determine the effect of the environment on the child
- to note the ways in which the child is smart

The observation may take many forms. Informal, unrecorded observation is frequently applied as it can be done while the observer participates with the children. Narrative (long and descriptive) accounts of behaviour do not rely on highly developed observational skills, and they are open-ended. Alternatively, observers looking for particular behaviours might use a prewritten chart, checklist, or scale. (I will deal with all of these methods in later chapters.)

Focus on the individual

"Did they like the creative activity?" a teacher asked an ECE student who came into her office. As the student replied, the teacher realized that she hadn't asked a very useful question. Imagining that each child's response to a situation is identical can be a mistake. We must focus on the behaviours of an individual child far more frequently than we do on the group.

If you can see only the general flow of action, you will not have insight into the set of individuals in your care. Without singling out children to observe closely, you are very likely to miss the particular skills that they have acquired and fail to acknowledge the areas of their development that you can address.

However, individuals do function within groups. Group dynamics can be better understood when the individuals in the group are first observed separately. For this reason, adults must learn to work at observing individual children and avoid making assumptions or generalizations. In time your observations can centre on the interactions within the group, but first you will need to refine your skills by observing one child at a time.

Observation as authentic assessment

The strengths of systematic observation as a form of **authentic assessment** are numerous. Observation

- enables adults to take responsibility for the process of the child's development
- is the key to evaluating development
- is important because adults can bring about changes in a child's behaviour
- focuses on what a child can do

- forms the foundation of effective individual program-planning and group-planning
- allows for variation between and the individuality of children in their development and needs
- presupposes no curriculum theory but can support almost all types of program-planning
- behaviour can be seen in context
- can be more objective and tends to be less biased than standardized tests
- allows for understanding of each interacting aspect of development
- enables the observer to carry out evaluation in familiar surroundings
- can be faster and more effective then other methods of gaining information about development
- encourages parents' involvement and professional teamwork

The Observer's Role

"Watching the kids" is a phrase sometimes used to mean looking after or caring for children. It is interesting that the nonprofessional term accentuates our responsibility for observation.

We face inevitable conflicts in our jobs as caregivers, teachers, and parents. Consider a parent who spends a lot of his time watching his children and pointing out to everyone how advanced they are. He does not take responsibility for interacting or even being with them but observes and expresses his pride in their accomplishments. Other parents and caregivers may be so busy doing practical domestic jobs that they don't take time to "stand and stare"—to watch their children with any sense of wonder or intrigue. Some are so involved with their children's activities that they do not notice their changing behaviours and increasing skills.

All adults involved with children need to observe those children constantly. Only a small amount of the information observed can be recorded or analyzed. An adult's active involvement with the children can make more formal observations difficult. Some methods enable us to be interactive as we observe, but these require a more refined skill.

Nonparticipant observation

Early attempts at the more formal types of observing and recording need to be done while the observer is detached from the children. Students and skill-building teachers need to remove themselves from the children for this **nonparticipant observation**. Through the practice of observation, student educators' perspectives will alter and they will gradually notice things that they missed before, become more objective about what they do see, and become more analytical about the information they record. This nonparticipant role is a necessary part of learning how to observe effectively.

Practising teachers should, from time to time, remove themselves from direct contact with the children. This helps the teachers watch more carefully what is happening and usually makes them more responsive to those children. Taking the time to be a nonparticipant in the program does not mean prolonged time away from the children, however, and should never be an excuse to ignore a child's needs.

With young children, you may find it useful to be a noninteracting observer from time to time. As long as the children's needs are met, they should not be particularly affected if you remove yourself just far enough to be out of their personal space but within their sight and earshot. Sit on a small chair in a position that does not interfere with their activity and is not in a significant traffic area. Here are some suggestions:

- Avoid making the facial expressions and eye contact that initiate communication with the children.
- Wear comfortable, fairly plain clothes; avoid wearing anything that will attract a child's attention.
- Try to avoid obvious staring at a child, which could make him feel uncomfortable.
- Distance yourself so that you can see and hear the children without being in their play area or personal space.
- Ensure that sufficient appropriate supervision is provided so that all the children's needs are met while you observe.
- If a child draws you into conversation, respond in simple sentences to explain what you are doing. Remember to follow through with any promises you make to her regarding later activities.
- Make regular times for your nonparticipant observation so that the children get used to your doing it. Older children may learn to observe by imitating you.
- Never use nonparticipant observation as an excuse for not involving yourself with the children when you should be responsible for their care.

Early childhood education students use an in-class opportunity for nonparticipant observation of infants. Skill in objective recording needs to be gained from practice.

Participant observation

Teachers who have gained skill in observing may make only brief recordings from time to time. Mostly they practise **participant observation** while they are involved with the children. Those teachers who have developed their skills will be more responsive to casually observed information.

For training purposes, there are more ways of improving your skills of observation. Visit child-care agencies and schools for opportunities. Use a college's on-site lab-school facilities as a particularly helpful setting. A laboratory school can help students with their skill development in several ways:

- Children can be brought to class for a "set-up" observation opportunity. All the students will see the same behaviour at the same time and can learn to record and analyze appropriately.

- Observations in the lab school can be recorded for later replay in class. Reviewing the material as a class can be good practice, as what is seen is the same for everyone.

- Students can go into the lab school and observe as nonparticipants. Situations can be set up so that they can all focus on the same aspect of development.

- Observation booths can enable students, individually or in groups, to observe children. Ideally, a sound system would enable the students to hear language and other sounds. This is a nonintrusive way of observing, which does not influence the recording. Students can observe while others play the interactive role, setting up activities for the children.

- If the centre is large enough, students may be able to do a placement practicum or internship at the lab school. As they get to know the children better than they would as visitors, students can try out different observational styles in nonparticipant and participant approaches.

The parents and teachers of the children to be observed may require some explanation of the purpose of focused observation by the students in a class situation. Of course, those students should gain their permission beforehand.

Professionalism and confidentiality

When you receive a psychological or medical report, it may arrive with a confidential sticker attached, making it clear that the report contains information to which access should be limited. An observation is also confidential material and should be treated as such. The circle of stakeholders involved in an observation, or those who require a degree of access to the information it contains, may be wider than you might at first imagine. This situation can present some challenges.

Who has, or should have, access to the formal records or informal notes that teachers and caregivers need to keep? While legal requirements vary, you must ensure that you interpret and practise **professionalism** and, when appropriate, **confidentiality** regarding all the information that is stored or shared. Follow the basic principle that information about a child is the concern of only that child, his or her custodial parent or guardian, and anyone with whom the parent consents to share it. In taking responsibility for the care or education of a child, you must ensure that any legal requirements regarding access to information and privacy are met. Your school or other agency must have a policy that determines who has access to what information and under what circumstances.

At enrolment, most agencies and schools enter into an agreement with parents and guardians that observations and information-gathering will be carried out. Student educators, however, must always request and gain parental permission before carrying out their observations, documentation, and record-keeping relating to a child. As a professional courtesy, students should provide parents with corrected copies of any such studies.

All written records need to be kept in secure, preferably locked, files. They should be labelled and dated. Files need to be updated regularly; the contributors should sign all their entries. Any significant content must be communicated to the parents in an appropriate manner with any necessary explanations. Parents should have open access to their children's files at any reasonable time. If you think that there is any reason to withhold information from a parent, that information is probably inappropriate and possibly **subjective**.

It is easier to accept the need for confidentiality with formal documents. Practising teachers find the challenge is to maintain the same level of confidential treatment with all pieces of information regarding a child. Parents' comfort level regarding privacy is very personal and may be culturally determined. Avoiding risks is essential and may require careful organization. While you may think that a posted chart recording the feeding, sleeping, and elimination pattern of the day is acceptable for infants, you will need to work out an appropriate practice for your setting with the parents.

In the days when children ran out of school clutching their readers of varying proficiency levels, it was quite clear to the parents—as well as to the children themselves—who was at the "top" or "bottom" of the reading class. You can avoid this kind of practice today.

Briefing parents about their children's challenging behaviour might be an excellent idea. While it is useful to share daily observations, you must be sensitive about timing. The end of the day might be the wrong time to deliver what could seem to be bad news; offering the comments when others might overhear them is also inconsiderate.

Students are in a difficult position with regards to confidential record-keeping. Their observations should not reveal the identity of a child to anyone who might accidentally come across the record. As student educators are learners themselves, their observations might not be as objective as they could be, and the inferences they contain might not be appropriate. The deductions the students make might be based on insufficient information or analyzed on the basis of an inaccurate explanation of a child's behaviour.

Schools and agencies have different attitudes to student educators' access to children's records. In some cases, the students might be considered to be in a better position to appreciate a child's behaviour depending on the contextual information offered; however, to many in supervisory roles, this access presents an unnecessary intrusion into the families' privacy.

Centres working with students need to decide how to seek permissions regarding these observations (see the permission form on page 9) and the amount of information about the child that is made available. Certainly some information, and the observer's bias, may influence the objectivity of the person making the record. An agency might request that a staff member countersign students' observations to indicate that permission has been given to make the observation and that the observation is consistent with that staff member's knowledge. Feedback can be very useful for students; without breaching confidentiality, they may find that they contribute new insights to other professionals' knowledge of the child or children being observed.

Permission Form

Child Observations, Case Studies, and Portfolios

Student and Parent Agreement

Without written permission I will not observe and record information about your child. Please sign in the space provided if you agree that I may make observations and study your child. It would be helpful if you could initial each of the boxes if you are willing for me to undertake any or all of the techniques of information gathering.

I _____ *(student name)* will not refer to the child in any written manner by his or her real name. Information recorded will be written objectively, treated professionally, and kept confidential.

_____   _____
(student's signature)   *(date)*

I _____

  (parent's name)

agree to have _____

              (child's name)

observed ☐   photographed ☐   audiotaped ☐   videotaped ☐

by _____

  (student's name above)

at _____

  (agency/home)

for the purpose of study in child development at _____

(school/college) for a period of _____ *(weeks/months)* on the consideration that copies are made available to me, the parent, if I so request.

_____   _____
(parent's signature)   *(date)*

Objective Observation

You may be relieved to hear that it is impossible to be completely objective when observing children. But it is a hard task to reach an acceptable level of **objectivity** in all your observation and recording. Cohen and Stern (1978) address this truth:

> For teachers observing the children with whom they work and live, absolute objectivity is impossible, and objectivity itself becomes a relative thing. As a matter of fact, it is to be hoped that no teacher would ever try for so much objectivity that she would cease to be a responsible and responsive adult to her group.

No two people will see the same child in identical ways. Two open and honest teachers can be asked to observe the same child. What they see and the interpretation they impose will depend on what they decide to look for and on their own particular perspectives. To scientists, this might appear to be an unacceptable variation; however, observers of children need to decide what is an acceptable degree of objectivity. According to these teachers, both tell the "truth," or their own version of it.

How can you ensure that you keep to the truth when others see the child's behaviour in a different light? How you see depends on your skill in observing, what you are seeking, and your own perspective. If these are the variables, you can improve your reliability as an observer by increasing your skills, determining what you are looking for, and reviewing your personal perspective.

The Objectivity Continuum

Objectivity ←————————→ Subjectivity

- There are no absolutes.
- All observations fall between the two opposites.
- Objectivity is usually desirable.
- Subjectivity is not always "wrong."
- Appreciation of the reasons for the degree of objectivity is always essential.

Bias

Whatever stage we are at in our professional or adult lives, we have all had experiences that shape our perceptions. The way we take in information is determined by our previous experience and knowledge. We bring to situations previously acquired attitudes and beliefs. Some of these are well founded; others are born of some **bias** that derives from incorrectly understood information, negative experiences, or inappropriate generalizations. Most biases are subtle, and other people may not even recognize them. Some may be much more blatant and recognizable to others. Some may even be considered acceptable.

Observers can eliminate or reduce many of their biases by acknowledging and confronting them. Eventually, observers will realize that there is more to observation than seeing. What separates human observation from a mechanical means of recording is how we perceive what we observe. The selection of how, when, and what to observe is a skill we must work on. **Perception** involves seeing and making meaning. The educators' task is to fine-tune their perceptions so they see, and process what they see, through experiences and well-informed sensory and mental functioning.

TAKING A SPECIAL LOOK: Observing exceptional children

How we see people may be shaped by our experience and our emotions. If we have little knowledge of **exceptional children** (children who have special needs), we could be fearful or negative about observing them. Recognizing this helps both you and the exceptional child speak positively about who he is and be clear about his abilities, rather than focus on his disabilities. Getting to know the child and increasing your knowledge about his condition will usually reduce any fears and help you relate to him. Children with below-average skill levels in one or more domains may have abilities in other areas that you can see more easily if you observe with a positive outlook.

Teamwork

Many people have a role in caring for, nurturing, and educating each child. Where there is responsibility for a child, there is also a need for observation and assessment of that child.

Parents are the most significant stakeholders in children's lives. They may be the adults who take the leading role in observing their children and responding appropriately to their needs. Quite naturally and spontaneously, a mother or father will watch a child; such observation may elicit a wide range of feelings and responses. This informal monitoring of the child's behaviour, and of changes in health or development, may well be the most significant assessment that is ever done. The professional involved in the child's care must never forget that the child is the member of a family and that the family may be able to offer closer insights than the trained caregiver. No assessment could ever be complete without including the parent's observations.

Front-line caregivers need to consider their observations in the light of what is known about the child. This is done most usefully in discussion with co-workers and parents. Interested parties may be able to exchange observations in a relatively informal way—frequently at the start or end of the day, or perhaps at nap-time for a younger child.

Supervisors and others involved in the delivery of care and education may add their own observations or help make objective inferences about the child. When observed behaviour causes concern or is difficult to interpret, an "outside" professional, such as a psychologist, may be brought in. Legislation varies, but professional principles and good practice indicate that this should be done only after seeking parental permission, support, and involvement. Psychologists, occupational therapists, child-care consultants, and social workers will not be able to make a fair and appropriate assessment without input from the day-to-day caregiver or teacher and the parents.

The transdisciplinary play-based assessment (TPBA) model (Linder 1990) offers the idea of holistic assessment, with the involved professionals working with the parents in a way that enables all parties to observe simultaneously and take the time to discuss deductions that have been made. Linder states, "Team discussion is critical, and having the same foundation improves team communication" (1990, p. 17).

Not all observations are, or could be, conducted when all those involved with the child are present. Communication systems should be in place to share information in convenient ways.

The team approach increases the reliability of inferences made from observation. This model also encourages each adult to take responsibility in the process. An indicator of good-quality childcare is the practice of teamwork in observation and program-planning.

The role of the parent

Within a home setting it is always the responsibility of the parent(s) to care for and protect the child or children. Nieces, nephews, and/or children of neighbours in the home may increase that responsibility. This requires constant observation! The love and feelings of protection that a parent has toward her child, along with her general sense of responsibility, are most important. These come quite naturally to most adults; to others, knowing how to observe and respond is more difficult. In their ideas of observational and nurturing responsibilities, adults who have experienced poor parenting in their own early years, or perhaps have experienced or experience times of stress in their own lives, can be influenced by ingrained patterns in their own behaviour.

Most parents do a wonderful job of observing and responding to their children's needs. However strong their observation skills, it is likely that they can improve their perceptions by becoming more knowledgeable about child development and by watching the development they see in their children. One of the best-known educators and observers was Piaget, who used his own children as subjects. His intensive observation, documentation, and analysis of his own children's behaviour forms a basis for our current understanding of developmental psychology today!

All parents will encounter a range of adults who play a role in the lives of their children. Some of these people will have advanced training in child development or in other professional fields. Others will have less preparation but copious amounts of experience with children. Parents can find sharing the responsibility of the care of their children very difficult. It's easy to appreciate that the intense relationships between parents and children are forged in ways that, at first, exclude others. As families vary in their complexity, parents may perceive somewhat different boundaries of responsibility for their children.

Child-care centres, schools, home childcare, and all programs for children deliver quality service when teamwork is effective within the program. Reaching beyond the program's delivery to parents is essential: parents must be considered key partners in the child's life and in their children's program. How the parent enters and functions within the circle of caregivers and educators is vital to the success of the child, as well as the program as a whole. The agency or program concerned must take this into account when devising its policies and in ensuring that its practices promote mutual understanding.

Communications from home to the agency, as well as from the program to home, form the core of this reciprocal relationship. This two-way exchange of information needs to include observations that the parent has made of the child at home. More than the exchange of information, there must be a sharing of values and personal goals. Miscommunication or the lack of communication can be at the root of many disagreements that can disrupt the program and upset the families.

Daily, weekly, and, on a formal basis, monthly exchanges of observations and information are necessary. Some of these will be spoken exchanges, while other important data should be recorded in the child's portfolio. While gossip is counterproductive, some chatting and exchange of personal information can help the parent get a sense of the philosophy and practice of the educator. Likewise, the program for the child can benefit from the input of either or both parents.

Formal records can seem intimidating to parents, but the records should be able, in an atmosphere of trust, to offer the agency staff a wealth of information about themselves, their child, their culture, and way of life. Some parents may be reluctant to complete long forms that ask intrusive questions, yet the information requested is intended to offer the children a better and more appropriate program. Personal and contextual information is particularly important for programs that offer care, education, or other programs for children from diverse backgrounds. Getting to know the children's food preferences, sleep cycles, religious requirements, play patterns, and so on may seem odd at first, but these are all particular and individual to each child. Parents and educators need to talk, trust, and share with each other so that they form a true partnership; the child will subsequently feel comfortable in both the home and the program, which will contribute to his **holistic** development.

Choice of Observation Method

There is a wide range of methods of recording information. As you read this book, you might want to try some new ways or practise some of those familiar to you. When choosing a method, ask yourself the following questions:

1. Are you playing a nonparticipatory role or do you have responsibility for the children as you observe?
2. Do you have the language skills to enable you to write detailed narrative descriptions?
3. Why are you observing? What are you looking for?
4. Is your purpose in observing to increase your skill or to benefit the child directly?
5. Do you appreciate what the various methods of information collecting will tell you—and can you choose appropriately?
6. Have you developed strategies to summarize and make sense of the observational information collected?

If in doubt about where to start, work through the methods presented in this book. They are offered in a sequence that is appropriate for observation students or for skill-developing educators. Since informal observation is what everyone has done without training, continue to do this. Your skill will improve as you record, and your casual observations will gradually take on greater meaning as you continue the process. Narrative recordings require little interpretive skill and so may be the method of choice for the relatively unskilled. As you find new ways of charting behaviours, checking off behaviours on lists, and using styles that require inference in their recording, your understanding of child development will also expand. Your learning will accelerate if you study theories of child development at the same time as you improve your observations. Each will benefit the other.

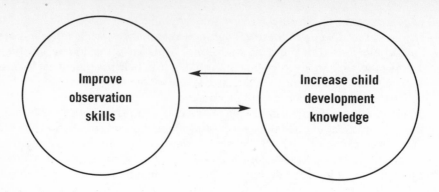

Improve observation skills

Increase child development knowledge

Observation as Part of an Assessment Procedure

Early childhood specialists focus more on the process of the child's learning than on its products. Observation of the process can tell us much about the child that would not be revealed by viewing only such products as the child's artwork and writing. It is important, however, not to disregard the significance of such products. If you can gather information about the child from various sources, and in a variety of ways, you will be in a better position to make evaluations.

Formal **assessment** may require tests. (Tests are dealt with in Chapter 10.) The best of these have an observation component. Even in a structured play situation, children are in a better position to be evaluated more fairly than in a testing situation. A restrictive "testing environment" can create stress. Children can demonstrate their skills more readily in a situation that resembles what they are used to. Members of an assessment team are wise to get their data through a variety of methods to ensure that they include naturalistic observations.

The **portfolio** technique combines the best of the evaluation styles. A portfolio can contain observations, charts, products of the child's efforts, test results, psychologists' reports, parental contributions, medical notes, and any other pertinent information. It forms a record that can be added to at any time. The portfolio forms long-term documentation of the child's education, health, and experience to which those involved with the child may refer. As the child grows, she may choose items for inclusion in her own

TAKING A SPECIAL LOOK: Emerging skills

Whatever the developmental progress of a child, we need to support the skills that are emerging. Sometimes, when a child takes longer than average to acquire a new skill, the achievement seems even more amazing than it does for the child who had no particular challenge in that domain.

Observing the ongoing progression of skill development should lead us to respond. When we see new behaviours, we need to find ways of supporting them. We are not trying to get the child to develop faster—development is not a race! Rather, we are trying to ensure that we maximize the child's potential in a nurturing way.

Observation Cycle

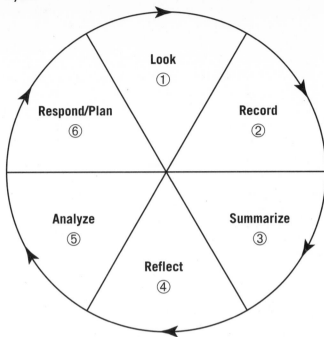

portfolio to form a personal record of achievement. Looking back at the child's life experience can stir the emotions and can supply significant information about her patterns of behaviour. (A full explanation of the portfolio method is given in Chapter 8.)

1. Look: Focus on current behaviour.

   Observation is not necessarily an exercise to identify "strengths" and "weaknesses" in children's behaviour. Such value judgments are usually inappropriate in **naturalistic** observation. Observers should look at the skills that are present rather than focus on what a child cannot do. Programs are more positive and more likely to be effective if they are planned to enable the child to build skills from "where he is" rather than from what he has failed to do. A more developmentally appropriate curriculum plan should result from focusing on **emerging skills**. It is not necessary to have an observational goal but you might want to look for particular types of behaviour.

2. Record what you see.

   Document what you see using a format that suits your purpose. Include enough detail according to the method used. Ensure accuracy and **objectivity**. (See Chapters 3 through 8 for methods of recording.)

3. Summarize information gathered.

   Often confused with analysis, the observation **summary** is a categorization or organization of the essential parts of the observation. In many open-ended observations, the summary may try to bring together information to identify and list the behaviours seen. It is not an interpretation but a review and organization of objectively recorded behaviours. Developmental domains might be used as categories in the summary.

In a more structured observation that looks for particular identified behaviours, the summary might contain information such as the number, frequency, **duration**, or triggers of those behaviours. The summary is intended to briefly outline significant observed behaviour.

4. Reflect on the observation and your summary.

   Review the observation to determine whether you saw and recorded any behaviour or category of behaviour you were seeking. Consider the data in relation to the child's acquisition of new skills, how the context affects the behaviour, and your own feelings, intuition, and expertise. Be aware of your **biases**.

5. Analyze the content of the observation.

   Here is the opportunity to use your critical thinking skills. Decide on a framework for analysis. Typically this framework might include identifying developmental changes, explaining behaviours, using theoretical models, comparing behaviours to the norm, assessing the achievements of the child with reference to specified standards, and/or identifying challenging behaviours or ones that need to be addressed. Your style of analysis must match your agency's philosophy and practice.

   There are a few basic rules of **analysis**:

   1. Focus on what was observed and recorded, not on other less accurate "bits of information."

   2. Always separate the observation from its summary and analysis.

   3. Do not make **inferences** unless you can support them; that is,

       a. identify the specific behaviour(s) that lead(s) to such a deduction.

       b. support your inference with reason(s), using inferential language carefully: "It appears that… on the basis of… I think that… demonstrates behaviours in excess of… norm for his age."

       c. **validate** each statement with the use of at least one (preferably all) of the following:

           i. observations made by others with similar inferences

           ii. use of theoretical explanations

           iii. comparison with a recognized **norm**

       d. state the source of the validation (professional input or book reference)

   4. Put on paper only what you consider professional and could defend against challenges. Avoid judgments, assumptions, and generalizations that cannot be substantiated regarding background, social, or contextual information. For example, do not say, "This occurs because he is an only child" or "He is much smarter than his brother" or "Her English is poor because her parents don't communicate with her."

   5. Keep the analysis as well as the observation confidential. Some people may find the word "analysis" quite off-putting or coldly scientific.

   "Analysis" is more easily understood as the "making sense of what I saw" section of the observation process. The easiest way to go about an analysis is to ask yourself, and then answer, a series of questions about what was observed. If the observation is set up to seek particular information, then that question needs to be addressed first. Unless you cite the source of "extra" information, it is best to stick to analyzing only what was in the observation just completed.

Attention deficit, hyperactivity, and attention deficit disorder (ADD) are terms used rather casually by some parents, teachers, and caregivers. These terms are very specific diagnoses and are not for the nonmedically trained to diagnose. Consequently, we should be careful about making inferences using these labels. It is better, without the benefit of a professional diagnosis, to describe behaviours objectively. Use your observation skills and describe exactly what you see!

Structuring the analysis in a way that considers each of the developmental areas is helpful. Any section where there is no significant information can be left out. In practice, you might find the following developmental analysis plan a good idea. Adapt it to fit your needs. Write it up according to the required style, either as an essay or in notes under organized headings. Of course, the more contextual data you have collected and the greater the number of observations you have recorded, the more valuable the analysis.

6. **Respond to observational data and analysis.** Responses to observed behaviour vary. They might include planning further observation, devising a program to fit a child's needs, making a referral, checking with parents, using appropriate guidance strategies, or developing a different teaching technique.

Plan to Assist the Analysis of an Observation

BACKGROUND
- What was the reason for observing? (Was I seeking specific information?)
- Did the observation occur spontaneously? Was the child aware of being observed?
- What is my role as observer? (nonparticipant, etc.)
- Did I have any preconceived ideas about what I was going to see?
- What contextual information might be helpful?
- Who gave permission for or input into the process?

METHOD
- Why did I choose this method of observing?
- Were there any concerns regarding the procedure?
- Did the method reveal what I wanted? What was it?

CONTENT
Physical development
- What gross motor skills were demonstrated?

- What fine motor or manipulative skills were seen?
- What activity was the child observed doing?
- What responses did the child make to any sensory experience (seeing, hearing, touching, smelling, or tasting)?

Social development

- What evidence was there of the child's sense of self?
- What kinds of connection was the child making

  a. with adults?

  b. with other children?

- What adult interaction did I observe?
- Describe the quality of the interactions.
- What kind of self-help skills were seen?
- Were there any examples of independence or dependence?
- What did I see that indicated understanding of social roles and behaviour?

Emotional development

- What demonstrations of feelings did I observe

  a. in language?

  b. in posture and body language?

  c. in gestures?

  d. in facial expressions?

- Was there indication of control of feelings?
- What attachments were evident?
- What moods did I see?

Play

- Did I see the child in onlooker, solitary, parallel associative, or cooperative activity?
- What type of play (if any) was observed? (One or more of imaginative, imitative, pretend, fantasy, sociodramatic, superhero, social constructional, functional, physical, or other.)
- How long and involved were these sequences?
- Was the play self-initiated and self-supported?
- What props were used?

Language and communication

- What utterances were made? In what language?

- What indications of nonverbal communication did I observe?
- What kind of structure did the language have?
- How extensive was the child's vocabulary?
- How effective was the communication?
- What was the child's interpersonal style?

Moral and spiritual development

- Did any of the observed behaviours indicate an understanding of "rights" or "social justice"? If so, how?
- Were any of the behaviours pro-social in nature? (Empathetic, altruistic, sharing, taking turns, helping others.)
- Was there evidence of beliefs about any philosophical issues, such as the creation of things, in the child's world?
- Did I see the child's curiosity and sense of wonder?
- Did the child demonstrate respect for the dignity of others?
- What indication was there of the child's categorizing himself or herself into a sub-culture? (Racial, belief system, family make-up, dialect, etc.)
- What demonstration was there of an understanding of, compliance with, or rejection of any kind of rules or guidelines?

Personality

- Did I observe any behaviours that indicate temperamental type? (Slow to warm, extroverted, orderly, etc.)
- What reactions to stimuli did I see?

Cognition

- What drew the child's attention? How long was the span of concentration?
- What behaviours indicated a thought process?
- Did I notice any "mistakes" the child made?
- Did the demonstrated language or behaviour show understanding of any of the basic concepts? If so, what? (Colour, shape, time, space, classification, relativity, seriation, conservation, etc.)
- Did the child "experiment" with materials?
- Was there evidence of conditioned responses?
- Did I see any trial-and-error strategies?
- What evidence might there be of an understanding of symbolism in language or behaviour?
- Was there evidence of use of memory?
- Was any of the child's art representational?

- What behaviours indicated to me how the child perceives the world?
- Did the child use concrete objects to help perform tasks? Can the child use any forms of abstraction?
- What humour did the child initiate or respond to?

The whole child
- What outside influences affected what I observed?
- In what ways did I see aspects of the child's development interact?
- What developmental stage did I observe? (What evidence?)

Responses to the above questions should incorporate deductions that cite the section of the observation to which they are related and that are validated appropriately. For practice, you might like to use the following flow chart, which follows the process of critical thinking required in analyzing observations. The sample on page 34 shows the analysis of an observation, while that on pages 36–37 shows the analysis of a number of behaviours in chart form.

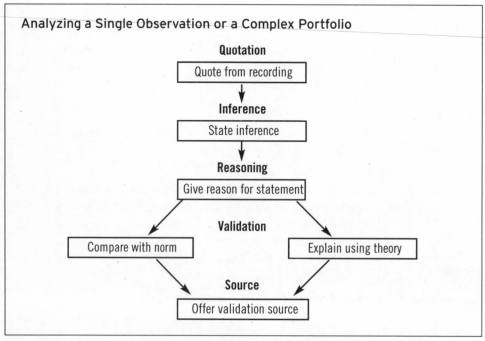

Analyzing a Single Observation or a Complex Portfolio

Quotation
Quote from recording

Inference
State inference

Reasoning
Give reason for statement

Validation
Compare with norm   Explain using theory

Source
Offer validation source

In each of the areas you will explore, ensure that all deductions and inferences can be supported. If such inferences are "checked" using this model, they can be evaluated for their objectivity and the likelihood of their being accurate. If your inferences cannot be validated, they should not be stated.

Using Observational Data to Plan

Those who teach teachers often say that students need to learn how to set goals and objectives for children. Such a philosophy makes people believe that achievement is only possible with goal-setting. It disregards the idea that children will progress through the developmental stages, given appropriate support and open-ended experiences that enable them to operate at their own levels. Learning and skills development do not depend only on our overt intervention. There is a difference between making appropriate curriculum provision based on observation of the child's developmental needs and goal-setting that presumes that you know what the child's "next stage" is. However knowledgeable you are about patterns of development, it is rarely useful to set specific goals for children who are in the mainstream of our education and care agencies.

Children with **special needs** who are identified and diagnosed may benefit from a more structured goal-setting approach because **objectives** can break down skills into component parts. These objectives can be addressed separately, one at a time.

Interpretation of observational information is essential for all planning and curriculum design. Many inappropriate assessments have resulted in poor provision; the teacher's focus should be on supplying appropriate experiences and guidance to support children in their own efforts to struggle with new skills.

Whether or not you set goals may be inconsequential in shaping how children actually behave. Merely setting goals does not bring about their achievement. However, thoughtful programming must always have some deliberate intention.

TAKING A SPECIAL LOOK: Early identification and intervention

Observing and recording development has a purpose beyond that of the school or child-care agency working directly with a child. Sometimes observation leads to the identification of potential concerns that need to be reviewed outside the agency. After repeating observations to see if the results are consistent, teachers and caregivers may suggest to the parent that further assessment from another professional might be helpful. Early identification of many conditions can be extremely beneficial for the child. In some cases, it may mean that an appropriate **assistive device** is supplied; in other cases, the teacher may follow the professional's directions to support the child more responsively. The long-term outcome is likely to be much better if action is taken early.

In some situations, a special plan of **early intervention** may be developed to support an infant, toddler, or preschooler. The plan can involve many different strategies to support the child's development and relationships. Psychologists or psychiatrists may try to assist before any potential problem rears its head. In other cases, where a developmental problem already exists, they will work with the child, parent, and caregivers or teachers to find appropriate ways of providing support.

Individual program plans (IPPs)

Individual program plans and **individual education plans (IEPs)** are commonly devised for children with identified special needs. But all children have individual needs that should be met. The IPP helps you in that task, by formalizing the process of converting observational and other assessment information into an action plan.

An IPP requires a team approach to piece together all available information about a child and come up with an appropriate response to the child's individual needs. At its best, it is a dynamic ongoing process that changes and is adapted in the light of new information.

Informal IPPs are devised regularly with parents and teachers working cooperatively to observe, evaluate, assess needs, and respond to them. In this case, it might not be a recorded plan. If there are specific concerns about the child's development, the IPP can be a much more thorough, written teamwork process with clearly defined intentions and practical suggestions or objectives.

A sample IPP can be found on page 35, and a sample IEP on pages 38–39. You might develop these to suit your own needs or use standard IPP/IEP forms used in your education or child-care region or authority.

TAKING A SPECIAL LOOK: IPPs for children with special needs

The idea of the individual program plan is borrowed from the philosophy of those working with children who have special needs. We should find ways to support emerging skills so that we assist development from the child's current skill level rather than jump ahead to the next stage. Designing activities to get a child to where he "should" be is not very helpful. For example, Juan, who is currently struggling to stand despite having malformed feet, is better assisted if we plan his individual program to include lots of activities to help him perfect this skill rather than set the goal of walking, which he may not reach for some time.

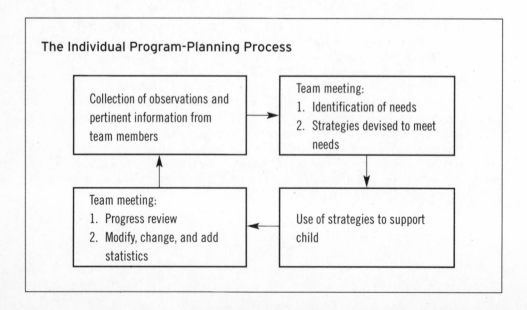

The Individual Program-Planning Process

Collection of observations and pertinent information from team members

→

Team meeting:
1. Identification of needs
2. Strategies devised to meet needs

Team meeting:
1. Progress review
2. Modify, change, and add statistics

Use of strategies to support child

Individual Program Plan

Child's name: _____ Teacher: _____

Age/D.O.B.: _____ Date: _____

Persons participating: _____

Reason for program development: _____

_____

Developmental domain	Observation summary (skills present)	Needs	Intentions	Practical supports	Person responsible

---

Individual Program Plan Review

Child's name: _____ Teacher: _____

Age/D.O.B.: _____ Date: _____

Persons participating: _____

Reason for program development: _____

_____

Developmental domain	Previous intentions	Observed skills	Progress made	Newly devised supports	Person responsible

Observation as part of curriculum-planning

A child's **curriculum** is his or her whole experience of life. What you may have thought of as "the program" or even "planned activities" forms only a small element of that whole experience. When you take care to observe children in every aspect of their days, from waking through all kinds of family interactions and domestic scenarios as well as more carefully designed day-care or school experiences, you can appreciate the children's styles, individualities, and social contexts, and how these affect their responsiveness and developing skills. As a trained observer, you may make useful inferences from observation in an agency or school setting. Those observations will be much more revealing if you have some previously acquired information about the child's family and background. Observing a child as widely as possible pays off in a picture of the whole rather than unconnected bits of information about some specific area of development.

The great challenge for teachers is to take the time to observe the individual within the group while acknowledging the dynamics of that group and endeavouring to provide for the needs of each child. Teachers need acute observational skills, an understanding of the more **"normal" patterns** of development, and a philosophy of curriculum that recognizes that everything they provide, including themselves, is part of the curriculum provision. If children are enabled to operate at their own levels, the variation of development within the group can be addressed; if changing environments are provided, children are able to build their own knowledge.

Translating what is observed into plans for meaningful activities and experiences is challenging for many reasons:

1. Observational information can indicate only the child's current **competency** level—this does not, of itself, dictate which skills need enhancing or what new ones could be acquired.

2. Observation and evaluation techniques require detailed analysis of the data if accurate inferences are to be made; analysis requires training and practice.

3. Naturalistic observation puts the emphasis for evaluation on the shoulders of the recorder.

4. The fact that a child is functioning at a particular level does not mean that the child will always develop in a particular sequence within a certain time frame or will always progress and not regress.

5. Programming for groups of children, each of whom is at a different developmental level, can be challenging if the variation is so great that the needs differ.

6. Where teachers believe that programming should focus on developmental needs, they may find that working toward determined learning outcomes or the curriculum of a school board or other authority is not only limiting but impossible.

7. A process needs to be established to move observational information into programming. This is a time-consuming activity that requires observational recording and analytical skills.

These skills are attainable, but teachers have to devote much time and hard work to achieve them. While teachers may struggle against making compromises, they should realize that some compromise is necessary in the most effective curriculum design.

Process of Curriculum Design

Observe ⟶ Record ⟶ Interpret ⟶ Plan ⟶ Implement

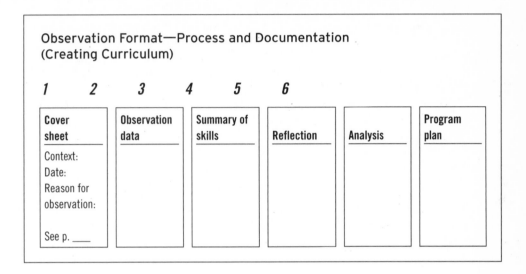

Observation Format—Process and Documentation (Creating Curriculum)

1	2	3	4	5	6
Cover sheet Context: Date: Reason for observation: See p. ___	**Observation data**	**Summary of skills**	**Reflection**	**Analysis**	**Program plan**

As part of curriculum design, observation provides ongoing evaluation of each child's environment for development. By observing, teachers can know if their intentions for the children's learning are being fulfilled. How the children respond to experiences helps teachers see how the environment might be changed or modified to facilitate learning.

Teachers and caregivers may use observation as a means of assessing the achievement of previously set goals and objectives. While this may work for some teachers, it may not work for others, particularly if their education philosophy is not one that embraces goal-setting.

Curriculum-planning models

The most effective planning models are rooted in observation and an appropriate evaluation of the child. Such evaluation can be used to indicate current competence in each developmental domain, attempt to predict the sequence of skill acquisition, and provide open-ended experiences from which the child can consolidate or build on skills.

Planning processes should ensure that the needs of the child and the focus of the program are met. Some directions may be set within a developmental context.

Sequential models make assumptions about the stages in which component parts of a competence are acquired. These models work most effectively when planning to support physical skills. Even with a clear step-by-step explanation of the stages through which the child will develop, they show little sensitivity to the concepts of learning readiness or levels of **maturation**. Children cannot always master skills even when the stages are specified and the necessary experiences are provided.

You may sometimes find that administrators' expectations regarding specified curriculum, competencies, or goals are not a "good fit" developmentally. If you program for the goal rather than the child, you may be unsuccessful. A compromise can be reached in an **input/outcome planning model**, which factors in both the child and the expectations. Teachers under pressure to conform may find this model expedient; they need not lose their integrity in their developmental focus. Ongoing, well-documented observation of the children may lead the administrator to change the expectations so that unrealistic or inappropriate outcomes are dropped. (See Chapter 9 on outcome-based education.)

Webbing models take into account the child's observed performance and curriculum goals. They try to relate all curriculum areas through a single topic or focus. These plans can generate many good ideas for constructing the learning environment; however, although they are intended to factor in observed information, their structure does not allow for it in any clear manner.

Topic planning may be based on notions of what is appropriate or desirable for the children to learn. This approach does not encourage optimal learning because it does not grow from the children's needs, interests, and abilities. Children may well get something from the topic, but it is likely to be limiting. Thematic approaches may have similar limitations but do acknowledge, at least, the need for interrelated learning experiences. Where the theme focus lends itself to open-ended activities, the children can operate at their own levels.

The gap between what the child can do independently and what she can do with support should be understood when planning experiences. Vygotsky (1978) offers an excellent model for responsive curriculum in the theory of the **zone of proximal development** (see pages 74–75). Sensitive observation of a child's behaviour will indicate when and how to move in to assist learning.

Using planning models

Advantages

- Visual presentations enable teachers to conceptualize the plan easily.
- The plan can offer programming process rather than random "good ideas."
- Teamwork planning can be effective when a common planning model is used.
- A model can be selected to fit the program's philosophy.
- The model may offer planning for developmentally appropriate experiences while meeting program outcomes.
- Most models are circular and ongoing.
- A model may easily build in a component for evaluation of its success.
- Team members can share a vision more readily.

Disadvantages

- Planning models depend on an understanding of curriculum design.
- The easiest options may be the least developmentally appropriate.
- The plan may be too abstract or not sufficiently flexible.
- If the plan is based on observation, perceptions may vary.
- Models may be used without an understanding of their underlying premise.
- The model may not conform to the needs of administrators.

Planning models based on observation

The role of the teacher is as important to the curriculum as the materials and set-up are. These planning models based on observation may help you in your responsibility. More specific samples, showing a curriculum web and an integrative planning model, can be found on pages 40 and 41.

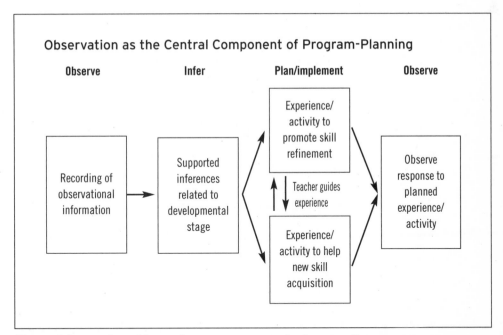

Observation as the Central Component of Program-Planning

Observe	Infer	Plan/implement	Observe
Recording of observational information	Supported inferences related to developmental stage	Experience/ activity to promote skill refinement — *Teacher guides experience* — Experience/ activity to help new skill acquisition	Observe response to planned experience/ activity

This model is one desired by teachers practising in a developmentally appropriate program, who use naturalistic observation as their primary tool for evaluation. The planning and implementation of learning experiences is supported by the teacher's guidance.

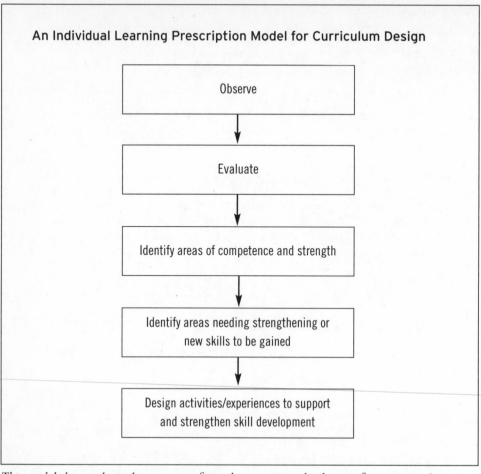

An Individual Learning Prescription Model for Curriculum Design

Observe

↓

Evaluate

↓

Identify areas of competence and strength

↓

Identify areas needing strengthening or
new skills to be gained

↓

Design activities/experiences to support
and strengthen skill development

This model shows a logical progression from observation to the design of an activity. It requires thorough analysis of observational data to identify "areas needing strengthening" or "new skills to be gained."

Current directions in curriculum design

Some educators who believe in developmental programming have been disheartened by the recent trend toward a standards-based curriculum. A prescribed curriculum may take into account the variations in children's development. However, inappropriate practice demands that young children acquire a particular knowledge base or set of skills; this can produce justifiable concerns. While skills may be acquired according to the curriculum, it is the underlying construction of their meaning that may be out of reach. We know that every child's learning is sequential and developmental, and those programs that facilitate this learning most effectively are holistic, child-centred, and developmental. Teaching skills or trying to impart knowledge outside the child's level of maturation is a waste of time. Take a look at the child's emerging skills and support him with exemplary practice, not formal lessons!

Why should we have research-based practice that includes observation and portfolio assessment for young children?

The short answer to this question is that we have plenty of evidence that observation and portfolio assessment are essential to high-quality practice in centre-based child-care, home childcare, education settings, and a variety of other programs and agencies for infants, toddlers, preschoolers, kindergarteners, and children in grades one to three and higher.

Institutions of education, professional bodies, and government agencies spell out their standards of practice, occupational standards, entry-to-practice requirements, pre-service teaching profiles, professional development portfolio structures. Head Start Regulations and many other reputable associations base their professional mandates on both developmentally appropriate practice and developmentally appropriate assessment that depend on refined observational skills.

Observation and portfolio assessment are cited in the following documents as part of a professional standard of practice:

- Canadian Child Care Federation Draft Child Care Occupational Standards 2002 (Canada):

  Draft Child Care Occupational Standards 2002
  "The ability to use observations to access children's skills, abilities, interests, and needs"

REQUIRED SKILLS AND ABILITIES	REQUIRED CORE KNOWLEDGE
Child care practitioners are able to:	Child care practitioners know:
a) use observation in an objective, non-judgmental way to assess children's skills, abilities and interests;	1) methods for the observation of children;
b) use observations to plan specific culturally–and developmentally–appropriate experiences for children;	2) methods for recording, sharing and using observations of children; and
c) communicate the results of their observations to others in a factual way that also helps to identify goals and/or jointly plan program experiences; and	3) the factors to take into account—such as a child's developmental level, past experiences, and cultural background—when interpreting observations.
d) use observation to determine whether program experiences are appropriate, useful and accepted by the children, and to modify them if necessary to better meet the children's interests, abilities and developmental needs.	Draft Child Care Practitioner Occupational Standards, March 25, 2002

Standard 4: Use observation to assess children's skills, interests and needs.

These standards are currently being drafted to improve the portability and transferability of early childhood professional status across Canada. They are also intended to underline professionalism and to support high-quality childcare. The standards have evolved from the work of the Canadian Child Care Federation (CCCF) in conjunction with the Association of Canadian Community Colleges (ACCC) as well as the key stakeholders in early childhood care and education communities across Canada.

- U.S. Department of Health and Human Services: The Administration for Children and Families Head Start Policies (USA):

  This agency outlines program-delivery requirements and also offers a clear rationale for why elements of practice should be as stated. For example:

  > Parents increase their observational skills through participation with their children in group settings and in the home, and through training with staff to become more effective in using child observations to plan the curriculum.

- *The Early Childhood Educator in British Columbia: A Guide to Registration and Renewal Procedures* (1998) (BC, Canada):

  > Observing and recording children's physical growth, cognitive skills and functioning, language development, interactions with adults and peers, dramatic play and behaviour.

  This is one of the required areas of ECE instruction in the training program that must be completed before registration as an early childhood educator in British Columbia.

- ACEI Position Paper: *Preparation of Early Childhood Education Teachers* (1998):

  > Assessing and evaluating children's total development (intellectual, social/emotional, aesthetic, physical) using authentic, performance-based assessment.

  This is an integral part of the Association for Childhood Education International's Position Paper that outlines requirements for the teaching and learning process for learners preparing for work with young children (pre-kindergarten through third grade) in the teaching profession.

- Ontario Ministry of Education and Training, College Standards & Accreditation Council (1996):

  > The graduate has reliably demonstrated the ability to utilize a variety of observation techniques to enhance work with children, families and co-workers.... *Elements of the Performance* [include]:
  >
  > - select appropriate data collection technique(s);
  > - utilize appropriate technique(s) to identify children's skills, abilities and interests;
  > - plan developmentally appropriate experiences based on the results of observations;
  > - design and modify, where necessary, physical environments for children;
  > - implement developmentally appropriate experiences;
  > - monitor children's progress;
  > - revise curriculum to support the observed developmental needs of the child(ren);
  > - apply effective information-gathering techniques to interactions involving parents, family members and others.

The points articulated in this section of the ECE Program Standards are required of all community colleges offering Early Childhood Education diploma programs that are approved by the Ontario government through the Ministry of Training, Colleges and Universities.

- NAEYC Position Statement: *A Conceptual Framework for Early Childhood Professional Development* (1998) (USA):

  observe and assess children's behaviour in planning and individualizing teaching practices and curriculum.

  This is part of the framework that the National Association for the Education of Young Children presents as its Position Statement that applies to "all individuals working in all early childhood settings...."

- National Association for the Education of Young Children's Position Statement: *Guidelines for Appropriate Curriculum Content and Assessment in Programs Serving Children Ages 3–8* (1990):

  Assessment is the process of observing, recording and otherwise documenting the work children do and how they do it, as a basis for a variety of educational decisions that affect the child. Assessment is integral to curriculum and instruction. In early childhood programs, assessment serves several different purposes: (1) to plan instruction for individuals and groups and for communicating with parents, (2) to identify children who may be in need of specialized services or intervention, and (3) to evaluate how well the program is meeting its goals.

  The U.S.-based National Association for the Education of Young Children issued these statements as its position on what constitutes developmentally appropriate curriculum and assessment within child-care settings. The document details both the guidelines for appropriate assessment and the links with program-planning, communication with parents, identifying children with special needs, program evaluation and accountability, and it indicates the teacher's role in these matters.

- National Council for Accreditation of Teacher Education (NCATE) (USA): *Program Standards for Elementary Teacher Preparation*:

  Candidates know, understand, and use formal and informal assessment strategies to plan, evaluate, and strengthen instruction that will promote continuous intellectual, social, emotional, and physical development of each elementary student.

  Candidates know that assessment is an essential and integral part of instruction. It defines the beginning point; helps identify objectives, materials and effective teaching methods or techniques; and informs the need to re-teach or adapt instruction. They understand the characteristics, uses, advantages, and limitations of different types of assessment appropriate for evaluating how K–6 students learn, what they know, and what they are able to do in each subject area. Candidates recognize that many different assessment tools and strategies, accurately and systematically used, are necessary for monitoring and promoting learning for each student. Elementary teacher candidates appropriately use a variety of formal and informal assessment techniques (e.g., observation, portfolios of elementary student work, teacher-made tests, performance tasks, projects, student self-assessments, peer assessment, and standardized tests) to enhance their knowledge of individual students, evaluate students' progress and performances, modify teaching and learning strategies, and collaborate with specialists on accommodating the needs of students with exceptionalities. Candidates use formative and summative assessments to determine student understanding of each subject area and take care to align assessments with instructional practice. They are aware that technology can facilitate appropriate forms of assessment and provide evidence across multiple dimensions of student performance. They use technology to improve the efficiency and effectiveness of assessment practices and in management of instruction. Candidates also monitor their own teaching strategies and behaviour in relation to student success, modifying plans and instructional approaches accordingly.

- Resources for Infant Educarers (RIE) (USA):

  This California-based organization was founded in 1978 by Magda Gerber and a colleague to promote the philosophy and methodology of Hungarian researcher Dr. Emmi Pikler. Magda Gerber coined the term "educarer" to describe the role of the caregiver in embedding education in the process of caring for infants. One of the key elements in this process is:

  > Sensitive observation of the child in order to understand his/her needs.

- Principles for Early Years Education: Curriculum Guidance at the Foundation Stage: Qualification and Curriculum Authority (UK):

  > Practitioners must be able to observe and respond appropriately to children.... This is demonstrated when practitioners (a) make systematic observations and assessments of each child's achievements, interests and learning styles; (b) use these observations and assessments to identify learning priorities and plan relevant and motivating learning experiences for each child; and (c) match their observations to the expectations of the early learning goals.

Summary

We all observe other people. Most of the time we do it informally. With practice, and with increasing knowledge about how children develop, we know both what to look for in a child's behaviour and we also refine our observation skills. While it is necessary to know why we are looking so intently at children—ultimately so that we can support their development, protect them, or perform our role in their lives more effectively—we are constantly amazed at the individuality we see. Because children's behaviour is so complex, we will find it challenging to understand one child's action, let alone that of a group of children, so that our skill-building develops from looking at one child at a time to how children behave and interact within a group.

Systematic observation can be used as a type of "authentic assessment." In other words, we can appreciate the child's behaviour within a natural environment and without the stress that testing might produce. Adults play a variety of roles and assume different responsibilities in their work with young children. At times we can be most useful as non-participants who can stand back and notice more about the children's behaviour. At other times we are actively engaged with the children; we exercise most of our professional responsibilities when we operate this way. The parental role is paramount and any interaction with parents should demonstrate partnership with them.

Professionalism, which includes asking for permission to observe and record, is essential in any aspect of working with children. We must determine how we can be discreet and confidential in our conversations and in the record-keeping that is part of our jobs. We wish to be as objective as possible in our observing and recording, while we leave some room for intuitive thinking about what we see.

Recording children's behaviour is part of the cycle of designing appropriate programs for them, both individually and in groups. By summarizing recorded data, we can organize the material in meaningful ways. By reflecting on what we have recorded we can carry out the thinking and feeling parts of our professional roles. A challenging process of critical thinking stands as the core of this analytical phase of the cycle. However, the cycle is not very useful if we have not developed a planned response. We design activities and programs based on what we have seen and interpreted. We continue the cycle with further observation, summarizing, and so on. Whether or not we record our observations formally, we must use observation skills as a central element in our practice as educators.

Key Terms

analysis

assessment

behaviour

bias

confidentiality

curriculum

early intervention

emerging skill

exceptional child

holistic

individual education plan (IEP)

individual program plan (IPP)

inference

input/outcome planning model

naturalistic

nonparticipant observation

norm

normal patterns

objectives

participant observation

perception

portfolio

professionalism

sequential model

special needs

subjective

summary

topic planning

validate

webbing model

zone of proximal development

Weblinks

www.acei.org
The Association for Childhood Education International (ACEI), a national association whose philosophy is to promote and support the optimal education and development of children, from birth through early adolescence, in the global community.

www.cayc.ca
The Canadian Association for Young Children (CAYC), a national association focusing on the well-being of children, from birth through age nine.

www.cccf-fcsge.ca
The Canadian Child Care Federation (CCCF) aims to improve the quality of child-care services to Canadian families.

www.childcarecanada.org
The Childcare Resource and Research Unit focuses on early childhood care and education research and policy.

www.healthcanada.ca/chr
Health Canada provides links to a variety of child-related sites. This particular page provides information on Canada's Child Health Record.

www.rightsofchildren.ca
The Canadian Coalition for the Rights of Children site offers information about the rights of children for people who work with children in specific areas.

Observation Sample

This sample shows how a student uses a prepared form to assist her critical thinking. She makes an inference from her observation and supports it with a quotation from a theory.

Analysis Chart: Observations

Child's name: *Zoe*   Date: *November 4, 2003*

Child's age: *2 years, 8 months*   Inference # *7*

Domain(s) of development *(If possible, state inferences in each developmental area.)*

The following inference concerns this/these area(s) of development:

Social-personal skills; imitative behaviour

Having examined the evidence *(Make a statement that assesses the child's development—is it typical, atypical, or can you explain it using a theoretical model?)*

I infer that *Zoe shows some signs of preoperational thinking. She has internalized a behaviour and imitated it.*

The source of my inference *(Which observation or bit of information led you to the inference?)*

Because I recorded *that she engaged in deferred imitation, where she imitated how her grandfather had placed a plastic cat-face mask on his face.*

My reasoning *(Give your own reasons for stating the inference.)*

I think this because *when I babysat a toddler, she held a baby doll in her arms and fed it with a toy bottle, just as her mother had done with her baby brother earlier that day when I had visited.*

Quote from norm (if applicable) *(Validate your inference with the use of either a norm, a theory, or both.)*

I found this quote from a normative development profile to support my inference:

N/A

Quote from theory (if applicable) *(Validate your inference with the explanation of a theory.)*

I found a theory that supports my inference. The theory is called *preoperational stage of cognitive development.*

This is a quote from the explanation of the theory: *"Many children between 24 and 30 months are entering Piaget's preoperational stage of cognitive development. The first sub-stage . . . is preconceptual, which occurs from about 2 to 4 years of age. . . . In deferred imitation the child imitates another person's behavior, even when that person is no longer present."*

The name of the theorist is *Piaget*

Author I found this in a book by *LaVisa Cam Wilson*

Title The book is called *Infants and Toddlers: Curriculum and Teaching (2nd ed.)*

Source The book/journal/article is published by *Delmar Publishers Inc.*

Date of publication: *1990*   Page # of quote: *276–277*

Observer/assessor/recorder's name: *Wanda*

Observation Sample

This simple IPP is based on behaviours recorded in observations. The child's needs have been determined. Activities are suggested to support skill development.

Individual Program Plan (IPP)

Child's name: Arjumand

Caregiver: Casz

Age/D.O.B.: April 9, 2003/1 year old

Date: April 15, 2004

Area of Development	Needs	Activities
Explores environment using fine motor skills (pincer grasp)	Small objects	Activity pillow with buckle, zipper, shoelace, and velcro Wind-up toys Putting small blocks in a bucket
Transfer objects from hand to hand	Small objects Chance to explore	Offer toys to Ashley when already has one Passing games (adapted version of "hot potato")
Feed self using a spoon	Opportunity Encouragement Exposure to spoons in a variety of situations	Kitchen play Sensory activities using spoons (e.g., oatmeal play)
Walk alone (began at the end of March)	Open space Encouragement	Gross Motor Room Walks of the center Nature walks outside Pull toys (e.g., wagons)
Climb on, over, and through objects	Climbing equipment Carpeted/padded areas Sturdy furniture	Slides Cushion ramps, stairs, and blocks Pillows Tunnels
Imitate actions and sounds	Music People Mirrors Toys with sounds	Songs with actions (e.g., "Row Your Boat") Copycat games; if he does something, you repeat it Walks outside so nature sounds can be imitated
Nod for "yes" and shake head for "no"	Opportunity to decide for himself Encouragement Reinforcement	Ask questions and let him tell you when he is done Repeat nods accompanied by you saying "yes"
Follow simple directions	Opportunity Praise Encouragement	Simple "Simon Says" games Head and shoulders, knees and toes Clean-up activities (e.g., put the toy on the shelf) Ask him to do things (e.g., "Please sit down" or "Come here, please")
Openly show affection toward others and his toys (likes to cuddle)	Trust Consistency Soft toys Praise Love	Songs about loving (e.g., Barney song, "I Love You") Pillows Teddy bears (washable) Cuddle Ashley throughout the day

Observation Sample

This excerpt from an analysis chart shows use of a structured approach to critical thinking. Observations are broken down by developmental domain. Explanations of behaviours use recognized theories and norms.

ANALYSIS OF DEVELOPMENT

Child's name: Carolina   Child's age: 18 months

SPEECH AND LANGUAGE DEVELOPMENT

Behavior observed	Inference	Reasoning
Followed caregiver when caregiver asked her to come	It's typical for children of this age to follow simple requests.	I believe this to be true because I have observed other children following simple requests.
Said hello on toy phone	It's typical for a child almost 12 months to start to use single words.	Children at this age learn through imitation, and the child hears "hello" many times a day.
Would sing before falling asleep	It seemed that the child was soothing herself before falling asleep.	Developmental Profiles states the child will do this as a way of releasing tension.
Would engage in rhythmic singing	It seemed that the repetitive sounds were the beginnings of speech.	David Elkind has noted that babbling and rhythmic sound speed up the acquisition of speech.

PERSONAL-SOCIAL DEVELOPMENT

Behavior observed	Inference	Reasoning
Watched the delivery man come in and followed him	Child seemed not to have a fear of strangers.	Child felt safe in her environment and does not have the concept of danger yet.
Imitated the adult's action by clapping hands	It's typical behaviour for children of this age to imitate adults.	Child observed what adult was doing and then repeated the action.
Followed caregiver when caregiver asked her to come	It's typical for children of this age to follow simple requests.	I believe this to be true because I have observed other children following simple requests.
Clapped hands and danced to a familiar song	It's typical for children of this age to enjoy rhymed activities.	I have observed other children, and they all seem to like dancing and singing.

BIBLIOGRAPHY
Allen, K.E., & Marotz, L.R. (1994). Developmental profiles: Pre-birth through eight (2nd ed.). Albany, NY: Delmar.

Observer's name: Ken   Date: November 6, 2003

Validation by theory	Validation by norm	Source	Bibliographic reference
	Carries out simple directions and requests	K. Eileen Allen & Lynn Marotz	Developmental Profiles, p. 73
	Names everyday objects; imitates sounds	K. Eileen Allen & Lynn Marotz	Developmental Profiles, p. 63
	May sing as a way of winding down	K. Eileen Allen & Lynn Marotz	Developmental Profiles, p. 75
The inability to babble during the early months of life delays language acquisition.		David Elkind	Sympathetic Understanding, p. 21

Validation by theory	Validation by norm	Source	Bibliographic reference
Children will show fear only after they have the concept that they are an object that can be destroyed.		David Elkind	Sympathetic Understanding, p. 12
	Often imitates adult action in play	K. Eileen Allen & Lynn Marotz	Developmental Profiles, p. 74
	Carries out simple directions and requests	K. Eileen Allen & Lynn Marotz	Developmental Profiles, p. 73
	Children enjoy simple songs, dance, and music.	K. Eileen Allen & Lynn Marotz	Developmental Profiles, p. 64

Elkind, D. (1994). A sympathetic understanding of the child: Birth to sixteen (3rd ed.). Boston: Allyn & Bacon.

Observation Sample

This thorough IEP was created for Jamilla, who has been identified as needing special support. Jamilla's resource teacher recorded the chart with Jamilla's regular teacher.

Individual Education Plan (IEP)

Child's name: Jamilla

Age/D.O.B.: 5 years, 7 months

Recorder: Ms. Jessop

Caregivers/Teachers: Ms. Trainor, Ms. Jessop

Date: May 7/04

Date of last IEP: April 9/04

Comment on success of previous IEP: Jamilla achieved the skills that were needed to perform the activities. There remains some concern about Jamilla's lack of social skills.

Developmental domain	Observation	Support	Response
Physical development: • gross motor	Jamilla watches other children in the playground. Walks around with adult supervisor.	Jamilla needs opportunities to become engaged with other children's activities.	Try parachute games and other noncompetitive games.
• fine motor	Jamilla has started to copy letters and joins in with drawing and "writing." She does some scribble shapes like letters in her name. She notices that other children can write their names.	Opportunities to develop fine motor control (and build self-esteem) are needed.	As Jamilla likes dramatic play, we could introduce a "post office" and writing center with writing pads, "stamps," envelopes, etc.
Cognition • number	Counting in sequence is no problem 1-20, but Jamilla can only count to 4 or 5 when actually counting objects.	Jamilla needs the chance to have fun with counting experiences.	Sociodramatic play could also have a table (for 6?) to set. Jamilla would enjoy "preparing" a meal for "guests."
• seriation	Jamilla gets confused when putting objects in any kind of sequence. She makes up her own reasons for pictures or objects to be the way she wishes.	Opportunity to seriate in play might add meaning to this.	Provide picture cards of growing seeds, buds opening, etc. (link with spring theme).
• patterning, matching, and sorting	When given assorted items, she can sort them according to color and kind but not according to two characteristics together. Jamilla likes to play with buttons, shells, and pine cones, making patterns with them. She plays with the materials by herself and rejects involvement with others.	The materials are already available, but these could be extended with other items.	Jamilla can be asked about her patterns--these involve sorting and patterning. She can be encouraged to articulate her reasoning for the patterns.

Developmental domain	Observation	Support	Response
Language • literacy	Jamilla appears to enjoy stories; she wants the same ones re-read. She follows the stories page by page. When sitting alone, she "reads" the story. At other times, Jamilla recognizes word shapes.	Provide other stories and opportunity to talk about the ones she likes. Pick up and reinforce her understanding of words in context.	Offer picture books for Jamilla to create stories. Provide books she likes and reinforce key words. Link words with everyday objects.
• language	Jamilla listens at circle time but only talks confidently one-to-one with an adult. She tends to play alone with a lot of self-talk.	She needs to build confidence.	Avoid forcing Jamilla, but provide opportunity for closeness with an adult.
Social development • play behavior	Jamilla tends to play alone. Sometimes she will play alongside others if she is interested in the activity (e.g., cooking).	Jamilla needs confidence to communicate, but her thinking tends to be egocentric. She needs time and play experience.	Encourage parallel play and provide opportunity for some association. Sharing tools may help.
• relationships with adults	Quiet moments alone with the teacher are the most happy times for Jamilla. She jumps up and down with enthusiasm when she starts talking. Soon she is immersed in conversation and she becomes composed again.	She needs one-to-one contact to build trust so that she can become more autonomous.	The new assistant could try to spend extra time so that Jamilla can build trust and begin to "branch out."
Emotions	Jamilla expresses her feelings in quiet communication but does not project her wishes to other children. At times, she is left out of the "girl play" because she can't negotiate.	Jamilla would be happier if she could find her way into the play with her peers.	Role-play situations may help. Strategies to overcome communication problems can come in children's stories.

Observation Sample

This web outlines an individual curriculum plan for a child in Grade 1. Moving out from observing the child's interests and abilities, the teacher plans activities to lead to desired achievements or learning.

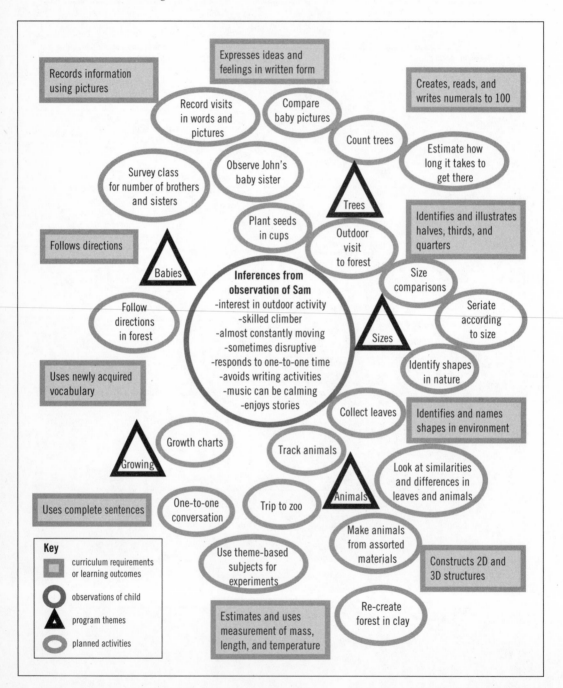

Records information using pictures

Expresses ideas and feelings in written form

Creates, reads, and writes numerals to 100

Record visits in words and pictures

Compare baby pictures

Count trees

Estimate how long it takes to get there

Survey class for number of brothers and sisters

Observe John's baby sister

Trees

Identifies and illustrates halves, thirds, and quarters

Plant seeds in cups

Outdoor visit to forest

Follows directions

Babies

Size comparisons

Seriate according to size

Follow directions in forest

Inferences from observation of Sam
-interest in outdoor activity
-skilled climber
-almost constantly moving
-sometimes disruptive
-responds to one-to-one time
-avoids writing activities
-music can be calming
-enjoys stories

Sizes

Identify shapes in nature

Uses newly acquired vocabulary

Collect leaves

Identifies and names shapes in environment

Growth charts

Track animals

Look at similarities and differences in leaves and animals

Growing

Animals

Uses complete sentences

One-to-one conversation

Trip to zoo

Make animals from assorted materials

Constructs 2D and 3D structures

Use theme-based subjects for experiments

Re-create forest in clay

Estimates and uses measurement of mass, length, and temperature

Key

curriculum requirements or learning outcomes

observations of child

program themes

planned activities

Observation Sample

This integrative-planning model focuses on the whole experience of the child related to a theme rather than on particular curriculum areas. The model leads to planning experiences and environments but does not determine expected outcomes; the open-ended activities allow each child to learn what he or she is developmentally ready to do. Teachers and caregivers can use their observations of the children to help plan motivating experiences and to intervene appropriately to support each child's learning. Observation of the children's responses also leads to modified or new activities.

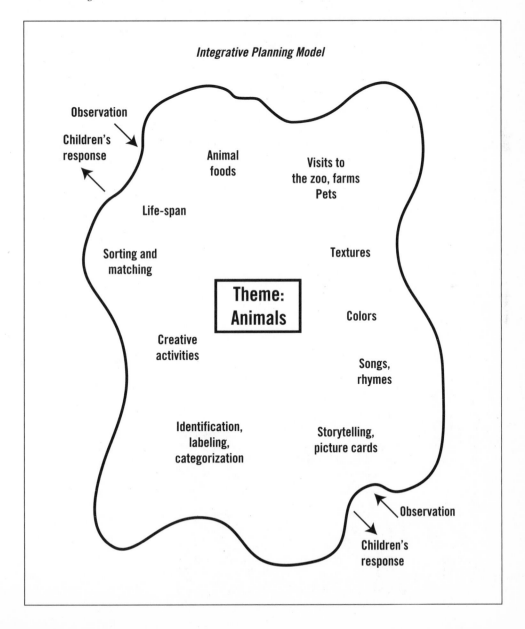

Integrative Planning Model

Observation
Children's response

Animal foods

Visits to the zoo, farms Pets

Life-span

Sorting and matching

Textures

Theme: Animals

Colors

Creative activities

Songs, rhymes

Identification, labeling, categorization

Storytelling, picture cards

Observation
Children's response

Observing
Development

chapter 2

*And so we see that if we can develop a more delicate faculty of observation,
we can really gain an insight into the true essence of human existence.*

Rudolf Steiner (1924)

*Early life experiences have disproportionate importance in organizing the
mature brain and are directly connected to children's optimal development.*

B.D. Perry (1996)

*Success is achieved if one is faithful to life, observing and
examining it in its individual and general reference.*

Friedrich Froebel (1826)

Any activity can
demonstrate a child's
development in various
domains. A careful
observer of these children
playing together could
comment not only on
their physical skills but
also on their social,
emotional, and
communication skills.

Observing the Development of Young Children

What we see when observing young children depends on what we know about how human beings grow and develop. The philosophy of observation and authentic assessment, and of this book, is based on the following principles:

Human beings

- are unique and individual and yet have characteristics that are common to all.
- need to form attachments and develop within a social network.
- tend to share patterns of maturational change.
- inherit many attributes and potentials, but their experiences of life influence how they develop.
- require early interactions and experiences that will decisively affect the structure of their brains and the type and extent of their adult capacities.
- are diverse in their appearance, patterns of development, beliefs, lifestyles, occupations, and needs.
- demonstrate individual temperamental styles that tend to remain fairly constant throughout life.
- develop within, shape, and are shaped by social contexts that are part of wider ecological systems.
- adapt to changing environments and circumstances, creating an individually constructed knowledge of the world.
- develop in patterns of continuous and discontinuous change, some elements of development increasing gradually and constantly and others changing in surges and plateaus.
- depend on having their basic physical and psychological needs met.

- are especially sensitive to particular kinds of stimuli at certain times in their development.
- undergo many changes during their lives, some observable and others internal.
- function in remarkably different ways and demonstrate a broad range of ways they can be creative, solve problems, and accommodate life experiences.
- are influenced by **social**, **biological**, and **psychological clocks**.
- demonstrate similar basic emotional expressions whatever their cultures or locations, whereas they learn social emotions within a context.
- continue to develop throughout their lifespans, each stage of which is equally significant.
- perceive the meaning of their lives and what is socially acceptable according to a myriad of different social, emotional, and spiritual factors.
- can be raised in environments that support and optimize development, but they cannot progress faster than their own timetables for development.
- may deviate from expected patterns of growth and development or have **special needs**, and they may sometimes require special health, nurturance, or education interventions.

The developmental process

DEFINITION: Child development

Child development is the dynamic process of change and progression that enables each individual to become increasingly independent, knowledgeable, skilled, and self-sufficient.

Child development depends on maturational processes and environmental conditions that can optimize each individual's genetic potential. Theories of child development, like those of lifespan development, consider each human being as highly individual in appearance, style, and needs, while recognizing reasonably predictable patterns of adaptation, changes in thinking structures, and skills acquisition among most members of a population. Child-development models can help us understand the role we can play in observing young children and supporting their development.

The biological clock is set by the individual's heredity. It shapes the person's pattern of **maturation**. The family and the wider community determine the social clock by their expectations. The complex inner self, beliefs, and motivations drive the psychological clock. As each clock "ticks," all three clocks influence the individual's development, interacting with one other.

At three years of age, Jerry, for example, is expected to be ready for nursery school (social clock). But he still wets himself because he does not yet have full bladder control (biological clock). Jerry wants to go to nursery school as the other children do and he

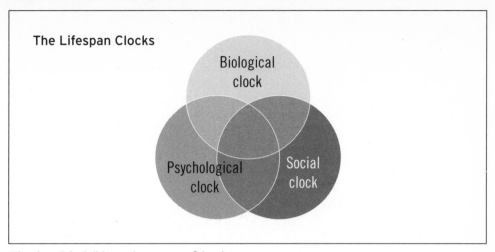

The three "clocks" drive the process of development.

feels bad whenever they see him wet himself (psychological clock). Soon he will be able to control his bladder and will go to nursery school. His motivation will help his ability to read the signs of a full bladder.

TAKING A SPECIAL LOOK: Developmental delay

For a variety of reasons, some children may have slower-than-average development. The developmental delay may be general or specific in one or two domains. The caregiver or teacher may identify a cause for concern and approach the child's parents, or a parent may bring a concern to the caregiver's or teacher's attention. It then becomes the professional's responsibility, along with that of the parent, to observe the child closely, focusing on the particular area in question and the child's development in general.

Developmental Domains

One way to look at a child's development is to consider the developmental domains and how they interact. Although we divide the domains for ease of study, they also need to be seen as a dynamic whole. Within each person, this development happens differently, with external factors influencing developmental outcomes.

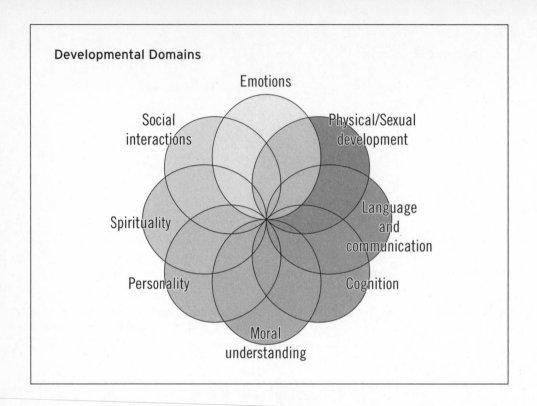

Developmental Domains

Emotions

Social interactions

Physical/Sexual development

Spirituality

Language and communication

Personality

Cognition

Moral understanding

TAKING A SPECIAL LOOK: The use of norms

Looking at the typical behaviours of children at particular ages and stages gives us an idea of what is average, but this **norm** does not imply that children "should" be at a certain level of achievement. The norm is just one way of viewing children's skill development, and it can give us an idea of how they are progressing. When we use the yardstick of the norm over a period of time, we can identify the children's rate of development in each domain. The fact that a child takes nine months to achieve skills that the average child accomplishes in about six months can tell us about the child's pattern of development.

If we can see that a child's skills are lagging behind those of other children her age, we may need to pay closer attention. Whatever the skills she demonstrates, we need to support that development, document further observations, and, if necessary, refer the child to a specialist.

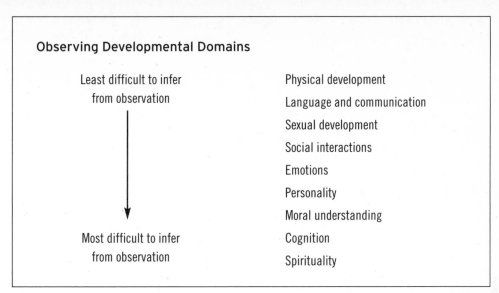

Observing Developmental Domains

Least difficult to infer
from observation

↓

Most difficult to infer
from observation

Physical development

Language and communication

Sexual development

Social interactions

Emotions

Personality

Moral understanding

Cognition

Spirituality

This sequence is offered to highlight the observer's challenge in making sense of observational information. It is based on the idea that behaviours that are clearly observable are easier to interpret. The sequence focuses on the evaluation of the child's progression through developmental stages. (It is not intended to be a hierarchy of difficulty in attributing theoretical explanations as to why the behaviour is demonstrated.)

Physical development

Physical development has two basic aspects: the development of **gross motor skills**, which refer to the large muscles of the body; and the development of **fine motor skills**, which concern control of the small muscles. The **cephalo-caudal principle** explains that the typical sequence of bodily control starts with the head and proceeds from there down; according to the **proximo-distal principle**, control usually begins at the centre of the body and proceeds to the extremities. **Sensory acuity** changes rapidly in the early months of the infant's life, with all five senses operating at an optimal level by the age of about two years. Bodily proportions change throughout development, with the head in infancy being larger in proportion to the rest of the body and the body gaining in proportional size through later stages.

Growth is an integral part of development and concerns only increase in size. Even with good nutrition, a child may demonstrate individual patterns of weight gain and height increase. The child's basic needs of food, shelter, clothing, and protection must be satisfied so that she develops physically in a healthy way. Children can fail to thrive if their physical or emotional needs are not met.

Sequences of skill development are common to most children, but they may take place at differing rates. Physical development is the most easily observed group of developmental changes. A sample observation can be found on page 83.

Observe:

- reflexive movements
- appearance: skin tone, quality, and clarity; posture; facial expression; hair colour and texture; nail quality; eye brightness and clearness, pupil dilation; facial symmetry; ear positioning and cleanliness; sweat, personal odour
- teeth: number, type, colour, and health
- skin marks: freckles, spots, birthmarks; cuts, bruises; acne, milia; urticaria, heat rash, cradle cap, diaper rash, etc.
- neck: angle and symmetry
- body temperature
- level of consciousness: uptime, downtime, trance, and sleep
- sleep: types, times, rhythms, and length
- appetite
- responses to foods: allergies, sensitivities, indigestion, colic, etc.
- abdomen: shape, protrusions, etc.
- increases in height
- body symmetry
- weight
- distribution of body fat
- muscular tone and definition
- alterations in body proportions
- sexual characteristics
- use and acuity of senses: sight, hearing, touch, taste, smell, and multimodal sensory acuity
- responsiveness to stimuli
- mouth and palate: shape, colour, and symmetry
- sound production
- levels of activity and passivity
- heart rate
- respiration
- bowel movements: continence, colour, consistency, frequency, and amount
- urination: continence, colour, frequency, and amount
- bodily fluids: drooling, discharges, etc.
- fontanels (in children younger than two years)
- mobility
- leg positioning and straightness
- large-body skills: walking, running, jumping, kicking, etc.
- foot position: inward pointing, outward pointing
- right- or left-footedness
- endurance
- hand coordination
- fine motor/manipulative skills: holding, throwing, catching, squeezing, drawing, piano-playing, etc.
- right- or left-handedness
- self-help skills: dressing, undressing, toileting, feeding, etc.
- repetitive behaviours: habits and patterns of physical behaviour

Observing Physical Development

Child's name:_____   Observer: _____

Age/D.O.B.: _____   Date: _____

Context/setting: _____

What gross motor skills do you observe? _____

_____

_____

_____

_____

What fine motor skills do you observe?_____

_____

_____

_____

_____

Describe the child's physical appearance and health indicators.

skin color/tone:_____

hair color/texture/length and condition: _____

eyes: _____

senses: _____

nails: _____

teeth: _____

foot position (inward/outward pointing): _____

head size in proportion to trunk/legs:_____

body shape: _____

body fat distribution:_____

posture/alignment/body symmetry: _____

legs (straight/bowed): _____

injuries (scars/bruises/etc.): _____

bowel control:_____

bladder control: _____

self-help skills: _____

observable habits: _____

identifying features: _____

height: _____

weight: _____

respiration: _____

health signs (and symptoms): _____

left/right hand preference: _____

Observing the children's activity—such as the ones pictured here—gives us some idea of their fine motor skill development, but it may also indicate their interests, personality, and social skills. Developing in one domain usually influences development in other domains.

Sexual development

Adults may have difficulty in thinking of very young children as "sexual" because sexuality is associated with adult activity and reproduction. However, any individual's sexuality starts in infancy. In a baby we see this in the attachments he makes with adults, the intimacy of close relationships, the sensuality of touch, multi-sensory experiences, and the physical discovery of the baby's own body. Healthy child sexuality involves learning about bodies, their functions, and gender. Most important, **sexual development** involves nurturance and the meeting of a child's physical and psychological needs. It is necessary for children to learn by experience and example that sensations can be pleasurable and that sexual activity, at the right time and in the appropriate place, is enjoyable. Above all, the child needs to feel loved, to learn to build trusting relationships, to build positive attitudes, and to discover what behaviours are socially acceptable. Privacy, respect, and personal space are essential for healthy sexual development; children need to find out what behaviours they can demonstrate in front of others and what behaviours are private. Answering children's questions about sex must be appropriate to their individual development, as should be any learning experience about sexuality.

Observe:

- attachment behaviours
- eye-gazing (gazing into space with or without focus, into another person's eyes or at an object)
- being soothed by touch/rhythmic movement
- accepting adult touch
- responding positively to massage
- initiating attention
- responding to adult cues
- discovering parts of the body
- assuming different postures for urination
- sensory discovery
- sensory repetition
- recognizing own body parts
- recognizing other children's body parts
- willingness to remove clothes
- sexual curiosity
- self-esteem
- sudden phobias
- self-help skills
- naming body parts
- categorization of self ("I'm a boy")
- identifying body functions
- masturbating
- choosing to be alone during toileting/bathroom times
- desire to be private
- request for personal space for personal belongings
- sharing/refusing to share
- physical distance between child and adult or other child
- asking questions about bodies or sexuality
- expressing emotions
- simulating "adult" sexual activity
- correct or incorrect statements about sexual intercourse
- child's conversation about television, movie, video, or DVD sequences
- doll play
- adult role play
- role reversal play
- unexpected displays of guilt, anger, shame, or sadness
- being "baby"
- gender-related play
- dressing up as member of the opposite sex
- "bathroom talk" ("poo-poohead")
- telling or repeating smutty jokes
- giggling or whispering ("Hazel loves Jason!")
- pro-social or helping behaviours
- exhibiting forceful behaviour to others/dolls
- communicating understanding of socially acceptable behaviour ("Only mommies and daddies do that")
- somatic symptoms ("I've got a headache")
- repetitive play
- worrying about mom or sister, etc.
- activity level
- separation anxiety
- response levels to stimuli
- repeated mention of fairness
- telling of "stories," real or imagined
- aimless behaviour or wandering
- need to see siblings
- functioning within a group of peers

- friendliness to strangers
- emotion expressed to or about parent
- quality of sleep
- use of sexual language
- habitual behaviours (such as nail-biting)
- eating patterns
- adjustment to new situations
- kissing (the way the child kisses parents, teacher, sibling, or child)

- touching (how, where, or the way the child touches others)
- swearing or using sexual terms
- sexual discovery (access to books or other media)
- inappropriate and appropriate actions
- relationship problem-solving
- same-sex relationships
- opposite-sex relationships
- group composition (male and female)

This list highlights elements of sexual development. Fortunately, most children demonstrate healthy development in all domains. If the observer has concerns about a child's health or behaviour that may indicate the possibility that the child has suffered abuse, the adult must report those concerns to a child-protection agency. An observer must follow the policies of schools and child-care centres in situations of potential abuse. They do not need proof that a child has been abused—only the reasonable concern that the child might have been abused. Confidentiality must be assured and no accusations should be made.

Language and communication

Language development leads to two-way interpersonal communication. It includes both hearing and the physical ability to produce sound, but it also concerns the other sensory abilities. Language requires experimentation with sound, the repetition of human sounds, the attachment to adults, and various forms of reinforcement. There appear to be **sensitive periods** early in life for language development. It is thought that human beings are "pre-wired" to acquire language as long as certain conditions allow it to flourish. Stages of first-language learning are clearly observable, while the underlying explanations of how language is acquired are more complex. Learning language is the precursor of literacy. Children who are exposed to more than one language may be at an intellectual advantage in later development.

Observe:

- crying: types and length
- eye-gazing
- eye contact
- two-way communication
- cooing
- vowel-type sound production
- babbling
- seeking adult company
- responding to "mother-ese" or "parent-ese"
- attaching to adults
- game-playing
- modulated babbling
- listening
- repeating consonants
- pointing
- gesturing
- making requests
- protesting
- drawing attention to self
- experimenting with sounds
- imitating sounds
- understanding language
- using holophrases (single words that, when uttered, imply the meaning of whole sentences)
- taking turns
- making pronunciation errors
- producing whole words
- language with gesturing
- uttering two-word phrases
- using phrases of three or more words
- asking questions
- answering questions
- using grammar/rules of language
- listening to stories
- labelling objects
- naming people
- rhythmic sound production
- repeating rhymes
- creating stories
- creating rhymes
- singing
- pretend-playing
- role-playing
- storytelling
- cooperating with other children
- communicating in associative play and activity
- social conversation
- responding to social overtures
- initiating social relationships
- expressing feelings
- collaborating on projects
- making grammatical errors
- clarifying misunderstandings
- mixing two languages
- recognizing written letters
- recognizing own name
- writing own name
- understanding the experiences and feelings of others
- reporting and planning
- lying and variations of telling the "truth"
- comparing and interpreting
- inferring
- decoding
- encoding
- imagining
- reasoning
- predicting sequences

- inquiring about people, places, objects, and ideas
- socially acceptable communication
- drawing conclusions
- copying word shapes
- early writing

- story- and letter-writing (simple or complex)
- symbolizing (using symbols but not always ones that have meaning to others)
- representing ideas

TAKING A SPECIAL LOOK: Responding to cues

Young children can send out different **cues** or messages to us through their body language, gestures, and expressions. They have individual ways of communicating. Children with some special needs may need to be supported with communication strategies and sometimes **assistive devices** so that they can be understood better. For example, a visually impaired infant may not maintain eye contact, smile, or imitate an adult in the same way that a sighted infant would. Caregivers will have to observe any visual responses she does make and provide communication means that she can perceive, perhaps through her other senses. If caregivers observe such a sensory deficit in a child, they should share their observations with the parents, who may have similar observations, and seek further professional assessment. In this example, the child will probably need glasses.

Although infants cannot express themselves through language, they communicate in other ways. Their development in this domain can be observed through such signs as facial expressions, gestures, eye contact, and crying.

Social interactions

Social development involves both the concept of self and the individual's relationships with others. Early **attachments** to primary caregivers are necessary for children to start building a sense of themselves. There may be particularly sensitive periods for the formation of these personal relationships, and long-term consequences if such relationships are not established. Children need other people so that they can learn what is socially acceptable. Much of this knowledge is gained through imitation. Social learning involves internalizing role models, so **social play** through pretend games is very important. **Social interactions** can be readily observed when children are at play, in domestic situations, or in their natural environment with other adults or children. A sample observation can be found on page 84.

Observe:

- eye-gazing
- reciprocal communication
- bonding to adult
- cues for attention
- egocentricity
- relationships with primary caregivers
- relationships with family members
- multiple attachments
- relationships with strangers
- stranger anxiety
- separation of "self" from others
- self-concept
- onlooker activity
- solitary play
- trial-and-error learning
- personal achievement
- individual problem-solving
- identification of own needs
- articulation of personal needs
- strategies for meeting personal needs
- parallel play

- genderless play
- recognition of the existence of others
- perspective-shifting
- associative playing
- sharing skills
- imitative learning
- acknowledgment of similarities and differences
- same-sex friendships
- acceptance as member of a group
- identification with group activities or beliefs
- opposite-sex friendships
- categorical self
- pretend-playing
- role-playing
- team activity and problem-solving
- cooperative playing
- developing strategies for collective success
- caring for others
- unconditional love

Observing Social Interactions

Observer: _____ Date(s): _____

Context(s)/setting(s): _____

	Child's appearance	Activity/materials	Involvement with self/others	Category of social play or activity
Infant				
Toddler				
Preschooler				
School-age child				

Observing Cooperative Activity

Children's names: _____ Ages/D.O.B.: _____

_____ _____

_____ _____

_____ _____

Observer: _____ Date: _____

Context/setting: _____

Type of activity: _____

Materials: _____

_____

How the play/activity started: _____

_____

How the activity progressed: _____

_____

_____

Adult involvement (if any): _____

_____

Evidence of leadership: _____

_____

Evidence of following instructions: _____

_____

How "rules" were set or followed: _____

_____

What agreement or disagreement was demonstrated: _____

_____

How difficulties were resolved: _____

_____

Evidence of sharing/empathy: _____

_____

Emotional development

Emotional development involves the expression and control of feelings. All infants express basic **emotions** in similar ways. However, feelings become more complex as children understand more about themselves, others, and the world. A parent's relationship influences early emotions. Children experience typical stages of emotional conflict throughout childhood. At first, infants strive for a trusting relationship; then they focus on becoming independent and showing initiative, and struggle for a clear sense of self-worth. **Social emotions** express feelings shaped by social experiences. Emotions can be observed by interpreting behaviours, expressions, posture, and gestures, but inner conflicts and the subtleties of complex emotions may be harder to analyze.

Observe:

- facial expressions
- eyes: openness, direction, pupil dilation, symmetry
- eyebrows: shape and position
- creases on forehead
- mouth: open or closed, tilted
- head tilt: direction and angle
- nose: flared or relaxed
- cheeks: puffy, pinched, etc.
- skin: patchiness, colour, sweat, etc.
- breathing: rate and depth
- posture
- positioning of arms
- state of consciousness
- attachments
- separations (being separated from a person, the child might behave in a way that shows the kind of attachment he has to this individual)
- patterns of sleep
- eating patterns and appetite
- speed of movement
- gestures
- cues
- regression and progression in play, language, or other developmental domain
- response to stimuli

- egocentricity
- perspective-changing
- pretend-playing
- intentional communications
- role-playing
- control of anger
- building confidence
- expressions of love
- use of comfort objects
- habitual behaviours
- labelling of emotions
- congruence between stated feelings and behaviour
- fantasy-playing
- making friends
- recognizing own emotional needs
- meeting personal needs
- sustaining friendships
- reactions to sensory experiences
- self-regulation
- creativity or destructiveness
- response to guidance strategies
- returning to plateau states of emotion
- coping with crises
- using personal style to advantage
- acknowledging the feelings of others

Observing Attachments and Separations

Child's name:_____   Observer: _____

Age/D.O.B.: _____   Date: _____

Context/setting: _____   Caregiver(s)/parent(s):_____

Child's routine contact with adults (e.g., 6 p.m.–8 a.m.: Mom; 8 a.m.–6 p.m.: 2 ECE teachers):

_____

_____

_____

Indicators of attachment (e.g., eye contact, physical closeness, etc.) to:

Adult #1: _____   Role: _____

_____

Adult #2: _____   Role: _____

_____

Adult #3: _____   Role: _____

_____

Adult #4: _____   Role: _____

_____

Behaviors at the time of separation from:

Adult #1: _____

Adult #2: _____

Adult #3: _____

Adult #4: _____

Behaviors one hour after separation from:

Adult #1: _____

Adult #2: _____

Adult #3: _____

Adult #4: _____

Personality

Personality involves the individual's **temperament**, awareness of self, patterns of response, and ability to manage life's challenges. Temperamental styles tend to be observable soon after birth and are thought to remain fairly constant throughout life. However, life experiences can alter how people deal with their temperaments, and adults can influence how children see themselves and cope with events. Temperamental styles have observable characteristics, whereas personality types can be difficult to label, because personal characteristics and patterns of behaviour need to be observed over a prolonged period. Chess and Thomas (1996) offer a useful model for identifying temperamental types for teachers and caregivers trying to respond to different temperamental styles (see page 190). A wide range of personality assessments are available, but there is merit in observing a child naturally rather than performing tests that disregard variables from situation to situation.

Observe:

- activity level
- rhythms and daily patterns
- pace of activity
- timing of responses
- adaptability and openness to new experiences
- extroversion or introversion
- response to success or failure
- response to being touched
- emotional stability or instability
- intensity of reactions
- agreeableness
- consistency of reaction patterns
- personal space (physical)
- need to be with others or to be alone
- pattern of self-control
- responses to stressors
- pro-social or antisocial style
- reality or fantasy
- positive or negative perceptions
- self-concept
- identification with adults
- leading or following others
- sex-role performances
- creativity
- optimism or pessimism
- confidence or diffidence
- habits
- honesty or dishonesty
- seeking of emotional or practical support
- conscientiousness
- role-playing
- degree of autonomy
- mood quality and changes
- distractibility
- attention span
- persistence
- sleep and wakefulness
- body type: ectomorph, endomorph, or mesomorph
- responses to auditory stimuli
- reponses to visual stimuli
- intensity
- stability
- sensitivity

Moral understanding

Moral understanding involves the intellectual and social skills of understanding the difference between right and wrong and being able to behave according to those principles. **Morality** develops from understanding social roles and responsibilities and may be shaped by religious beliefs and culturally determined roles. Because cognitive skills are required to be able to think from the perspective of others and to manipulate ideas about what is ethical or morally right, this developmental domain is difficult to observe. **Pro-social skills** are easier to observe, but the ability to behave appropriately or desirably do not necessarily indicate moral understanding. It is thought that stages of moral understanding can be observed through children's responses to moral dilemmas.

Observe:

- concept of self
- egocentricity
- perspective-taking (ability to understand the viewpoint of another individual—a cognitive function—as well as having a personal point of view)
- attachments
- guilt
- view of punishment
- response to consequences
- response to lack of consequences
- appreciating the concept of winning and losing
- pleasure-seeking or pain-seeking
- pleasure-avoidance or pain-avoidance
- cause-and-effect understanding
- risk-taking
- thrill-seeking
- labelling of "good" and "bad"
- understanding the role of authority
- remembering parameters of behaviour
- control over own emotions and behaviour
- metacognitive processes concerning morality
- choosing to demonstrate "good" behaviour or "bad" behaviour

- linking events to causes
- identification with adult figures
- role-playing
- superhero-playing
- fantasy-playing
- understanding specific rules
- following rules
- identifying emotions and feelings
- apologizing
- accepting apologies
- making up rules
- lying
- cheating
- behaving unsociably (the child might not yet be of a stage or disposition to absorb what is socially acceptable)
- matching "punishments" and "crimes"
- inflicting "punishments" on others
- justifying behaviours and actions
- internalizing religious beliefs
- internalizing philosophical perspectives
- making moral judgments on the basis of abstract ideas
- stating personal beliefs
- advocating for what is "right"
- advocating for social "causes"

Cognition

Cognition involves the process of knowing, thinking, and understanding. Early learning is shaped by experimentation, play, imitation, stimulus-response, and reinforcement. Stages of cognitive development differ in their complexity as well as in the amount of information that is learned. Infants' understanding is acquired through their sensory exploration of the world and is highly egocentric. Later, thinking patterns change as children are able to deal with concrete ideas and some symbolism. Through intellectual stimulation and brain maturation, children gradually learn to deal with abstract ideas and multifaceted tasks. Information is processed according to these changing mental structures; the child creates an internal construction of the world. We can understand what children are thinking according to what they say, what they do, and the mistakes they make.

Recent advances in neuroscience are helping parents and professionals understand the importance of early experience and the dynamic capacities of the human brain. Cognitive development is an extremely difficult process to observe and to make appropriate inferences about. We can observe brain activity through various types of electronic scans and we can study it in the form of neurological activity, but this doesn't help us understand thinking in everyday situations! Theories of cognition can help us untangle the complexities of children's thought processes. A sample profile using the theory of multiple intelligences (see page 75) can be found on page 87.

Observe:

- reflexive behaviours
- consciousness
- exploration
- levels of awareness
- experimentation
- curiosity
- sensory acuity
- sensory discovery
- attachment behaviours
- responses to stimuli
- imitation
- constructing meaning
- object and people permanence (the cognitive process by which a person can exercise complex recall and the ability to hold the idea of another person or an object in mind)
- trial-and-error behaviour

- use of symbolism
- pretend-playing
- role-playing
- attention span
- emergence of language
- use of language to express ideas
- response to ideas
- concrete thinking
- classifying
- sorting
- matching
- seriating
- counting
- one-to-one correspondence
- cardinality
- magical thinking
- sequencing
- spatial relationships

- decoding
- encoding
- conserving ideas
- concentrating or focusing on single ideas
- identifying people, objects, and places
- asking questions
- discriminating
- patterning
- discovering properties of materials
- using logic
- predicting outcomes
- following sequences
- estimating size, time, quantity, etc.
- convergent problem-solving
- creative problem-solving
- aesthetic understanding
- following instructions
- understanding time sequences
- remembering people, objects, and places
- considering others' viewpoints
- construction
- searching for challenges
- expressing a problem
- goal-setting
- reading and understanding
- investigating a problem
- producing ideas
- using rational arguments
- combining ideas
- designing objects
- making models
- using metacognitive strategies
- using metalinguistic strategies
- arranging the learning environment
- developing strategies for problem-solving
- carrying out plans
- cooperating in activities
- investigating nature
- recalling facts
- learning by rote
- overextending rules
- creating rules
- pressing individual interests
- using research methods
- scribbling
- attempting to spell
- making errors
- identifying and solving problems
- making free associations
- scientific discovery
- awareness of own thinking processes
- recording events
- brainstorming
- debating
- paraphrasing
- comprehending
- making inferences
- refining solutions
- identifying elements of "the mind"
- summarizing information
- making objective comments
- making value judgments
- deferring gratification
- stating hypotheses
- analyzing research
- assessing situations
- synthesizing ideas

Observing Mathematical Thinking

Child's name:_____   Observer: _____

Age/D.O.B.: _____   Date: _____

Context:_____

Observation task	Original presentation	Transformation	Observed response
Number	Are there the same number of pennies in each row?	Now are there the same number of pennies in each row, or does one row have more?	
Length	Is each of these sticks just as long as the other?	Now are the two sticks each equally as long, or is one longer?	
Liquid	Is there the same amount of water in each glass?	Now is there the same amount of water in each glass, or does one have more?	
Mass	Is there the same amount of clay in each ball?	Now does each piece have the same amount of clay, or does one have more?	
Area	Does each of these cows have the same amount of grass to eat?	Now does each cow have the same amount of grass to eat, or does one cow have more?	
Weight	Does each of these two balls of clay weigh the same amount?	Now (without placing them back on the scale to confirm what is correct for the child) do the two pieces of clay weigh the same, or does one weigh more?	
Volume	Does the water level rise equally in each glass when the two balls of clay are dropped in the water?	Now (after one piece of clay is removed from the water and reshaped) will the water levels rise equally, or will one rise more?	

Source: Laura E. Berk, <u>Infants, Children, and Adolescents</u>. Copyright © 1994 by Allyn & Bacon. Reprinted by permission.

This observation chart provides the opportunity to see how a child "conserves" ideas. Some pre-school children understand constancy, while others will not grasp the concept until they are older. Remember that responses may reflect language limitations rather than conceptual errors.

TAKING A SPECIAL LOOK: Patterns of development

We gain skills in almost always the same sequence, even though we may demonstrate them at varying rates. For a child with special needs whose development is somewhat uneven, you may observe that his domains of development are more advanced than the rest. Frequently, one aspect of development will affect another, so we sometimes need to respond in different ways. For example, you may need to arouse the interest of a child who has a hearing deficit by providing visual rather than auditory stimulation. Watch closely to see the reactions to your stimuli and respond accordingly.

Spirituality

Spirituality is concerned with personal reflections, a connection or relationship with a power or person outside the self, and an appreciation of the significance of people and things. Not all child-care professionals consider this developmental domain significant, and those who do may have difficulty defining it. For some, spirituality involves appreciating beauty, developing aesthetic values, and demonstrating care for the world and its people. For others, it is strongly associated with a religion or philosophy of belief about our creation, the nature of existence, and our role in the world. Spiritual development can involve an increased awareness, understanding, or practice in any of these areas.

Spiritual development is possibly the most challenging area of human development to observe. Philosophical thought obviously involves cognition, but there is more to spirituality than logic and mental gymnastics, and even that part of spiritual thought is not easily observed. Our observation of children's actions and words may only hint at a surface explanation for something that runs much deeper.

Observe:

- curiosity
- levels of consciousness
- appreciation of beauty
- meditation and prayer
- listening to music
- appreciating art forms
- acknowledgement of nature
- wonder
- joy
- connection with predecessors
- insights regarding the future
- symbolism
- recognition of signs
- premonitions
- intuition
- identification with culture or ethnicity
- rituals
- ceremony
- social responsibility
- rites of passage
- imagination

- discussion of the meaning or purpose of life
- philosophical thought
- religious understanding
- appreciating the efforts of others
- pro-social behaviour
- fantasy
- magic and imagination
- interest in literature
- creative activity
- expressing love
- experiencing the intensity of emotions
- forgiving
- accepting forgiveness
- appreciating movement and dance
- experiencing success or failure
- poetry
- magical thinking (which indicates a level of pre-operational thought that enables a child to create magical or imaginary interpretations of events because he makes incorrect associations between ideas or lacks the ability to think logically as a more mature person would)
- connectedness with family, friends, etc.
- romance
- striving for justice
- fun experiences
- transcending the "here and now"
- advocating for peace
- stillness
- membership in a group
- enjoying myths and legends
- appreciating the "essence" of an experience

- birth experiences
- belief in the sanctity of human life
- dreaming
- being solitary
- giving thanks
- celebrating
- fasting
- reciting mantras, creeds, scriptures
- metaphysical thought
- comparing and contrasting world religions
- analyzing why events happen
- making a pilgrimage
- attributing "bad" things to the devil or Satan
- knowledge of nirvana, heaven, hell, the underworld, etc.
- singing and chanting
- acknowledging and respecting icons, symbols, altars, and other holy objects
- belief in an afterlife
- worshipping
- belief in the soul or other immortal element of human beings
- listening to an inner voice
- social advocacy
- mysticism
- punishment and retribution
- belief in sacraments and other practical signs of spiritual occurrences
- knowledge or wisdom
- belief in being saved
- belief in reincarnation
- healing
- mindfulness

- communication with the "creator"
- interpreting dreams
- belief in God, the Divine, Krishna, etc.
- near-death experiences
- expressing or experiencing wholeness
- atoning
- acknowledging auras, karmas, atmospheres
- expressing ethical perspectives and behaving according to ethical principles
- identifying a moral in a story
- interest in the supernatural or occult
- communion
- love for people or for God
- giving to the poor or needy
- belief in immortality

- animism
- identification of archetypes
- initiations
- belief in extraterrestrial forces
- arguing from a specific religious or moral standpoint
- visiting historic and holy places
- superstitious beliefs and practices
- perspective-taking (indicates a particular level of cognition, beyond pre-operational thought, rather than willfulness or negative personality)
- expressing emotional experiences or ideas
- being in a state of depression, sadness, bereavement, loss, etc.
- living in the moment
- interpreting scriptures, holy books, and moral stories

The interaction of the domains

When we observe any child, we see a flow of behaviour that is not labelled as part of any one developmental domain. In fact, we should make sure that we do not think of any behaviour as solely physical, cognitive, and so on; every behaviour involves interacting domains. Since no area of development should be considered without seeing how it might relate to the others, we need to observe carefully and consider the **whole child**. If, for example, we observe language skills, we must remember that they depend on social skill development, cognitive processes, emotional ties, and the physical skill of sound production. The sample observation on page 85 shows how we can observe various domains in play.

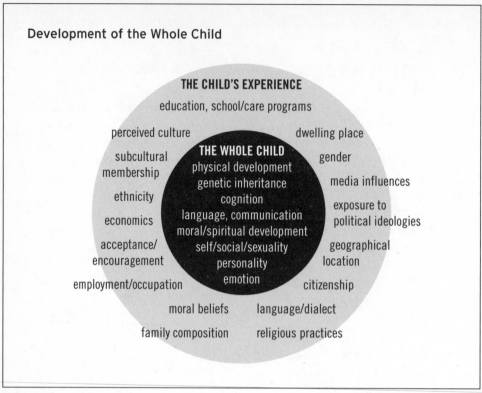

Development of the Whole Child

THE CHILD'S EXPERIENCE

education, school/care programs

perceived culture

dwelling place

subcultural membership

THE WHOLE CHILD
physical development
genetic inheritance
cognition
language, communication
moral/spiritual development
self/social/sexuality
personality
emotion

gender

media influences

ethnicity

exposure to
political ideologies

economics

acceptance/
encouragement

geographical
location

employment/occupation

citizenship

moral beliefs

language/dialect

family composition

religious practices

The child stands at the centre. Each interacting aspect of the child's development is affected by all of the environmental factors that contribute to her experience of the world. You observe the behaviours that help you make inferences about the whole child's development.

Principles of Development
Understanding developmental theories

We should be aware of the developmental domains while also keeping in mind some other important ideas that can shape how we observe, what we see, and how we interpret that information.

Behaviour as a key to development

The way to learn about young children is to be with them and to observe them. Observing a child's behaviours is the best way of appreciating the child's development and needs. Earlier in this chapter we explored the domains of child development and determined some of the things we might look for that fall within those domains. By watching the child in action in various situations we can come to know and understand her better. Surface behaviours are what we can see, but inner psychological and cognitive

Observing a Preschooler's Development

Child's name: _____ Observer: _____

Age/D.O.B.: _____ Date: _____

Context/setting: _____

Appearance: _____
_____

Sensory exploration/discovery: _____
_____

Physical skills:

    a. gross motor: _____
_____

    b. fine motor: _____
_____

Language/communications: _____
_____

Evidence of pre-operational thinking: _____
_____

Demonstration of conceptual understanding: _____
_____

Self-help skills: _____
_____

Social/pre-social skills: _____
_____

Demonstration of emotions: _____
_____

Personal style/temperament: _____
_____

Play behaviours: _____
_____

Personal interests: _____
_____

Observing an Adult's Assistance in a Child's Learning

Child's name:_____   Observer: _____

Age/D.O.B.: _____   Date: _____

Context/setting: _____

Observe a child in a play sequence or semi-structured learning activity. _____

_____

What can the child do without adult assistance? _____

_____

_____

Describe how the adult "moves" in the situation. _____

_____

_____

What strategy is the adult using to support the child's understanding or skills? _____

_____

_____

How does the child respond? _____

_____

_____

What can the child do now with the adult's support? _____

_____

_____

How can the child become able to do this independently?_____

_____

_____

Observing Play

Child's name: _____   Observer: _____

Age/D.O.B.: _____   Context/setting: _____

What interests the child? _____
_____
_____

Describe the kinds of play the child engages in. *(isolate, onlooker, parallel, interactive, explorative, physical, functional, pretend, cooperative, sociodramatic, etc.)* _____
_____
_____

Describe the complexity of play. *(use of symbols, use of tools and objects, complexity of rules in interactive play, etc.)* _____
_____

What are the emotional characteristics of this play? *(smiles a lot, talks during play, aware of others; follows, leads; etc.)* _____
_____

What knowledge does the child have to possess to play this way? *(how things work, units of measurement, social roles, etc.)* _____
_____

Describe the use of materials. *(appropriate, inappropriate; destructive, creative; repetitious; imitates others, shows others; etc.)* _____
_____

What skills does the child have to possess to play this way? *(drawing, constructing, creating, measuring, etc.)*
_____

What is the use of language during play? *(quiet, talkative; positive, negative; talks to self, talks to others, responds verbally to others; asks questions, explains, describes, labels items; uses words/phrases/sentences; etc.)* _____
_____

Describe the social characteristics of the child's play. *(relationship and involvement with others)* _____
_____
_____

processes are happening that we cannot see directly. However, we can draw inferences from the things the child does, what she says, and often by the mistakes that a child might make. Behaviourists such as Watson and Pavlov focused on the demonstration of behaviours to help them understand their "subject"—the child. Their understandings can be useful to us, but appreciating some of her underlying motivations, thought processes, and feelings can help us understand the individual child more sensitively. Freud offers a **psychoanalytic** framework that provides further insights; Bandura, founder of the social learning approach, helps us understand the importance of imitation and role-modelling. Piaget, perhaps the most important developmental psychologist, supplies a complex model for grasping the dynamic processes that underpin the observable behaviours that we can record. Many other theorists also provide constructs that assist in our interpretation of the behaviours we see. We need to ensure that we separate our observation of behaviour from our interpretations of that behaviour; we may be correct in our interpretations but our application of a particular theory to observed information may not lead to a complete, full, or correct analysis.

Ages and stages

Any casual observer will notice that children change while they grow. An adult is more than just a large baby! Infants become toddlers, and in time they become preschoolers, and later they become school-age children. They increase in age, grow in height, gain weight, and develop in many ways as they acquire skills, construct knowledge, and acquire values and attitudes. These things happen simultaneously as all the domains of the child's development interact. The changes that we see follow a sequential pattern; in nearly every case the child makes these gains progressively. Children do not always undergo these changes at the same chronological age (actual age), but the order of their acquiring these skills remains much the same. We see that there are qualitatively different levels of development. For example, the toddler solves problems differently than an older child does. The periods of time that can be characterized in different steps we call stages. Ages and stages are not necessarily the same. Observing a child's behaviour indicates better her stage of development than her age does. Some stages refer to an approximate age-range—such as "toddlerhood." Other stage labels refer to abstract ideas such as "the sensori-motor stage." Significant stages of development, or the acquisition of particular skills, may be referred to as "**milestones**."

Clarify your meaning when you use any stage description because the meanings of such terms vary considerably. Variations come about because of culture, social expectations, research methods legislation, and child-care and education program delivery.

Stage constructs
Model A: Broad stages commonly associated with child-care provision

infancy	birth to 12 months (or walking)
toddlerhood	12 months (or walking) to 30 months
preschooler	30 months to 5/6 years
school-age children	5-6 years to 11-12 years

Model B: Freudian stages/Psychoanalytical approach

oral stage	birth to 12 months
anal stage	12 to 36 months
phallic stage	3 years to 5 years
latency stage	5 years to puberty
genital stage	from puberty onwards

These are age approximations. Each stage involves complex interactions between the id, ego, and superego. These stages are for reference only; students should research Freudian ideas after gaining an overview of his theory.

Model C: Erikson/Psychosocial approach

trust versus mistrust	birth to 18 months
autonomy versus shame	12 to 24 months
initiative versus guilt	2 to 5 years
industry versus inferiority	elementary years

These are age approximations. Each stage involves a profound inner conflict that has to be resolved. These stages are for reference only; students should research Erikson's ideas after they gain some understanding of the structure of his theory.

Model D: Piaget/Developmental Psychology model

sensori-motor stage	birth to 2 years
pre-operational period	2 to 7 years
concrete operational period	7 to 11 years
formal operational period	11 years to adulthood

These are age approximations. Each stage involves development through qualitatively different ways of thinking and behaving. The stages are for reference only; students should research Piaget's theory after having studied its structure.

Model E: Allen and Marotz age/stage profiles

This is a model based on levels of maturation and developed from surveying large numbers of children. Gesell (1940) initiated this style of profile; Sheridan (1992) created a similar model using a different population of children. Other maturational profiles can be accessed for assessment purposes.

Pre-natal	(first, second, and third trimester)
Birth	
Neonate	birth to 28 days
Infant	1 to 4 months
	4 to 8 months
	8 to 12 months
Toddler	12 to 24 months
	the 2-year-old

Preschool child	the 3-year-old
	the 4-year-old
	the 5-year-old
School-age children	the 6-year-old
	the 7- and 8-year-old

Model F: Greenspan's chart of milestones in emotional development

Self-regulation and interest in the world	birth to 3 months
Falling in love	2 to 7 months
Developing intentional communications	3 to 10 months
The emergence of an organized sense of self	9 to 18 months
creating emotional ideas	18 to 36 months
emotional thinking	30 to 48 months

These are age approximations. Each stage involves significant emotional experiences and reactions. The stages are for reference only; students should research Greenspan's concept based on <u>First Feelings</u> (1985).

Attachments   Bowlby (1965), Ainsworth (1972), and others have done significant research on the necessity of early attachments. Caregivers should observe the processes of attachment and separation that children experience. Without recognizing the emotional ties of attachment, an observer may believe all other aspects of development are irrelevant. With infants, the attachment relationships with primary caregivers should be strong and well supported. With children of all ages, caregivers must observe how the children make transitions from one adult they know well to another adult and find ways of supporting them through such separations. Strong emotional ties will lead to trusting relationships.

The child as the constructor of knowledge   Piaget's (1954) theory of developmental psychology offers a profound view of children's **construction of knowledge**. He observed and described play sequences that indicate that young children learn through direct experience. Their understanding must come from firsthand experiences; caregivers may orchestrate the events but the children must play themselves. Piaget's theory reinforces the need to observe children's activities and to be present during those activities to ensure that the children can construct meaningful learning. Where necessary, caregivers have to intervene, reconstruct the physical environment, and then continue to observe.

The adult's role as facilitator of learning   Froebel (1826) described the adult as a gardener in the child's garden. Teachers and caregivers must watch what is happening and supply the nurturance, tools, or practical help as required. They must be keen observers and learn when and how to assist the children's development.

The zone of proximal development and scaffolding   Vygotsky (1978) discusses a **zone of proximal development** that explains how children can be supported to acquire new learning. Through observation, caregivers identify what each child knows or can currently accomplish. The caregivers employ a variety of strategies to help the children perform at a new level of skill or acquire new knowledge. Bridging the gap between what each child can do with and then without assistance allows caregivers to help learning and allows the children to be successful. This principle underlines the need for careful observation and appropriate intervention in the children's activity.

Bruner (1966) developed a theory of **scaffolding** by studying how adults help children gain new language skills. He noticed that many mothers aided their children's language by extending the learning that the child has already been gained. Mothers observed their infants closely and provided a "scaffold" for new language by using various support strategies. This model applies to many different situations in which caregivers observe children and can help the children's learning. A sample observation of scaffolding can be found on page 86.

Neuroscience   Neuroscientific research currently under way is offering exciting insights into how the human brain works. This has major implications for parents and professionals involved with infants and young children. A number of reports, including *Rethinking the brain: New insights into early development* (Shore 1997), *The early years study: Reversing the real brain drain* (McCain & Mustard 1999), and *Brain research and childhood education: Implications for educators* (Bergen & Coscia, 2001), have helped educators translate the highly technical and scientific data into material that is understandable and that offers clear implications for practice.

Fortunately, these reports have not contradicted our previous understanding as offered by Piaget, Vygotsky, and other eminent figures. The reports are challenging to condense to essentials: educators need to reinforce their understandings of the immense capacities and the **neural plasticity** of the brain and to provide optimal learning environments to help maximize the brain's potential. However, **neuroscience** does not suggest that overly structured and targeted programs be developed for children; this science underscores the need to provide developmentally appropriate environments. We can observe children's responses to the experiences that we provide and mediate them according to the children's needs as they become apparent.

Multiple aspects of intelligence   In recent years, interest had increased in Gardner's (1993) work on **multiple intelligences**. He hypothesizes that there are eight or more different forms of intelligence including the spatial, logical/mathematical, linguistic, bodily/kinesthetic, musical, interpersonal, and intrapersonal. He suggests that, if we observe the styles of different children, the way they think, we can see that they think and operate in different ways. Without valuing any intellectual type over another, teachers and caregivers should offer different learning experiences to accommodate all types of learning; each child will vary in both his approach to learning and the content of what he is to learn. The work of Goleman (1997), on what he calls **emotional intelligence**, reinforces our need to observe and value ways to control, manage, motivate, and recognize emotions in others and to handle relationships. Both theories clearly indicate that caregivers must observe and identify personal styles in order to meet the children's needs. See the sample multiple-intelligence profile on page 87.

Sleep   Much of what there is to know about sleep remains a mystery. Some interesting studies have been conducted on the types and qualities of sleep, and the effects that they have on adults. Infant sleep-studies have also enlightened us about the body's need for sleep and its regenerative powers. Studies in the United States have recently determined that many adults and children are getting inadequate, poor-quality, or too little sleep. Sleep hygiene may seem an old-fashioned concept, but it seems that negative sleep experiences are having a profound effect on children's learning and safety, and may negatively affect all-round development. The science of sleep can help our understanding of the processes of sleep, and watching children sleep may help us determine the sleep patterns of individuals. At the same time we must appreciate that adults need to provide an optimal environment for children that balances their stimulation and relaxation, their social activity with space to be alone, and to ensure that children's differing needs for sleep, naps, downtime, and uptime be accommodated. Without adequate, good-quality sleep children cannot benefit from the programs and experience that we offer.

Cultural diversity   Many of the children we care for and educate come from backgrounds very different from our own. This **cultural diversity** can be positive for us all. We benefit from both the breadth of experience of our community and from the multicultural climate that stops us making assumptions about those who may seem to be unlike ourselves. We can observe the behaviour of people from different cultural groups, while we must avoid employing **stereotypes** and generalizations from one family's behavioural patterns. Those behaviours may be particular to a family or even to an individual. Asking questions can supply us with really helpful information; a person will rarely reject a genuine inquiry, but approach the parent in an appropriate manner. Invite parents to participate in whatever way they can, and you may find you get to know each other better and provide a stronger bridge between the child's home and the child-care facility or school.

A pro-social ethos   Moral understanding depends on children's stages of maturation as well as their environments. Although parents are usually the strongest influence on their children's value systems, children also receive many strong messages from the media and from the other adults around them. Social learning theorists such as Bandura (1977) explain this process as imitation and deferred imitation, yet the way children construct their own set of values is more involved than mere imitation. A complex interplay between children and their environment enables them to search for meaning. Their cognitive level shapes how this happens; children can only internalize "right" and "wrong" according to their own personal realities.

Positive guidance strategies and strong role models can influence how children learn to behave; children acquire much of their moral and pro-social learning through conversation with adults. When we listen to what they tell us and respond thoughtfully, children know that we take their thinking seriously and care about them. In addition, we can observe their play behaviours and intervene to label a behaviour, clarify a moral issue, or nurse hurt feelings.

Ecological systems   Because human development occurs within a social system, caregivers must know about children's social networks and as much as possible about their broader ecological systems. Bronfenbrenner's (1979) **ecological systems model** of concentric circles explains how a child's development is influenced by a wide variety of social, political, economic, and religious aspects of the environment (see page 193). Caregivers should do their best to appreciate these interrelated factors that shape the development of the children they care for. Possible strategies include conducting socio-

TAKING A SPECIAL LOOK: Assessing children from diverse cultures

Children from other cultures can face social and linguistic challenges in North America. If such children also have special physical or developmental needs, caregivers and teachers must approach the assessment process with extra care. Methods of authentic assessment will allow a child to demonstrate her abilities and needs clearly. If at all possible, the child should be assessed in her native language to avoid misunderstandings and to ensure that a limited command of English is not interpreted as a limited ability to communicate or understand. Similarly, a person from, or at least familiar with, the family's culture should be present at meetings with the family, both to help the family understand the child's needs and to ensure that the family's beliefs and values are understood and respected by the caregivers and other professionals involved with the child.

logical studies, observing local environments, keeping up to date with economic and employment issues, finding out about social challenges in the community, and establishing good communication with parent groups. Contextual questionnaires can supplement this data (see pages 262–64).

Early intervention   Until recently, it was thought inappropriate to interfere with a child's development in its very early stages. Any remediation or accommodation was thought unnecessary unless the child had a severe physical disability. The Greenspans' (1985) work demonstrates great success in early intervention with infants and toddlers who are experiencing emotional and social challenges in their relationship-building. Recent studies show that "intensive, well-designed, timely intervention can improve the prospects—and the quality of life—of many children who are considered to be at risk.... In some cases, effective intervention efforts can even ameliorate conditions once thought to be virtually untreatable..." (Shore 1997). Caregivers need to observe many aspects of early development, especially those involving how babies relate to adults. Early observation and identification of social difficulties may have lifelong effects.

Sensitive periods of development   The entire lifespan provides a time for a flow of change, and certain sensitive periods are particularly important for learning specific skills and acquiring cognitive processes. Observations of the imprinting behaviours of young birds led Lorenz (1937) to develop this theory, which can also be applied to other aspects of development. Language learning, in particular, is much easier for a young person acquiring a first or subsequent language. Bowlby (1985) believed that maternal bonding with a newborn needs to happen immediately after birth, or subsequent attachments will be spoiled.

Although some people debate whether a child will actually miss the stage or skill if he does not develop it during the sensitive period, it may not be possible for him to make up for some early deprivations. A neglected child who was not exposed to language or social learning may show severely reduced ability to gain a full language; in one such case, the child was able to say only a handful of words when she received concentrated teaching. Some mechanisms do exist to overcome certain short-term deprivations or limitations; in principle, however, some key experiences need to be provided at the right moments. We can observe the "prime times" (Shore 1997), critical periods, or whatever we may call the best time for particular experiences, when the child's response to an experience elicits a desired learning. Educators waste precious time when they try to "teach" a child something when the timing is not right for him.

Developmental diversity   As more children diagnosed with special needs are integrated into mainstream settings, we see a greater need to accommodate a wider range of development within any group of children. **Developmental diversity** can be positive for society and education as teachers and caregivers are more likely to treat the children as individuals. At the same time, the integration presents a challenge in terms of the curriculum and the assessment. Observation skills need to be finely honed, and a wide range of assessment tools is necessary. Conducting some standardized assessments may be helpful, depending on the caregiver's role and responsibilities (see Chapter 10). It will always be necessary to read reports from education psychologists and to be able to interpret the summary or results. Any **individual program plan (IPP)** that has been developed will have to be carried out. It is preferable that such a plan be a team activity; however, teachers can also find themselves carrying out the plans of psychologists or other interventionists, so they must be able to understand what is required and to observe and record the child's responses.

We discussed ages and stages earlier in this chapter. Now we revisit the age/stage approach whereby we consider the variety of individual developmental patterns. The age and stage profiles can be useful when we compare a child's demonstrated behaviour and chronological age with any of the stage charts—they give us an idea of where the child "is" in his development. The charts do not indicate what a child "should" be able to demonstrate; they illustrate what the "average child" can do at a given age. There is no such child as the average child. It is appropriate to measure a child's performance in a constructive manner—in terms of what competence he has, rather than what he cannot yet do! The concept of the norm is useful for parents and professionals as a benchmark and a reference point; it is not acceptable to judge a child's development in such a way that the child "fails" in some manner.

Again, the concept of "normal" is also open to misapplication. There are no normal children. The "norm" is an abstract measurement. A positive attitude is essential, just as we must remember that many of the world's great thinkers have performed in ways considered well below accepted norms at some time in their lives. Focus on competence, the behavioural evidence of development, document this progress, and find ways of responding appropriately.

Health issues   In order to notice that a child is looking or behaving in ways that are different from usual, caregivers need to know about typical appearance and usual patterns of behaviour. Baseline observations are usually made on a daily basis. They can give us clear information about a child's state at the start of the day, which then acts as a useful reference point for later physical or behavioural changes. Pimento and Kernested (1996) suggest that caregivers take the time to observe and assess growth, personal hygiene, emotional health, developmental skills, and a range of physical and behavioural signs and symptoms.

Resilience and children's needs   Children do not always respond to the same situations in the same ways. Recent studies show that some children fare better in adverse situations. These children who do better despite difficult circumstances are considered "**resilient**." Parents and professionals need to appreciate the factors that contribute to making children more resilient. We don't want children to experience difficult circumstances; if challenges arise, we want them to cope well, adapt themselves to the situation, and go on succeed in every aspect of their lives. Steinhauer (1996) considered the task of raising competent children a collective responsibility that benefits society, the child, and the family. The framework that Steinhauer offers us may seem like common sense, but it needs to be stated nevertheless. Children have primary needs that include biological, physical, cognitive, and emotional/social elements. As he found in his work, and as is echoed in the work of numerous others, many children do not have these needs met and consequently fail to develop in ways that will enable them to become resilient.

When we think about basic needs we might first think of the physical ones, such as air, food, protection, and so on. Recent studies have elaborated upon these items. Children's real needs appear to include enriched relationships and experiences as well. Brazelton and Greenspan (2000) have collaborated to produce a useful model. They identify the significant needs of all children in terms of being "irreducible," or an absolute minimum. These include the need for ongoing nurturing relationships, physical protection, safety and regulation, and experiences tailored to individual differences; the need for developmentally appropriate experiences, limited setting, structure and expectations; and the need for stable supportive communities and cultural continuity.

These **irreducible needs** seem much more than basic; if they are not met, society suffers along with the individual child and family. Brazelton and Greenspan urge that these irreducible needs be considered "the highest international priority, alongside human rights, as a 'right' for all.... [They] can serve as a framework (a report card) for nations and regions within nations and the international community as a whole to monitor current status and provide incentives for progress" (2000).

Assessing development through observation

Advantages

- The observer knows what to look for.
- Recorded information is detailed.
- The observer is both teacher and assessor.
- Analysis of data is more straightforward.
- Data collection can meet the needs of educators.
- Observation is an open-ended process.
- The approach is holistic.
- The data collected are focused and pertinent.
- Data are reviewed within the construct of developmental principles.
- Information is set into context.
- Observational information is recorded immediately.
- Intuitive and educated opinion is valued.

Disadvantages

- The observer may be biased by a particular developmental theory.
- Developmental knowledge takes time to acquire.
- Analysis may disregard pertinent information that was thought irrelevant.
- Prescribing learning requirements based on open-ended observations can be too subjective.
- The data are collected using formats that are not tested as valid or reliable.

Summary

As we learn more about children, we know more about what behaviours to look for, and how to interpret some of the behaviours we see displayed. All the time we are observing we need to remember some basic philosophical beliefs about human beings. Our particular philosophical perspectives shape how we understand children. These beliefs indicate our own values and must be based on sound research, experience, and tested theories; they encapsulate how we think development occurs.

There are several aspects, or domains, of development. These include the physical, sexual, language and communication, cognition, emotional, spiritual, social, and personality. Even though we can identify behaviours that fall within these categories, many behaviours demonstrate an interaction between several different domains. The child is a whole person exhibiting integrated behaviour; her behaviour does not occur in separate, neatly labelled boxes. We can look for many behaviours, but children will often behave in unexpected ways; we need to be prepared to observe and record these too.

There are observable characteristics of development that can be readily seen by even a casual child-watcher. Studying children usually involves understanding the ages and stages of their development. Although there is a pattern of development common to all children, the rate of the progression of each child is highly individual.

Behaviourists focus on demonstrated behaviour rather than the inner thoughts of the child. Social learning theorists suggest that imitative learning and the internalizing of role models explain some of a child's behaviours. Psychoanalytic thought leads people to consider the individual's deeper drives and motivations. Developmental psychologists also operate on this complex level of behaviour analysis. They appreciate the qualitatively different stages of thinking and behaving that emerge from a close scrutiny of actions. Surface behaviours tell us about acquired skills and indicate changes at a deeper level as well.

As science and a variety of research studies inform our work with children, we develop a set of principles of development. These may change over time while underlying our best understanding about children. We must express them so that our observational frame of mind is apparent. We consider the child an active creator of her own knowledge and the adult plays a clear role in facilitating the child's learning. A prosocial ethos helps us to value and encourage moral understanding and appreciate it within a developmental construct. We know there is a gap between what children know and what is "to be learned"; we can assist children to cross this zone of proximal development with a variety of strategies. We can provide a scaffold to gain new skills. Children have a variety of ways of being smart, and children are stronger in some areas than others. We have to accommodate these multiple aspects of intelligence once we have observed them.

Neuroscience has updated our thinking about children and learning. Fortunately, it underscores what we already know about the importance of a child's early years to his later development. We warmly appreciate the emotional needs of young children, particularly their need for attachment to certain adults. The cultural context of a child's upbringing and schooling influences his behaviour, attitudes, and thinking; these should be celebrated. The ecological system into which every child is born is different. Educators must be mindful of that ecosystem when trying to determine and meet the needs of children. There are some irreducible needs for all children, although the ways in which they are met may differ widely; these differences are both physical and psychological. When a child's needs are met she is likely to be more resilient when any challenges present themselves. Although there are some sensitive periods that are a prime time for a child to experience particular things, parents and educators can take comfort in the fact that there is also some flexibility in this development and in the child's brain plasticity. Early intervention programs can ameliorate the effects of previous damage. We can observe a wide range of development in any group of children, even children of similar ages. All children need to have experiences and programs designed for their particular capabilities.

The importance of adults' observing and responding to the health, growth, and development of each child underlies all the principles of child development.

Key Terms

attachment	fine motor skills
behaviourism	gross motor skills
biological clock	irreducible needs
cephalo-caudal principle	language
child development	maturation
chronological age	milestones
cognition	morality
construction of knowledge	multiple intelligences
context	neuroscience
cue	norm
cultural diversity	personality
developmental diversity	(neural) plasticity
developmental psychology	phenomenology
early intervention	physical development
ecological system model	pro-social skills
emotion	proximo-distal principle
emotional intelligence	psychoanalytic (theory)
environment	psychological clock

psychosocial development	social interaction
resilient	social play
scaffolding	special needs
sensitive period	spirituality
sensory acuity	stereotype
sexual development	temperament
social clock	whole child
social emotions	zone of proximal development

Weblinks

www.childstudy.net/cdw.html
Overview of the "Classic Theories of Child Development" of Freud, Mahler, and Erikson.

www.ecewebguide.com/child.html
This child development page offers pages about curriculum help, program management, anti-bias resources, and professionalism among others.

www.nncc.org/
The National Network for Child Care (NNCC) site is categorized into age groups (infants to school-age), developmental domains, ages and stages series, brain development, observing, and assessing children, among others.

www.hrdc-drhc.gc.ca
The Aboriginal Relations Office of Human Resource Development site features a child-care page describing First Nations and Inuit Child Care Initiatives. It offers excellent links.

www.hc-sc.gc.ca/hppb/familyviolence/bilingual.htm
Health Canada's National Clearinghouse on Family Violence site offers links to resources and publications related to family violence in Canada.

Observation Sample

This recording documents the child's physical attributes and skills that were observed during recess time. The recording is written fairly objectively with useful details.

How might this information help the teacher individualize her program for James?

Observing Physical Development

Child's name: _James_   Observer: _Danielle_

Age/D.O.B.: _6 years, 2 months_   Date: _March 3, 2004_

Context/setting: _recess for Grade 1 class_

What gross motor skills do you observe? _Walking, standing, running forwards, to the right, and swerving; jumping down from the climber, sitting, jumping over skipping ropes on the ground, kicking a large ball (right foot)_

What fine motor skills do you observe? _Grasping with left and right hands, pointing to an item, pincer grasp (right hand), throwing ball through hoop, catching small ball, threading grasses through fencing with fine motor control, holding hands, pressing hands down on ground, shoveling sand_

Describe the child's physical appearance and health indicators.

skin color/tone: _fair skin, pink flush on cheeks (cold day), downy face_

hair color/texture/length and condition: _light brown, straight, somewhat lank, "bowl cut" style_

eyes: _gray-brown, long eyelashes, eyes set wide apart_

senses: _response to sound, visual stimuli, smell (fish tank), taste? touch?_

nails: _short and bitten on left hand; left thumb is sore_

teeth: _white, full set of first teeth, need cleaning, no cavities/fillings?_

foot position (inward/outward pointing): _slightly inward pointing, right more pronounced_

head size in proportion to trunk/legs: _1:6_

body shape: _slim build_

body fat distribution: _chubby cheeks but fairly flat abdomen and little fat on legs_

posture/alignment/body symmetry: _appears symmetrical with upright posture_

legs (straight/bowed): _straight legs_

injuries (scars/bruises/etc.): _knees have small grazes_

bowel control: _yes_   bladder control: _yes_

self-help skills: _can dress himself, use bathroom, wash, brush teeth; difficulty with shoelaces_

observable habits: _nail biting_

identifying features: _bushy eyebrows, small mole on upper lip_

height: _4 ft. 8 in._   weight: _44 lb._

respiration: _22 (30 after running)_

health signs (and symptoms): _normal temperature, active_

left/right hand preference: _right-handed, right-footed_

Observation Sample

This chart allows the teacher to review an entire play sequence to highlight its important characteristics. The recording contains some inferences as well as objective recording.

What further information would help the reader appreciate what actually happened during this activity?

Observing Cooperative Activity

Children's names: _Damian_   Ages/D.O.B.: _5 yr., 6 mo._

Cara   _4 yr., 11 mo_

Jessie   _5 yr._

Malachi   _5 yr., 3 mo._

Observer: _Shakila_   Date: _May 28, 2004_

Context/setting: _Preschool room, 3:30 p.m._

Type of activity: _Dramatic play_

Materials: _Dress-up clothes including hats, capes, and old shoes_

How the play/activity started: _Jessie was pretending to bake muffins when Cara asked if she could join._

How the activity progressed: _Jessie said Cara should do the dishes. Cara said she wanted to bake. Damian walked by and said boys are chefs, not girls. Damian continued conversing and entered the pretend kitchen area._

Adult involvement (if any): _The ECE asked Damian what made him think only boys were chefs. He shrugged and continued to take items out of the oven._

Evidence of leadership: _Jessie tends to initiate play activity; others follow, but she does not sustain interest._

Evidence of following instructions: _Cara followed Jessie's suggestion to wash dishes, but she soon found "baking" more interesting. She said she would "make eggs and ketchup" so Damian set the table and Malachi sat waiting to be served._

How "rules" were set or followed: _All group members agreed to the social rules of domestic play._

What agreement or disagreement was demonstrated: _Jessie did not pursue her direction to Cara; they were caught up in the play._

How difficulties were resolved: _Because each child took a "role," there was little to resolve._

Evidence of sharing/empathy: _The playthings were shared as was taking turns in conversation and the division of domestic "tasks."_

Observation Sample

This play observation was recorded during and after the sequence observed. This structure allows the teacher to look at the most important aspects of development that can be seen in play.

How might you use this observation to extend Rachel's play?

Observing Play

Child's name: *Rachel*   Observer: *Jerry*

Age/D.O.B.: *2 years, 8 months*   Context/setting: *Child's home, April 10/04*
Rachel is home in the afternoon after nursery school. Rachel is diagnosed as being "gifted." Observed for 48 minutes.

What interests the child? *Rachel focuses on two puzzles--one 8½ x 11 of Pooh Bear and the other a large floor puzzle of Piglet.*

Describe the kinds of play the child engages in. *(isolate, onlooker, parallel, interactive, explorative, physical, functional, pretend, cooperative, sociodramatic, etc.)* *Rachel plays by herself in solitary activity except when she engages her mother.*

Describe the complexity of play. *(use of symbols, use of tools and objects, complexity of rules in interactive play, etc.)* *Rachel follows a left-to-right sequence using trial and error, guessing, and matching pieces.*

What are the emotional characteristics of this play? *(smiles a lot, talks during play, aware of others; follows, leads; etc.)* *Rachel appears to have little expressed emotion except when she tries to get her mother's attention. She is then excitable and whines.*

What knowledge does the child have to possess to play this way? *(how things work, units of measurement, social roles, etc.)* *She needs to understand what the puzzle demands of her. She needs a knowledge of space and shape, and the ability to match colors and fit shapes together using a variety of cognitive strategies.*

Describe the use of materials. *(appropriate, inappropriate; destructive, creative; repetitious; imitates others, shows others; etc.)* *Rachel handles the material (puzzle pieces) with care, manipulating them in her hands.*

What skills does the child have to possess to play this way? *(drawing, constructing, creating, measuring, etc.)* *As well as the cognitive skills, she needs to be able to sit for a prolonged period and use fine motor skills.*

What is the use of language during play? *(quiet, talkative; positive, negative; talks to self, talks to others, responds verbally to others; asks questions, explains, describes, labels items; uses words/phrases/sentences; etc.)* *She talks as she plays. At times she focuses on the real world and what she is doing. At other times she talks to Pooh and Piglet as though she is "in" the pictures. She uses complex sentences with correct grammar, tense, etc. "Piglet wants to go on a picnic; he liked it when Pooh shared his honey last time."*

Describe the social characteristics of the child's play. *(relationship and involvement with others)* *Content playing by herself, Rachel appears to want her mother's company more than her practical assistance. She wants Mom to do it "her way."*

Observation Sample

In this sample, both the child and the adult have been observed. The recording focuses on the specific responses that the adult makes to assist learning. This is an example of scaffolding.

What other strategies might the adult use to assist Pegah's understanding of animals?

Observing an Adult's Assistance in a Child's Learning

Child's name: *Pegah*　　　　　　Observer: *Cory*

Age/D.O.B.: *1 year, 11 months*　　　Date: *June 8, 2003*

Context/setting: *Home child-care setting--in living room with two older children. Caregiver is present.*

Observe a child in a play sequence or semi-structured learning activity. *Pegah is looking at a small bound book.*

What can the child do without adult assistance? *She can point to pictures in the book (of baby animals) and say "dog, dog."*

Describe how the adult "moves" in the situation. *The caregiver sits by Pegah and says "lamb" and "calf" for the appropriate pictures.*

What strategy is the adult using to support the child's understanding of skills? *The caregiver repeats "lamb" and makes the sound "baa, baa."*

How does the child respond? *Pegah looks at the book, points to the lamb, and says "log." The caregiver repeats "lamb" until Pegah says "lab."*

What can the child do now with the adult's support? *Pegah says "lab" for "lamb."*

How can the child become able to do this independently? *If she is supported in hearing "lamb" and seeing the picture, singing songs about lambs, seeing a stuffed toy lamb, and seeing lambs on television, this may reinforce "lamb."*

Observation Sample

This multiple intelligence profile demonstrates the child's intellectual type. This information will help teachers and caregivers provide appropriate learning experiences.

Although this profile does not offer the observations on which it is based, we can assume that this summary represents what was recorded. From what you know about Tam, what special programming ideas might be successful for him?

Multiple Intelligence Profile

Child's name: Tam   Observer: Ryan

Age: 6 years, 11 months   Date: May 17, 2004

Sources of data: Running records, conservation test, checklist observation, and interview

Contect: School-age child care and Grade 2 class

Summary: The observational data pointed to Tam being strongly mathematical; he has intense and prolonged interest in all types of construction and the drawing of architectural diagrams. Although competent in language, Tam prefers the media of music and movement to express himself. He appears interested in making social relationships as long as they focus on his interests. If not, he soon loses the base for the relationship. He seems independent yet is not particularly reflective on his own abilities. When asked about what he liked doing, he mentioned the construction games, but he wasn't sure if his skill was strong in this area.

Tam responds to physical challenges and, although he did build intricate structures, his fine motor skills are not particularly well developed. It appears that his activity derives from his thought processes and problem solving rather than his physicality. Tam has interest in playing the piano, but he is frustrated that he cannot get results quickly.

Recently Tam has become involved with camping with his family. Tam enjoys building campfires, putting up tents, and pretending to be in the wilderness. Although he likes outside pursuits, he can often watch others rather than be involved in action; when he cannot lead, he opts out rather than follow directions.

chapter 3

Narratives

What is important in collecting anecdotes is that one develops a keen sense of the point of cogency that the anecdote carries within itself.

Max Van Manen (1990)

The Montessori Method is a system of education born from the observation of the needs of the children at every stage of their physical and psychological development. Its objective is to help the child with the enormous task of inner construction necessary to pass from childhood to full adulthood.

Mario M. Montessori, Jr. (1977)

Observing young children at play, one is struck by the length of time that a child can spend blowing bubbles and learning about their characteristics, dressing up in adult or super hero clothes and trying on various roles, exercising creative talent while making a collage of found materials, figuring out how to build a snow creature or listening attentively to a story.

Ada Schermann (1990)

Narrative observations help us notice what the child is doing in a more objective, detailed way. A narrative of this girl's play will help evaluate her fine motor, language, and cognitive skills.

Narrative Observations

DEFINITION: Narrative observations

Narrative observations are a written sequential account of what is perceived.

Describing behaviour

In most cases, recording a child's **behaviour** in a narrative description is a direct, non-interpretive method. The skilled observer can make an accurate record of the behaviour; for the less practised observer the method can lend itself to accidental **inferences** and **assumptions**. The greatest challenge of all narrative recording is to include sufficient detail to describe what happens and the way in which it happens, so that readers of the record can get an accurate "visual" impression. The goal will be to record very much as a video camera does. (Using a video camera is covered in Chapter 7.)

And narrative recording goes further. By looking for the minute details of behaviour, you as observer will perceive details of behaviour more closely than you would by recording the same behaviour on tape. The process of narrative recording makes you a better observer and furthers your own learning.

Pestalozzi (1894) coined the term "Anshauug" to capture the "verbosity" of meaningless words and to help the adult appreciate direct and concrete observation of children. This term should be revived—or another like it—to assist teachers in writing what they see, and only what they see!

Narratives can be helpful in observing and recording

- gross motor skills

- fine motor skills

- social interactions

- spontaneous language

- play patterns

- interests

"But I can't write down everything," many students say—and they are correct! It is impossible to describe every muscle movement, blink of the eye, and breath of a child. Describe as much as you can of what is going on—you are exercising a degree of selection, whether it is inadvertent or owing to the limitations of language. By recording, you learn to see more clearly.

Even when you intend to record all the nuances of the behaviour you are watching, in practical terms you must use whatever skill you have by writing down as quickly as possible everything that seems significant. Your early observations will likely contain a lot of information relating to the child's **gross motor skills** and **language**. Later, you may add some detail about **fine motor skills**. As you practise, you will be able to add descriptions of posture and eye contact, and more details regarding the subtleties of communication. You will also develop your ability to "see" with new eyes.

Another observational concept useful to us is that of the teacher as "**contemplative observer**" (Brown 1998). The teacher contemplates—which provides a role model for the child—as she observes. This is not considered a subjective process; it is one that brings the observer closer to the child who is being observed. Coming from a Buddhist tradition, Brown suggests that teachers take time to eliminate the thought that constantly fills our minds. These thoughts "interrupt our direct experience. Observation is about untangling our experiences" (1998). To highlight this observational approach, Krishnamurti (1981) explains, "To understand a child we have to watch him at play, study him in his different moods; we cannot project upon him our own prejudices, hopes, fears and mold him to fit our desires." Although we may think of our observational role within the context of our homes, schools, or child-care centres, and all that those small communities demand of us, we might want to refresh our ideas about objectivity and decide on our own philosophical perspectives.

Finding the right words can be difficult when describing behaviour and expressing the quality of actions. A review of some of the components of narrative may help you:

1. **Adjectives:** These are the describing words, words used to qualify or define. Use them to describe how something is being done—for example, a "loud" noise made the "sleeping" infant start.

2. **Verbs:** These are the action words; they tell what is being done. These are the most important words in a narrative as they indicate the type of behaviour observed—she "skipped," he "ran," she "jumped," he "sorted" the counters.

3. **Adverbs:** These words describe the quality of an action or modify a verb—he rose "quietly" from the chair, not saying anything, straightening his knees "slowly" and twisted his ankles "sharply" as he passed the book to the teacher.

4. **Sequencing:** This can be a hurdle to those people who are not good at telling stories in the order in which they happen. Some cultural groups find this a particular challenge, as their language or tradition may emphasize different elements of a storyline. Writing down what happens, as it happens, can help with sequencing difficulties.

5. **Tense:** Purists would have us write what is happening in the present tense—"he squats down and picks up the book." Others are concerned that the tense be consistent—"he squatted down and picked up the book." Unless otherwise directed, use the tense that you find most comfortable.

6. **Observer bias:** The direct recording of behaviour in narrative styles allows less scope for **bias** than the interpretive methods, such as sampling. However, the observer risks seeing from a perspective that is slanted. Descriptive words may themselves seem biased—to describe a child as "smiling" may suggest happiness whereas the word "grin" may have broader connotations. The observer may feel subjectively about the observed child and consequently record as a fact something that might actually be a negative interpretation—for example, describing a child as whining might be a subjective observation. Selecting one anecdote rather than another may in itself express further bias—for example, the anecdote you select shows a preschooler being uncooperative when more often she is observed cooperating and sharing.

   Biased data presented for analysis make for inadequate, invalid, subjective inference of little use. (See Chapter 1 for a more detailed explanation of observer bias.)

Types of narrative observations

Narrative observations can take the following forms:

A **running record** (pages 94–99) is a written description of the child's behaviour. The observer should be physically separated from the child to be observed and without immediate responsibility for the child or for other children in the area; this is **nonparticipant observation**. The observer records exactly what the child says and does in sequence as he or she watches. The observer can attempt this method with little previous observation skill, but increased practice enables the observer to record more detail, to describe more accurately, to avoid assumptions, to be aware of personal biases, and also to make better use of the **data** that are collected.

An **anecdotal record** (pages 100–104) requires that the observer, usually a practising teacher or a student teacher, write a brief account of a selected incident or behaviour soon after it occurs. These records are frequently used because they can be written up at the end of the working day and are an appropriate method of recording developmental stages. They require some expertise on the part of the recorder in choosing significant sequences of behaviour.

A **diary record** (pages 104–106), or a day-by-day written account of the child's behaviour, which is dated and timed, may incorporate features of the running record or anecdotal record as the observer thinks appropriate. This record can offer some of the **contextual information** that could help explain the behaviours observed. It may serve as a vehicle for an ongoing dialogue between caregiver and parents. Particularly useful for caregivers working with infants or children with **special needs**, this method enables rigorous record-keeping.

A **specimen record** (pages 107–108) documents in precise detail the play or other behaviour of one child with such description and clarity that reading the account evokes a mental image of what the observer saw. This method may be carried out for a particular reason and therefore be undertaken at a time designated in advance—say, to determine the child's attempts to communicate or to use a particular limb. Alternatively, the observation may have no specific focus but offer an opportunity for thorough observation of the child in **spontaneous play** to investigate interests, choices, or **play patterns**. Most often, a psychologist or teacher not working directly with the child uses this intensive recording method.

The concept of **personal narratives** covers a different type of narrative writing that includes self-observation, or what the teacher might think of as self-reflection. There are at least two kinds of personal narratives considered in this book.

The first is the teacher's own documentation of the experiences, programs, interactions with parents, involvement with children, teaching strategies, activities developed, and other elements of her own practice. Most importantly this kind of documentation includes, as part of the writing, self-evaluations—reflections on what was successful or not, feelings about her responsibilities, and so forth. All of these contemplations contribute to serious teacher reflection, which is the essence of good practice. While the process of writing may start with anecdotal records, lists, and reminders, the narrative will be complete only when the teacher has examined her reality of experience. Personal narratives frequently form part of a teacher's **professional portfolio**. This form of narrative allows the teacher to think critically, both objectively and subjectively, about her role and the experiences of those children and families for whom she is responsible. This is a **phenomenological** process—one that leads the teacher to construct a thorough, personal, re-creation of her experience. Through writing the narrative the teacher becomes more aware of her own needs and is able to focus clearly on how she sees the needs of the children in context; she can then plan for a continued relationship shaped by her realizing her own philosophy of practice.

The second type of personal narrative is the one that is authored by a child. It shares some similarities with that of the teacher in that it encourages self-reflection and self-discovery, and it builds self-esteem that leads toward success. Clearly, very young children cannot write narratives. However, they can take steps towards personal narrative in oral (taped) recordings and they can also begin the narrative process through pictures. Teachers can assist children by writing the words each child speaks alongside their visual representations of the experiences. While early narratives seem to be little more than a few words and pictures, children encouraged to represent their world and their feelings about it are underscoring their own construction of their realities. Some personal narrative contributions can be included in the child's developmental portfolio along with teacher observations, samples of "work," and other evidence of development.

Personal narratives will not be discussed in further detail in this chapter as they fall outside a strict definition of observation methods.

Running Records

KEY FEATURES: Running record

- observation of one child
- open-ended
- written account recorded at time of observation
- detailed
- records most actions
- records all speech
- records whatever occurs
- naturalistic
- nonparticipatory
- as objective as possible

Writing descriptive sequences of children's activity is particularly useful for teachers or caregivers whose philosophy is a **child-centred** approach to planning the curriculum. Open recordings enable observers to record whatever behaviours are demonstrated rather than look for specific categories of behaviour. Children's play is unstructured and directed by the children themselves. If we can observe children in action in their natural setting, we see the children being themselves.

Observers face the challenge of recording whatever they happen to see, since the focus is not on specific behaviours. They must have good descriptive skills and the ability to record a number of behaviours in quick succession. A running record is the method students often choose when they start an observation course, because it does not require a strong knowledge of child development.

When looking for a particular behaviour, you may well see it because you are expecting to. If you are looking for nothing in particular, you run the risk of not interpreting correctly what you do see—but you are more likely to be more objective.

Depending on when you undertake your running record, you are likely to see a variety of behaviours. As you write down what you see, do not include any inferences.

Observing one child at a time can allow us to see more detail and make useful recordings. But the way the group interacts is also important, so you'll need to find ways of using a narrative form to capture this.

Leave them for your **analysis**, where you will have to validate your comments. Sample running records can be found on pages 113–17 and 118–20.

In the effort to write what you see, you might find yourself writing "he played" or possibly "she went." Such phrases do not describe with sufficient accuracy what actually happened. Write down specifically how the child moves and what he does rather than use vague interpretive terms.

Running records are useful when planning parent interviews. Caregivers and parents work together better through sharing some substantial information. At this time, teachers may request the parents' informal observations and add them to the collection of information about a child.

Making regular **assessments** may mean employing the running record with other assessment or observational tools. These records may be presented at a case conference with the parents, at which a multidisciplinary or co-worker team may plan the required curriculum.

The running record is the method most frequently used for learning about children in every aspect of their development. Teachers, students, and parents gain; the process benefits everyone.

Narrative methods of observation and recording are sufficiently open-ended to
make them suitable for children who have special needs. For example, Rianna–
who was diagnosed with cystic fibrosis as a toddler and is now three years and
five months old–has a fluctuating activity level. On some days, she is very mobile
and plays alongside other children of her age; on other days, she is quiet, more
reflective, and less active. Rianna's teacher is keen to record her development
in each domain. A running record allows for detailed recordings without any
intrusion into Rianna's activity.

Using running records

Advantages

- This method can be used by untrained observers.
- Observation is less likely to be affected by bias when written at the time the behaviour occurs.
- A description of a child's behaviour can be used for a variety of purposes—developmental assessment, parent meetings, program-planning, or learning about child development.
- Observational data can be used by other professionals for objective analysis.
- This method provides the opportunity to record all behaviour, including the unexpected.
- The record may indicate the need for further observation and/or assessment using other methods.

Disadvantages

- Successful recording requires fluent use of language.
- Observer bias may not be obvious where assumptions are made.
- The observer needs to be removed from responsibilities with the children.
- Writing the record can be a long and laborious task.
- Inferences may be difficult to draw from a bulk of data.
- Observation can be undertaken with only one child at a time.

Method charts for running records

Split-page format

Running Record

Child's name: _____   Observer: _____

Age/D.O.B.: _____   Date: _____

Reason for observation: _____

_____

Context: _____

_____

_____

_____

Time	Observation	Comment/explanation

This chart enables the observer to log the time of events described. The "Observation" column is used for a detailed description of the behaviour, recorded as it occurs. The right-hand column allows for comments that clarify or explain what is happening (this section is not to make inferences).

Full-page format

Running Record

Child's name: _____   Observer: _____

Age/D.O.B.: _____   Date: _____

Reason for observation: _____

_____

Context: _____

_____

_____

_____

Time	Observation

Although a running record can be written on any paper, an organized chart can be helpful. The left-hand margin keeps track of the time.

Categorizing format

Running Record

Child's name: _____   Observer: _____

Age/D.O.B.: _____   Date: _____

Reason for observation: _____

_____

Context: _____

_____

Category of behaviours: _____

_____

Classification: _____

_____

Time	Observation	Classification

This chart offers the possibility of writing a running record in the form of a note or a detailed narrative. Time is recorded as behaviours occur. After the recording, the observer categorizes each play or behaviour sequence according to the required classification (for example, for social play, the categories would be Onlooker, Solitary, Parallel, Associative, or Cooperative). The classification section should focus on such categories as play behaviours, developmental domains, communication type, or other teacher-intended focus. It should not be used for unfounded inferences.

Anecdotal Records

Although open to **subjectivity**, the anecdotal record is often used by psychologists, teachers, caregivers, parents, and students because of its focused efficiency.

The most basic forms are those that parents record in a **baby book** or log book of development. As the child gets older, caregivers and parents can use this method of formal record-keeping for meetings with parents or, most effectively, to maintain a log of developmental or behavioural changes. Students may learn from recording anecdotes while working with children or during opportunities to observe when they are not otherwise engaged with the children.

Piaget recorded anecdotal observations of his own children in the 1920s. Later, his observations were more systematic and focused on asking children questions. His early observations enabled him to formulate his cognitive theory. Recording what seemed noteworthy enabled him to study the child's behaviour, by noticing the child's mistakes or misunderstandings.

The choice of event to record can challenge the untrained or inexperienced. Parents may be able to identify a significant behaviour worthy of recording because of the change it exhibits from previous behavioural patterns. The child may demonstrate a new strategy or an **emerging skill**. These would be opportune moments to record.

The anecdote dictates the degree of description required in its essential elements. You can test the appropriate level of detail by having other people read the anecdote, to see if they can appreciate its significance. Similarly, there is no set length of narrative for an anecdotal record. Usually a paragraph or two is adequate, as the context and behaviour can be captured in that space. (See a sample anecdotal record on pages 121–123.)

Researchers and psychologists can keep anecdotal records and classify them according to behavioural types, social play categories, temperamental styles, cognitive activities, child's age, and so on. In this way, these records can be resourced or cross-referenced so that key elements can be drawn together as required.

Practising teachers may have a card index system, record information on tapes for each child, or keep a daily log book that parent and child can complete. Caregivers responsible for infants may find this a particularly easy and effective way to pass information back and forth between home and agency.

Caregiving in a private home environment is particularly challenging because there is little time to write up observations. The anecdotal record enables the caregiver to make a few written notes while remaining a participant. Daily **"baseline" observations** can be recorded using the anecdotal method. These provide a benchmark for later changes in a child's health or behaviour. Many child-care centres require that baseline observations be made at the start of each day as policy.

Time constraints make any written recording difficult for all those who work with young children. Toddlers' teachers may find the anecdotal record convenient and efficient. Fragmented bits and pieces of activity typical of the toddler can be written up as anecdotal records. If the caregiver is lucky, he can record these anecdotes at naptime.

Accidents, potential child abuse, or serious incidents may be written in anecdotal form. A court of law may require dated anecdotal records of a child's behavioural changes and health observations as evidence, considering those records important documentation.

TAKING A SPECIAL LOOK: Observing indicators of abuse or neglect

Observations may lead teachers and caregivers to think that a child has suffered some kind of abuse or neglect. It is not for them to investigate the situation; that is the task of the child-care protection agency, which must be notified if there is proof or evidence of abuse and also if there is reasonable cause for such concern.

Particularly useful observations in these cases include dated anecdotal records or diary accounts that detail the observation of physical marks, unusual or disturbing behaviours, anything significant that the child tells you, or artwork that the child has produced. Be very careful not to question the child, which can be counterproductive in the long term even though you might think that doing so could be therapeutic for her. Questioning can plant suggestions in the child's mind and could also undermine possible legal action.

Using anecdotal records

Advantages

- A brief account of what happened is easy to record.
- Short anecdotes are efficient.
- The observer can record behaviour soon after it occurs.
- This is a useful means of recording behaviour for record-keeping and communicating with parents.
- Data can form a useful selection of significant behaviours.
- Almost everyone can use the anecdotal method.
- The observer can concentrate on more than one child.

Parents and caregivers may wish to write down what they judge to be significant. An anecdotal record can capture the essence of the moment.

- The observer can participate in the program at the same time.
- The record may form the basis of documentation for legal purposes.
- This method can be used as a learning tool for students.
- Anecdotal records containing baseline information can be made daily.

Disadvantages

- The observer needs to decide what behaviour is pertinent to record.
- Any time delay can increase observer bias.
- This method relies on the observer's memory.
- Selective recording can be biased.
- The record may offer insufficient contextual information.
- The observer must be skilled in recording most significant behaviours.
- The observer may find it irresistible to mix observed information with opinion.

Method charts for anecdotal records

Basic recording system

Anecdotal Record

Child's name: _____   Observer: _____

Age/D.O.B.: _____   Date: _____

Reason for observation: _____

_____

_____

Time/date: _____

Context: _____

_____

Observation anecdote: _____

_____

_____

Time/date: _____

Context: _____

_____

Observation anecdote: _____

_____

_____

Time/date: _____

Context: _____

_____

Observation anecdote: _____

_____

_____

These anecdotal forms can be used in a card index system or in a log form for each child.

Accident/serious occurrence

Anecdotal Record						
Date	Time	Name of child	Incident	Teachers present	Action	Parent informed (sign)

This chart is useful when spread over the open pages of an accident book. Describe the incident as fully as possible—you might include a drawing.

Diary Records

KEY FEATURES: Diary record

- observation of one or more children

- selects highlights of activity

- written account recorded regularly after observation

- as objective as possible

- may contain reflections or analysis within text

- naturalistic

- nonparticipatory or participatory

Diaries may be the oldest of all narrative-recording methods. The diarist requires little technology or expertise and chooses to record what he considers significant. Diaries usually involve a series of anecdotal recordings; the degree of detail can vary. A diary may be an open communication or a private record of events.

The same diary technique can be used for keeping an up-to-date account of the development of an individual child or a group of children. The significant area of development is selected and written up on a frequent, usually daily, basis. The style is often anecdotal, but other forms of recording can be included. We can learn from the diary records of many figures in our history of education. Pestalozzi, Montessori, Steiner, Froebel, and Piaget, among others, offer us the legacy of their diary observations.

A parent may initiate a process of diary-keeping that produces a valuable document. Teachers and others may also want to keep an open diary as a dialogue between themselves and parents; the diary may encourage more parental involvement.

Developmental changes become evident when regularly documented. Patterns of behaviour are frequently revealed when the recording was made for other reasons.

Using diary records

Advantages

- Observations are easy to record.
- This method leads to a daily record of behaviour.
- The diary becomes a valuable tool for communicating between parents and care-givers.
- The diary provides a valuable record or "keepsake" for parents and/or the child-care agency.
- This method may be used along with other methods of observation.
- The diary can be used as a learning tool for students as part of a child study.
- The record is useful in identifying behavioural changes and revealing patterns of behaviour.
- Observations may be written about one or more children at a time.
- Diaries can frequently help teachers review previous months' or years' programs and/or children's progress.

Disadvantages

- The choice of content might be subjective.
- The observer must be consistent in keeping the record daily.
- The need to interpret data is easily overlooked.
- Situations usually require further observation. A diary alone may provide insufficient information.
- Inferences may be drawn too easily.
- The selection of information may be influenced by observer bias.

Method charts for diary records

Daily log

```
                              Diary Record
    Date: _____
    Caregiver observation: _____
    _____
    _____
    Caregiver signature: _____
    Parent signature/comment: _____
    ────────────────────────────────────────────────────────────
    Date: _____
    Caregiver observation: _____
    _____
    _____
    Caregiver signature: _____
    Parent signature/comment: _____
    ────────────────────────────────────────────────────────────
    Date: _____
    Caregiver observation: _____
    _____
    _____
    Caregiver signature: _____
    Parent signature/comment: _____
```

This system allows recording a daily anecdote that is shared with the parent. You could include equal space for parent observations. Similarly, a parent can give the caregiver an update of what has occurred at home.

Infant observation log

```
                         Infant Observation Log

    Child's name: _____   Date: _____
    Age/D.O.B.: _____   Caregiver's name(s): _____
    Feeding: _____
    Diapering: _____
    Sleeping: _____
    Played with: _____
    New interests/achievements: _____
    Caregiver signature: _____
    Read by parent (signature): _____
```

These sheets can be copied and left on a clipboard for each infant each day. After a week, the sheets can be kept in a binder, for each child, which the parent may want to keep. The "New interests/achievements" category can be completed as an anecdotal record.

Specimen Records

KEY FEATURES: Specimen record

- very detailed narrative that focuses on one child
- written account recorded at time of observation
- records <u>all</u> actions including expressions, gesture, vocalizations, etc.
- may use codes for ease of recording
- requires skill and practice
- naturalistic or test situation
- the observer is nonparticipatory

The most detailed narrative recording, the **specimen record**, is described by Goodwin and Driscoll (1980) as "a comprehensive, descriptive, objective and permanent record of behaviour as it occurs." It is the most challenging of the narrative forms because of its comprehensive and open-ended nature.

An observer cannot undertake this type of recording while she has responsibilities for the child or other children. It requires skill on the part of the observer to record all the child's behaviours. All possible detail should be recorded, including all gross and fine motor movements, actions and reactions, descriptions of posture, gesture, facial expression, and all utterances, using the child's exact words.

Specimen records can use a variety of coding systems by which the observer captures details. Coding systems can be harder to read yet form a more detailed picture of the behaviour. They may be written by re-running a video-recorded sequence—particularly in a detailed movement study. Rarely if ever do practising teachers have the time or motivation to conduct this kind of observation. Sometimes, however, they will read specimen records prepared by psychologists; such records offer greater depth than normal classroom observation usually allows.

Using specimen records

Advantages

- The specimen record gives a rich, detailed narrative description of all behaviour.
- The data collected can be analyzed by one or more professionals.
- These records are useful for case conferences and may be used in research work.
- They are less likely to be affected by observer bias than other narratives.
- The record may focus on one category of behaviour or be entirely open-ended.
- This method provides an opportunity to observe unstructured play.
- The record may establish causes of behaviour.

- The observation may indicate development in one or more domains and show the necessity to employ other methods of observation.
- Specimen records may provide behavioural details that identify concerns not revealed through more superficial recordings.

Disadvantages

- The observer requires refined skills to record.
- The observer must be a nonparticipant in the children's program.
- This method depends heavily on the writing and language skills of the observer.
- The observer can observe only one child at a time.
- The observer record may incorporate complex coding in order to include sufficient detail.
- Professionals frequently keep specimen records without including full contextual information and may not represent the whole child fairly.

Recording Narrative Observations
Steps to take to record, summarize, and analyze a narrative observation

1. Decide on your reason for using the narrative method.
2. Choose one of the narrative styles that fits your purpose.
3. Check that you have parental permission.
4. Prepare a method chart to meet your needs.
5. Write the observation as it happens, or as you select behaviours to record after they occur, in a rich, descriptive narrative.
6. Write up your "neat version" of the observation as soon as possible, making only additions that you are certain help your description without changing the content.
7. Review your data, sort it, and summarize the information according to developmental domains. (List, without explaining, behaviours you have observed in each domain.)
8. Explain the observed behaviours with referring to norms and theories.
9. Make inferences about the behaviours following the process of analysis outlined in Chapter 1 (page 16).
10. Develop an action plan or learning prescription based on your findings.

Ways to make narrative recording easier

- **If your handwriting is a problem:** Try using a tape-recorder. Speak your observation into it, using rich, descriptive language. Write up the observation as soon as possible before you forget any of the details.

- **If English is your second language:** Try writing your observation in your own first language, using the method as described. You may have to translate your work if it is for an assignment or for record-keeping. Be aware of how translation can affect objectivity.

  Or tape-record your observation in your first language to capture the detail and then translate as you put it down on paper.

- **If you cannot write fast enough:** Try using a map to indicate the child's movements to accompany your observations.

  Or videotape the observation and take your time in writing your version on paper, using the pause and replay buttons frequently until you have the descriptive narrative written down.

  Or observe the child with another observer recording simultaneously. Afterward, sit down together and discuss your perceptions. If possible, write a narrative together.

  Or use a form of shorthand. If you do not know standard abbreviations, study or invent your own. Try using "R." instead of "Richard," "chdn." instead of "children," and so on.

- **If your language lacks sufficient descriptive powers:** Write your observation in point form and add the adjectives, adverbs, or whatever is missing afterward with the help of a teacher or colleague who observed at the same time or from whom you can get language support.

  Or prepare lists of adjectives, adverbs, and even verbs to help you write up your observation.

- Work with another adult and share your observational data, but avoid accepting another person's biases.

- While practice may not make your observation skills perfect, it helps!

Each of the above strategies can help students or teachers who have particular difficulties in writing. Always acknowledge the skill-building ideas you employ in your actual observation, as they may affect the accuracy of your recording.

TAKING A SPECIAL LOOK: Terminology for exceptionality and differences

Positive language can help shape our attitudes to children with special needs. A child is a person first and foremost; her individual identity should come before any descriptive term denoting ability or any professionally diagnosed condition. It is more sensitive and appropriate to speak of "a child who is partially sighted" than to say "a blind child." Observe children and describe their behaviours from a positive perspective.

Inappropriate language can be demeaning, teasing, impersonal, or judgmental; it often ignores the child's potential and focuses on disability rather than ability. Appropriate language considers the child first and then describes her condition, family, ability, or behaviour as objectively as possible.

More appropriate terms	Inappropriate terms
Dana has epilepsy.	an epileptic
Percy has a hearing deficit.	the deaf kid
Bert's social skills are sometimes inappropriate.	a "behaviour" child; a misfit
Kinga needs special help with...	a slow learner
Dora has learned to tie her shoelaces.	educable retarded; trainable
Rivka has a developmental delay.	a below-average child
Cory (child's name alone)	spotty Scotty (or other rhymes)
Ho is new to the country.	a "Chink" (or other demeaning references to country of origin)
Sharina's skin is a rich brown colour.	ethnic children; "fuzzy tops"
a child who has exceptionalities	a special-ed kid
a child with a disability	a handicapped child
a child with a disorder/delay	an abnormal child
developmentally delayed	a "retard"/"retarded"
a child who is unwell	a sick kid
developmental diversity	normal and subnormal
focus on ability	focus on inabilities
focus on person	focus on disorders
living with HIV/AIDS	dying of AIDS
inclusion	exclusion
building on competence	identifying failures
celebrating successes	pinpointing "incorrect" behaviour
authentic assessment	dependence on standardized tests

Summary

There are a number of different methods of documenting observations in written form. Each of these narratives—running records, anecdotal records, diary accounts, and specimen records, as well as personal narratives—has its strengths and weaknesses. Deciding which method to use depends on the observer's reason for recording. The specimen record is the most detailed written record, and although it is potentially revealing, its detail makes it cumbersome and time-consuming, and typically the data need to be coded. Teachers and others who want a detailed account of behaviour prefer the running record, yet accept that they cannot record every tiny nuance of the behaviour they observe. Typically, teachers aim to write running records that incorporate as much detail as possible. The writer's biases can compromise each of the narrative styles. The recorder's bias is particularly evident in anecdotal records, in her choice of a particular sequence to document, as well as in the difficulty in separating observational information from opinion. Anecdotal records are useful for those professionals and parents who want to record what they think important after it has occurred. The long stream of behaviour and the interactions between children typical of the level of activity within classrooms, child-care centres, homes, and play spaces also make it difficult for adults to collect as much information as they might like. The anecdotal record is quick, focused, and efficient.

The diary recording offers the observer the regular opportunity to document a series of observations. Over time these records may become more revealing than at first obvious. Clearly the diary allows greater flexibility in the selection of observational information, and this is also its challenge—the diary-recording process is open to unfocused recollections, biases, assumptions, and unsupported inferences. However, neither the professional who wants to view what is happening nor the parent who wants to document the daily progress of his child should discount its usefulness.

Personal narratives can take two or more different forms: one for the teacher and one for the child. The teacher's personal narrative is a full document containing observations and reflections that merge fact and opinion. This might form part of a teacher's professional portfolio as well as provide information about the effectiveness of her role and responsibilities. Young children do not have the power of self-reflection at first. Through visual representations, oral recordings, and adults' assistance, children can become more reflective about their learning in a way that can lead to their greater success in making their records. Neither of the personal narrative forms constitutes typical observational methods.

Narrative recording can be used to record situations such as this intimate sequence where an adult and two children share a moment with a book.

Key Terms

analysis

anecdotal record

assessment

assumption

authentic assessment

baby book

baseline observations

behaviour

bias

child-centred

contemplative observer

contextual information

data

diary record

emerging skill

fine motor skills

gross motor skills

inclusion

inference

language

narrative observation

nonparticipant observation

personal narrative

phenomenology

play pattern

reflective practice

running record

special needs

specimen record

spontaneous play

Weblinks

www.naropa.edu/brownessay2.html
Dr. Richard C. Brown of Naropa University describes contemplative observation and the role of the observer.

www.temple.edu/CETP/temple_teach/a-observ.html
Various assessment techniques include a brief but accurate description of anecdotal records.

www.sims.berkeley.edu/courses/is190-2/f96/kuntay/assign1/narrative.html
Useful Internet resources for academic researchers interested in the field of narrative psychology and narrative development in child language.

kerlins.net/bobbi/research/qualresearch/syllabi.html
Qualitative-research site provides links to courses and syllabi on qualitative research, along with links to qualitative research journals.

www.us.edu/newreading/runrec.htm
Complete description of running records developed by Marie M. Clay, a developmental researcher.

Observation Sample

This sample running record offers an extremely objective and descriptive recording of the child's behaviour. A diagram aids the recording process. The student then summarizes the data and provides a self-evaluation.

All observations need to include sufficient background information, such as that given here on the first page, to make the recording meaningful. Permission to record must always be sought from the parents, as shown on page 2 of this assignment. Note that the permission form shows the child's real name, while the observation form uses a pseudonym to preserve confidentiality. How does this cover sheet support the observation assignment?

---

1 of 5

Observation Assignment

Front Page

Student name: _Sue Fung_ Student number: _000-888-000_

Section number: _062_

Assignment method: _Running Record_

Date due: _February 12, 2004_ Date handed in: _February 12, 2004_

Child's name (pseudonym): _Patrick_

Child's age (years/months): _2 years, 8 months_

Date of observation: _February 2, 2004_ Time of observation: _2:10-2:25 p.m._

Setting: _Day-care setting. Children are in free play time. There is a wide_ _choice of activity_

Parent's name: _Mr. P. Yuen_ Phone # if released: _N/A_

* _The observation recording is translated from Chinese._

Each assignment has specific criteria. Please check with the assignment description and direction given in class.

Declaration by student

I have followed the assignment description and instructions given in class about confidentiality and privacy. I confirm that appropriate processes for making this observation have been undertaken and that permission has been gained from the parents. A copy of this observation will be given to the parents if they desire.

Sue Fung
_____
Signature of Student

Why is it necessary to use a form for permission—wouldn't oral permission be adequate?

Permission Form

Child Observations, Case Studies, and Portfolios

Student and Parent Agreement

Without written permission I will not observe and record information about your child. Please sign in the space provided if you agree that I may make observations and study your child. It would be helpful if you could initial each of the boxes if you are willing for me to undertake any or all of the techniques of information gathering.

I ___Sue Fung___ *(student name)* will not refer to the child in any written manner by his or her real name. Information recorded will be written objectively, treated professionally, and kept confidential.

___S. Fung___   ___Feb. 2, 1998___
(student's signature)   *(date)*

I ___Peter Yuen___
(parent's name)

agree to have ___Johnny Yuen___
             (child's name)

observed ☑   photographed ☒   audiotaped ☒   videotaped ☒

by ___Sue Fung___
   (student's name above)

at ___University Settlement Recreation Center-ESL child-minding division___
   (agency/home)

for the purpose of study in child development at ___Centennial College___

(school/college) for a period of ___1 week___ *(weeks/months)* on the consideration that copies are made available to me, the parent, if I so request.

___Peter Yuen___   ___Feb. 2, 2004___
(parent's signature)   *(date)*

Is the level of detail recorded below sufficient? Is there any content that might be missing?

OBSERVATION RECORDING

Patrick is sitting with his legs beneath his buttocks; then he stretches both legs and sits on the floor. He holds a plastic strawberry in his left hand and a knife in his right hand, and he uses the knife to cut the strawberry in half. He grasps the two pieces of strawberry in his left hand and puts them on a plate. Then, he puts the knife down on the floor; he picks up a cup with both hands, moves the cup toward himself and puts the straw, which sticks in the cup, in his mouth. It appears that he is sucking something from the cup.

He puts the cup down on his left side, and he bends his body forward and stretches his left hand to get a plastic tomato and holds it in his palm. He moves his upper body backward and turns it to his left side. He puts the tomato on the floor and uses his left thumb and forefinger to support the tomato. Then, he holds the knife in his right hand and cuts the tomato. He releases one half of the plastic tomato from his left hand and uses his thumb and forefinger to get a plastic lemon. He puts it on the floor, supports it with two fingers and cuts it with the knife he is holding. He puts the knife down, grasps a half of plastic tomato and sticks it with the half of lemon. He holds the knife in his right hand and cuts the tomato-lemon, which is put on a plate and supported by his left thumb and forefinger.

He puts the knife down again, leans his upper body and stretches his left hand toward John, who is sitting opposite him. He frowns and grasps the plastic fruit that John is holding and pulls it toward himself. After getting the fruit from John, Patrick holds it in his left hand. He raises his left hand and uses it to hit John's head. After an instructor tells him not to hit others, he throws the fruit away.

He stands up, bends to the floor and picks up a cup using both hands. He straightens his body and walks to the instructor; he lifts the cup and has the straw touch her lips. The instructor asks him, "What's this?" He replies, "Orange juice, for you." After the instructor asks him to get an apple juice for her, he smiles and bounds to the place where all the plastic fruits and plates are located. He holds the cup in his left hand; he puts his right palm on top of the cover, seizes the edge by the fore-finger, middle finger, ring finger and baby finger of his right hand, and pulls the cover away. He moves the cup toward his nose; it seems like he is smelling something in the cup. Then, he uses his right hand to press the cover on top of the cup. He holds the cup with two hands, walks to the instructor and stretches both hands toward her, smiles and says, "Apple juice." After the instructor has finished the juice, he throws the cup away, as he smiles and hums a tune.

He runs and then jumps into the play tent. He sits with his legs beneath his buttocks among balls and holds a ball in each hand. He raises both hands, looks up and says, "Cinderella" in a loud voice. He throws the balls away, leans his body forward and puts his hands on the floor. He stretches both legs; I think that he is trying to stand up. However, his right foot steps on a ball, and his body leans to the left. Then, he puts his hands on the floor again, stands up and jumps out of the tent.

He laughs and runs after John and says, "Goooo . . ." in a high-pitched loud voice. He runs around the room, stops next to the slide and jumps up and down with both hands raised. At this moment, John is throwing balls from the tent. As the instructor asks John to stop throwing and pick up the balls, Patrick helps them to pick up the balls near him and throws them overhand into the tent. Then, he laughs and runs after John, follows John, creeps under the slide and lies with his chest down. He puts both elbows on the floor and both palms under his chin.

When snack is ready to be served, he creeps forward and puts both hands on the floor to help himself stand up. Then, he runs to the right side of the room, grasps the back of a chair with two hands and walks with his body leaning backward. He puts the chair next to the table and sits down. He stretches his right hand and grasps a cup by using thumb, forefinger and middle finger. He pulls the cup toward himself; after the instructor asks him to wait for others, he pushes the cup forward next to the plates, moves his hands back and puts them on his thighs. While waiting for the instructor to allot the food, he puts his right hand on the edge of the table and says, "I want to eat." Then, he pulls the plate toward himself with thumb and forefinger. He grasps a cookie by using his thumb, forefinger and middle finger and puts the cookie in his mouth. He holds his cup with his hands and moves it toward his lips.

How does the diagram assist the observation? What could have been included in this illustration?

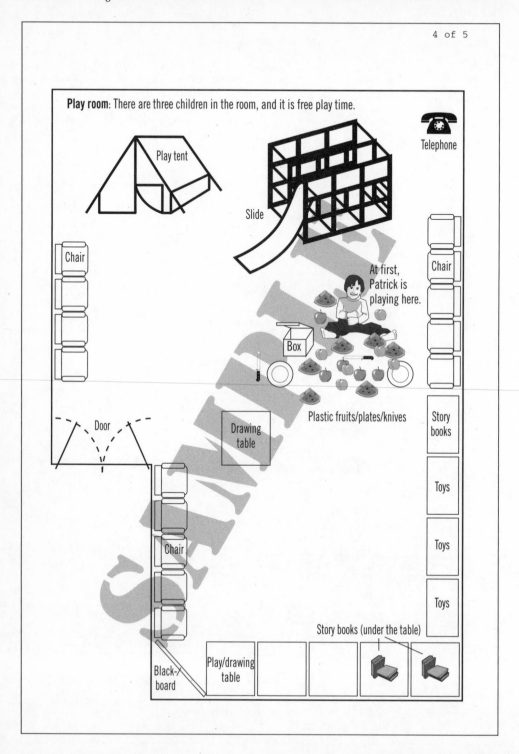

Play room: There are three children in the room, and it is free play time.

Telephone

Play tent

Slide

Chair

Chair

At first, Patrick is playing here.

Box

Plastic fruits/plates/knives

Story books

Door

Drawing table

Toys

Toys

Chair

Toys

Story books (under the table)

Black-board

Play/drawing table

Are there any skills missing? Are there any developmental domains missing? The categorization of skills in this summary is helpful; what is the next step in the process of documentation?

SUMMARY

Physical Skills

Gross Motor:
- sits with his legs beneath his buttocks (squats)
- moves his body forward and backward when he sits
- pulls a plastic fruit toward himself from another child
- bends his body to pick up an object when he is standing
- walks steadily
- jumps out from the play tent and jumps up and down
- throws balls overhand into the play tent
- runs without falling
- creeps under the slide

Fine Motor:
- holds a plastic fruit in his left hand and a plastic knife in his right hand
- holds a cup with both hands and puts straw in mouth
- uses thumb and forefinger to support a plastic fruit
- holds an object in each hand and sticks the two objects together
- pulls a cover off a cup by using four fingers to seize the edge and putting his palm on the top
- picks up an object by using thumb, forefinger and middle finger (tripod grasp)
- uses thumb and forefinger to pick up food and feeds himself without assistance

Social Skills:
- grabs a plastic fruit from another child and hits the child with the fruit
- offers a cup of "juice" to another person
- friendly, eager to please, for example, gives the instructor an "apple juice"
- helps other children pick up balls
- plays parallel to another child (runs after the child and follows him to creep under the slide)

Emotional Skills:
- frowns when he grabs a plastic fruit from another child
- smiles and hums after the instructor drinks the "juice"
- laughs and says, "Goooo" loudly when he runs after another child

Cognitive Skills:
- sticks two pieces of plastic fruit together
- cuts a whole plastic fruit in half by using a plastic knife
- identifies the name of the object in the cup
- knows a cover should go with a cup
- picks up his own chair before having snack

Language and Communication:
- pushes the cup toward another person and lets the straw touch her lips
- tells her, "Orange juice, for you"
- laughs and says, "Goooo" in high-pitched, loud voice
- says, "Cinderella" loudly when playing alone in the play tent
- tells the instructor, "I want to eat," and puts his right hand on the edge of the table

Observation Sample

This running record offers an objective, flowing description of activity. Beside it the recorder offers explanations of what is happening and some inferences about the child's behaviours.

Some educators are uncomfortable with documenting reflections at the same time as the observation. Do you consider the "Comments" appropriate or too subjective?

Running Record

Child's name: _Mandy_   Observer: _Daisy C._

Age/D.O.B.: _2 years, 6 days/October 30, 2001_   Date: _November 5, 2003_

Reason for observation: _____ To observe all of Mandy's behaviours as they spontaneously occur during observation period, to help assess her development in all domains (emotional, social, physical, cognitive).

Context: _____ Observation took place outside in the playground after afternoon snack. There were thirteen toddlers in the playground at the time of the observation. The weather was sunny and cool, so the children were dressed in coats, hats, and mittens. Five other children were also in the same play space with climbers and tricycles.

Time	Observation	Comments/immediate reflections
3:50 to 4:10	Mandy is sitting on a tricycle with her feet placed flat on the ground, facing forward. She is grasping the handles, wrapping her hands around the handlebars. She climbs off the tricycle, swinging her right leg over the seat, both hands remaining in same position as above, while looking in the direction of another tricycle.	She has physical skill of sitting astride tricycle. Puts her feet on the ground rather than on the pedals. Good coordination allows her to climb off tricycle with ease, while appearing to focus visual attention on another object (tricycle).
	Mandy runs toward the other tricycle, climbing on by swinging her right leg over the seat, hands placed on the right side of the handlebars. Putting each foot on a pedal, she attempts to propel the tricycle forward. Her right foot slips off the pedal. She takes her left foot off the left pedal and moves the tricycle forward, using her legs and feet, both feet forward, pushing backward at the same time.	Effective coordination also displayed in her ability to run toward the other tricycle. Appears to understand that tricycle can be propelled by using pedals; however, has difficulty keeping her feet on pedals and quickly resorts to using her feet on the ground to move forward.
	Stops tricycle and looks over left shoulder in the direction of another child's father. She	Appears very aware of what is happening around her, implying her ability to scan her

Time	Observation	Comments

says, "John, your daddy is here!" Continues to sit on tricycle, watching John's daddy. After a moment, Mandy climbs off the tricycle and runs toward the riding car John had been sitting in. She climbs in and pulls the car door shut with her left hand and grips the steering wheel, one hand on each side, and propels forward using her feet, one in front of the other, to push the car forward.

She places her left hand on the back of the car, puts her left foot on the ground, pushing the door open with her right foot, and climbs out. A caregiver comes over to Mandy and takes her hand, saying, "Come, Mandy, we'll wipe your nose." Mandy takes her hand and walks to the Kleenex box. She stands and lets caregiver wipe her nose. Mandy stands beside caregiver for a moment, then walks toward another caregiver.

Caregiver says, "Hi, Mandy. Your shoe is untied; let me tie it for you." Mandy says, "No, I want Daisy to do it." Caregiver says, "Okay, Daisy will do it!" Once her shoe is tied, Mandy climbs the stairs on the climber, holding onto the railing with her left hand, alternating feet up the stairs. She sits down at the top of the slide and pushes herself down, each hand on one side of the slide. At the bottom, some other toddlers begin screaming, and Mandy stands up and screams as well. She runs back to the stairs and climbs to the top again, sliding down the slide. Lands on her bottom, flips over on hands and knees, looking up the slide. Gripping sides of slide, Mandy climbs up on hands and knees, sliding her hands up as she goes. At the top, lets her feet slip into a straight position, lying prostrate on the slide. Lets go with hands and slides down on her belly. Repeats this activity two more times.

surroundings to assess what is going on.

The above is further supported when Mandy immediately runs to the riding car as soon as John vacates it. When she looked for John after seeing his dad, she also noticed the toy he was using.

Good large muscle coordination once again displayed. Mandy easily climbs into the car, using a series of twisting, supporting, and maneuvering motions to get herself in and out.

Mandy understands simple instructions--both the instruction to go with the caregiver and what was going to happen (wipe nose).

Mandy is able to assert her independence by making her wishes known, verbally.

Good large motor control displayed here. Mandy climbs stairs with ease, alternating her feet. She easily maneuvers her body down the slide.

Joining the other children by imitating their screaming indicates, once again, that Mandy is aware of what is happening around her and is prepared to join in when she feels she would like to. May indicate her enjoyment of other toddlers' company.

Mandy enjoys using her motor skills in creative ways, exploring new ways of doing things.

Time	Observation	Comments
	At the bottom of slide, Mandy stands up from a crouch position, runs to climber stairs and climbs, using alternating feet and left hand on rail. Another child is sitting at the top of the slide. Mandy begins to scream in a frustrated voice. Caregiver says, "Mandy, Paul will slide down, then it is your turn." Mandy watches Paul slide down, then she slides down, on her bottom. Stands up from crouch position and walks toward a caregiver. She says, "I want to go on bike" (looking at a "big wheel" trike).	Evidence of Mandy's egocentricity. She has difficulty "sharing" the slide with another child, but understands that she will get her turn when Paul slides down. She accepts this and waits her turn.

Evidence that Mandy can express herself verbally. |
| | Caregiver holds bike steady while Mandy climbs on. Mandy tries to propel trike forward with her feet, but the front wheel is turned sideways. The caregiver says, "The handles are backward, Mandy. Let's turn them around." Mandy climbs off trike, helping caregiver turn handles around. She climbs back on the trike and moves it forward using alternating feet. Goes a short distance, then climbs off. | Climbing onto yet another style of trike/riding toy, Mandy displays typical 2-year-old curiosity and exploration skills. |
| | She stands and looks around the playground. Walks toward another child on a tricycle and says, "Ride bike?" Other child pedals away. Mandy walks toward a mom picking up her child. She walks to caregiver and says, "I get up," while her arms stretch out in caregiver's direction. Caregiver picks her up. Mandy smiles and laughs. Stays in caregiver's arms for a couple of minutes, until caregiver says, "I have to put you down, Mandy, to see what is wrong with Michael, Okay?" Mandy gets down and follows caregiver in the direction of Michael. Stops and looks toward two other children, who are standing facing each other. Mandy walks toward them, stops, and observes. Walks away and wanders around the playground. Walks toward two children playing with a wagon. She follows the wagon as another child pulls wagon around the playground. | Behavioral indication of Mandy's comfort level with her environment and the people in it. She approaches another toddler with confidence, then a caregiver for some personal attention. Indication of her emotional well-being—she is able to approach a caregiver for a cuddle when she feels she needs one.

Understands why caregiver needs to put her down; but, stays close until she finds something of interest to her.

Evidence that Mandy enjoys the company of other children, but still tends to play solitary.

Evidence of onlooker-type social play. She doesn't join in, but remains close to the action. |

Observation Sample

This student has used anecdotal records to record significant behaviours in different developmental domains. The summary comments make tentative inferences about the child's performance.

What do you think of the student's choice of events to record and how she has documented them?

Anecdotal Records

Observer's name: Sherry Lacroix

Child's name (pseudonym): Jenna

Age: 6 years, 4 months

Date: Thursday, January 29, to Friday, February 20, 2004

Setting: Child Care Center, Preschool room

   17 children and 2-3 adults

Purpose of observation: To observe the child in a natural setting to record behaviours unique to her. To select from the anecdotes the specific behaviours, and to use these for the purpose of the final analysis of her portfolio.

Date of observation: Thursday, January 29, 2004

Time: 10:40 a.m.

Context: Preschool room during circle time with all the children.

Jenna is sitting down cross-legged in a circle with all of the other children; she is listening to the caregiver read them a story. After the story is finished, several of the children, including Jenna, put up their hands and offer questions and comments. Jenna puts up her hand; the caregiver asks Jenna what she would like to say. Jenna says, "I think Jeremy is having a very good day. I think he deserves a round of applause." The caregiver says that it is a good idea, and all the children clap their hands for Jeremy.

Summary: Jenna appears to be showing signs of some pro-social behaviour; she seems to be able to see things from another child's perspective and feel empathy for him. Jenna appears to have the ability to think about other people's feelings and show a sensitivity toward them. This can be seen in the above anecdote; Jenna seems to recognize the type of day a particular child is having and acknowledges it in her own way. Jenna appears to be becoming less egocentric; she now is able to put others in a primary role, showing increased pro-social behaviour.

Date of observation: Friday, January 30, 2004

Time: 11:15 a.m.

Context: The children are going to the gymnasium for gross motor activities.

The children walk to the gymnasium and sit down on the floor. Jenna puts up her hand; the caregiver acknowledges Jenna and asks her what she would like to say. Jenna asks, "Can we do exercises?" The caregiver says yes and asks her what kind of exercises they should do. Jenna pauses; she stands up with her legs straight and her feet slightly apart. Jenna bends at the waist and reaches her hands to touch her toes. The caregiver says,

"All right, let's touch our toes ten times." The children touch their toes. Jenna then says, "How about leg lifts?" Jenna lies down on the floor and demonstrates to the caregiver what she has said. The children follow Jenna and do five leg lifts.

Summary: Jenna appears to have improved gross motor skills and coordination. She seems to be able to demonstrate specific exercises with relative ease and confidence. Jenna seems to use her cognitive abilities to think of different exercises, and to use her gross motor skills to carry them out in front of the class.

Date of observation: Friday, February 6, 2004

Time: 4:05 p.m.

Context: Preschool room at a table. Earlier in the day, Jenna and a caregiver had put together a puzzle; it was time for clean-up and the caregiver told Jenna they could do another puzzle later.

Jenna comes over to the caregiver she was playing with earlier in the day and asks, "Remember when you said we could finish the puzzle--well, could we finish it now?" The caregiver says yes. Jenna and the caregiver walk over to a table with two other children. Jenna picks out a Mickey Mouse puzzle containing 100 pieces. Jenna tries to fit several pieces together until she finds the one that will fit. The puzzle is completed and the caregiver asks, "How many pieces of the puzzle are we missing?" Jenna points to the empty spaces with her fingers; she replies, "One, two. Two pieces are missing." Jenna then says, "Let's keep this one together on the table. Let's do another one." Jenna stands up and walks over to the shelf and picks up another puzzle.

Summary: In the developmental area of social competence, Jenna appears to be able to interact positively with both adults and peers. She seems to be able to work cooperatively in a group all striving for one goal. Jenna appears to have a good sense of memory when she asks the caregiver about the puzzle they could not complete earlier in the day. Jenna seems to have an expanded concentration span to finish a large puzzle and wants to do another; she seems to be able to solve math questions the caregiver asks her. Jenna appears to have well-developed fine motor skills to fit together the small pieces in the puzzle. Jenna appears to enjoy cognitive games such as puzzles; this is seen when she remarks, "Let's do another one."

Date of observation: Friday, February 20, 2004

Time: 11:55 a.m.

Context: Just before lunch is about to begin, the caregiver asks the children to go to the washroom and wash their hands.

Jenna is sitting on the floor; she stands up and begins to walk to the door. Jenna stops and turns her head, looking behind her, then turns around and walks to a younger child who is standing still. She takes his hand and says, "Come on, Benjamin." Jenna takes Benjamin's left hand and walks with him out the door. The two children turn left and walk down the hallway and turn right into the bathroom. Jenna puts her hands under the fountain sink and washes her hands. She walks over to the paper-towel dispenser and pulls out one paper towel, dries her hands, and throws the paper towel into the garbage. Jenna turns around and walks toward the

Each anecdote is documented and summarized separately. What further considerations might follow this series of observations?

water fountain where Benjamin is standing. She bends down slightly, puts her arms around Benjamin's waist, and carries him over to the paper-towel dispenser. Benjamin grabs a paper towel; she puts him on the floor; he disposes of the paper towel. Jenna walks back to class beside Benjamin.

Summary: Jenna appears to have acquired many pro-social skills. She has developed a positive relationship with her peers; she shows sensitivity toward a younger, smaller child who has trouble reaching the paper-towel dispenser. She seems to be becoming less egocentric and has the ability to see things in a new perspective and help out when she can. Jenna appears to show her cognitive abilities when she responds to certain situations. She realizes the need for this child to get a paper towel; he cannot reach it, so she implements her own plan to fix the problem. Jenna shows her emotional development in a sensitivity toward others and in her general interaction with her peers; she seems to try to help others whenever the need arises.

chapter 4

Samplings

Just as the word "time" is central to time sampling, so the word "event" is central to event sampling. Although both methods use the word "sampling," their procedures and results can be quite different.

Warren R. Bentzen (1993)

For those students for whom typical interventions have not been successful, developing an understanding of the cause of behavior may be key to helping them learn new behavioral skills.

Parent Advocacy Coalition for Educational Rights (1994)

This method [event sampling] proves to be very efficient in reducing observation time and has the added bonus of providing data that could be summarized easily and subjected to statistical analysis.

D. Michelle Irwin and M. Margaret Bushnell (1980)

Cooperative play can be encouraged if time, space, opportunity, and materials are available. Sampling this type of activity can help in understanding the children's social skills and assist in programming.

Sampling Observations

DEFINITION: Sampling observations

Sampling observations are those in which (a) examples of behaviour are recorded as they occur or (b) behaviours are recorded as they are demonstrated at previously decided intervals or (c) "work" samples are gathered.

Sampling behaviours or events is an indirect or interpretive style of observing children. Practising teachers may choose to record them frequently because of their very specific nature and their speed in producing results. Recording information while involved in activity with the children can be challenging; you can do some samplings without disengaging yourself from the children for any significant length of time. Gathering examples (or samples) of the products of a child's work can provide insight into that child's interests and thought processes.

CHILD DEVELOPMENT FOCUS

Samplings can be helpful in observing and documenting
- patterns of behaviour

- what triggers or causes a behaviour

- examples of the products of a child's activity

Samplings may assist in

- avoiding negative behaviour sequences

- behaviour reshaping

- evaluating both the process and the products of behaviour

Some educators ignore samplings because they consider them only suitable in special education settings. Reluctance in using what might have once been considered a technique associated with behaviourism might also prevent teachers from recognizing their potential effectiveness.

Event Sampling

Event sampling is a method of observation that records occurrences of behaviours called **events** or target behaviours, which are examples of a previously selected category of behaviour. Event sampling most frequently focuses on one child at a time but may be constructed to record behaviours of a number of children simultaneously. Varying formats mean that the following aspects of the behaviour can be highlighted:

- frequency: how often the behaviour occurs
- duration: how long the behaviour continues
- causality: what triggered the behaviour
- severity: the degree to which the behaviour can be considered serious or a cause for concern

Event sampling is frequently used to analyze behaviours that present a challenge, but it can be used for other observational purposes as well.

KEY FEATURES: Event sampling

- focuses on behaviour of one child
- defines the behaviour to be sampled
- records occurrences on a chart
- aims to establish behavioural causes and patterns
- naturalistic
- participatory or nonparticipatory
- interpretive method of recording

ABC format

The ABC format is possibly the most useful of the event sampling methods:

A: the antecedent event—the "happening" just before the behaviour example cited

B: the behaviour—the example of the category of behaviour you are looking for

C: the consequent event—the effect, consequence, or event that occurs after the example given

Event samplings can indicate clearly the causes of the behaviours recorded. With the ABC format, the trigger or cause of the behaviour may become apparent through application of the ABC format. By viewing the antecedent we can see whether there is an identifiable pattern in which responses are elicited by particular stimuli. The child may initiate the stimulus-response pattern but the teacher's behaviour, a routine occurrence, or an environmental factor could also produce the pattern. This method enables the observer to see possible effects as well as causes of the behaviour. See examples of event samplings using the ABC format on pages 144–148 and 149–150.

Behaviour categories

Sampling techniques involve categorizing sets of behaviours. An **operational definition** of the behaviour to be observed is essential for the success of the observational recordings; without, it the observation will be built on quicksand. More than a list of behaviours that fall within a broad category; the definition must offer a clear explanation of what will be recorded.

Choosing, and then defining, the behaviour category can be troublesome. Behaviour is a continuous flow of activity, so it is hard to segment, so observers must be clear about what they seek to watch and to record. Categories can be broad or specific according to needs, as long as they are precise. To clarify your thinking, ask yourself, "What range of behaviours am I expecting to see?" The commonality of the set of behaviours should become apparent.

For example, if you expect to see examples of hitting, biting, and shouting, you will see that the common denominator of these qualities is anger or aggression. Consider the following definitions of "anger" and "aggression":

Anger: a behaviour in which the individual demonstrates rage and passionate resentment.

Aggression: a behaviour in which the individual demonstrates acts of violence or anger in words.

You might find it useful to create your own definition of aggression. Your definition could be more open-ended and therefore likely to cover other examples of behaviours you might see.

You might identify narrower categories if you are looking for a specific behaviour. In that case, you might choose a precise category. If you were seeking examples of altruism or empathy, you would not choose a category such as social behaviours.

Defining the behaviour you want to observe both limits the parameters of the observation and supports its objectivity. You may discover that the examples of behaviour that fall into a category may be more than you anticipated—and the operational definition would allow for that.

A special targeted way of looking for the reasons for, or purpose of, a behaviour is called "**functional assessment**." This precise event sampling leads to the development of an intervention to help change the child's behaviour that is the focus of the observation. You aim to establish priorities of the troublesome behaviours so that you target the most challenging ones first. Teachers and psychologists work together with parents, team members, and, if possible, the child himself, to identify the frequency, intensity, and context of the behaviour.

TAKING A SPECIAL LOOK: Behavioural challenges

Sometimes a behaviour makes us wonder what is making the child act this way. We can be so frustrated that we believe the behaviour is happening more often than it actually is. Consider this situation an excellent opportunity to conduct an event sampling. This will enable us to examine the possible cause or triggers of the behaviour, try to determine how significant the behaviour is, and see how frequently it really is happening.

For example, Karl, aged five years and seven months, has been diagnosed as visually impaired, so various strategies have been employed to help him become independent. Recently, Karl seemed to withdraw from the other boys with whom he usually played. Sitting alone, he would rock himself back and forth, bang his head repeatedly, and sometimes rub his eyes and shake his hands in front of them. After carrying out an event sampling over several days, documenting each occurrence of these solitary and self-destructive behaviours, the teacher could see a pattern and a possible cause: the behaviours denoted a decrease in Karl's visual acuity. Karl could not sustain the relationship he had previously had with the other boys because he could not see well enough. The teacher's observation led to his referral to an ophthalmologist. With a much stronger prescription for his glasses, Karl regained some of his sociability and entered into activities with the other children.

Using event sampling

Advantages

- This method of recording is quick and efficient.
- The targeted behaviour can be charted in convenient units.
- Information can be recorded more quickly than with narrative observations.
- Sampling may be blended with other methods—with a detailed narrative account, rating scale, and so on.
- This method may reveal behavioural patterns, frequency of behaviour, and cause and effect of behaviour and event.
- It is possible to observe and record more than one child at a time.
- The results are easily converted into appropriate program planning and/or behaviour modification strategies.
- An observation can be recorded at the time or soon after its occurrence.
- Teachers interacting with children can record as they interact within the program.
- Sampling may offer information about the duration of particular behaviour.
- Sampling may indicate the severity of the recorded behaviour.
- Consulted professionals can select some basic formats and, with only a little instruction, parents and caregivers can carry out those formats.

Disadvantages

- Sampling lacks the detail of narrative recordings.
- A high degree of selectivity and inference is required in categorizing observed behaviour.
- Sampling breaks up the natural continuity of behaviour into separate units.
- This method may encourage judgmental inferences.
- Sampling relies on the repetition of behaviour—not useful for infrequently observed behaviours.
- Any time lag in recording data might lead to inaccurate documentation.
- Sampling relies on the skill of the observer to choose an appropriate methodology, define the category of the behaviour, and evaluate the child's behavioural patterns.

Seemingly happy as he eats his lunch, this boy, who has Down's Syndrome, suddenly burst into tears a moment after the photograph was taken. An event sampling of these occurrences revealed a significant behaviour pattern.

Method charts for event sampling

ABC format

Event Sampling

Child's name: _____ Observer: _____

Age/D.O.B.: _____ Date(s): _____

Behaviour: _____

Operational definition: _____

_____

Examples of behaviour: _____

_____

Reason for observation: _____

_____

Time	Antecedent event	Behaviour	Consequent event

*This chart enables the observer to record the behaviour under examination as it occurs, giving information about what was observed immediately before the sample behaviour and what happened afterward. By detailing the surrounding events the observer gains clues to the possible causes or triggers for the behaviour, gains a **tally** of occurrences, and can produce a detailed set of information that may be helpful in understanding the behaviour of the child.*

Frequency count

Event Sampling

Child's name: _____ Observer: _____

Age/D.O.B.: _____ Date(s): _____

Behaviour: _____

Operational definition: _____

_____

Examples of behaviour: _____

_____

Reason for observation: _____

_____

Time	Tally count	Total

Here the observer records the occurrences of the selected behaviour as they happen. A practising teacher can employ this method efficiently, without a break from her responsibilities with the children. No detail about the behaviours can be recorded.

Duration chart

Event Sampling

Child's name: _____ Observer: _____

Age/D.O.B.: _____ Date(s): _____

Behavior: _____

Operational definition: _____

_____

Examples of behaviour: _____

_____

Reason for observation: _____

_____

Day/date	Time (from–to)	Total in minutes

This chart gives the observer a sense of the duration of the selected behaviour, although no other explanation of the occurrences of behaviour can be offered. The observer might find it advantageous to calculate average duration as well as to analyze the pattern of behaviour examples.

Group samples

Event Sampling

Names: _____ Ages/D.O.B.: _____

_____ _____

_____ _____

_____ _____

_____ _____

_____

Observer: _____ Date: _____

Context: _____

Behaviour: _____

Operational definition: _____

_____

Examples of behaviour: _____

_____

Reason for observation: _____

_____

Time	Antecedent	Behaviour	Consequence

Recording information about more than one child at a time has its practical limitations. Here the observer can record a set of examples of a preselected category of behaviour. It is wise to limit the breadth of categories used in this method or the set may provide too many examples. In other variations, the observer can simply document the frequency of the behaviour, record the behaviour's duration, or, if the observer is not directly involved with the child, apply the full ABC format.

Severity recording

Event Sampling

Child's name: _____ Observer: _____

Age/D.O.B.: _____ Date(s): _____

Behaviour: _____

Operational definition: _____

Examples of behaviour: _____

Reason for observation: _____

Inference Coding Rating Scale

1	3	5	7	9
Mild		Moderate		Severe

Date	Time	Behaviour	Rating	Comments

This chart uses a combination of an event sampling technique and a rating scale. Charting the severity of behaviour can reveal more information than some other sampling methods because the observer is required to evaluate the behaviour's severity as he records it.

Complex behaviour sampling

Event Sampling

Child's name: _____ Observer: _____

Age/D.O.B.: _____ Date(s): _____

Behaviour: _____

Operational definition: _____

Examples of behaviour: _____

Reason for observation: _____

Inference Coding Rating Scale

1	3	5	7	9
Mild		Moderate		Severe

Date	Antecedent event	Behaviour example	Consequent event	Duration	Severity	Comments

This chart can be too demanding for the caregiver of a medium or large group of children. Parents, student observers, and psychologists whose focus is on only one child at a time find this an appropriate method of recording detailed information. It is particularly useful for challenging behaviours for which guidance strategies need to be developed as part of **behaviour modification**, *cognitive therapy, or another management or therapy technique.*

Time Sampling

Time sampling is a method of observing and recording selected behaviours during previously set periods. These observations can be used for recording information about one or more children simultaneously. Time samplings are usually structured to record behaviours at regular intervals though they may also be undertaken at randomly chosen times. See sample time samplings, recorded in two different ways, on pages 151–152 and 153–156.

KEY FEATURES: Time sampling

- focuses on behaviour of one child
- records behaviour at preset time intervals
- records behaviours on a chart
- aims to identify behavioural patterns
- naturalistic
- participatory or nonparticipatory
- interpretive method of recording

Time intervals for samplings

Time sampling observations need to be set up even more rigorously than event samples do, because the interval at which the behaviours are to be sampled must be structured in such a way that they produce the information required. A sampling made over several days at 15-minute intervals may give information about an infant's pattern of sleep and wakefulness, but it may not give such useful insights into a seven-year-old's levels of concentration. Those experienced in doing time sampling suggest that, as a rule of thumb, the younger the child, the more frequently she will select shorter time intervals. This tendency, however, is not a hard-and-fast rule; circumstances may suggest other timings.

Using time sampling

Advantages

- This method provides frequency data about behaviours.
- Information can be recorded quickly.
- Time sampling is more likely to allow for a representative sample of behaviour appropriate for students and researchers to use.
- Results tend to be more reliable over time.
- Time sampling provides an overview of a wide range of behaviours.

Disadvantages

- Time sampling does not provide qualitative information.
- The recordings may be misinterpreted because of the lack of contextual information.
- Behaviour observed infrequently may not be recorded effectively.
- Sampling relies on the skill of the observer to structure observations appropriately to elicit the most important information.

Method charts for time sampling

Interval recording

Time Sampling

Child's name: _____   Observer: _____

Age/D.O.B.: _____   Date(s): _____

Context: _____

Behaviour: _____

_____

Reason for observation: _____

_____

Date	Time/interval	Behaviour	Comments

This chart presents a standard format that can be adapted to various uses by altering the time/interval designation as required. Here the behaviour category could be open-ended or quite specific. An observer may wish to see the general pattern of activity during the course of the day or look for types of behaviour to see if they are exhibited or absent in the sample period.

Group interval recording

Time Sampling

Names: _____   Ages/D.O.B.: _____

_____   _____

Observer: _____   Date: _____

Context: _____

Behaviour category: _____

Reason for observation: _____

#	Child	Behaviours (Time/units/intervals)	Comment (Total)
1.			

A group of children can be observed in this time sampling. The detail of activity that can be recorded is quite limited.

How to Use Event or Time Samplings
Deciding what sampling methodology to use

1. Become aware of the various techniques; know their advantages and disadvantages, and what information they could give you.
2. Assess your need for a sampling: What do you need it for? These are some of the most obvious uses:
   - to help you learn about sequences of development
   - to support understanding of an individual child's behaviour
   - to look at the behaviours a group of children demonstrate
   - for formal record-keeping
   - to support communications with parents, colleagues, and other professionals
   - to help evaluate the program offered to an individual or group
   - to provide information for behaviour modification plans or for learning prescriptions
3. Choose the method of preference, use it, and evaluate its usefulness for the required purpose.
4. Practise using sampling techniques and build skills in the component parts of objectivity, clarity, and accuracy of recording, checking with others on their perceptions of the validity of your work.

Event sampling versus time sampling

Event sampling	Time sampling
• can be used to study any event or behaviour	• can record any demonstrated behaviours
• is less likely to give information about frequency of behaviour over longer periods of time	
• is more likely to give qualitative information	• may make it easier to quantify behaviour
• may indicate causes of behaviour	
• may indicate effect of child's action	
• is often used by practitioners	• is often used by researchers
• includes every natural occurrence of target behaviour	
• may offer information about duration of behaviour	• may offer behavioural pattern
• may indicate severity of behaviour	
• can be user-friendly and easily carried out by parents and paraprofessionals	• may require professional background in child development to structure behaviour-coding systems

How to record a time or event sample observation

1. Decide on your reason for sampling behaviour.
2. Select the behaviour category or time frequency that applies.
3. Prepare a method chart to meet specific requirements.
4. Write your operational definition of the behaviour category, if necessary.
5. Record as soon as possible the precise details of the examples of behaviour observed.
6. When sufficient examples are recorded for your purpose, take time to analyze your findings.
7. Write your objective **inferences** as clear statements—but support your statements.
8. Use the inference statements to devise a plan or learning prescription.

The analysis: Interpreting data collected from process samplings

Remember that your inferences rely heavily on the **objectivity** of your recording. Before you start to analyze the data, evaluate its **validity** and **reliability**. Review the effectiveness of the sampling before you proceed to analyze the content. Some samplings require

Patterns of behaviour, such as this one when a baby imitates her caregiver, can be recorded easily using a sampling method.

you to select specific behaviours. Your decision to observe a particular behaviour may prove ineffective because you didn't see the behaviour you expected. The operational definition of the behaviour category can also cause difficulty—perhaps you could have selected a suitable category without defining it clearly to cover the samples you include.

Focus the **analysis** on some of these issues:

1. determining the frequency of the events
2. considering what prompted the events (which may be different from the actual cause)
3. finding a cause for the behaviour
4. measuring the duration of the events
5. examining the developmental significance of the events
6. evaluating the necessity of responding to the events
7. identifying the pattern of behaviours and/or events
8. determining further observation and assessment needs

The samplings on pages 144–148, 149–150, and 153–156 include analysis of the observations.

Using inferences drawn from the analysis

Other than for purposes of dry record-keeping, there is little point in recording copious numbers of observations without putting them to some use. There is a wide range of reasons to record samplings, and often more than one reason for each observation.

Having checked the inferences for their detail and general objectivity, you will be ready to make use of your analysis. The sampling on pages 151–152 includes an inference chart.

You can use the inferences in a similar way to those produced by other methods of observation (see Chapter 1, pages 21–28). Samplings are frequently used as forerunners to devising a learning prescription or individualized program plan for children.

TAKING A SPECIAL LOOK: Reinforcement

- Melinda's family came on "meet the teacher" night. Melinda showed her parents around the room and introduced them to the teacher. Both her parents and the teacher thought that Melinda had behaved very well and praised her beautiful manners.

- Ellie was just past her second birthday, and her parents were concerned that she had not yet said a "real" word but tended to repeat the same string of sounds. Her caregiver saw Ellie point at the shelf above her crib and say "bo-bo" repeatedly. "That's your bunny rabbit, bunny rabbit," the caregiver said. Ellie later said "bun-bun," and the caregiver said, "Yes, your bunny rabbit," and gave it to her.

- Craig, at 6 months, liked to hold his own bottle. But he didn't like to hand back the bottle when it was empty. His mother played a game with Craig in which they passed items back and forth. The next time his bottle was empty, he handed it to his mother.

These examples suggest that behaviours can be reinforced through positive feedback or some kind of reward. More structured behaviour modification also employs **reinforcement.** Be aware that this method is not used everywhere, because of concerns about manipulating behaviour. The following example illustrates how sampling can be used in a classroom where behaviour modification is practised.

Gareth, aged seven, has been diagnosed with a social adaptation difficulty, based on detailed narrative observations, a psychological test, and meetings with his parents and teacher. Recently, he has faced some new challenges in sharing art materials. He snatched items from other children, and the class disintegrated into a fight. He also took home a pair of scissors, which he used to cut up an album of family photographs. When Gareth met with the psychologist, his parents, and his teacher, they decided that he would be "rewarded" for behaving appropriately and "corrected" for behaving inappropriately. Gareth agreed that he wanted to "behave himself." In the following days, he demonstrated positive behaviour, such as helping hand out the snack, waiting in line for the washroom, and helping a younger child find his lost coat. Each time the teacher observed such behaviour, she recorded it on a sampling chart and allowed Gareth to have "privileges," such as staying outside for longer than the rest of the class or being first to select afternoon activities. For each negative behaviour, Gareth was asked to do a clean-up job, made to sit away from the other children, or denied his choice of book at circle time. Gareth understood this plan, which seemed to reinforce some of his better behaviours; his behaviour overall was being modified to what was considered socially acceptable.

Work sampling

A **work sample** is the product of the child's activity. Although the term "work" might make us think of formal classroom activities, the term also applies to items a child might produce during times of creativity and play. Typically these "work samples" might include

paintings	drawings and diagrams
early writing and letter formations	pattern-making
card-sewing or fabric-sewing	weaving
project work	collages
group-made creative materials	models
pictorial representations (early math)	masks
story-writing	mathematical work, scale drawings, etc.
tape-recordings of early reading or music-making	photographs of large-sized constructions

Parents, teachers, other professionals, or students who are studying the development of one or more skills may wish to collect work samples. They may do so rather than compiling a complete portfolio (see Chapter 8 on portfolios) or to enrich a rounded portfolio. In collecting most effectively, consider:

1. what the child produces on a regular basis
2. the child's "best" work (using her own opinion of her efforts)
3. items that illustrate **progression** or **regression** in skill development

The **products** of a child's play activity may not give us an accurate picture of that child's process of discovery and learning in creating them. Adults can focus too much on the product because they need to identify art that is **representational** or that corresponds to their idea of what is beautiful or worthwhile. Too much emphasis on the products of a child's activity may lead children to think that what they produce is more important than the thinking they put into their activity. Educators prefer to honour both the child's work and its products.

The Work Sampling System is a trademarked performance-assessment system that is "used in pre-school through fifth grade. Its purpose is to document and assess children's skills, knowledge, behaviour, and accomplishments across a wide variety of curriculum areas on multiple occasions in order to enhance teaching and learning" (Meisels 1997). Teachers who wish to adopt a systematic approach to work sampling and reporting may find that this system meets their needs for observing, documenting, and assessing learning. Those wanting a more open-ended work-sampling approach might establish their own systems to fit their own philosophies and the outcomes expected of their programs.

Mathematical Thinking

Area of Learning	Child's Work/Representation
Understanding and applying classification and seriation skills	• Record of child sorting beads
	• Photo of child's arrangement of rods, buttons, or crayons in order of size
	• Photo of child putting away blocks or other equipment according to size, shape, or use
	• Anecdotal record of child's comment about the rule used for classifying
	• Anecdotal record of child's comments at snack time or out on the playground that demonstrate understanding of seriation or classification
	• Child's drawing that shows classifying skills (these are all toys, this is my family, or these are all the kinds of leaves we collected)
	• A collage of categorized items (shapes, colours, foods, animals, or "the things we do on the playground")
Understanding and using number concepts to solve problems	• Anecdote describing child's method of arranging cups and napkins for snack
	• Description of child counting children at sand table to see if there is room for a friend
	• Record of child's solution to a question about distributing class supplies for a project
	• Record of child's counting children at circle and remarking that "there are more girls than boys"
Understanding and applying size and measurement concepts	• Record of child's comments comparing sizes of blocks
	• Photo with note of child measuring own height or the growth of a plant
	• Anecdote depicting how child compared heights of classmates
	• Photo of child measuring amounts of ingredients during a cooking project, potting plants, or making playdough
	• Child-created measuring tape for determining the length of a block structure or the snack table
	• Photo of child using balance scale

When used successfully, work samples can offer

- a glimpse (for adults) into the thinking of the child as he created the work
- a time when the child and the adult discuss the child's work and how it was created
- concrete examples of the child's progression and skill development over time
- a collection of materials to share with parents and families that helps re-create a learning experience
- the feeling for the child that her work is valued
- additional insights into the developmental portfolio process

Summary

There are three basic types of sampling. The first focuses on recording an event and the time in which it occurs (event sampling), the second looks at what behaviour is happening at designated times (time sampling), and the third considers the products of a child's activity (work sampling). Each sample offers a glimpse of a child's behaviour—concentrating on the frequency, duration, and severity of a particular behaviour, or on what behaviour is occurring at predetermined times, or seeking what the child has produced in order to supply us with insight into the child's skills and general behaviour.

Samplings of each kind can give us a hint of the interests, significance, and development of the child being observed. The decisions that need to be made about how to sample behaviour are challenging, but the results can offer insights into the possible cause of the behaviour, the recurrence of the behaviour, and, most important, possible means of managing the child's behaviour. The samplings can help a child to understand better his own behaviour and so acquire skills of self-regulation. Most educators can discern patterns of behaviour from the samplings that lead them to make appropriate decisions about interventions, guidance, and curriculum.

Event samplings make it possible to discern patterns of behaviour and identify behaviour triggers and causes. This means of recording depends on the observer's identifying and developing an operational definition of the behaviour under examination. Time samplings often highlight a suspected pattern of development that needs careful guidance. Both of these techniques are the traditional sampling methods used by a variety of behavioural specialists, educators, and psychologists.

Work sampling is a method of gathering samples of a child's "work." The term "Work Sampling" is the registered name of a system for collecting children's work as part of a portfolio. However, sampling children's products is a widely used technique in the portfolio-documentation process, and it includes a variety of observation and documentation approaches to each assessment.

analysis

antecedent event

behaviour

behaviour modification

causality

consequent event

duration

event

event sampling

frequency

functional assessment

inference

objectivity

operational definition

process

product

progression

regression

reinforcement

reliability

representational

sampling

severity

tally

time sampling

validity

work sample

Weblinks

www.acm.org/chapters/trichi/newsletters/nov96/behavior.obs.html
Explanation of the use of systematic observation methods with reference to time sampling, with a brief description of how and when to use the technique.

http://ici2.umn.edu/preschoolbehavior/strategies/fa.htm
Description of functional assessment focusing on three areas: indirect assessment, direct observational assessment, and environmental manipulations of analog assessment.

www.rebusinc.com/work_sampling.html
Overview of the work sampling system.

www.uws.edu.au/learning/earlychildhood/mod3.htm#d
Introduction to observation techniques, including: running records, anecdotal records, time sampling, and checklists.

www.earlychildhood.com/Articles/index.cfm?FuseAction=Article&A=255
Step-by-step procedure for performing a functional behavioural assessment.

Observation Sample

This observational recording is a clear example of an ABC event sampling. The operational definition is clear, and the examples of behaviour are specific. The analysis explains the behaviours in paragraph form. Note how the observer has outlined the assignment on the first page and included a signed permission form from the parents. The child's identity is kept confidential through the use of a pseudonym in the observation.

Is there any other information that might support the observation that follows?

Observation Assignment

Front Page

Student name: *Donna Francisco*   Student number: *000-111-000*

Section number: *061*

Assignment method: *Event Sampling (ABC format)*

Date due: *October 24, 2003*   Date handed in: *October 24, 2003*

Child's name (pseudonym): *Margaret*

Child's age (years/months): *1 year, 11-1/2 months*

Date of observation: *Oct. 8 and Oct. 15*   Time of observation: *Throughout day*

Setting: *Toddler room at child-care center and main entrance hallway at the center*

Parent's name: *Wayne and Jane White*   Phone # if released: *(203) 987-6543*

Each assignment has specific criteria. Please check with the assignment description and direction given in class.

Declaration by student

I have followed the assignment description and instructions given in class about confidentiality and privacy. I confirm that appropriate processes for making this observation have been undertaken and that permission has been gained from the parents. A copy of this observation will be given to the parents if they desire.

Donna Francisco

Signature of Student

If the permission form is stored with the observation, how might confidentiality be compromised?

Permission Form

Child Observations, Case Studies, and Portfolios

Student and Parent Agreement

Without written permission I will not observe and record information about your child. Please sign in the space provided if you agree that I may make observations and study your child. It would be helpful if you could initial each of the boxes if you are willing for me to undertake any or all of the techniques of information gathering.

I ___Donna Francisco___ *(student name)* will not refer to the child in any written manner by his or her real name. Information recorded will be written objectively, treated professionally, and kept confidential.

___Donna Francisco___   ___Oct. 1/03___

(student's signature)   *(date)*

I ___Wayne White___

(parent's name)

agree to have ___Jennifer White___

   (child's name)

observed ☑   photographed ☑   audiotaped ☑   videotaped ☑

by ___Donna Francisco___

   (student's name above)

at ___Grenadier Child-Care Center___

   (agency/home)

for the purpose of study in child development at ___Northern College___

(school/college) for a period of ___2 weeks___ *(weeks/months)* on the consideration that copies are made available to me, the parent, if I so request.

___Wayne White___   ___October 1/03___

(parent's signature)   *(date)*

Read the recording of the observation. Does the analysis reflect the pattern of autonomy that the student is seeking?

Event Sampling

Child's name: ___Margaret___ Observer: ___Donna Francisco___

Age/D.O.B.: _1 yr, 11-1/2 mos/Oct.30/01_ Date(s): ___October 8 and 15, 2003___

Behaviour: Autonomy _____

Operational definition: _This is a behaviour in which the child displays initiative_ _to perform tasks independently to help herself achieve something specific._

Examples of behaviour: __Self-help skills: for example, independent toileting or__ _identifying her need to have her diaper changed/sit on toilet; feeding_ _self; washing/drying own hands without help; dressing self_

Reason for observation: ___To see if Margaret is succeeding in her attempts at_ _autonomous behaviour(s)._

Time	Antecedent event	Behaviour	Consequent event
(October 8)			
9:45 a.m.	Sitting on floor playing with "linking stars."	Turned to caregiver and said, "I need help with this one."	Caregiver showed Margaret how to attach the star and handed it back to her, and she tried to put the pieces together.
2:45 p.m.	Margaret sitting on floor pulling on her sock.	Said to caregiver, "I am fixing my sock."	Caregiver said, "You did it all by yourself, Margaret!"
3:45 p.m.	During gross motor activity in hall, Margaret went to her cubby and took out her hat.	Margaret pulled her hat onto her head.	Looked at caregiver and said, "Look, I put on my hat!"
3:50 p.m.	Children had just re-entered toddler room to find a place at the tables to sit for snack.	Margaret, sitting at her place at the table, said to caregiver, "I want juice please; I want milk please."	Caregiver poured a cup of milk for Margaret and put it in front of her. She picked it up with both hands and drank.
(October 15)			
11:10 a.m.	Margaret, while seated at the table at lunchtime, was sorting through the plastic bibs.	Margaret chose a green bib.	Margaret said, "I want this one," while she was trying to put it on for herself.

Time	Antecedent event	Behaviour	Consequent event
11:20 a.m.	Margaret's lunch was placed in front of her.	Margaret picked up her spoon, scooped up some pasta, and put it in her mouth.	Margaret successfully placed food in her mouth and ate it.
2:30 p.m.	Margaret had just awakened from her afternoon nap.	She walked to the caregiver standing at the door and said, "Change my diaper?"	Caregiver said, "Yes, Margaret, let's change your diaper."
2:40 p.m.	Margaret returned to the toddler room after having her diaper changed.	She walked to her cot and picked up her shoes.	Margaret sat on the floor and tried to put her shoes on, saying, "Put shoes on."
3:35 p.m.	Caregiver had just placed coats on the floor in preparation for going outside.	Margaret went to where her coat had been placed and picked it up.	She tried to put her coat on, putting her right arm into the sleeve of the coat. She looked at caregiver and said, "I need help."

Observation Analysis

This is the age of the drive for autonomy. Children at this age are often heard to say, "Me do it myself!" They are striving for independence, while still needing lots of support from caregivers and parents. They make many attempts throughout the day to do things for themselves, and it is important that caregivers recognize their attempts in a positive and supportive way. According to Erikson, this is the stage of a child's social/emotional development where the struggle for autonomy versus shame and doubt takes place (Barrett, 1995, p. 264). To avoid power struggles with toddlers, which may impede their ability to achieve autonomy, caregivers need to offer children "yes" choices instead of those requiring "yes or no" answers. Leading them to the choices one wants them to make in a positive manner (for example, "I bet you can put the blocks away all by yourself!") is much more effective than making direct demands. When children feel that they have made decisions to perform specific tasks on their own, it contributes to their ability to think for themselves.

Throughout the observation period, Margaret displays many attempts to make decisions and do things for herself. The observation was limited to observing "self-help" skills and there were many to see. Each of the behaviours recorded shows that Margaret consistently tries to perform tasks for herself and that she is aware of the order and routine in her day. For example, she tries to put on her socks, her coat, and her shoes at different times in the day. Once she completes the toileting routine after nap, Margaret knows that it is time to put on her shoes, and she looks for them as soon as she re-enters the room. While she still requires the assistance of an adult in her dressing routine, she knows what to do and consistently practices the skills she needs to do these things for herself (October 8, 2:45; 3:45; October 15, 2:40; 3:35).

The caregivers in the room recognize the importance of facilitating and supporting the children's self-help skills. For example, coats are placed separately on the floor of the toddler room when it is time to go outside. This gives the children the opportunity to find their own coats and attempt to put them on. Words of encouragement are also given consistently throughout the day, as when Margaret is successful at pulling her own sock back up her foot when it is falling off (October 8, 2:45). In each behaviour recorded, Margaret's attempts at independence are recognized and positively reinforced. As she makes her attempts to help herself, she often seeks the attention of a caregiver. Caregiver responses support her attempts, and she knows that her requests for support/help will receive a positive response resulting in the help she needs. For example, she asks for help with her coat; she receives milk at snack time as she requests; her need for a diaper change is acknowledged verbally and accommodated immediately; and her success with the sock is verbally acknowledged. At the same time, caregivers do not interfere with Margaret's attempts to help herself until she asks for the help. Margaret is consistent in her requests for help and asks immediately when she requires adult assistance (October 15, 2:30; 3:35).

Margaret's attempts at self-help skills are developmentally appropriate for her age (almost 2 years old): "Self-help skills improve during this time period (18 months to 2 years). As far as dressing is concerned, toddlers can do a few things for themselves, but for the most part, they require the assistance of an adult" (Barrett, 1995, p. 213). Finally, "Erikson believed that if toddlers are allowed to learn to do things for themselves, such as walking or dressing and feeding themselves, they gain a feeling of autonomy. If they are not allowed to do so, feelings of shame and self-doubt will haunt their sense of themselves, and they will have trouble with the next phase of development" (Barrett, 1995, p. 204). Margaret's positive approach to helping herself and her comfort level at asking an adult for help are indicators that she is achieving success in her drive for autonomy, paving the way for the next stage of development, "initiative versus guilt," which she is moving into on the eve of her second birthday.

References Cited

Barrett, K.C., et al. (1995). Child development. Westerville, OH: Glencoe.

Biracree, T., & Biracree, N. (1989). The parents' book of facts: Child development from birth to age five. New York: Facts on File.

Martin, Sue. (1994). Take a look: Observation and portfolio assessment in early childhood. Don Mills, ON: Addison-Wesley.

Woolfson, R.C. (1995). A to Z of child development: From birth to age five. Toronto: Stoddart.

Observation Sample

This excerpt from an event sampling documents a "negative" behaviour. The analysis examines a behavioural pattern and offers a good rationale for the inferences made. However, these inferences are not further validated.

When looking to record a "negative" behaviour like the one in this sample, you might create a problem. Why is this?

Event Sampling

Child's name: ___Kyle___   Observer: ___Damian___

Age/D.O.B.: ___3 years, 2 months___   Date(s): ___March 20, 2004___

Time of observation: ___9:50 a.m.–4:00 p.m.___

Behaviour: ___Aggression___

Operational definition: ___This is a behaviour in which inappropriate words or actions are displayed by the child himself as a result of his anger or frustration. These actions are harmful and usually hostile to those around him.___

Examples of behavior: Hitting, kicking, pushing, spitting, pinching, destroying property

Setting: ___Preschool room at The Briars nursery school___

Time	Antecedent event	Behaviour	Consequent event
9:51 a.m.	A peer comes to say hello. Kyle grunts at her. Adult says that he is "Mr. Grump."	Kyle hits the adult on the shoulder.	Adult moves away from Kyle and says good-bye to him.
9:55 a.m.	A child comes and tries to take Kyle's shovel from him.	Kyle attempts to hit the child with the shovel.	Teacher tells him not to hit and to keep his shovel down.
9:56 a.m.	Kyle is told not to hit with his shovel.	Kyle rakes the ground roughly and rapidly.	Kyle stops raking and walks over to another child.
9:57 a.m.	Kyle walks over to a boy after raking aggressively.	Kyle picks up sand in his shovel and throws it at the boy.	Teacher comes and takes the shovel away from him.
10:01 a.m.	Asks a child if he can play with him. The child says "no."	Kyle kicks the child's sandcastle over.	The child tells him not to do that. Teacher tells Kyle not to ruin the child's work.
10:05 a.m.	A student waves at Kyle through the window.	Kyle hits the window with his hand.	Teacher encourages Kyle to move on.
10:52 a.m.	Kyle is playing in the dramatic play area with a friend. The friend asks him not to pull the sink back.	Kyle hits his friend on the head.	Kyle makes the boy cry. Teacher comes over and sends both children out of that area.

Time	Antecedent event	Behaviour	Consequent event
10:54 a.m.	Kyle walks to the door after being instructed by teacher to get his jacket.	Kyle hits his friend on the back on his way out the door.	Kyle's friend tells him not to do that.
11:12 a.m.	Kyle's friend gets his bicycle wheel caught on Kyle's scooter wheel, preventing Kyle from moving.	Kyle catches up to his friend after getting free and bangs into the back of the child's bike.	Kyle's friend turns around and tells Kyle that he didn't like that.

Observation Analysis

I chose to observe Kyle's aggressive behaviours because of my past encounters with him and because of recommendations from regular teachers. I hoped to find the cause of Kyle's aggression and the regular intervals of occurrence.

Through my observation, I discovered that Kyle tends to act aggressively when he doesn't have much to do and when he may be bored or bothered.

Upon Kyle's arrival, he began his aggressive behaviour. This continued until later that morning when we went inside and some students did an activity with the children. During this time period between 10:05 a.m. and 10:52 a.m., Kyle was occupied with many things to do. He did not display any acts of aggression until he had done all of the activities and appeared to be getting bored. The cycle of aggressive behaviour then began again.

Kyle's aggression is displayed physically rather than verbally. He mainly takes his anger out on other children and on his teachers. Instead of using words to express himself, he prefers to use actions involving his gross motor skills such as hitting and kicking.

Kyle appears to use his aggressions to get even with others. On occasions when a child does or says something that Kyle does not like, he acts back aggressively by kicking, hitting, or pushing. Kyle appears to have a difficult time expressing himself verbally.

Kyle appears to be one of the most aggressive children in his junior preschool room, with twenty-one acts of aggression displayed over the course of this particular day. Most of these behaviours were displayed through violent and harmful acts.

The cause of this child's aggressive behaviours appears to stem from boredom, upset, and frustration, as well as possibly a lack of confidence in his language skills. The transition from home to day care could also be having an effect on his behaviour, but the first act of aggression was displayed to an adult from home, possibly suggesting that this behaviour carries on at home as well.

Through my observations, I have come to the conclusion that Kyle is a child who requires a constant, fulfilling curriculum with cooperative and group play regularly involved to encourage constant cooperation and teamwork. I think that it would be ideal to encourage acceptable behaviour by praising Kyle for using words instead of actions, instead of focusing on his aggressive behaviours. Kyle would also most likely benefit from a full curriculum to reduce the frustrations he feels from being bored and to enhance his social well-being.

I have concern about the frequency of these aggressive behaviours and the length of time it takes Kyle to get over his aggressive outbursts. I will continue to observe his behaviour and talk with the teacher and his parents about what we can work on together to support Kyle in gaining more pro-social behaviours.

We cannot expect Kyle, at his age, to understand the perspectives of others; he does not yet have the cognitive skill to do this. However, he needs to know that his actions have consequences. I want to try to shift his behaviour so that he can feel positive.

Observation Sample

The "snapshot" style of this time sampling can be useful to determine behavioural patterns. Further examples on other days might have offered more information. The brief analysis uses the flow chart outlined on page 20 in Chapter 1. How effective is this type of time sampling?

Time Sampling

Child's name: _Cassidy_   Observer: _Donald_

Age/D.O.B.: _15 months_   Date(s): _Sept. 25 and Oct. 1, 2003_

Context: _Toddler room, morning_

Behaviour: _Infant development_

Reason for observation: _Cassidy has recently moved to the toddler room; we want to look at her gross motor skills and how she is fitting in._

Date	Time/interval	Behaviour	Comments
Sept. 25	10:48 a.m.	Plays with push-pop toy with other child	Engaged in parallel play.
Sept. 25	10:51 a.m.	Mouths a plastic bracelet	Other child moved off.
Sept. 25	10:54 a.m.	Mouths books	Crossed the room to quiet area.
Sept. 25	10:57 a.m.	Rubbing eyes and crying	ECE had said book not for mouth.
Sept. 25	11:00 a.m.	Throws telephone on the floor	Seems to be looking for reaction.
Sept. 25	11:03 a.m.	Pulls self up to stand and jumps	Holds on to house while jumping.
Sept. 25	11:06 a.m.	"AAAAA" touches ECE's face	Having her diaper changed.
Sept. 25	11:09 a.m.	Mouths an abstract colorful toy	ECE is holding her on lap.
Sept. 25	11:12 a.m.	Sucking thumb "AAAAA"	ECE is rocking her.
Sept. 25	11:15 a.m.	Thumb in mouth, eyes heavy	Thumb in mouth, but not sucking.
Sept. 25	11:18 a.m.	Eyes are closed, appears asleep	ECE moves her to crib.
Oct. 1	10:50 a.m.	Pulls self up to standing position	Holding on to windowsill.
Oct. 1	10:53 a.m.	Crawls across room and stops and sits	Seems to change her mind.
Oct. 1	10:56 a.m.	Banging two wooden puzzle pieces together	Seems frustrated that she can't put them together.
Oct. 1	10:59 a.m.	Same as above	Did not want help from ECE.
Oct. 1	11:02 a.m.	Throws puzzle and cries	Refused comforting from ECE (a).
Oct. 1	11:05 a.m.	Mouthing abstract colored toy	ECE (b) had given it to her to soothe her.
Oct. 1	11:08 a.m.	Puts face in ECE's chest and rubs	ECE holding her while sitting.
Oct. 1	11:11 a.m.	Sucks thumb and holds toy	Sitting on ECE's lap; seems to watch other children.
Oct. 1	11:14 a.m.	Sucking thumb "AAAAA"	Has her head on ECE's shoulder.
Oct. 1	11:17 a.m.	Eyes are closed and sucking thumb quickly	Seems still awake.
Oct. 1	11:20 a.m.	Eyes are closed; sucking has stopped	In her crib; seems asleep.

Making Inferences About Development

Behaviour observed	Inference	Reasoning	Validation by theory	Validation by norms	Source	Bibliographic reference
The child would sing herself to sleep by singing "AAAA" each time before falling asleep.	I infer that the child was soothing herself by saying a rhythmic "AAAA" sound.	Because the sound was rhythmic and consistent and repeated each time before falling asleep, it appears to be a form of singing.		Child will use singing as a way of winding down before falling asleep.	K. Eileen Allen and Lynn Marotz	Developmental Profiles, 2nd ed., p. 75
The child mouthed the same colorful plastic toy before falling asleep.	I infer that the child had formed an attachment to the abstract colored toy.	Before falling asleep each day, the child would find her toy and mouth it to soothe herself to sleep.		Child will make requests for special bedtime items.	K. Eileen Allen and Lynn Marotz	Developmental Profiles, 2nd ed., p. 75
The child jumped up and down and threw things.	It seemed that, as the child became tired, her aggressive behaviour increased.	As sleep approached each day, the child would bang and throw things. At times she also jumped up and down, perhaps to release tension as a way of preparing for sleep.	Children who have not burned off enough energy might find that their body won't let them sleep.		Susan Quilliam	Child Watching, p. 87
The child fell asleep at approximately the same time each day.	It seems that the child has formed regular sleeping patterns.	Regardless of activities, the child's internal clock caused her to fall asleep each day at the same time.	Children quickly develop regular patterns of sleep.		David Elkind	Sympathetic Understanding, p. 12
The child sucked her thumb while holding toy.	It seemed that the thumb sucking was a sign that she was becoming tired.	Each day, minutes before the child fell asleep, she would start to suck her thumb.		Thumb sucking is normal for an infant during sleep.	K. Eileen Allen and Lynn Marotz	Developmental Profiles, 2nd ed., p. 49
The child mouthed the abstract toy given to her by ECE.	It seemed that the child had formed an attachment to this toy and it soothed her.	Each day before the child fell asleep, she would seek out this toy. It also comforted her when she was crying.		Objects offer comfort when a baby is tired.	Eisenberg, Murkof, and Hathaway	What to Expect the First Year, p. 119

Observation Sample

This time sampling offers a narrative description rather than brief notes. This style is useful if the recorder wants more than a "snapshot." The analysis recognizes the significance of the behavioural patterns and tries to validate its statements. Read the entire time sampling and its analysis.

What are the strengths and weaknesses of this particular recording?

TIME SAMPLING

Child's name: Tyler   Observer: Hana Nakagawa

Age/D.O.B.: 11 months/March 29, 2003   Date(s): February 19 and 20, 2004

Context: The infant room. Tyler was sitting, mostly on the carpeted floor, near toys and other kids.

Behaviour: Whatever is observed.

Reason for observation: To discover behavioural patterns and what they reveal about Tyler's development.

Time	Behaviour/comments

Feb.19

10:00 a.m. Tyler is sitting beside the padded mat on the floor, both feet extended in front of him. He is mouthing a small elephant car, taking turns holding it in each hand and looking at another infant sitting near him.
* Tyler appears content as he sits watching the other infants and mouthing a toy.

10:10 a.m. Tyler is still sitting beside the mat, and he smiles as he looks at the teething ring in his right hand. He throws the ring and murmurs as he reaches out his left hand to pick up the teething ring and places it in his mouth.
* Again, Tyler appears pleased with the teething ring and seems happy.

10:20 a.m. Now lying on his tummy, Tyler is kicking his feet in the air behind him and is crying slightly, as he seems to be stuck.
* Tyler's mood has changed slightly from seemingly happy to unsettled and restless.

10:30 a.m. Sitting on the mat now, Tyler has a push toy pulled up onto his lap and is playing with the balls and toys on the front of the push toy. During this, he is smiling and talking to himself.
* Tyler's mood has changed once again from unsettled to content.

10:40 a.m. Again, Tyler has managed to maneuver himself onto his tummy and is kicking his feet while reaching for a ball in front of him. After a few seconds without success, he starts to cry slightly again as he bangs at a nearby toy in an attempt to reach the ball.
* There has been another mood change as Tyler seems frustrated that he cannot reach his toy.

10:50 a.m. Sitting on the floor near the teacher, Tyler is mouthing another teething ring. He is trying to put the whole ring in his mouth.
* Tyler's mood is still unsettled. Although he seems more content with the teething ring, he is still crying slightly and has teary eyes.

Time	Behavior/comments

11:00 a.m. Tyler is sitting on the floor and is still mouthing the teething ring as he watches the other infants around him. While watching the others, Tyler talks to himself and reaches out to a child with his left hand, almost pulling the child to him, smiling as the child laughs in response.
* Once again, Tyler has gone from unhappy to happy, and this seems to occur when he has a teething ring and is sitting up.

Feb. 20

10:00 a.m. Tyler is sitting on the floor near the mat and the toys, where he is mouthing a teething ring and playing with a ball in his right hand. He puts the teething ring on the floor next to him and takes the toy from his right hand, with his left hand, and places it in his mouth. This seems to please him and he laughs to himself.
* Tyler seems to be experiencing some discomfort with his teeth, and he is trying to ease that pain by mouthing the toys and frozen rings.

10:10 a.m. Tyler is crying as a teacher is hugging and trying to comfort him. The teacher offers him his teething ring, and Tyler takes it, rubbing it in his mouth.
* Again, Tyler seems to be unsettled and restless. He gets some relief from the teething ring but is still unhappy and crying slightly.

10:20 a.m. Now sitting in a sit-in boat, Tyler is watching an infant in front of him. With a half-smile, Tyler plays with the steering wheel and the horn on the boat while pulling on the gearshift with his right hand.
* He appears to have calmed down and has moved on to something new.

10:30 a.m. Still sitting in the boat, Tyler is watching the other infants in the room and is smiling at some of their actions, while talking away.
* Tyler appears to be enjoying himself playing in the boat and watching the others.

10:40 a.m. Now sitting on the floor with a basket of toys in front of him, Tyler tries to reach for another toy that Beth is playing with. In doing so, he ends up on his tummy and begins to cry slightly. While crying, he tries to lift himself up by pushing with his arms and kicking his feet and legs.
* Here, Tyler becomes upset when he cannot reach a toy and then cannot get up from his tummy.

10:50 a.m. Tyler is sitting on the floor and is playing with his teething ring. He is moving the ring back and forth between his hands and throwing it in front of him then retrieving it again.
* Tyler seeming content with himself again as he plays with his teething ring.

11:00 a.m. Tyler is sitting on the floor, mouthing his teething ring. While doing so, he is talking to himself and smiling when he gets most of the ring in his mouth.
* Tyler still seems content as he plays with his teething ring.

TIME SAMPLING ANALYSIS

Throughout the observations on both days, there are various recurring behaviours that outline examples of Tyler's development. The first behaviour noted was the repeated mouthing of toys and objects.

Mouthing objects is normal for infants aged 8 to 12 months (Allen & Marotz, 1994, p. 62). This mouthing can be attributed to teething. From a note taken in class on February 12, 2004, the primary teeth start breaking through the bone of the jaw and the gums between the ages of 4 and 8 months. Allen and Marotz (1994, p. 134) state that the first two teeth to break through are the lower front, and the upper front follow those. The note taken on February 12 also states that between the ages of 9 and 12 months the surrounding teeth, on either side of the upper and lower front teeth, begin to break the skin as well. Although we may not remember this experience, we can imagine the pain and discomfort it can cause. Teeth breaking through the skin is known to cause flushness in the cheeks and, in extreme cases, a slight fever. Children who are teething are known to be unsettled and cranky. To alleviate the pain, children are often given frozen teething rings to soothe the swollen gums. Many children, whenever possible, will put whatever they have in their hands in their mouths to rub along the gum line. According to Laura Nathanson (1994, p. 132), "[Children] want to mouth everything and chew" when the teeth start coming through. Tyler was constantly putting toys in his mouth, and this seemed to comfort him. When given teething rings, Tyler would rub them along his gums and chew on them. Thus, Tyler's mouthing and discomfort can be attributed to the pain of the surrounding teeth breaking through, which is common in an infant aged 11 months based on the references stated above.

Another behaviour observed was Tyler looking and watching the other children in the room. This behaviour is typical of a child aged 11 months, based on data in Allen and Marotz (1994). This behaviour is classified as perceptual-cognitive development. An infant between the ages of 8 and 12 months typically "watches people, objects, and activities in the immediate environment" (Allen & Marotz, 1994, p. 62). Therefore, watching and looking at the infants in the center is normal for an 11-month-old infant.

The final behaviour observed and noted was how Tyler became frustrated when he could not move around on the floor. This behaviour was observed on several occasions. At 10:20 a.m. on February 19, Tyler was lying on his tummy and was unable to pull himself up from that position. According to Nathanson (1994), children between the ages of 9 and 12 months should be able to bear weight on their legs, and when on their bellies, "should be able to push way up and roll over in both directions. They should be able to get from lying down to sitting up. They should be trying to pull up to a standing position" (p. 130). Tyler showed that when he was lying down, after a few moments of trying to help himself, he would cry slightly for someone to help him sit up again. Tyler appears to be frustrated when he cannot move himself around like the other children; evidence of this is that he cries for help after trying to help himself. Not being able to creep, crawl, or walk at 11 months is atypical, according to Allen and Marotz (1994), but not necessarily a developmental alert. Nathanson (1994) states that it is okay that children do not walk at earlier ages, and that some children "don't [walk] until nearly 16 months" (p. 130). She goes on to say that some children don't ever crawl, but may pass this stage and "cruise" around the furniture, or use alternative methods of moving, eventually walking from there (p. 130). Allen and Marotz (1994) state that children between the ages of 8 and 12 months should be "creeping and crawling on their hands and knees, walking with adult support, beginning to pull self to a standing position, beginning to stand alone, leaning on furniture for support" (p. 62).

Although Tyler is not walking or completely mobile, he is trying and becomes frustrated when unable to do so. However slow Tyler may be at his mobile development, he is developing in accordance with some of Allen and Marotz's (1994) developmental norms; for example, Tyler has good balance when sitting and can shift positions without falling, which is stated as a profile of motor development (p. 62). Tyler is also able to "reach with one hand" (p. 61) and manipulate objects by moving them from one hand to the other (p. 62). Infants who are larger than average "may lack in motivation and delay motor skills" (Barrett, 1995, p. 145). This could be an explanation for Tyler's delay, since he is a large infant. Another explanation, according to Child Development, could be that Tyler is the second child born in the family, since "firstborn children tend to develop motor skills at an earlier age than their younger siblings" (p. 147).

Therefore, although Tyler is slow in his motor skills, such as crawling and walking, he is developing according to the other norms stated as references in the above paragraphs. There is no need for immediate alert as far as his motor development is concerned; however, observations and involvement on the part of the parents and caregivers is necessary to watch for possible problems in the future.

SELF-ASSESSMENT

This was a difficult assignment, in my opinion. I feel that I have met all the required components of the Time Sampling Observation; however, I am unsure if I did them correctly. Tyler's behaviours seemed to be those of any late-starting infant, and I found that it was difficult to describe those behaviours in this manner. Stating and validating inferences was not the hard part. I found the hardest part of the assignment to be the "pulling" of behaviours from the observations recorded. Although the assignment was difficult to put together, now that it is complete, I am able to see the relevance of the observations and the inferences made regarding the infant's development.

BIBLIOGRAPHY

Allen, K.E., & Marotz, L.R. (1994). Development profiles: Pre-birth through eight (2nd ed.). Albany, NY: Delmar.

Barrett, K.C., et al. (1995). Child development. Westerville, OH: Glencoe.

Nathanson, L.W. (1994). The portable pediatrician for parents. New York: Viking.

chapter 5

Checklists

Contemporary assessment approaches ask teachers to use checklists to enhance the process of observation and make it more reliable.

Samuel J. Meisels (1993)

Checklists can reflect a particular theoretical perspective and provide a biased view of the observational situation.

A.E. Boehm and R.A. Weinberg (1987)

Checklists are closed, because they reduce raw data to a tally that indicates the presence or absence of a specified behaviour.

Warren R. Bentzen (1993)

Checklists allow observers to make quick records of a child's behaviours and skills. This boy's outdoor play could lead to checklist observations related to his gross motor skills and personality.

Focus Questions

1. How could you record behaviours quickly when you are looking to see whether a child exhibits a particular skill?

2. If you listed some behaviours, how could you determine whether they were in an appropriate developmental order?

3. If you had to observe and record using a ready-made checklist concentrating on gross motor and fine motor skills, how would you know whether the checklist was any good?

Learning Outcomes

- Learners will develop appropriate checklist criteria.
- Learners will use prepared checklists as tools to identify the developmental characteristics of young children.

Types of Checklists

DEFINITION: Checklists

Checklists record the presence or absence of particular predetermined behaviours demonstrating skills, attributes, competencies, traits, reactions, achievements, or stages of development.

The observer may use a checklist she has prepared for a certain purpose, a prepared checklist by a well-known authority, or a checklist written by a group of users who have a common reason for observing.

In this interpretive style of observing, the observer records a demonstrated **behaviour** by checking off the item on the checklist. This may be done at the time the behaviour was demonstrated or a short time afterward.

CHILD DEVELOPMENT FOCUS

Checklists may help the observation and recording of

- physical skills (gross and fine motor)

- self-help and social skills

- emotions and temperamental style

- cognitive skills

- language and communication

A knowledge of the **patterns of development** is essential for observers using checklists. These recordings can be only as useful as the items in them are sound; reference to recognized authorities on child development will support the writing of the checklist criteria. The items in the checklist must be **developmentally appropriate** and designed to supply the information the observer seeks.

The homemade checklist

The homemade checklist is a useful tool for teachers or students to record developmental information about one or more children quickly and efficiently. Observers may want information about the children's skills in particular areas such as **language**, **fine motor skills**, **gross motor skills**, or shape recognition. A list of such skills, developmentally appropriate and complete, will give the observer some insights into a child's **skill acquisition**. These results may be used as part of a program-planning change if teachers think that new activities or experiences might enable the child to gain the skill.

Parents might want to keep a record of the sequence in which, or dates by which, their children achieve particular **milestones**. In this case, a checklist can be prepared to indicate key achievements; these can then be checked off when they occur, and they should also be dated.

KEY FEATURES: Homemade checklist

- designed to record developmental information about an individual child
- lists expected behaviours
- used to check off observed behaviours
- interpretive method of recording behaviours
- naturalistic or "set up"
- participatory or nonparticipatory

Developmental Checklist

Child's name: _____   Observer: _____

Age/D.O.B.: _____   Date: _____

Context: _____

Source of checklist: _____

Age/stage designation: _____

Age/level	Behaviour	Date	Evidence

Prepare the checklist before you need to record the evidence. You might want to use a developmental profile to select items. Make sure you state the source of the checklist items.

The prepared checklist

Many well-designed checklists are available for use with young children. For ready-made observational tools, the same criteria apply for appropriate categories. If the items are not developmentally appropriate or do not fit the job you need done, then they will not produce useful information.

Teachers, psychologists, caregivers, students, or parents may wish to carry out checklist observations for different reasons, but they might find part of a prepared checklist sufficient for their purposes; they do not have to use the whole schedule.

Besides a specifically prepared checklist, you can look for checklist criteria in a variety of resources. An annotated list of prepared checklists and sources of checklist items appears on pages 167–168. You can also use developmental profiles or schedules for this purpose.

KEY FEATURES: Prepared checklist

- uses a standardized list of behaviours to record information about an individual child

- behaviours listed have been checked for their validity and reliability

- interpretive method of recording behaviours

**Teacher Observation Form and Checklist for Identifying Children
Who May Require Additional Services**

Child's name: _____   Recording teacher's name: _____

Birth date: _____   Date: _____

LANGUAGE	Yes	No	Sometimes
Does the child			
1. use two- and three-word phrases to ask for what he or she wants?	☐	☐	☐
2. use complete sentences to tell you what happened?	☐	☐	☐
3. when asked to describe something, use at least two or more sentences to talk about it?	☐	☐	☐
4. ask questions?			
5. seem to have difficulty following directions?	☐	☐	☐
6. respond to questions with appropriate answers?	☐	☐	☐
7. seem to talk too softly or too loudly?	☐	☐	☐
8. Are you able to understand the child?	☐	☐	☐

PREACADEMICS

Does the child

	Yes	No	Sometimes
9. seem to take at least twice as long as the other children to learn preacademic concepts?	☐	☐	☐
10. seem to take the time needed by other children to learn preacademic concepts?	☐	☐	☐
11. have difficulty attending to group activities for more than five minutes at a time?	☐	☐	☐
12. appear extremely shy in group activities (for instance, not volunteering answers or answering questions when asked, even though you think the child knows the answers)?	☐	☐	☐

MOTOR

Does the child

	Yes	No	Sometimes
13. continually switch a crayon back and forth from one hand to the other when colouring?	☐	☐	☐
14. appear clumsy or shaky when using one or both hands?	☐	☐	☐
15. when colouring with a crayon, appear to tense the hand not being used (for instance, clench it into a fist)?	☐	☐	☐
16. when walking or running, appear to move one side of the body differently from the other side? For instance, does the child seem to have better control of the leg and arm on one side than on the other?	☐	☐	☐
17. lean or tilt to one side when walking or running?	☐	☐	☐
18. seem to fear or not be able to use stairs, climbing equipment, or tricycles?	☐	☐	☐
19. stumble often or appear awkward when moving about?	☐	☐	☐
20. appear capable of dressing self except for tying shoes?	☐	☐	☐

SOCIAL

Does the child

	Yes	No	Sometimes
21. engage in more than two disruptive behaviours a day (tantrums, fighting, screaming, etc.)?	☐	☐	☐
22. appear withdrawn from the outside world (fiddling with pieces of string, staring into space, rocking)?	☐	☐	☐
23. play alone and seldom talk to the other children?	☐	☐	☐
24. spend most of the time trying to get attention from adults?	☐	☐	☐
25. have toileting problems (wet or soiled) once a week or more often?	☐	☐	☐

VISUAL OR HEARING

Does the child

	Yes	No	Sometimes
26. appear to have eye movements that are jerky or uncoordinated?	☐	☐	☐
27. seem to have difficulty seeing objects? For instance, does the child			
• tilt head to look at things?	☐	☐	☐
• hold objects close to eyes?	☐	☐	☐
• squint?	☐	☐	☐
• show sensitivity to bright lights?	☐	☐	☐
• have uncontrolled eye rolling?	☐	☐	☐
• complain that eyes hurt?	☐	☐	☐
28. appear awkward in tasks requiring eye–hand coordination such as pegs, puzzles, colouring, etc.?	☐	☐	☐

29. seem to have difficulty hearing? For instance, does the child
   - consistently favour one ear by turning the same side of the head in the direction of the sound? ☐ ☐ ☐
   - ignore, confuse, or not follow directions? ☐ ☐ ☐
   - pull on ears or rub ears frequently, or complain of earaches? ☐ ☐ ☐
   - complain of head noises or dizziness? ☐ ☐ ☐
   - have a very high, very low, or monotonous tone of voice? ☐ ☐ ☐

GENERAL HEALTH   Yes   No   Sometimes

Does the child

30. seem to have an excessive number of colds? ☐ ☐ ☐
31. have frequent absences because of illness? ☐ ☐ ☐
32. have eyes that water? ☐ ☐ ☐
33. have frequent discharge from
   - eyes? ☐ ☐ ☐
   - ears? ☐ ☐ ☐
   - nose? ☐ ☐ ☐
34. have sores on body or head? ☐ ☐ ☐
35. have periods of unusual movements (such as eye blinking) or "blank spells" that seem to appear and disappear without relationship to the social situation? ☐ ☐ ☐
36. have hives or rashes? ☐ ☐ ☐
   wheeze? ☐ ☐ ☐
37. have a persistent cough? ☐ ☐ ☐
38. seem to be excessively thirsty? ☐ ☐ ☐
   seem to be ravenously hungry? ☐ ☐ ☐
39. Have you noticed any of the following conditions:
   - constant fatigue? ☐ ☐ ☐
   - irritability? ☐ ☐ ☐
   - restlessness? ☐ ☐ ☐
   - tenseness? ☐ ☐ ☐
   - feverish cheeks or forehead? ☐ ☐ ☐
40. Is the child overweight? ☐ ☐ ☐
41. Is the child physically or mentally lethargic? ☐ ☐ ☐
42. Has the child lost noticeable weight without being on a diet? ☐ ☐ ☐

Source: K. Eileen Allen et al., Exceptional Children: Inclusion in Early Childhood Programs (1998). Reprinted with permission of ITP Nelson.

Features of a Checklist

A checklist can give you worthwhile information if the items it indicates are appropriate to the child. To work out the usefulness of a checklist, you will need to assess its appropriateness, **validity**, and **reliability**.

Theoretical perspective

All checklists have an underlying perspective, set of values, or beliefs. Even a simple list of behaviours indicates that the teacher considers those behaviours important. The way items are selected, the sequence in which they are written, and the way they are observed and documented are all shaped by the adult's beliefs, even if those beliefs are not articulated. If an authority of some kind developed the checklist, that list will also reflect a perspective on what is important and will reflect beliefs about the way that children develop. Because all checklists are **theory-bound**, those we use or develop must reflect our beliefs about children and their development.

Developmental sequences

Most checklists used by educators have lists of behaviours that form the criteria for what they want to look for when they observe. The checklist should indicate:

- the domain of development to which it applies
- the age/stage of development for which it is intended

The behaviours listed must be in a developmental sequence that is consistent with current knowledge about the step-by-step progress made by most children—what is considered the "**norm**." There should also be scope for recording behaviours that fall outside this typical sequence. This detailed developmental sequence allows the observer to record specific behaviours that might otherwise be lost. The success of this method of recording depends entirely on the adequacy of the developmental criteria and should not be considered an open-ended observation.

Ideally the checklist should offer space to record "evidence" of what was actually observed that makes the recorder think that the child demonstrated the behaviour. This evidence elaborates on the "present" or "absent" checks.

Appropriateness

To judge the suitability of a prepared checklist, determine the following:

1. The checklist covers the areas of behaviour you wish to record.
2. The items cover a suitable developmental span of behaviours in the selected domain.
3. A sufficient blend of behaviours will be recorded to show a pattern, rather than simply whether a behaviour is absent or present.
4. The checklist will fit your purpose—in the form of reports, record-keeping, program-planning, identifying a concern, and so on.

Validity

Checklist items must measure effectively the behaviours that they intend to assess. First, look at a checklist's broad categories and consider how they will provide information in those areas. There should be a sufficient number of subcategories, graduated in their level of difficulty. Without these, the criteria will likely not measure what you desire. (See also Chapter 1, page 16, and Chapter 10 regarding the notion of validity.)

Reliability

Prepared checklists have usually been tested for reliability, but do not assume this has been done. While standardized measures may be useful in many situations, their reliability may be affected by a built-in **bias** not easily detected. Most significant, but least easily detected, is a cultural bias that can lead an observer to believe that a child is either more advanced or less skilled than he actually is. Even supposedly "standardized" measures may not have eliminated these biases. For example, if you were to assess self-help skills as part of competence, you could find that some children lack experience dressing themselves because this is not considered a desirable early skill in their cultures of origin. Similarly, when a child's first language is not English, it is unfair to evaluate her communication skills in English. She may be far more competent in her own language; consequently, her cognitive skills may also be more advanced than your observations might suggest.

To be reliable, a checklist should evaluate a child's behaviour in a way that does not fluctuate from one observation situation to the next. Look for some short-term consistency among outcomes of the checklist recordings. Observers recording information about a child should produce consistent results.

Checkmarks

We use **checkmarks** to record whether we have seen a behaviour. A simple ✓ is not really enough because it does not offer any detail. In addition to writing some "evidence" you might develop a code to assist your documentation. Educators find the following marks useful, and you can develop your own as well. Remember to date everything!

Skill demonstrated	SD
Not yet demonstrated	ND
No opportunity to observe	NP
Attempts unsuccessfully	AU
Can perform with support	CS
Emerging skill	EM
Seen by third party	3D

Checklist Observations

Recording observations

Observers need to interpret the checklist criteria and match the observed behaviour to each of the items. Observers mark the presence or absence of the behaviour; behaviours may be coded as noted above. This recording may be done all at one time, or over a period of a few days, if a wide variety of behaviours is sought.

Checklists may also form part of a complex developmental assessment. We then focus on basic developmental checklists useful for educators and parents. See pages 170–173, and 174–176 for sample checklist observations.

Items are usually checked off as a result of the child's spontaneous activity. Occasionally, the child will not demonstrate some desired behaviours, so the observer may set up a situation in which the behaviour may occur or organize a more formal "testing" situation to elicit the desired response. In any situation, the observer should record the contextual information that might have had an impact on the behaviour.

Checklists are frequently used to evaluate information gathered from informal observations, and they may be compiled from a narrative recording or from other documentation as well. The direct method is more likely to generate accurate results.

How to record a checklist observation

1. Decide on the purpose for using the checklist method and review its underlying theory.

2. Choose a prepared checklist or devise a list of behaviours that fits your purpose.

3. Assess the checklist for its developmental appropriateness, validity, and reliability.

4. Prepare the checklist and place it where you can record the behaviours as they occur or soon afterward.

5. Check off the items you see demonstrated and use codes where appropriate.

6. Date all entries.

7. Make a note of any areas about which you are uncertain because of difficulty in interpreting the criteria or because the behaviour is just emerging.

8. If more than 80 percent of the items are checked, you may find that the child's behaviour has developed beyond the scope of your checklist. If so, use a more advanced checklist.

9. When behaviours are not demonstrated, set up experiences so that you will see them. Document the results.

10. Make appropriate, validated **inferences**, remembering that the absence of a behaviour does not necessarily indicate that the child is incapable of performing the behaviour.

Using checklists

Advantages

- Recording is quick and efficient.
- This method can be used in a variety of settings.
- All details need not be recorded.

- A clear picture of the presence or absence of behaviour is given.
- The observer can choose the criteria to observe.
- The observer can record observations while responsible for the care of the children under observation.
- The observer can choose to record information about more than one child at a time.
- Coverage of a range of developmental aspects may offer an overview of the whole child.
- The information produced can be used for program-planning.
- Prepared checklists that are valid and reliable may be available.
- This method can identify concerns when an individual is not performing in keeping with the norm.

Disadvantages

- Recording is so simple that errors are not easily seen. The detail and context of the observed behaviour are lost.
- Recording may require a degree of inference or interpretation.
- Criteria can easily be inappropriate, invalid, or unreliable.
- Criteria may reflect a theoretical perspective other than the one that the observer holds.
- Interpretation typically focuses on what the child cannot do rather than on the skills she has mastered.
- The checklist requires evaluation and preparation beforehand.
- A checklist tends to represent a selection of isolated fragments of behaviour.
- Information about a child's skill development does not necessarily translate into appropriate goal-setting or -planning.
- Checklist criteria may be difficult to validate for developmental appropriateness.
- This method typically relies on norm referencing, which some educators consider a dubious tool.
- Recorded behaviours may require a qualitative description in addition to a statement of presence or absence.
- The absence of a behaviour does not necessarily indicate an inability to perform the behaviour.
- Recording might be affected by emotional conditions or illness that might not be evident.
- Teachers and parents tend to "remember" behaviours and record them as present from previous occasions; these may be expectations rather than objectively recorded examples.

The analysis: Interpreting the data collected from checklists

Inferences should not be drawn from the information unless the checklist has been assessed for its suitability and the recording has been made with **objectivity**. A typical **analysis** might cover the following areas:

1. Draw deductions from the pattern of skills present on or absent from the checklist. Highlight the strengths demonstrated.

2. Make inferences about the child's skill level using comparisons with expected performance. This **norm-referenced assessment** needs to make clear supporting statements that are thoroughly validated.

3. Depending on the reason for making the observation, evaluate the effectiveness of the checklist and examine its outcome.

   a. Focus mainly on what the child can do.

   b. Look at any supposed "lack" of skill development. Ask yourself whether the child has not acquired the skill or the skill was perhaps present but not demonstrated.

   c. Verify the checklist with information from others.

   d. Consider the child's behaviour within his cultural experience and expectations.

   e. Follow up with a variety of other observation methods and attempt to match the outcomes.

   f. Develop an **individual program plan (IPP)** that devises activities and experiences to enhance the child's skills.

   g. Ask the parents, school, or another interested party to offer insights or other informal observations to help explain the behavioural pattern recorded.

   h. If the child demonstrates all the criteria, little information about the stage of development can be elicited. Use another checklist more developmentally appropriate for that child.

Sources of checklist items

Allen, K.E., & L.R. Marotz. (2003). *Developmental Profiles: Pre-birth Through Twelve* (4th edition). Albany, NY: Delmar.

Six one-page developmental checklists for children at 12 months, 2 years, 3 years, 4 years, 5 years, and 6 years. Each contains broad categories of behaviours—good for an overview but not very refined. The emphasis is on easily observable skills rather than cognitive activity, which requires more interpretation. The text of the book covers more detailed profiles of growth and development in each developmental domain, offering age/stage divisions. These could be adapted for use as checklists.

Beaty, J.J. (2002). *Observing Development of the Young Child* (5th edn). Upper Saddle River, NJ: Prentice-Hall.

Textbook written around a developmental checklist called "Child Skills Checklist," appropriate for three- to five-year-olds in any setting. Each developmental area is included with eight items in each of 12 categories. Broad categories may not reveal specific information, but the checklist is useful for any observer. The book explains how each skill may be developed by appropriate curriculum-planning.

Furuno, S., et al. (1995). *HELP [Hawaii Early Learning Profile] Checklist (0–3)* (revised). Palo Alto, CA: VORT Corp.

VORT Corp. (1995). *HELP for Preschoolers Checklist (3–6)*. Palo Alto, CA: VORT Corp.

Two detailed checklists covering hundreds of behaviours. Supporting resources include the *HELP Activity Guide* and *HELP at Home*, which give those working with children practical suggestions for supporting skill development. HELP charts present checklists in an easy-to-interpret format. Both checklists are intended for the majority of children who fall within the age ranges—not necessarily those with developmental concerns.

Herr, J. (1998). *Working with Young Children: The Observation Guide*. Tinley Park, IL: Goodheart–Willcox.

Several prepared age-related (birth to five years) checklists itemized by developmental domain, designed for students learning about children's development. Practising teachers, caregivers, and parents could also use these.

Ireton, H. (1995). *Child Development Inventory*. Minneapolis, MN: Behavior Science Systems.

A brief overview of developmental domains for the age ranges one to two years, two to three years, three to four years, four to five years, and five to six years. Parent questionnaires supplement an observational checklist. There are also an open-ended "other skills" section and the identification of possible "problems."

Summary

Checklists may either be developed by an educator or borrowed from a prepared standardized measure. A checklist is only as useful as its appropriateness for the age/stage of the child, its focus on the appropriate domain of development, its reliability in measuring what it intends to measure, and its effectiveness in improving the child's development. Essentially the checklist records the presence or absence of the skills, attributes, or other characteristics of development.

In practice, checklists usually offer more useful information if they are accompanied by clear evidence, or note exactly what it was that made the observer check off or mark the item. Although completing this kind of checklist can take longer, such detail improves the checklist, makes it easier to share with others, and leads to strong curriculum decisions.

Prepared checklists can offer educators and parents a valid and reliable measure while homemade checklists can be tailored to the particular needs of the educator and children. All checklists require that their criteria be interpreted and those items be related to the actual behaviours observed. These requirements can be harder to meet than might be apparent at first. An experienced observer makes these necessary interpretations better. Practising the use of narrative recordings helps you complete checklists as well because the latter hones your skills of recording without interpretation.

All checklists are created according to a theory about how children develop. Not all checklists will be appropriate or reflect your philosophy as educator. Take care when selecting and using a checklist to ensure that it actually measures what you consider important. As with other observational recordings, collect data using a variety of different methods and at different times. Use the checklist to prompt action in terms of general curriculum design along with individual program-planning.

analysis

behaviour

bias

checklist

checkmarks

criterion-referenced assessment

developmental sequence

developmentally appropriate

evidence

fine motor skills

gross motor skills

individual program plan (IPP)

inference

language

norm-referenced assessment

objectivity

pattern of development

reliability

skill acquisition

theoretical perspective

theory-bound

validity

Weblinks

www.pcc.cccoes.edu/dept/eceforms.htm
A series of "Early Childhood Education and Early Childhood Professions" forms.

www.sasked.gov.sk.ca/docs/kindergarten/kindshar.html
Techniques for sharing evaluation information with parents and family members.

www.bmcc.org/Headstart/As_I_Am/appendix.htm
"Observing Skills for Living" checklist.

These two children are enjoying experimenting with dough and comparing it to flour without water—this provides evidence of their parallel play.

Observation Sample

The recorder has selected a checklist appropriate for the developmental level of the child. The prepared checklist allows room for supporting evidence when items are observed. This sample shows excerpts from the complete checklist.

How might parents and professionals work together to complete a "Child Skills Checklist" for a preschooler?

Child Skills Checklist for Preschoolers

Child's name: Jimmy   Observer: Cody

Age: 5 years, 9 months   Dates: 25 and 30 June and 2 July, 2003

Setting: Laboratory School

Key: A–agree   D–disagree   N–not observed

* Observation of day-care teachers   ** Observation of mother

Item	Evidence	Date
1. Self-identity		
A Separates from parents without difficulty	Mother tells him good-bye; he says bye and continues to play.*	30 June
A Does not cling to classroom staff excessively	Plays at the assigned areas on his own	30 June
A Makes eye contact with adults	Looks teacher in the eye as she explains how to stop the tricycle	30 June
A Makes activity choices without teacher's help	Hollers out, "I want to paint!" after the teacher explains their options for play	25 June
D Seeks other children to play with	Will seek out an activity, not a playmate	25 & 30 June
N Plays roles confidently in dramatic play		
A Stands up for own rights	Teachers say he often expresses anger if he does not get his way.*	30 June
A Displays enthusiasm about doing things for self	Holds up his artwork to show another student	30 June
2. Emotional development		
A Allows self to be comforted during stressful time	During play, when Jimmy is running around wildly not listening to the teachers, he allows an instructor to pull him onto her lap. He remains there until he is more settled.	25 June
A Eats, sleeps, toilets without fuss away from home	Uses the bathroom and eats lunch at the day-care centre with no fuss	25 June
N Handles sudden changes/startling situations with control		
D Can express anger in words rather than actions	Jimmy has hit teachers and peers when he is angry or is not getting his way.*	30 June
D Allows aggressive behaviour to be redirected	Teachers say it is difficult to redirect his anger and aggressive behaviour when he is upset.*	30 June

Item	Evidence	Date
A̲ Does not withdraw from others excessively	Eager to do activities even when they involve the entire group	25 June
A̲ Shows interest/attention in classroom activities	Asks teacher to read a story again that involves imitation	25 June
A̲ Smiles, seems happy much of the time	Often smiles while playing	30 June

3. Social play

Item	Evidence	Date
A̲ Plays by self with or without objects	Plays with a paper airplane while other children are around or alone	2 July
A̲ Plays by self in pretend-type activities	Pretends his tricycle is an automobile	30 June
N̲ Plays parallel to others with or without objects		
A̲ Plays parallel to others in pretend-type activities	Pretends his tricycle is an automobile; other children are present	30 June
A̲ Plays parallel to others constructing or creating something	Colouring and cutting out a picture at a table with other children	30 June
A̲ Plays with a group with or without objects	Pretends to dig in sand with a shovel during a circle reading activity	25 June
N̲ Plays with a group constructing or creating something		

7. Cognitive development: classification and seriation

Item	Evidence	Date
A̲ Recognizes basic geometric shapes	Can identify triangles, squares, and circles**	30 June
A̲ Recognizes colors	Can identify the main colors	2 July
A̲ Recognizes differences in size	Will tell his mother he wants a big cup not a small cup**	30 June
N̲ Recognizes differences in musical tones		
D̲ Reproduces musical tones with voice	Will sing a song but does not noticeably change his tone**	30 June
N̲ Sorts objects by appearance		
N̲ Arranges events in sequences from first to last		
N̲ Arranges objects in series according to rule		

8. Cognitive development: number, time, space, memory

Item	Evidence	Date
A̲ Counts by rote to ten	Counts by rote up to one hundred**	30 June
A̲ Counts objects to ten	Can count at least up to ten with a one-to-one ratio**	30 June
A̲ Knows the daily schedule in sequence	Has to make his bed and brush his teeth after breakfast so that he can play before he goes to school**	30 June
N̲ Can build a block enclosure	Child has never tried to build one. He builds bridges and airplanes with Lego.**	30 June

Item	Evidence	Date
A Knows what happened yesterday	Can recount events of days that have passed**	30 June
A Can locate an object behind or beside something	Finds the Slinky that is behind a bigger toy	25 June
A Recalls words to song, chant	Can repeat/sing popular country songs that he hears frequently**	30 June
A Can recollect and act on directions of singing game	Participates in a group activity that involves singing and acting out parts of the song	25 June
9. Spoken language		
A Speaks confidently in classroom	When the teacher asks the group a question about a story she is reading, he answers the question with, "It's a wave."	25 June
A Speaks clearly enough for adults to understand	Same as above	25 June
A Speaks in expanded sentences	Tells his mother, "I have an airplane. Ben made it for me."	2 July
A Takes part in conversations with other children	Talks to a child sitting next to him while he is colouring a picture	30 June
A Asks questions with proper word order	Asks the teacher, "Can we go in this room to play now?"	2 July
N Makes "no" responses with proper word order		
A Uses past tense verbs correctly	Tells the teacher, "I used my feet to stop the bike."	30 June
N Plays with rhyming words		
10. Written language		
N Pretends to write by scribbling horizontally		
N Includes features of real letters in scribbling		
A Identifies his own name	Can point to things that have his name and recognize his name written**	30 June
N Identifies classroom labels		
A Knows some of the alphabet letters	Knows the entire alphabet and can recognize most of the letters**	30 June
A Prints real letters	Can print his first name**	30 June
A Prints letters of name	Can print his first name**	30 June
A Prints name correctly in linear manner	Can print his first name**	30 June

Item	Evidence	Date
12. Imagination		
<u>N</u> Pretends by replaying familiar routines		
<u>N</u> Needs particular props to do pretend play		
<u>N</u> Assigns roles or takes assigned roles		
<u>N</u> May switch roles without warning		
<u>D</u> Uses language for creating and sustaining a plot	Mother says she's never heard him make up stories about an event.**	30 June
<u>N</u> Uses exciting, danger-packed themes		
<u>A</u> Takes on characteristics and actions related to a role	Makes sounds like a car while riding a tricycle	30 June
<u>D</u> Uses elaborate and creative themes, ideas, and details	Mother says she's never heard him make up stories about an event.**	30 June

Observation Sample

This school-age child has been observed using a checklist developed from a normative profile. The recording contains quotations in the child's (and recorder's) first language. The observer found a way of addressing language differences in her recording.

How might you complete a developmental checklist if you do not share a common language with the child?

DEVELOPMENTAL CHECKLIST

Observer: Ki Wan A Yau

Child's name: Mei Lin
Age/D.O.B.: 8 years, 8 months (June 10, 1995)

Date of observation: March 2-16, 2004
Time of observation: throughout day
Setting: March 2-16 at her home and her aunt's home; March 4, 9:25-11:30 a.m. in her classroom and gym

Source of checklist items: Allen, K.E., & Marotz, L.R. (1994). *Developmental profile and growth pattern* (Appendix 2). In *Development profiles: Pre-birth through eight* (2nd ed., p. 171). Albany, NY: Delmar.

Designated age/stage of checklist items: 8 and 9 years

Key: ✓ Observed

✓₂ Observed by caregiver or parent

N No opportunity to observe

✗ Behaviour not yet demonstrated

Behaviors	Key	Date	Evidence
1. a. Have energy to play	✓	March 4	She showed she had energy to play in gym. She climbed a rope, walked across a balance beam, jumped up and bent her knees on a boxhorse, turned somersaults.
b. Continuing growth	✓	March 2	Now, her height is 51.5″. Since last June, her height has increased 1.5″.
c. Few illnesses	✓	March 6	Last winter, she only had one cold.
2. Use pencil in a deliberate and controlled manner	✓	March 4	She can hold a pencil and marker using a tripod grasp. I saw this when she was drawing pictures in her journal.

Behaviors	Key	Date	Evidence
3. Express relatively complex thoughts in a clear and logical fashion	✓	March 2	She used macaroni to make a bracelet and talked at the same time. Quote: Chinese language: 她對媽說:「我用這條繩去度手腕的長度。」(她再度橡根,然後將通心粉串上)又說:「陣間我會油上顏色。」媽說:「你串好,十分難上色。」她說:「我要知道用幾多,然後拿出來再上色。」 Translation: She said to her mom, "I use this string to measure the length around my hand." After she had done, she cut a rubber band and threaded macaroni one by one. She said, "I will paint them later on." Mom said, "If you thread them all, you will find it difficult to paint afterward." She said, "I want to know how many I will use, then I will let them out and paint them."
4. Carry out multiple (4-5) step instruc-tions	✓	March 13	Quote: Chinese language: 媽對她說:「Tracy,去廚櫃拿一個碗和碟,放在枱上。然後去雪櫃,取兩隻蛋,兩塊 HAM。打蛋於碗內,至起泡,用剪刀把 HAM 剪絲。做完後,話我知,我會教妳煮蛋。」 Translation: Mom said, "Mei Lin, get one bowl and one small plate from the cupboard and put them on the table. Then, get two eggs and two pieces of ham from the refrigerator. Break the eggs into the bowl and stir them with a fork until bubbles appear. Cut the ham into stick-size pieces on the plate with scissors. After you finish, tell me. I will teach you how to cook it."
5. Become less easily frus-trated with own performance	✗	March 5	She was frustrated with her own performance when she did paper folding to make a turtle because she didn't remember exactly the steps.
6. Interact and play coopera-tively with other children	✓	March 14	She talked to her cousins when they played games together. They played Monopoly coopera-tively. She waited for her turn patiently.

Behaviors	Key	Date	Evidence
7. Use eating utensils with ease	✓	March 4	She can use her right hand to grasp chopsticks and left hand to grasp a bowl at the same time to eat food. She uses her right hand to grasp a knife and left hand to grasp a fork at the same time to cut food.
8. a. Have a good appetite	X	March 5-16	She could eat half a bowl of rice, lots of vegetables and meats.
b. Show interest in trying new foods		March 15	Mom mixed salad and tuna fish. She did not want to eat it.
9. Know how to tell time	✓	March 4	Quote: Chinese language: 在校裏，我問她:「recess 幾時完?」她說游泰十。 Translation: I asked her when she finished recess in her school. She said "10 to 11."
10. Have control of bowel and bladder functions	✓	March 2-16	She has control of bowel and bladder functions. I saw this when she went to the washroom regularly and independently without any problem.
11. Participate in some group activities a. Sports	✓	March 4	In gym, she participated in the group routines.
b. Plays	✓2	March 4	Every Monday, she joins the folk-dance club after school.
c. Games	✓	March 17	She played games with her cousins.
12. Demonstrate beginning skills in a. Reading	✓	March 6	She read a book to her baby sister. Sometimes she reads books borrowed from the school library.
b. Writing	✓	March 12	I saw this when she wrote letters to her classmates using handwriting.
c. Math	N		
13. a. Want to go to school	X		
b. Seem disappointed if must miss a day	X		

Charts, Scales, and Pictorial Representations 6

Mapping the children's movements on a floor plan of my room helped me to reorganize my space a bit better. The older children watched me watching them— they decided to record my movements so I gave them a copy of the floor plan.

ECE student (1993)

It is possible, by knowing the basic types of data graphs and understanding their limitations, to create visually pleasing charts that are also founded on sound principles.

Edward Tufte (1983)

Plotting on the chart shows a steady upward curve for each child. When this ascent either slows down abnormally, dips or flattens out, it tells the caregiver something is happening to that particular child.

Veronica Rose (1985)

Understanding a child's family and social context can help an observer interpret the child's behaviour. Family trees and other social maps can be used to chart the child's relationships.

Focus Questions

1. How might you devise a quick and efficient method of recording information about a child's daily routine?

2. How might a map of a room, outdoor play space, or other children's area be used to benefit the program or an individual child?

3. After interpreting data from observations of a whole class, the teacher wants to present the findings in a graphic manner. In what ways could this be done?

Learning Outcomes

- Learners will identify a variety of usual techniques to record observational data.
- Learners will recognize a range of graphic data displays.

Features of Charts, Scales, and Pictorial Representations

DEFINITION: Chart

A **chart** is observed information that is recorded onto a prepared format or map according to specified criteria.

DEFINITION: Scale

A **scale** is a form of measuring information that uses lists of behaviours or other items and rates them according to predetermined values.

DEFINITION: Pictorial representation

A **pictorial representation** is any form of recording or interpretation that uses a visual presentation to demonstrate collected data.

Charts, scales, and pictorial representations are all interpretive methods of recording observational data. They enable the observer to write down information quickly and efficiently as it is perceived. These methods depend heavily on the recorder's **objectivity**; frequently there is little way of validating the accuracy of the recording. These forms of recording can enable teachers to collect information that might be impossible to record using more time-consuming methods.

Some charts and many pictorial representations and scales are completed soon after the activity is over. Again, their easy use enables teachers to record some of the essence of what was observed without having to write down all the details. This recording requires professional skill in deciding what is relevant to record and what is not. Almost any untrained person could complete a rating scale or chart; some of the information might be useful and accurate, but it might not all be reliable. While the outcome may look fine, the chart may lack the objectivity of a professional's work. These observations alone should not be used to determine a child's program plan. They can be used in addition to other observation methods, as they may help in providing a fuller picture.

CHILD DEVELOPMENT FOCUS

Visual representation may assist in determining

- social relationships

- typical patterns of behaviour

- contextual influences on development

- mobility

- personal preferences

Useful recording methods

Charts, scales, and pictorial representations are methods for recording observational data or ways in which information is presented after analysis. They are all visual representations of information. The following are the most useful categories for the observer.

Observation charts (pages 180–188): These are prepared blank forms with labelled and sectioned categories used for charting behaviours, relationship dyads (connections/interactions between two individuals), routine events, and other significant information as it is observed.

Observation scales (pages 189–192): Commonly called **rating scales**, these are lists of behaviours or traits prepared in advance for scoring at the time of or after observation. These can be open to subjective recording. They may include forced choices, semantic differentials, **numerical scales**, or graphic scales.

Social maps (pages 192–198): Pictorial presentations of the composition of the child's family, history, social relationships, or life experiences are all helpful to the observer. These may include sociograms, ecomaps, genograms, family trees, and flow diagrams or pictorial profiles. Information is gathered from the child, family members, or those in other social relationships and is presented as a chart or diagram.

Mappings (pages 198–200): Trackings or mappings are records of a child's movement or activity within a specified room, zone, or space. By recording the path of movement on a prepared map of that space, the teacher documents evidence of the child's mobility, interests, and attention span. Mappings may also support a teacher's evaluation of the use of space.

Interpretive graphic representations (pages 201–202): In analyzing observational recordings, observers might wish to explain their findings visually. Graphs, block charts, and pie charts are simple methods designed to make evaluative comparisons.

KEY FEATURES: Charts, scales, and pictorial representations

- visual representations of observational data

- interpretive methods of recording information

- may focus on one or more children

- usually naturalistic

- mostly nonparticipatory

Observation Charts

Many teachers choose to record behaviour on a wide variety of **observation charts** because the method is quick and efficient and they can do so while the teacher continue to participate in the children's program. Routines and sequences of a child's day may be recorded to help indicate the child's personal rhythms and adaptation to a changing environment, and to assist a caregiver in responding to the child's needs. Using a prepared form or chart, the caregiver can check off when particular events have occurred, such as sleep, rest, feeding, periods of activity, diaper-changing, or bowel or bladder evacuation. The pattern of feeding, wakefulness, sleep, and toileting can give clues about the child's health and well-being. Observers often use these charts for infants, but do not underestimate their use with toddlers and older children when identification of behavioural patterns could help the caregiver appreciate the child's needs in a **holistic** sense. A sample infant chart can be found on page 206.

The effectiveness of charting observations relies on the philosophy on which the chart is based, the appropriateness of the chart in covering a range of predictable categories, the accuracy of the recording as the observer interprets what she sees, and the consistency of interpretation among the adults using the chart.

An obvious limitation of charts lies in their simplicity, as they offer little opportunity to explain behaviour. It is tempting to make efficient use of a chart and to avoid analyzing the resulting patterns and identifying any need for intervention. As records, charts must be used, not just stored. While we must observe indicators regarding individual needs, health, well-being, and disease in order to respond to a child's needs, we must also consider this information within its family and social context, and understand its impact on the interrelated aspects of the child's growth and development.

Participation charts can give teachers a good indication of the interests, motivation, and focus of individual children or groups. They frequently quantify involvements, while they may offer little opportunity to describe the quality of activity. Some charts allow for recording the number of children involved in a specified activity; others count activity in designated time slots or enable the teacher to determine who has participated. Charts may be designed to increase the children's own responsibility for their activity by having the children themselves check off what they have done.

Charts may be designed to increase parent–teacher communication or facilitate the exchange of information among caregivers. Separate charts for each child may be useful for focusing on an individual, and group charts can help with program-planning. In the latter case, exercise caution in making assumptions about the "average" or the "majority's" responses, and in planning a curriculum on that basis. "Averages" may in fact apply to nobody; the groups of children may have levels of competence and participation above or below that average, and your programming may not suit any of them. Similarly, focusing on the "majority" may leave out children who have other needs.

Caregivers, social workers, or teachers may make observations related to the children's health and symptoms, which information can then be offered to health professionals. A non–health professional can chart symptoms only if trained in what to look for. Children with a variety of special medical conditions—such as asthma, anemia, cystic fibrosis, diabetes, eczema, epilepsy, or allergies—may be in mainstream settings and need close observation and appropriate intervention when they exhibit particular symptoms. Many of these children may have mild conditions, others much more severe; in all cases, parents and caregivers should share observational information, and a connection to the health professionals should be maintained.

TAKING A SPECIAL LOOK: Health observations

Baseline observations should be made every day. These informal observations act as a foundation for measuring a child's change of behaviour or appearance later in the day and are particularly useful for children with special conditions that need to be monitored. These observations can be recorded as anecdotal records but are more often unwritten observations.

Using observation charts

Advantages

- Charts may enable observers to record behaviours quickly and efficiently.
- Behaviour may be recorded during or after observation.
- Charts may include routine information as well as behaviours—for example, feeding, diapering.
- The format is pleasant and user-friendly.
- Observations are usually easy to interpret.
- Charts may identify behavioural patterns.
- The format is useful for information exchange between caregivers and parents.
- Charts frequently offer health as well as developmental areas for observation.

Disadvantages

- This method requires a prepared chart that includes all predictable categories.
- Charts often require that inferences be drawn at the time of recording.
- The format may encourage observers to concentrate on domestic routines rather than on responses and learning.
- This method may be used for efficiency rather than depth.
- Charts tend to offer only superficial information, limited to observation categories that are expected.
- The format may encourage simplification of developmental issues.
- Charts should not be relied on as the sole source of observational information.

Types of observation charts

The following pages show several types of charts that can document general behaviour, social relationships, and health.

Caregiver-Parent Information Chart for Infants

Child's name: _____

Week of: _____

Age/D.O.B.: _____

Caregiver(s): _____

		Mon.	Tues.	Wed.	Thurs.	Fri.
Liquid intake	a.m.					
	p.m.					
Solid intake	a.m.					
	p.m.					
Sleep	a.m.					
	p.m.					
Activity	a.m.					
	p.m.					
Urination	a.m.					
	p.m.					
Bowel movements	a.m.					
	p.m.					
Behaviour notes	a.m.					
	p.m.					
Comments/ messages	a.m.					
	p.m.					

This chart offers essential information to parents. The caregiver keeps an ongoing record of observations of the infant's day. The format allows for a change of caregiver while sustaining the information flow. However brief, the notes can form the basis of a log, which can show developmental changes over weeks. The chart may also aid the caregiver's memory, prompting some oral anecdotal accounts to support the information. A sample information chart for a single day can be found on page 206.

Daily Program Implementation Chart

Children's names: _____   Age/D.O.B.: _____

_____   _____

Date: _____

Observer(s): _____

Activity area	Materials	Objectives	Observation
Creative			
Language			
Sensory			

This chart underlines the notion of a dynamic, ongoing process of observation and activity planning. The activity area will always show a response to the previous day's observations; the following day, these observations would be used to determine the new plan.

Activity Response Chart

Observer(s): _____   Date.: _____

Zone, activity, or room area	Children's names				
	1_____	2_____	3_____	4_____	5_____

*The activity response chart shares some features with **event sampling** but uses only a **tally** or checkmark to identify each child's involvement in an activity. As an alternative, have a separate chart for each activity or learning centre and check off the name as a child participates.*

Activity/Routine Chart for Infants

Name: _____

Age/D.O.B.: _____

Date: _____

Context: _____

Observer: _____

Time	Activity/routine	Imposed (I)/Choice (C)	Feeding	Personal care	Rest/sleep	Outdoor activity	Play	Other
6:00 a.m.								
6:30 a.m.								
7:00 a.m.								
7:30 a.m.								
8:00 a.m.								
8:30 a.m.								
9:00 a.m.								
9:30 a.m.								
10:00 a.m.								
10:30 a.m.								
11:00 a.m.								
11:30 a.m.								
12:00 p.m.								
12:30 p.m.								
1:00 p.m.								
1:30 p.m.								
2:00 p.m.								

The pattern or rhythm of a child's day needs to be considered with reference to the context and any imposed routine. Infant schedules may be structured or responsive; if flexible, the pattern will reveal the child's natural rhythm and may help indicate the child's personal style. This chart includes a column to indicate whether an activity is imposed or chosen by the child. Older children continue to have their own patterns; if accommodated, they may be happier and more able to maximize their learning opportunities. This chart is a form of **time sampling***.*

Immunization Record

Immmunization type	Date	Reaction	Given by

Parents may keep an immunization-record card for their own benefit, to be aware of their children's immunization needs. Agencies may wish to see the record with verification of the information.

Patterns of Relationships Within a Group

Date(s)/times: _____

Context: _____

_____

Observer(s): _____

Children's names: Ages/D.O.B.:

A: _____ _____

B: _____ _____

C: _____ _____

D: _____ _____

E: _____ _____

F: _____ _____

G: _____ _____

Child	A	B	C	D	E	F	G	H	I	J
A										
B										
C										
D										
E										
F										
G										

To complete this chart, observe the children in various activities in which they are free to choose their companions. Record interactions between children with a tally mark in the appropriate box. When two children interact for longer than five minutes, put a different mark. Patterns of interactions will enable you to identify children who are isolated from the rest and those who have made social relationships. This chart could also focus on initiating and responding to invitations to play. For example, if C initiates play with F, record "CF," but if F invites C to play, record "FC." You can classify positive, negative, or neutral interactions (with a colour-coded tally) to add a further dimension. This practice requires further interpretation, which has to be recorded during the process.

Components of Participation Chart

Children's names: _____ Ages/D.O.B.: _____

_____ _____

Observer: _____

Activity: _____

Names	Physically involved	Follows instructions	Attempts to solve problems	Cooperates in action/ verbally	Creative/ constructive	Keeps on task

This chart can be used to record participatory information about an activity for a group of children. Do not assume that each component of participation is, of itself, always positive. Appropriate and valid participation may include solitary activity, experimentation, and even destruction! Chart results can be useful if analyzed without imposing prejudgments and assumptions.

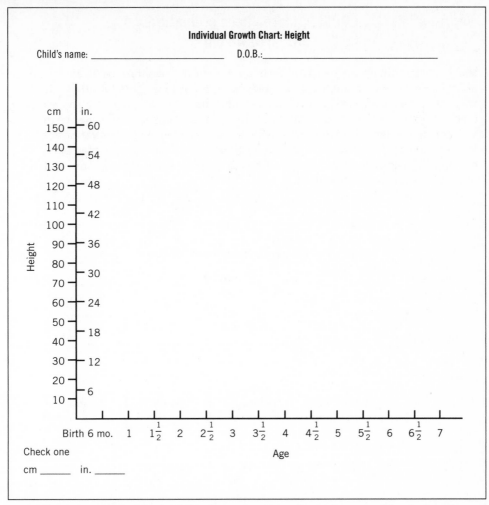

Individual Growth Chart: Height

Child's name: _____   D.O.B.:_____

Height

cm	in.
150	60
140	54
130	
120	48
110	42
100	
90	36
80	30
70	
60	24
50	18
40	
30	12
20	6
10	

Birth 6 mo. 1 $1\frac{1}{2}$ 2 $2\frac{1}{2}$ 3 $3\frac{1}{2}$ 4 $4\frac{1}{2}$ 5 $5\frac{1}{2}$ 6 $6\frac{1}{2}$ 7

Age

Check one

cm _____   in. _____

A child's height can be plotted on this chart. A pattern of growth is a useful consideration when evaluating aspects of gross motor-skill development.

A similar chart can be used for weight. Plotting a child's weight gain can help parents and professionals determine the child's overall pattern of change. Comparisons with norms can be helpful if those using the information understand the range of what constitutes an average; undue emphasis should not be placed on slight variations from a norm.

TAKING A SPECIAL LOOK: Children born prematurely or at low birth weight

Many babies, with expert pediatric assistance, survive premature birth, and some of them are extremely small. Other babies have low birth weights for other reasons. More than their size presents a challenge; many of these babies also have a range of medical and developmental difficulties. You will need to consider birth size and developmental history when you are interpreting your observations of infants, toddlers, and also older children. For example, some children may be developing at an appropriate rate, but their actual skill performance might match that of the norm for a younger child.

Symptom Chart for Chronic or Special Medical Conditions

Child's name: _____ Age/D.O.B.: _____

Observer(s): _____

Diagnosed condition: _____

Date(s) from: _____ to: _____

Reporting line: _____

Date	Behaviour symptom	Number of times observed	Severity	Comment

The parent, caregiver, or teacher may need to record observations of a child's specific behaviours or symptoms as they occur. If a child with a special medical condition is integrated into a mainstream setting, the caregivers should be taught to identify the behaviours that are important to record for that child, and they should ensure that such information is reported appropriately.

Observation Scales

You can rate observed information according to the degree to which a quality, trait, skill, or competence is demonstrated in various ways. The simplest **rating scale** may use a checklist-style inventory of items accompanied by a scale that elaborates a yes/no response. The scale may contain opposites on a continuum, numerical ratings, choices of levels of behaviour, or pictorial or graphic representations. More complex rating scales may have established criteria for grading a performance or demonstration of skill. Each type of scale is scored at, or soon after, the time of observation. Some require evidence to help validate the scoring.

All rating scales require the observer to make **inferences** at the time of recording. The complex inferences required in identifying a child's behaviour, labelling it, and evaluating the quality of the child's performance require considerable skill. The components of the inventory itself, coupled with the form of evaluation that goes with it, may not be sufficiently valid. It can be difficult to assess the **validity** and **reliability** of a rating scale; too often, a scale is chosen because of its apparent ease of use rather than its technical merit or appropriateness. A scale can be only as good as the philosophy, theory, and research on which it is based. Allocating a grading or scale to a checklist may alter its intrinsic reliability if it was not designed to be used that way. Also be aware that evaluating skills based on a pre-set scale presumes that the performance will fall within the bounds of that grading system. The sample scale on page 207 is accompanied by an assessment of the scale.

Using observation scales

Advantages

- Scales can be used to record information about a wide range of behaviours.
- Recording is efficient.
- Little training is required to implement the use scales at a basic level.
- This method can be used to measure behaviours not easily measured in other ways.
- Scales may be used to record information at the time of observation or shortly after and they allow for the observer's continued participation in the program.
- Scales may offer a large amount of information about children quickly.

Disadvantages

- The validity of items may be questionable.
- The format offers little contextual information.
- For effective choice and use, thorough training is necessary to evaluate behaviour.
- The rater needs to make qualitative judgments of behaviour.
- The position of items on the inventory may affect scoring.
- Inferences must be made rapidly and without full validation.
- A scale may be inconsistent in its wording or lead to assumptions about so-called **positive** and **negative behaviours**.

- Scoring may not be consistent over time.
- Scoring may depend on the observer's interpretation of an item.
- Evaluation should not stand alone as the sole information-gathering technique.
- Observer **bias** is not easily detected.
- Observer bias can take a variety of forms.
- There may be a tendency to rate well-known, liked, or attractive children higher.
- There may be a tendency to overcompensate for known and recognized biases.
- There may be a tendency to avoid extreme scores.
- Results can be affected by the order of inventory items.

Types of observation scales

1. **Forced choice scales:** Observers choose between predetermined ranges of behaviour to identify levels of functioning.

   Example

   handwriting (Circle the category most applicable.)

messy, ____	some ____	some ____	words ____	phrases ____	clear, ____
illegible most	letters	words readable	legible,	legible, tidy	legible
of the time	readable but	but quite	varying	most of	sentences
	untidy most	untidy most	tidiness most	the time	most of
	of the time	of the time	of the time		the time

2. **Semantic differential scales:** With a semantic differential scale, the observer chooses between two extremes or opposites, or at one of 3, 5, 7, or 9 points between them. Typically seven categories are used between the extremes. The categories may be numbered or may appear on an open continuum. See pages 207–208 for a sample semantic differential scale.

   Example

   a. cooperative   ☐☐☐☐☐☐☐   uncooperative

   b. sociable   ☐☐☐☐☐☐☐   unsociable

   c. honest   ☐☐☐☐☐☐☐   dishonest

   d. skilled   ☐☐☐☐☐☐☐   unskilled

   e. extrovert   ☐☐☐☐☐☐☐   introvert

3. **Numerical scales:** The inventory items may be rated according to a number system. Each item is graded in relation to a predetermined set of criteria. Assigning a number to a skill can indicate the level at which it is performed. Pre-assigning the grading can help ensure objectivity in the structure of the scale, although it does not ensure objectivity in the grading.

Example A

How well does the child dress herself/himself? (Choose one of the categories.)

1. Competent in all respects, including doing up buttons, laces, zippers.

2. Puts on clothes, tries to close fasteners, but lacks sufficient skill to complete task.

3. Attempts to put on clothes, cannot do fasteners, and needs help.

4. Does not attempt dressing.

Example B

Preschool physical skills (Circle the number as appropriate.)

1 = poor skill _____ 5 = highly defined skill

runs	1	2	3	4	5
skips	1	2	3	4	5
hops	1	2	3	4	5
climbs stairs	1	2	3	4	5

Example C

Communicates wishes and needs verbally.

1. Makes self understood with phrases and gestures.

2. Clear articulation in full sentences.

3. Attempts to make self understood with some success.

4. Attempts infrequently to make self understood.

5. Does not attempt to communicate wishes and needs.

Circle one: 1   2   3   4   5

Example D

Obeys simple instructions

Scoring

5   Clearly follows a series of instructions in order they are given.

4   Follows instructions/does not keep to sequence requested.

3   Attempts to follow instructions but makes some mistakes.

2   Makes limited attempts to follow instructions but makes many mistakes.

1   Makes erratic effort to obey instructions but follows them incorrectly.

0   Does not attempt to obey instructions.

4. **Graphic scales:** These points on a line indicate the degree to which the item is applicable. This evaluation form is frequently depicted as a scale between "always" and "never." Descriptions may also be used for clearer evaluation.

Example A

Speech fluent and grammatically correct.

←——————————————————————————————→

Never   Usually   Always

Asks meanings of abstract words

←——————————————————————————————→

Never   Usually   Always

Example B

Response to new activities:

←——————————————————————————————————→

| positive, inquiring, and exploratory approach, long attention span | erratic, inconsistent, varying attention, relatively easily distracted | negative, disinterested, does not respond to stimulation |

TAKING A SPECIAL LOOK: Temperamental differences

Children respond to the same situations in different ways. The style of response particular to an individual depends on his **temperament**. Although you may see fairly typical patterns of responses from a child, sometimes you will be surprised when he acts "out of character." Observing what is typical and also what is unusual for a particular child helps you determine his environmental influences and how he is coping.

Chess and Thomas (1996) review nine categories of temperament and three temperament "constellations." These categories can be scored on a rating scale—mild, medium, high—to develop an individual child's profile. The child is rated on activity level, rhythmicity (regularity), approach or withdrawal, adaptability, threshold of responsiveness, intensity of reaction, quality of mood, distractibility, and attention span and persistence.

Social Maps

The complexities of a child's social context can make professionals very wary of delving into her background. Recognize that conclusions drawn quickly can lead to very inappropriate judgments and assumptions. Nothing can replace the sensitive observations and recordings of an observer who has taken the time to delve into the home life and social background of a child to understand who she is and appreciate the range of factors that affect her growth and development. Social maps can offer a backdrop against which you can increase your understanding of what you observe directly.

The child's social context can be represented in various ways. These maps are not intended to replace more detailed study; they may help support an in-depth study. Diagrams can show key life experiences, family trees, social relationships, or factors affecting the child's world, providing a structure to help make sense of the whole. In themselves, they offer little detail of the child's life. They may serve to provide some basic hooks on which to hang observational information.

Family trees

Sentimental interest often motivates a person to research a **family tree**. Such research, however, may also produce some understanding of a child's genetic inheritance, life patterns, and history, which in turn can help medical professionals, social workers, caregivers, and teachers, as well as the child himself. A family tree provides historical background information gained through interviews, diaries, and archives. Name searches can be part of the research; surnames can help in tracking family members though they should not be relied on in determining a person's complete ancestry.

Families have become increasingly mobile since the last century. Immigration frequently complicates research. Information recorded in passenger ship lists and diaries can assist in tracing ancestors. Adoption, multiple partners and offspring, name changes, wars, changes of location, inadequate local record-keeping, translations, fires and other natural disasters, and individuals trying to cover up their ancestry are some of the common challenges we face in formulating a family tree. A typical one may look like this:

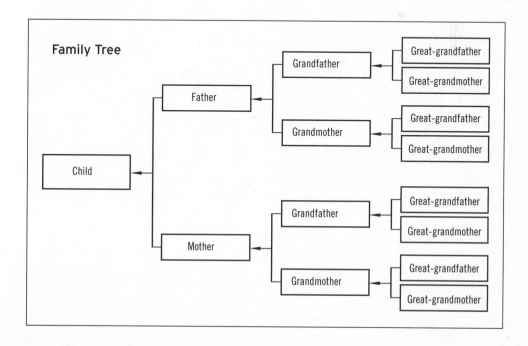

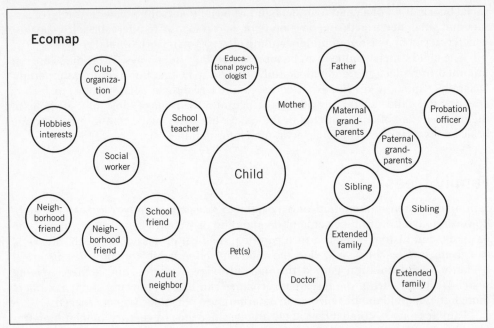

Ecomap

Source: Department of Health, Great Britain, <u>Protecting Children: A Guide for Social Workers Undertaking a Comprehensive Assessment</u> (1988).

Ecomaps

An **ecomap** is a diagram showing a child's world in the form of a diagram—the significant people, activities, and organizations in that world and the relationships between the child and those elements of his environment. For social workers, an ecomap might facilitate an understanding of how the family's demands and resources compare. Teachers, caregivers, and parents might find the exploration of the child's ecosystem enlightening in understanding how the immediate social setting (the family) and the more remote social settings (such as childcare, school, media, clubs, and so on) influence the child's development. A sample ecomap can be found on page 211.

Urie Bronfenbrenner's (1979) **ecological systems model** of child development helps identify the components of a child's environment. He describes four systems that influence the child's development. Based on these, a caregiver or other professional can construct an ecological model from which to study the child's environment. Perhaps it is impossible to include all environmental components and to determine their effects on the child. The ecomap attempts this, and we do need to acknowledge its limitations.

Genograms

According to McGoldrick and Gerson (1985), "a **genogram** is a format for drawing a family tree that records information about family members and their relationships over at least three generations." It is created through interviews, discussion, and research with the child's family members. Family structure and composition may be shown in a variety of

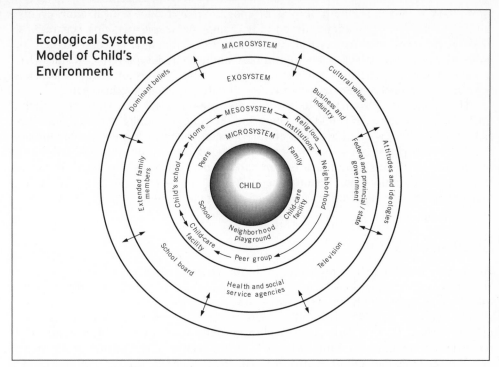

Source: Based on Urie Bronfenbrenner, <u>The Ecology of Human Development: Experiments by Nature and Design</u> (1979).

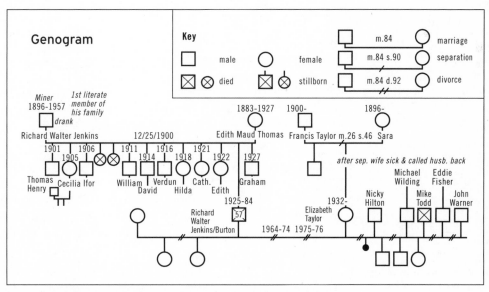

Source: Monica McGoldrick and Randy Gerson, <u>Genograms in Family Assessment</u> (1985).

forms, there being no "standard" format. A genogram may include critical family events, dates of birth, marriages, adoptions, custody arrangements, partnerships, separations, divorces, and deaths, and details of places of residence, occupations, and other significant information. It provides a clear view of complex family scenarios, patterns, and lifestyles. It is not intended to detail day-to-day interactions or to be a "snapshot" that evaluates the ways the family functions. Social workers often find the genogram a valuable tool.

The process of collecting the data from family members may be as important as the final product. Adults in the child's life may find the genogram enlightening themselves as it provides them with an overview of the connections between the family members and can identify possible stressors. Sensitivity to the privacy and range of styles and practice of families is essential when embarking on drawing a genogram. Both the researcher and family members must agree on the symbols to represent birth order, individuals, relationships, and living arrangements before a genogram can be drawn.

Sociograms

Sociometry is a research technique used for identifying children's acceptance by their peers and exploring their social status. A **sociogram** visually represents the child's perceptions of acceptance within his own group. A child in an organized setting may be asked to name the child who is his "best friend" or "person they do not especially like" or "like best" or "admire most." Results depend on the phrasing of the question and may be influenced by what the child thinks the adult wishes to hear. Information gathered from group members is pieced together and presented in a diagram. Popular children and those who are

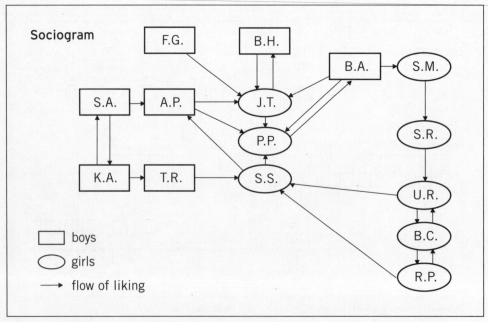

Information collected from a class of eight-year-olds (seven boys, eight girls). The children were asked, "Who are your two best friends?" The sociogram may indicate whether some of the children are isolated.

solitary or isolated may be identified quickly; some unexpected connections may come to light at the same time, leading the teacher to observe interactions more closely. Over a period of time, the sociogram may change quite radically. You may choose to use a sociogram at designated times during the year to assess the dynamics of your group. The children must be old enough to understand the questions posed, be able to give clear answers, and be mature enough to have formed social relationships within the group. The interactions or "friendships" of younger children tend to be transitory because the children are not yet able to communicate, appreciate the perspectives of others, or form social attachments with their peers. For these children, a sociogram would reveal little.

Life-experience flow charts

A person's significant life experiences can be reduced to a list of dates that offer a structure for understanding chronology, while providing no contextual information to explain why the events occurred. A **life-experience flow chart** explores the context, identifies key experiences, and labels and shows a sequence of events. The flow chart

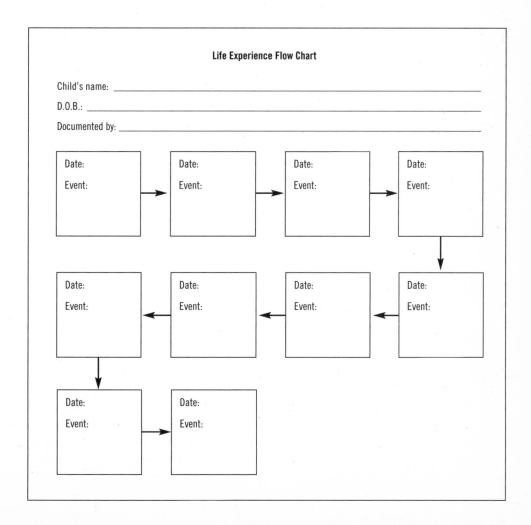

can reveal structure and patterns in a child's life. Teachers and caregivers can use such charts to help them appreciate the child's cultural identity, traumas, life stages, and happy experiences. As a result, they may become more sensitive to the child's needs and understand the child's own perception of reality.

Using social maps

Advantages

- Social maps are relatively easy to create.
- Social maps give a visual overview of the child's situation/context/environment.
- Families are usually helpful in supporting access to information.
- Social maps may appear clear and concise.
- The information is easily accessible.
- Individual and group contexts can be examined in this way.
- The child may be involved.
- The process of drawing up maps may have a therapeutic purpose.

Disadvantages

- Social maps depend heavily on professional sensitivity.
- The format can be overly simple and insufficiently supported by contextual information.
- Social maps rely on the accuracy of the information collected.
- Objectivity of recording is required.
- Inferences may be difficult to draw.
- Training may be needed to analyze family patterns.
- Inaccurate assumptions may be made by unqualified people.
- If support is not available, the child may be unnecessarily vulnerable.

Mappings

Sensitivity to the planning, set-up, and use of the children's environment leads educators and caregivers to evaluate what they provide (see Chapter 11). Part of a qualitative assessment of the use of space will be to create a map or **mapping** of the room or outdoor space to see how well it meets the needs of the children. The evaluation might consider the effectiveness of the learning environment, the aesthetics of the space for children and adults, the contrasts of activities in different areas, the degree to which the space allows for appropriate mobility and safety, its flexibility of use, and the construction of the environment based on an agreed philosophy of care and education.

Trackings can follow the movement of groups of children to see how they interact, move, and use the different parts of their environment. By tracking individual children, you might notice what interests them, their mobility, their concentration span, and their range of movements between activities. You can evaluate caregivers' roles within the room or play space by tracking their movements within the available space as well.

A simple line on a map can follow the movement of a child. Arrows can show the direction in which she was moving. You can represent movement back and forth in the same place with arrows in both directions (< >) showing the number of times the child travelled through that space. A circle containing the number of minutes or seconds can show how long a child stayed at a particular activity. More than one child can be tracked on the same map if the observer has sufficient skill and uses a different coloured line for each child.

A narrative description of the details of a tracking can explain the diagram recorded. This dual technique means the observer can elaborate on the "tracks" so that she can make a more qualitative evaluation later. The sample tracking on pages 209–210 includes a narrative account.

Using mappings

Advantages

- Mappings are easy and efficient to record.
- The tracking can focus on an individual child or the actions of a group.
- Mappings may be used to analyze traffic, use of space, or safety considerations.
- Analysis can help to identify
  - mobility
  - attention span
  - interests/motivation
  - child-to-child interactions
  - child–adult interactions
  - participation in specific areas of the program
- Maps can be layered to show change, compare activity levels, or identify traffic problems.

Disadvantages

- The space or room must be mapped beforehand.
- It is difficult to record the action of more than one child at a time.
- Qualitative evaluation is difficult without an accompanying narrative.
- Reasons for behaviour may not be revealed.
- Inferences must be drawn on little data.
- Participants in a program may find it difficult to make an accurate tracking.

Mapping templates

A mapping can show both the physical layout and the use for which each area is intended. Such blank maps can be used for observation or environmental evaluation. See pages 209–210 for a sample observational tracking of a child's movements.

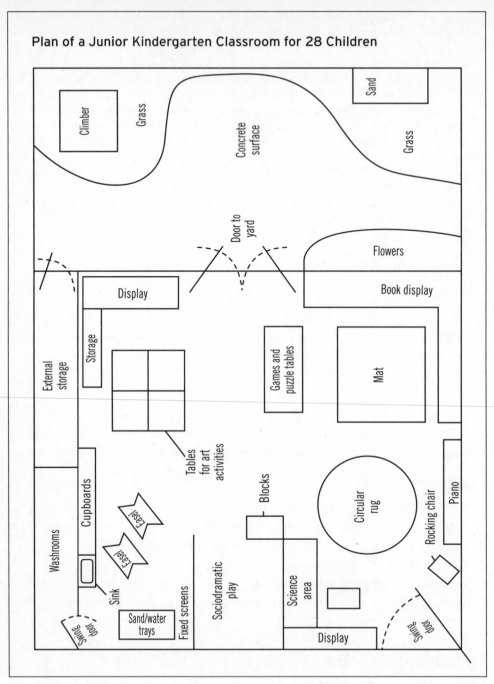

Plan of a Junior Kindergarten Classroom for 28 Children

This mapping could be used by a teacher to evaluate the use of space—for example, to consider whether all curriculum areas have been included or whether activities are allotted appropriate space. The plan could also be copied and used to track the movements of individual children.

Interpretive Graphic Representations

Rather than recording direct observational material, **interpretive graphic representations** aim to demonstrate numerical results, percentages, comparisons, variables, proportions, or other quantifiable outcomes from observation or evaluation. Pictorial representations are used to understand and analyze the content of assessment **data** (information). While there is a danger that observers could oversimplify such information without appreciating its context, the representations are intended to support the conceptualizing of large amounts of information.

Graphic representations are mathematical and statistical ways of presenting data clearly and objectively. Often easier to understand than to create, they may require some practice before they can be relied on for accuracy.

A wide variety of techniques might be used. Charted tally marks can form simple graphic representations. Block graphs, **bar charts**, flow diagrams, **pie charts**, chains-of-events charts, scatter graphs, line charts, area charts, organizational maps, triangular charts, 3D plots, Venn diagrams, cycle organizers, spider maps, fishbone-mapping graphs, picture diagrams, genetic maps, percentile charts, and picture symbols can all be used to present data. A sample graphic representation can be found on page 211. (For a more detailed explanation of these representations, refer to Tufte [1983].)

Using graphic representations

Advantages

- Graphic representations can display simple, easy-to-understand information.
- Certain formats may offer trends and comparisons.
- Mathematical data analysis may be more objective than anecdotal reports.
- Information from various sources can be pulled together.
- Large amounts of data can be represented meaningfully.

Disadvantages

- Graphic representations rely on valid and reliable data collection.
- Users may need to understand statistics in order to interpret the information.
- Results are quantitative rather than qualitative.
- Graphic representations may encourage comparisons with other children rather than an analysis of changes in the child's own performance.
- Results can be used for unwise program-planning.
- Comparisons may foster unnecessary parental anxiety.
- Trends may be analyzed without contextual information.
- Research psychologists may be able to use graphs more readily than practitioners.

Conducting research into child behaviour

Beyond carrying out their primary role, educators conduct research into the finer nuances of children's behaviour so that they can respond to the children more fully, understand the ways that they learn, and, consequently, furnish them with improved learning experiences. Such research may be either **quantitative** (considering behaviour in terms of counting repetitions of actions or the number of children behaving a particular way) or **qualitative** (looking at the subtleties of individual children's behaviour in particular circumstances).

Both approaches to this research rely on accurate, skillful observation and information-recording. Without either of these elements, the researcher cannot analyze the data and draw useful conclusions from them. The research analysis may be presented in the form of a graphic representation, particularly in quantitative research. The numerous types of graphic representation include those listed above, many of which are self-explanatory.

To pursue qualitative inquiry, refer to Creswell (1998) or Ely (1991) as starting points for effective research. Other inquiry methods that are more quantitative in style are described in Best and Kahn (1989).

Action research, a favoured **research method**, is a branch of qualitative research that teachers frequently carry out while attending to the children more directly. The teacher observes, records, and analyzes the program, curriculum, environment, interactions, or the children themselves. The information generated can assist the teacher's planning and lead to program improvements. It can also have larger implications when those data are shared with other teachers. To some extent all teachers are conducting action research as they carry out their roles and responsibilities. However, some present their data collection and findings more formally.

As discussed previously regarding basic observations of children, all research into human behaviour must be conducted ethically, confidentially, and with informed consent. Gain permissions for any research beyond the day-to-day notes teachers record in their roles as employees. Make the research data available to the participants—in this case, their parents. Educators should ensure that they do not use information gained while performing their roles as teachers in the interests of other research without gaining necessary permissions and using pseudonyms for the children being observed.

Types of graphic representations

The following examples show two of the most common types of graphic representations and suggest the types of data for which such graphs can be useful.

Summary

Charts, scales, and pictorial representations each have a visual component and need to be interpreted. They also serve a variety of different purposes, including the display of observational data or representation of an analysis of that data. At the day-to-day level, educators may gather information about the children with whom they work using easy-to-manage graphic forms. They may also be conducting action research with those (and possibly other) children. This might be a more comprehensive data-gathering process and would require that the person collecting the data understand complex research

Bar chart

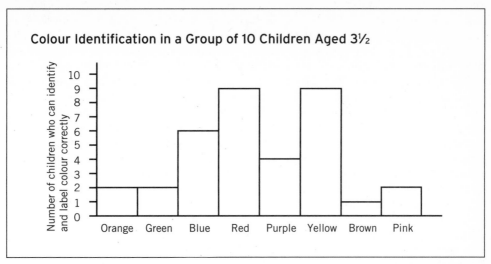

Colour Identification in a Group of 10 Children Aged 3½

Information charted is not designed to show which child knows which colours; the intention is to determine the number of children who can identify each colour. The bar chart can be used to present a variety of data.

Pie chart

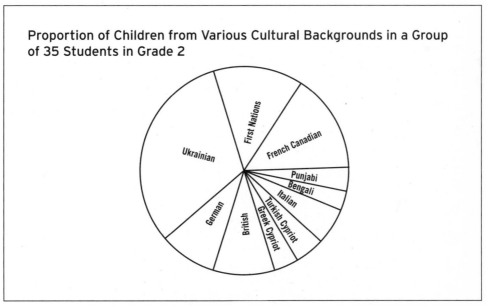

Proportion of Children from Various Cultural Backgrounds in a Group of 35 Students in Grade 2

This particular chart indicates heritage rather than origin or place of birth. A pie chart may need a key to explain the items. The "whole" must be identified; otherwise the proportions of the whole are meaningless. Percentages can be written into the pie for extra clarity.

methodologies. Whatever the observer's intentions, each of these forms incorporates some kind of observation strategy.

Prepared charts can help with recording observational information efficiently. These are often used for focused observations of individuals and children. Rating scales are the most frequently used type of scale. The observer can record information from observations as he conducts them, without influencing what is happening with the children. Scales indicate the degree of a specified characteristic in a child; several useful forms employ numerical or semantic differentials. Graphic scales visually represent the degree to which an attribute is present.

Social maps can reveal relationship patterns among groups of children or within families. Through family trees the educator, parent, or older child can show the family relationships over generations. Ecomaps consider the particular social networks within which the child lives; these networks include the individualized microsystem, mesosystem, exosystem, and macrosystem of a particular child. Genograms provide complex generational maps of the structure, composition, and relationships of a family. Sociograms are visual representations of a child's perception of himself within a social group. Life-experience flow charts document the significant life experiences of a child. Mappings are particularly useful for teachers who want to examine the use of the space available to them for their classes; through these they can track the movement of individuals or of groups of children.

Interpretive graphic representations can take numerous forms, many of which are borrowed from mathematics. These include bar charts, diagrams, 3-D plots, spider maps, Venn diagrams, area charts, and visual organizers. Those conducting research may represent their data, ideas, analysis, and theories using a variety of interpretive measures. Read the representations carefully and appreciate precisely what they indicate within the context of particular research.

Observational data, such as recording each child's hand preference and fine motor skills, can be recorded efficiently using charts.

action research

bar chart

bias

chart

data

ecological systems model

ecomap

family tree

forced choice scale

genogram

graphic scale

inference

interpretive graphic representation

life-experience flow chart

mapping

negative behaviour

numerical scale

objectivity

observation chart

observation scale

pictorial representation

pie chart

positive behaviour

qualitative

quantitative

rating scale

reliability

research method

scale

semantic differential scale

social map

sociogram

sociometry

temperament

tracking

validity

Weblinks

www.archives.ca/02/0201_e.html
ArchiviaNet is the National Archives of Canada's online research and consultation tool.

www.deakin.edu.au/~agoodman/sci101/chap12.html
Presentation of data and other major forms of non-quantitative charts in the form of graphs.

Observation Sample

This information chart provides daily information for parents and caregivers. A comparison of these charts as the weeks pass will provide more information about the infant's development.

Are there any other categories that you might include on this one-page chart?

Information Chart for Infants

Child's name: _Adrienne_

Age: _9 months_

Parents: _Lynn and Malcolm_

Other caregivers and students: _Michelle P., Jennifer, Carolie, Darlene, Michelle C._

Who brought the child to the center? _Malcolm_

Date: _January 18, 2004_

Observer: _Scott_

Time: _8:10 a.m._

Liquid intake	a.m.	Formula: 8:30 – 4 oz; 9:15 – 2 oz; 11:15 – 1/4 cup
	p.m.	Formula: 1:00 – 6 oz; 4:35 – 4.5 oz Water: 4:15
Solid intake	a.m.	8:30 – Cheerios; 11:15 – macaroni and cheese, breadstick, 2 oz. peas, 1/4 banana
	p.m.	2:50 – 4 oz. peaches mixed with 1 tbsp. of cereal
Sleep	a.m.	9:30–10:25
	p.m.	1:52–2:36
Health indicators	a.m.	Diaper rash, runny nose
	p.m.	Diaper rash, runny nose
Urination/diaper change	a.m.	10:30 wet; 11:55 wet
	p.m.	1:00 wet; 2:38 wet; 4:10 wet
Bowel movements/diaper change	a.m.	None
	p.m.	None
Behaviour notes	a.m.	Very happy (11:15 lunch – all smiles)
	p.m.	Happy *on walk Adrienne became slightly upset – carried rest of the way
Play activities	a.m.	Gross motor room, different types of boxes, floor toys – crawling
	p.m.	Jello cube play on the floor
Climate/environment	a.m.	20°C room
	p.m.	7°C walk, partly cloudy, mild; 20°C room

Who picked up the child? _Malcolm_

Time: _5:45 p.m._

* NOTE: Only three infants in today

Observation Sample

This semantic differential scale is used to record observations on a child's personality. The attached personality profile comments on the validity and reliability of the rating scale and elaborates on the results.

The observer used the following attributes as a guide to considering Tasha's personality. Can you see any issues related to these items on the semantic differential scale?

<table>
<tr><td colspan="9"></td><td>1 of 2</td></tr>
<tr><td colspan="10" align="center">**Personality Attributes Rating Scale**</td></tr>
<tr><td colspan="5">Child's name: Tasha</td><td colspan="5">Observer: Salma</td></tr>
<tr><td colspan="5">D.O.B.: 5-5-96</td><td colspan="5">Age: 7 years, 8 months</td></tr>
</table>

Circle the number that describes the degree of the attribute:

Outgoing	3	②	1	0	1	2	3	Reserved
Sensitive	3	②	1	0	1	2	3	Insensitive
Confident	3	②	1	0	1	2	3	Lacking confidence
Aggressive	3	2	①	0	1	2	3	Passive
Dominant	③	2	1	0	1	2	3	Submissive
Flexible	3	②	1	0	1	2	3	Inflexible
Patient	3	2	1	⓪	1	2	3	Impatient
Responsible	3	2	①	0	1	2	3	Irresponsible
Dependent	3	2	1	0	①	2	3	Independent
Imaginative	③	2	1	0	1	2	3	Unimaginative
Relaxed	3	②	1	0	1	2	3	Tense
Responsive	3	②	1	0	1	2	3	Unresponsive
Introverted	3	2	1	0	1	②	3	Extroverted
Generous	3	②	1	0	1	2	3	Mean
Trusting	3	②	1	0	1	2	3	Suspicious
Controlled	3	2	①	0	1	2	3	Uncontrolled
Serious	3	2	1	0	①	2	3	Easygoing
Courageous	3	2	①	0	1	2	3	Timid
Intelligent	③	2	1	0	1	2	3	Less intelligent
Emotionally stable	③	2	1	0	1	2	3	Emotionally unstable

Signature ___Salma Ahmad___   Relationship ___Student teacher___

Tasha's Personality

Validity of the rating scale: There are more "positive" attributes on one side of the scale than the other. This makes me think that my responses may have been skewed a little. Also, a few of the items are presented as opposites when they are not, according to my own definitions. I am not entirely confident that the scale can measure what it is meant to measure.

Reliability of the rating scale: I think that there needs to be a way of indicating what exposure to the child is necessary before undertaking the rating. I might have been influenced by the fact that I have known Tasha for only a short time. If her mother or teachers scored Tasha's personality with this scale, they might come up with different responses.

Strengths of the rating scale: The rating scale prompts me to evaluate some elements of personality that I might not have considered otherwise. I see it as a kind of checklist with a way of stating to what degree the attribute "fits." This kind of rating scale is very quick to do and could be replicated by other adults to determine common perceptions.

Weaknesses of the rating scale: There may be some bias in my scoring because the items are not effectively random. Also, my results cannot be validated on their own. My current positive outlook on life may bias me to see Tasha more positively than I would at another time. A few items are not typical of most personality inventories; for example, intelligence seems inappropriate as a dimension of personality.

My profile of Tasha's personality: Personality is a matter of relatively enduring behavioural characteristics. These are difficult for me to determine in Tasha because I have not observed her with her family or anywhere outside her class. I have seen patterns of behaviour that have repeated themselves. Some are sufficiently predictable that I have to alter my teaching strategies so that she cannot always be the leader of an activity! I think that Tasha tends to be warm and receptive to new ideas, but this wasn't scored on the rating scale. Her warmth may be seen as pro-social behaviour that is developmentally significant, as well as part of her personal style. Focusing on what the scale did indicate, I see Tasha to be very imaginative in her artwork and sociodramatic play. She frequently has ideas for new dramas that she initiates and draws her peers into. She is willing to cooperate with others, but she is persistent in wanting the play to go her way. Tasha leaps into new situations without being daunted and appears confident in approaching unfamiliar people. Her trusting nature could be potentially worrisome, so she needs close supervision. Curriculum challenges may allow Tasha to use some of her dispositions in new areas. I am hopeful that she will soon expand her artwork into storytelling because the necessary pre-reading skills are emerging. We are using a lot of stories in the classroom; she responds and acts out some of them in her play.

Observation Sample

This mapping tracks a child's movements in order to assess his participation in a program. The accompanying narrative provides details that will help the observer draw inferences from the mapping.

Although this mapping provides useful information, it may not offer a complete answer to the observer's reason for observing Peter. What should the observer do next?

Tracking in School-Age Program   1 of 2

Child's name: ___Peter D._____   Observer: _____Rena_____

Age/D.O.B: ___7 years, 2 months_____

Context: ___Peter has recently come, with his sister Kate (6 years),___
___to an after-school program in a housing complex. Both started___
___the program less than three weeks ago. Mom and Dad have___
___recently separated and there is now nobody at home until___
___approximately 6:00 p.m., when Mom returns from work.___

Reason for observations: ___We tracked Peter's movement to help us deter-___
___mine the level of his interaction in the program. There were___
___concerns about Peter remaining in an onlooker role while other___
___children were playing.___

Narrative account of tracking

Peter came out of the room just after 4:00 p.m., a few minutes after arriving from school. Standing at the door, he looked around outside at the children. Walking to the storage room, he said "Hi!" to his sister, who was talking to some girls. After a moment, Peter came out of the storage room carrying a ball, bouncing the ball as he walked. Peter looked up to see where everyone was and dropped the ball. Standing momentarily, he watched a girl playing catch by herself against the wall. When she finished, only a moment later, Peter took over her position and bounced his ball against the wall. A boy called to him from a swing. He went over to the swing and had a conversation about school until the other swing became available. Snack arrived a few moments later, so Peter left the swing in response to the caregiver's request. Walking slowly to the picnic table, he sat down, but was sent in to wash his hands. Following instructions, Peter came back after a few moments, ate a snack that was offered to him, but declined the drink. Walking around the backs of three seated children, he went to sit under a tree for some minutes as he watched the others staying at the picnic table. Another boy came up to him. They talked and walked together to the baseball diamond.

Peter's movements are tracked on the attached map.

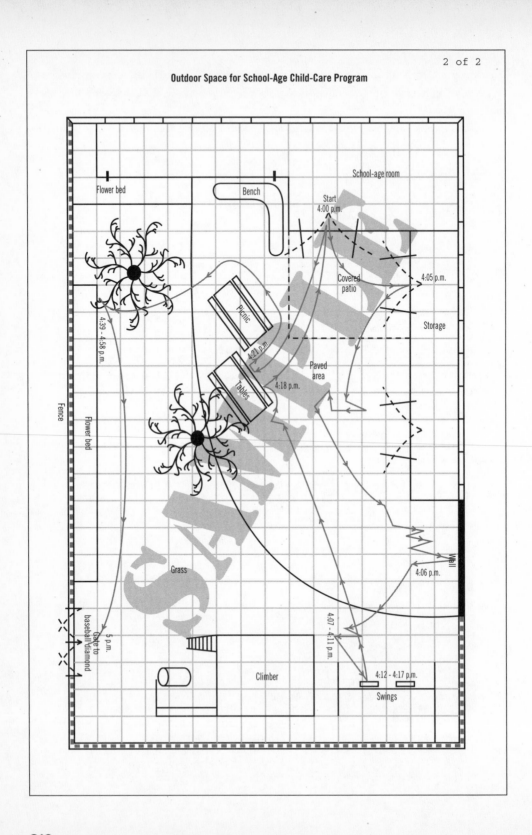

Outdoor Space for School-Age Child-Care Program

Flower bed

Bench

School-age room

Start
4:00 p.m.

Covered
patio

4:05 p.m.

Picnic

Storage

4:39 - 4:58 p.m.

4:21 p.m.

Paved
area

4:18 p.m.

Tables

Fence

Flower bed

Wall

4:06 p.m.

Grass

4:07 - 4:11 p.m.

5 p.m.
Gate to
baseball diamond

Climber

4:12 - 4:17 p.m.

Swings

Observation Sample

This sample ecomap represents the people and organizations that make up a child's world. The annotations provide further information to help the observer understand the child's relationships and their influence on his development.

What information should the observer have recorded that would have produced this ecomap?

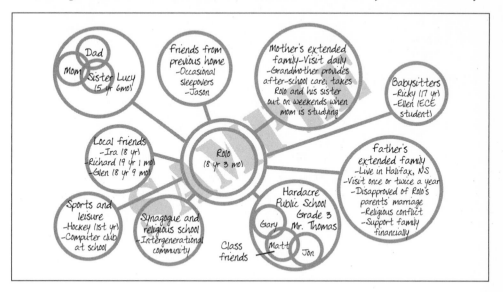

Observation Sample

This bar-line graph does not identify particular children or order the results. Such a graphic representation allows observers to make comparisons and consider trends without commenting on specific children.

Why might the observer have recorded these data? How do these data relate to the standardized norms for this age/range?

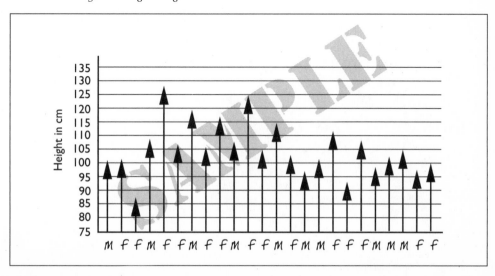

Media
Techniques

7

We think we remember the growth of our children, and we remember the high spots. The triumphs and minor tragedies. But how much we miss with the camera of our memory. For the life of a child is a kaleidoscope of changing moods, aptitudes, activities and developing personality and physical growth. Photographs help us capture these facets to enjoy ourselves and to pass on to our children and our children's children. But we must realize that the pictures we can chortle or sigh over tomorrow we have to take today.

George Hornby (1977)

If technology gets a too central role, the content and purpose of work [portfolio development] will fade out to the background...

Marja Kankaanranta (2002)

A teacher or parent will find it more informative and interesting to listen to a tape of a child reading a story than to review reading scores.

Brenda S. Engel (1990)

A video-recorder can be unobtrusive and help students in learning to observe. Here, an in-class observation opportunity is recorded so that replay can assist in making accurate inferences.

Focus Questions

1. What benefits might you have from using tape-recordings of a child's language rather than writing down what the child says?

2. What kinds of photographs of children are useful to the educator and parent?

3. What special issues of confidentiality must be recognized in using the newer technologies for recording observations?

Learning Outcomes

- Learners will identify a range of media tools for recording children's activities.

- Learners will develop strategies to ensure effective use of various technologies for observation and assessment purposes.

Features of Media Techniques

DEFINITION: Media technique

A **media technique** is any method of recording or storing observational data that is achieved by mechanical, electronic, or technical means.

An ever-widening range of methods of observing and **recording** information is becoming accessible to those working with young children. If used properly, these techniques offer the chance to gather information more quickly or effectively. They require the same degree of sensitive perception as traditional methods, because the choice of whom to observe and what to record remains the observer's decision. An observer requires varying amounts of skill to use the different media techniques. For example, the automatic functions of many cameras, digital cameras, or video cameras can mean you need little training before you start to employ them; practice is the most effective way of improving the quality of your productions.

Media techniques can provide a quicker, more efficient, more accurate, more detailed, and possibly longer-lasting and more meaningful record of the child, and one that can be more readily replayed. Not all the technologies available offer these benefits, however, so do not assume that technically assisted observations are, of themselves, preferable to narratives or samplings. Consider them a useful addition to our range of information-gathering tools.

It is tempting to let a videotaped observation "speak for itself." Even if the observation were self-explanatory when recorded, it would become increasingly meaningless if not labelled, dated, explained, summarized, and analyzed as any other significant data would be. We can choose the most effective methods of media techniques of observing and recording by acknowledging their limitations.

Recording and communicating using media tools

Here is an overview of most of the technologies currently available, what they are, and what they can offer to observers.

Type	Method	Special Recording Uses
audio tape-recording	• records sounds on magnetic tape • replays tape	• language development • rhyme and song • music: rhythm and pitch • music "corner" • sound experimentation

Type	Method	Special Recording Uses
video-tape-recording	• records audio and visual material on magnetic tape • replays tape	• social play • relationship dyads • group interactions • games with "rules" • dramatic activities • conversation • discovery learning • targeting "challenging" behaviour • process of creativity/ learning
photography: instant film	• takes photographic image using immediate processing technology	• children in action • portraits • physical skills • constructions • large artwork • children photograph each other • special achievements/ occasions • products of activity
photography: processed film	• takes photographic image using film that requires processing and printing in a laboratory	• As above—but less immediate
Internet	• World Wide Web	• access to program's web site • can have secured access to video/digitally recorded observations • virtual art gallery • program/school bulletin-board

Type	Method	Special Recording Uses
photography: digital	• records images on computer disk rather than film	• As above—but can record constantly • all activity (low cost)
CD	• most computers can "burn" text and images onto a compact disk	• more versatile and much greater storage than conventional "floppy" disk
closed-circuit television	• uses television screen at limited linked range to show video-camera images/sound • may have recording capability	• observation from a small distance (nonparticipatory) • replay for parents • replay for group discussion among children • research potential
computer: observational/recording software	• provides structure for record-keeping; • accessible for portfolio-building over time • can be accessible to parents	• observational recording systems simplify data storage and retrieval • some programs can sort and present data graphically
PowerPoint	• a computer program that uses and stores data and text in various display formats	• useful for group parent meetings: visual presentation of data; • graphic representations
personal computer	• provides electronic filing system • can be downloaded • can be accessed within classroom • parents may gain limited access	• can manage multiple files • can incorporate scanned data • various formats can be incorporated
overhead projection	• basic method of sharing information/images using transparencies/light/screen	

Type	Method	Special Recording Uses
overhead projection (continued)	• can present computer-generated images	• presentation of group data • photographic display
e-mail	• Internet-based communication system anyone with access to Internet provider can use • reasonably confidential	• quick communication with parents; • documentation of communications
intranet	• closed communication system for designated users	• up-to-date communications
computer scanner	• scans images and other paper documents to produce copied form for storage	• Storing of original children's work in accessible format • storage of letters, documents, and photos
video recording	• records moving images and sound • can replay	• children's interactions • play sequences • group action • adult–child interactions • dramatic play • most classroom-learning situations • captures action for later reply to professionals and parents • can provide opportunity to write an accurate narrative
sound systems	• strategically placed microphones • listening stations • recording capabilities	• enables observer to hear conversation across room • music/language/conversation can be analyzed later

Type	Method	Special Recording Uses
sound systems (continued)		• adult students can be led to observe particular sequences of importance • good practice for observational skill development
telephone/cellphone		• emergency communication • regular updates
video monitoring	• records sound/action without adults'/ children's knowledge	• spying on caregivers (unprofessional and unethical) • positive uses may include video recording, as above

Using media techniques

Advantages

- These methods offer detailed information not possible with traditional methods.
- The observations recorded may show more **objectivity** than those requiring the observer's description.
- A large quantity of information can be recorded quickly.
- The recordings can be analyzed by many professionals individually and collectively after the event.
- The observations can supplement and validate other traditionally recorded observations.
- Information can be shared with parents that replays the "real" situation.
- Data can be stored efficiently.

Disadvantages

- The costs can be high.
- The availability can be limited.
- Training is required.
- These methods can encourage quantity recording at the expense of well-analyzed quality recording.

- Knowledge of the recording may influence the children and alter their behaviour.
- **Confidentiality** issues are challenging to resolve.
- Storage and retrieval systems need to be established.

Ethical issues

Use of the new technologies presents some challenges related to **professionalism** and **ethics**. In the past it was much clearer who was responsible for what. Confidentiality was clear-cut; particular information was to be recorded and shared between parents and professionals only. Now personal information in the form of photographs, digital portfolios, scanned images, video-recordings, and other stored data has exploded in volume. Questions remain as to why and when this information should be made available, and to whom. Some of the technologies permit limiting access electronically, but this is not entirely reliable.

Members of the observation and assessment teams observing young children may also be more numerous than before. With parent helpers, assistants, technical resource people, and paraprofessionals, as well as the teaching team and consultants, the sheer volume of people accessing personalized data, as they are being collected, is potentially large.

Consequently, gaining permissions to collect or use those data, and ensuring their confidentiality, is not easy. Some parents might reasonably withhold their permission to feature their own children in a group video sequence because they do not want others to know about their behaviour. These people may feel the whole world is watching their children and their teachers! These concerns are not reason enough to avoid using technologies altogether to assist in record-keeping and the closer observation of children. All those involved with children must work together to develop policies to ensure confidentiality within certain parameters. Neither the educators nor the parents should feel that they are constantly being scrutinized in every aspect of their lives.

One use of video cameras causes particular problems: the hidden camera. Some education institutions use them for safety purposes or for a random documentation of activities. Although this may have become accepted practice, it does raise the invasion-of-privacy issue. Intrusively observing and recording personal information about parents, children, or educators is not acceptable. There is a fine line between educators observing children at a distance without their knowledge, and intruding in the private lives of people. As technologies develop, we can expect more ethical issues to arise. We will have to address these with proactive policy-making born of a common understanding of what is in the best interests of the children.

If parents feel the need to monitor their in-home caregivers or educators minute to minute, the two parties would appear to distrust one another. Videotaping the caregiver to ensure that a child is properly cared for is ineffective; parents will know there has been a problem only after some event. Sensational video footage has been shown on television of caregivers abusing the children in their care, and this has caused some alarm among those employing nannies. It is not recommended that parents record their in-home care providers. Instead, before hiring, parents should interview prospective caregivers, observe them in action, request and check references, and suggest a probationary period with the parents and the caregiver working together. Once a sense of trust has been established, parents can feel more comfortable about offering a contract. By that point both parties will have clear expectations. If you feel that you must videotape the caregiver and your child, explain this at the outset of offering the employment, and do it to capture some of the moments of your child's development you would otherwise miss or lose. Ideally, ask the caregiver to use the technology to make records to share with you later.

As an educator, you may encounter concerns arising from bad experiences related to recordings that make some parents particularly reticent to share information, have photographs taken, or use recording devices that collect material about their children. If your explanations of your purpose in making the recordings cannot satisfy a parent's concerns, then you must limit such documentation to the minimum necessary. As a parent you will need to build trust and confidence in the educators before you can feel comfortable sharing some information. Explain this to the teachers who are requesting your permission.

Another serious issue concerns access by other parties, governments, employers, and other powerful agencies to information about individual children and their families. While relatively unlikely, some people will particularly resist sharing personal data that might fall into "Big Brother's" hands. This fear should not be discounted, even if you consider the likelihood far-fetched. Again, limit the exchange of information and reduce documentation to only what is strictly necessary. As an educator, you may find this frustrating because you think that having more information about a child will help both you and the parents appreciate who she is and what she needs. While the authentic-assessment approach honours family information as integral to understanding the behaviour that the educator observes, parents may have valid reasons to shy away from what they believe would put them in a vulnerable position. Current technologies aggravate the problem, as they can store so much more information than was possible earlier, and unauthorized and unwanted people could gain access to it.

Photography
Uses for recording information

You will need to consider your intentions and the possibilities associated with the use of photographs. You can likely use photography in one or more of the following ways to help you perform your responsibilities or support your learning about children:

- as part of a **life book** to support a child's appreciation of his own "story"
- as evidence of a child's growth and changes in physical appearance
- to record significant life experiences and rites of passage
- to support traditionally recorded observations
- as part of a child's developmental **portfolio**
- to document stages in the process of an activity or project
- to record episodes of a child's activities
- to keep information about the products of a child's activity
- for file identification

- as a safety measure to ensure security
- to aid a child's memory of situations

General principles

Some basic guidelines might be helpful if you choose to use photography to support your child observations.

1. Choose a camera that fits your level of competence and your purpose.
2. Keep the camera loaded with film, stored safely and close to where it will be needed.
3. Always have spare film ready.
4. Choose your film and adjust your camera according to the lighting available.
5. Get lots of practice in taking pictures.
6. Get the children used to your taking photographs.
7. Be aware of your reasons for taking a photograph.
8. Design and use a consistent format for labelling and storing the photographs.
9. Ensure that every photograph is treated as a confidential document.

The basics of photography

Taking photos for use in childcare and education does not substantially differ from taking family photos. Just as you and your family will regard your photos as records of significant events or stages in your life together, so will child-care professionals taking photos of your children use those photos professionally. In making any kind of photographic record you aim to capture what you consider pertinent in a way that is accurate and easily understandable. Some people have a natural flair for photography, while for others even the "point and shoot" camera presents challenges!

Here are some suggestions for increasing your skill and artistry with this tool.

Choice of camera Many good pictures have been "lost" because of the time it took to set up a complex camera's speed, angle, and focus. Gifted and skilled photographers will get some marvellous results investing in expensive paraphernalia and lots of time, but most adults working with children want to capture a moment spontaneously. They may prefer a camera that is relatively small in size, has automatic functions and a built-in flash, and is loaded with a film intended to work both indoors and out.

With an automatic pocket camera, you can often take a perfectly adequate photograph that you might have missed with a camera with various attachments. A camera that meets the following specifications is ideal and can be used by any member of the work team:

- small, pocket-size with firmly attached cord for wearing around neck or tying to something
- automatic loading and automatic wind
- automatic shutter/exposure and automatic flash

- clear indicator for number on roll of film
- battery-tester buzzer
- clear and accurate indicator of image through lens
- relatively inexpensive

Film facts These points will help you choose the best film:

- "Professional" film is very similar to "amateur" but it may be fresher.
- Exposed, unprocessed film is vulnerable to image decay.
- Slight variations in temperature may damage film.
- High-speed films permit shutter speeds that enable you to take pictures with a hand-held camera even in dim light.
- "Slow" films have the finest grain and produce negatives of the highest contrast; they may require the use of a tripod.

The importance of lighting Adjust your technique to the lighting available. Ensure that there is sufficient light for your proposed shot and supplement it with the flash if necessary. Avoid taking photographs while looking toward the sun. The sun should be behind you, preferably not casting long, sharp shadows. The degree of light can be deceptive: light in snow and evening sun are particularly difficult to evaluate without a light meter. Indoor lighting can seem stronger than it actually is and can also make your photograph turn out in strange, unpredictable colours. You may not know this until you have your pictures processed (developed).

Instant cameras Instant cameras are frequently called Land cameras—after Edwin Land, who invented them—or Polaroid cameras—after the company that developed, manufactured, and marketed them.

Instant photographs have some obvious advantages. They enable you to

- tell immediately if you have taken an appropriate photograph without waiting for processing;
- avoid waiting for film processing and sending, delivering, or collecting film; and
- date and label the photograph immediately, and more accurately and rapidly share information with the subject of the picture, parents, and other professionals.

Against these points there are a few negative considerations:

- The cost per photograph is increased;
- The quality of the picture may not be as good;
- The photograph is thicker than a regular photo; and
- The photograph may not resist fading as well as a traditionally processed film would.

Photographic processing If you have a dark room and the appropriate equipment, you might want to develop and print your own film. More likely, you will use a commercial processing service.

A photograph that depicts a part of an activity can be a helpful addition to written observations.

The cost of service varies considerably, often according to the time you choose to wait for the processing: the faster the service, the higher the charge. Although photography experts may argue about the types of process and their results, your choice may be more a matter of personal preference than objective choice. You will also have to decide on the size of photograph, finish, and number of copies. It is a good idea to log the details of your photographs as you take them, because of the time lag between taking in the film and turning it into photographs.

Digital cameras These cameras store images on a computer disk rather than on film. No processing is required as the images can be downloaded and viewed (as well as stored) on a computer. They can also be e-mailed as "jpg" files and "burned" onto CDs. If you need conventional prints, you can make them from the stored file, either at a photo-processing lab, or at home or in the office, using an appropriate printer and photo-quality paper. Because the imaging process uses pixels, these images will not normally look as sharp when printed as copies made from conventional film.

Taking photographs for observational purposes

When to take a picture (being natural) Your purpose is likely to "capture a moment" of a child in action, to record interests, skills, relationships, learning, reactions, or some other educational consideration. Be patient; try not to attract the child's attention or disturb his activity in any way. The child's play and learning experience are always more important than the actual photograph. You cannot record the essence of the action by trying to direct what the children are doing for the sake of the camera. If you start to interfere, you become intrusive and work against the professed philosophy of early childhood education.

To achieve **naturalness**, to record a child's interactions within a natural setting, there is a longer list of what *not* to do than what *to* do. It may be helpful for the children to access "play" cameras or even to try their own photography. Their familiarity with the technology may help them accept your use of the camera around them more casually.

Capturing natural expressions Getting down to the child's level is very important in understanding what the child is doing. The child's eye level is exactly where you need to be; that angle allows you the most open view of the child's expression and allows you direct eye contact, which can help personalize the moment, if that is what you wish. Less appealing is an angle that looks down at the child and distorts the action rather than showing it as the child sees it. You may have to lie on the floor, squat, kneel, sit on a child's chair, or adopt some other uncomfortable position.

When children try to pose, they tend to overact. If you take several pictures within a short period of time, you are more likely to get a useful shot. At moments of discovery and engrossment, the children are less likely to be influenced by your presence, and the result should be more successful.

Recording child development To record child development, take regular and deliberate, rather than occasional or random, photographs of each child in your care. You might like to record a chart of your photographs so that you can check whether you have selected each child at regular intervals.

Early use of photography by child-care professionals frequently employed a static, impersonal, and posed technique. There are more effective ways of recording growth information than standing the child against a marked and measured wall for a mug shot; you can do that with a tape measure or a scale. What you want to do is take photographs of the child when she is involved in typical activities.

Using photographs to supplement other observational recordings can be helpful because they can give a more real sense of "who" the child is when you review the data.

Photographs for record-keeping You may wish to establish a photographic record system that uses a predetermined labelling system. Include the child's name and age, the date of the photograph, the names of other children/adults in the photograph, and the situation depicted. For observational purposes, you might have the photograph mounted on an accompanying form with additional information on the **context** of the photo. Try to avoid writing directly on the back of a photo, as the photo suffers from being handled and the writing may rub off or show through on the front. You could apply self-adhesive labels to the photos if you wish to cut down the bulk of paperwork, but even a preprinted label will not save the picture's being lost in a file folder with other information. If you have available shelf space, you could keep the photographs in albums, one for each child, with labels below each picture. You can also keep the photos filed in special boxes designed for file index cards and present them as wonderful gifts to the children's parents when their children leave the agency.

A sample photographic observation with contextual information can be found on page 240.

Video-Recording
Uses for recording information

There are a number of purposes for videotaping the child's activities or environment:

- to replay particular scenes when time allows for greater analysis
- to share information about the child's development with parents
- to create a long-term record of a child's progress
- to assist in observing groups of children so that attention can concentrate on each child's involvement and interactions
- for research
- to record important happenings or rites of passage in the child's life so that the child himself can review significant parts of his own life
- to support observations recorded in more traditional ways
- to recreate the child's activities and interactions to support a multidisciplinary evaluation
- to assist in evaluating the child's **environment**

The complexity of some play activity can be a challenge to record. These school-age children play a game involving rules. Video-recordings can capture such activity better than any other method.

General principles

You can gain skill in video-recording quite quickly once you get started.

1. Survey the market of available recording equipment, identify the features you need, and consider your finances.
2. Familiarize yourself with your recording device and its functions.
3. Allow plenty of time and tape for practice.
4. Build your vocabulary to include video terminology.
5. Desensitize the children who will be your subjects before making recordings you intend to keep. You might have the children actively participate in video-making.
6. Determine your purpose for recording.
7. Avoid **subjective** shooting that centres on what is "cute" or on children "acting up" for the camera.
8. Investigate possibilities for editing your video-recordings.
9. Design and use a format for labelling and storing the videotapes.
10. Ensure that every videotape is considered a confidential document.

The basics of video-recording

Some beginner's tips to get you started:

- Read and use the owner's manual so that you can appreciate the camera's features.
- Try using a tripod to hold the camera or brace yourself against a firm object to avoid a bouncing effect recorded on the tape.
- Use an autofocus or practise focusing manually. Be aware that the camera will focus on the nearest object when set on autofocus.
- Practise using the zoom to accustom yourself to the feeling that you are lurching back and forth, but do not overuse this feature.
- Compose your videotaping so that the context or background is clear before you go into a close-up.
- Set or move the camera at different angles in relation to the subject to create more interesting images.
- Use your camcorder to record movement that cannot be captured by a still camera.
- Hold static shots, particularly at the beginning and end of a sequence.
- When panning across an area (left to right or right to left), move smoothly to direct the viewer's attention, and limit the angle of movement to 90 degrees.
- Follow the children's action at their level for a more insightful view of their world.
- The pause button enables you to exercise a form of in-process editing. Practise using it.
- Try to capture meaningful sequences of activity while being aware of the simultaneous audio-recording.

Videotapes Blank tapes are not all the same. They vary in length, cost, quality, and type. Most of the guides to videotaping recommend using name brands sold by reputable dealers and buying them when their price is lowest. Alternatively, read a video magazine or consumer report for the "best buy."

Handle videotapes carefully. Use fresh tapes, if possible, because VCRs tend to wear out tapes. Protect tapes from extreme temperatures and humidity. Keep them clean, in their sleeves or cases, stored fully wound and vertical, and away from magnetic fields.

Video skills To learn how to make video-recordings, you may want to read "how to" manuals, but your starting point will probably be trial and error. Awareness of the most common mistakes will not necessarily help you avoid them, because you need to see how they come about before you can rectify them. Familiarize yourself with the functions of the camcorder on a try-out basis. Short of dropping the camcorder or applying physical force to it, you are unlikely to do it any harm.

In *Learn to Make Videos in a Weekend*, Roland Lewis suggests that the 14 basic skills of video can be learned in two days. He describes the sequence of holding and moving the camera through lighting and composition to editing, adding titles and soundtracks. Another good reference is John Hedgecoe's *Complete Guide to Video: The Ultimate Manual of Video Techniques and Equipment*, which is written for the newcomer and provides helpful detail.

Additional camcorder features

- **Age subtitles:** It is possible to program some camcorders to memorize an individual's birth date so that her actual age can appear on the video.

- **Date/time:** Camcorders usually record the date and time of the recording on the screen.

- **Title superimposer:** A memory function in the camcorder can record a title or picture over a scene.

- **Self-timer:** A timer allows the camera operator to "get into the action" for participant observation.

- **Insert edit:** New recordings can be made over the old with a sophisticated, dedicated insert-edit facility that you can pre-set to the point at which you want to add the new material.

- **Macro close-up/zoom:** Camcorders allow for varying degrees of close-ups. On some, this function can be controlled automatically.

- **External mike socket:** This feature can help picking up sound when the fixed microphone is too far away to pick up language.

- **Audio dub:** The recorded sound can be replaced with a narrative or voice-over on some models.

- **Auto exposure:** The iris diaphragm automatically adjusts the size of the aperture to suit the available lighting.

Making videotapes for observational purposes

When to make a video-recording As you develop your skill, you will start to see opportunities for recording the activities of the children in your care. You may find the flow of their action makes it difficult to decide when and what to record; the amount of time you have may well dictate your choice. It can be a challenge to maintain your supervisory role, participate in the activity, and also record what is happening. You can solve this problem if you have systems of shared care, time designated for recording, or a small, undemanding group of children. Somehow educators who are committed to videotaping usually manage to do it!

You may want to record some of the more domestic and routine elements of the children's day. In only a short time, these routines evolve as the children develop, and mere memories of them can be lost. Recording typical behaviours may be as rewarding as seeking new advances in development. The dated record will help you see developmental changes over a period of time. Capturing children's **spontaneous play** can be the most revealing and meaningful subject of videotaping. You can shoot what happens without any fuss by having the camcorder available in the children's play area. Indoors and out, you can record a variety of play sequences and social interactions.

Video-recordings may centre on the activity of one child. You will seldom record that child in isolation; she will usually be involved with others. If you make a videotape, you must decide how to pick out the individual child's behaviour from the general flow. Knowing how to edit forms the foundation of effective individual record-keeping.

What video-recordings can highlight Here are some suggestions for the types of observations you could record on videotape:

- any of the features of audio-recordings (see pages 233–234)
- play patterns
- body language/eye contact
- program effectiveness
- use of space
- group interactions and behaviour
- gross motor skills
- manipulative skills
- children's responses to activities
- discovery and curiosity
- experimentation with objects and materials
- mood changes
- independence skills or autonomy
- process of play and learning

American Sign Language (ASL) is the form of **sign language** used most commonly by people who are considered deaf (this does not always mean people who are completely nonhearing). Observing and recording the communication of children who use sign language is even more challenging than observing children who use spoken language!

To record sign language and other gestures, videotape the child and transcribe the communication. You can also write a full narrative description that includes all the child's gestures as well as any facial expressions and changes in posture; you will likely have to devise a coding mechanism in order to capture all the detail. Or you could record the use of sign language with a commentary that included the meaning of the signing rather than in a narrative that described the signing in full.

- products of activity
- creative activity and artwork in progress
- social groupings
- parenting styles
- separation or other anxieties
- any other aspect of development that can be revealed by other observation methods

Videotapes for record-keeping Video-recordings can form a history of the children's development, activities, or festivals. You can store the tapes, labelled and filed vertically in chronological order.

An educator's videotapes that record the activity of groups of children may require editing, but they can be very useful for program-planning for the group. These tapes can be stored simply and accessed by staff when necessary. They may also provide very good teaching material for student educators and caregivers.

Most important is record-keeping of such tapes for the individual child. Keep these recordings with, or alongside, an observation file or portfolio, and consider them an integral part of your observation and assessment system. To make these individual tapes, you must have an effective editing facility.

Confidentiality and professionalism must apply to the use of videotaped observations. You may need to use a permission form that addresses video-recordings specifically (see page 9).

Labelling and dating are often difficult with videotapes because they offer little space for detail. A reference card showing the same counter numbering as the tape itself could accompany the video in its sleeve or box.

Videotape Recording Log

Name:		Group:	
Date	Counter #	Context	Comment

Audio-Recording
Uses for recording information

You may have any of the following purposes in making audio-recordings:

- to support any traditionally recorded observation
- to record the educator's **narrative observation** of a child's behaviour
- to record a child's or children's verbal communications
- to facilitate close analysis of a language sample
- to record a child's or children's explorations and production of sound and music
- to keep records of a child's language, music, or reading skill development
- to communicate with parents in sharing direct recordings or anecdotal observations
- as part of a child's developmental portfolio
- for the student teacher to learn about the language, music, humour, and thinking skills of children

General principles

The following steps will help you get started with audio-recording:

1. Consider your needs and purchase a tape-recorder that is resilient and portable.
2. Set up the tape-recorder in a convenient place and use its portable feature to go where the children are when necessary.
3. Give yourself lots of time to practise tape-recording.
4. Familiarize the children with tape-recording and playback.
5. Organize time for replay and analysis.
6. Determine your purpose in recording.
7. Consider the possibilities of editing your recordings using specialized equipment.
8. Accept failures.
9. Design and use a format for labelling and storing the audio-recordings.
10. Ensure that every audiotape is considered a confidential document.

The basics of audio-recording

Some beginner's tips:

- An extended microphone with a jack will pick up sounds more clearly—try placing a pair of microphones at least 9 inches (23 cm) apart.
- Avoid constant rewinding and re-recording as this can stretch and distort the tape.
- Use the pause button for in-process editing.
- Set up your recordings in an area that minimizes sounds of background activity.
- Use a Dolby noise–reduction system if one is built into the recorder for better, clearer replay.
- Keep tapes and recorders in a dry place, in moderate temperatures, and away from magnetic fields.
- If the tape becomes unravelled, try to rewind it with a hexagon-shaped pencil, but be aware that damaged tapes can jam in the recorder.
- If a tape does get jammed in the recorder, do not try to force it out. Take the recorder to a dealer.
- For educators working in well-designed environments with sound systems, try linking a microphone with a recording device.

Choice of tape-recorder You may be familiar with a range of audio-recording machines. Reel-to-reel, cartridge, and cassette systems are available, the cassette being the most popular. The cassette protects the tape and makes threading simpler. Small portable cassette-recorders are most suitable for an observer.

Here are some features to look for in a basic tape-recorder:

- easy hook-up to microphones/sound system
- resilient, robust design
- battery- or power cord-operated
- simple operation
- a counter system
- Dolby noise reduction
- easy access to repair and servicing

Batteries can be expensive, so look into rechargeable batteries. If you have a machine that can operate on both batteries and a power cord, you can save battery power by plugging the unit into a wall socket when rewinding and replaying.

Choice of tape   More expensive tapes are often the best. To compare quality, try out a variety of tapes when they are offered at a discount. Avoid the cheaper copies of the well-known manufacturers' tapes. The brand-name tapes are usually superior because of their high-frequency response, high output, consistency of magnetic characteristics, freedom from squeal, absence of stretching, and accuracy of sound reproduction. However, they too vary in quality.

Set-up   The set-up of your recorder and microphones is important. You will sometimes miss opportunities for recordings because you are not ready, and you can limit these occasions if you make a point of being already set up to record.

Laboratory schools and agencies with built-in sound systems that allow students and teachers to "listen in" will be at an advantage. Not all of these systems are built for recording, so you might want to check into this. A good sound system has microphones a little above the children's heads, fairly evenly spread across areas where the children are active. Observers listen from a distance, usually from a one-way mirrored observation booth with speakers or headphones. Observers can select the microphone they wish to use and pick up the sounds they want. If your school or agency has an additional recording facility as well, you can store a lot of useful information this way.

You can use dangling microphones if you are doing straightforward recording. One mike might give you a "flat" sound-recording, while two or more give a stereophonic quality and can record a group of children more effectively. A mike propped up on a table usually picks up too much white noise. When the children move around, you might try the reporter's technique of following them with a hand-held microphone.

Making audio-recordings for observational purposes

When to make an audio-recording   You will need to decide what to record according to your purpose. The children may become so familiar with the tape-recorder that it does not bother them. You can desensitize them to the equipment by allowing them to record and replay by themselves, or by sharing your recordings with younger children. The replay may elicit squeals of delight from the preschoolers, but younger children may be confused when you replay their language.

You might like to make an audio-recording at many times during a child's day. Try not to miss the normal, average, and domestic aspects as well as the more structured peak-programming times. Be prepared to record spontaneously, and also acknowledge that you will have to be patient. Here are some suggestions on what to record:

- circle times
- greetings, separations, and reunions
- group-singing
- experimentation with sounds and instruments
- book corner—conversation, reading, storytelling
- spontaneous play activities
- crib sounds
- interactions with adults
- sociodramatic play
- imitative play
- transitions
- bathroom routines
- individual singing or reciting rhymes
- music activities
- hearing children read
- bilingual children's conversation
- toddlers' emerging language
- problem-solving activities
- outdoor play
- outings, picnics
- at home with parents/siblings/friends
- formal assessments
- examples of school-agers' jokes
- portfolio-assessment meetings

What audio-recordings can highlight While this list is not comprehensive or ordered, it offers some ideas of what you might look for in analyzing your recordings:

- pronunciation
- reading strategies
- MLUs (mean length of utterances)
- pitch discrimination
- experimentation with oral-sound production
- rhythm of speech/length of phrase
- accent/cultural patterns
- phraseology/speech patterns

- use of parts of speech/grammatical errors
- communication difficulties
- egocentric speech/egocentricity
- expression of ideas
- overextensions
- misunderstandings
- social relationships
- humour and incongruities
- moral views and attitudes
- social role play
- developmental level of thinking skills
- demonstration of feelings
- solitary activity/isolation/talking to self
- memory
- sequencing of stories or events
- imagination
- use of rhyme
- musicality
- concentration length
- interests
- play level
- fantasy or realism
- logic
- friendships and peer interactions
- imitation or repetition
- conversation with adults
- sibling interactions

Audiotapes for record-keeping Like any other observational material, audio-recordings must remain confidential. You may wish to have individual and group recordings. Remember that individual children's records are more effective in helping you determine developmental levels and programs in response to children's various needs and skills. Where you have the recordings of a group, you will find it almost impossible to edit the tapes for individual files. Instead, you could write a narrative account from the tape. Although it may be difficult to get complex language down on paper, you can replay the tape many times, and the resulting document would capture all the detail.

If you can organize taping so that you put into the record the child's "own" tape, you will gain some chronologically recorded bits of information for that one child. Use the counter and write down the numbers to keep track of where you are on the tape.

Tapes must always be labelled, dated, and accompanied by a numbered log. Keep them at room temperature in their boxes, having rewound them. Tapes may be kept in the child's portfolio, or, because of their bulk, in a storage system near the portfolio.

Computers and Recording and Storing Data
Uses of computers for recording and storing data

Computers can be used to retain data from observations, in various readable and presentable formats. Any of the available word-processing programs allows for easy input and storage, so you can retrieve and display the records quickly or print them in a wide range of styles. They also facilitate the addition of new data as part of an integral record (always a problem with handwritten notes) as well as the insertion of changes. One concern here is that it may not be obvious that these additions and insertions were made to the original recording later. Work around this drawback by using "read-only" protection and passwords to control access.

Files can be sorted alphabetically and/or by date. Mail management programs such as Microsoft Outlook allow you to send documents electronically between locations.

CDs and floppy disks Computer files are stored on the system's hard drive. If you need copies on other computers, you can either send them electronically (see above) or copy them to floppy or compact disks. The former is a straightforward exercise; the latter requires that the computer have CD-write capability.

Managing large quantities of observational data The storage capacity of most modern computers is huge—20 times or more what it was even a decade ago—and can be expanded if necessary. You can also store documents on floppy or compact disks. This means you can store a massive archive of records without paper files. By using a properly planned system of folders and files in the computer, you can locate materials easily and quickly, controlling access to them with passwords to ensure security. A further precaution is to "back up" all computer records by copying them to disk and keeping those disks in a separate location.

Software programs All computers come pre-loaded with word-processing programs (Word and WordPerfect are the most common) and spreadsheet software (Excel). Other widely used programs include Microsoft Access (for databases), Microsoft PowerPoint (for presentations), and Microsoft Outlook (for e-mail management). Educators and parents can use these to document their observations and their most necessary information in the form of more traditional methodologies, such as narratives, samplings, and checklists. Even complex portfolios can be managed using these tools.

Some purpose-designed software programs also meet the needs of observers and researchers. For example, the Creative Curriculum has a new integrated assessment system based on their developmental continuum, which has a software-reporting tool, CC-PORT (2002). Another software package available through a weblink, **earlylearner.net**, makes it possible to document observations, document portfolios, and recommend activities and support resources. This is available to schools and child-care centres;

another version is available for parents. Research into the effectiveness of these kinds of software still needs to be done; they look promising but have not been tested. Whether or not the expense of the software is justified is another matter—costs are usually cited on a per-child basis.

For research, some people have found software programs that do more than store information. Some programs can actually manage data, sort it, and produce printouts that can add meaning to data collection. NUD*IST—yes, that's its name!—is one of these programs. However, it requires complex coding of qualitative data and tedious inputting. You may find the results useful for some projects once you collect enough material to warrant investing in the program.

Scanners Scanners let you save documents and images on the computer's hard drive as facsimiles of the originals. This is extremely useful as a means of retaining a child's file copies of letters, forms, work samples, and photos.

Sharing Information with Parents Using Technology

The guidelines for communication remain the same with whatever media you're using for transmission of data. Keep the following points in mind:

- Frame all communications positively and focus on a child's progress.
- Avoid communicating anything through technology that you wouldn't say to a parent's face.
- Ask parents what they want to discuss or see.
- Remember that communication is a two-way process; you need to receive as well as send information.
- Make face-to-face communications a priority; technology should not take you away from personal interactions.
- Ensure privacy and limit access to any personal information.
- Make sure that you have permission to collect and store all information.
- Consider ethical considerations more seriously, not more casually.
- Personalize the information you transmit rather than send cold data.
- Provide the opportunity for parents' feedback and family discussion.
- Ensure that you include all team members in the communication circle.
- Communicate regularly during, rather than at the end of, a major project.
- Avoid comparing any child with another or commenting on the other children.
- Explain the purpose of your observations, record-keeping, and assessments.
- Present the information and your perspective professionally.
- Document the parents' responses.
- Develop your ongoing plan with the parents.

Audiotape Recording Log

Child's name: _____ D.O.B.: _____

Date	Counter #	Sequence	Narrative documents Yes No	Comment

Summary

Each year, new technologies and modifications of existing ones appear and become more accessible to the mass market. We can be dazzled by them and want to use them in our programs for children as novelties. For observation and recording purposes they may offer us significant advancements beyond traditional paper-and-pencil methods. Yet we need to use them carefully and spend money on them wisely, so that the medium does not take over the children's activity and our time as educators. Children must remain our focus!

All the media techniques available obscure the "real time" activity of the children who exist in the here and now. At the same time, traditional approaches using narrative, sampling, or other documentation cannot match the amount and quality of recording of children's activity possible through these newer technologies. We need to learn about what and how to record, and to acquire some understanding of the potential of each technology. Try to learn these skills outside your actual observation time as educator rather than devote precious program time to it.

Recordings made by any media are just that—recordings. They are not really observations and they are not interpretations of a child's activity. We must not let the technology "speak for itself"; educators must narrate what they record, find ways of categorizing the data, and develop ways to analyze what they have collected. The tools merely allow us to gather more information about children. We don't learn more if we don't do something with the information!

Simple audio-recordings can offer educators detail of conversation unparalleled by other methods. They also allow us to for replay the material and make sense of what we hear. Perhaps even more detailed, the video sequences of activity offer such a quantity of data that they may leave us no further ahead in our interpretation than when we were observing those same sequences in real time. At the same time they can allow us to focus on one type of behaviour or on one child at a time, by replaying a scene over and over again. We can gain insights this way that would otherwise be lost because we cannot process all that information as it actually happens.

Computers enable parents and professionals to record information quickly, easily, and accessibly. They can also allow parents and other team members access to that information through the same technology. Through video facilities linked to the computer we can gain a limited-access view of the children while the parent is at work or at home and the child is in childcare or in school. This suggests a new type of parents' involvement.

Digital portfolio systems are now being developed that move our authentic assessment process into more new territory. We still have to consider whether we are using technology to fulfill our needs, or using it simply because it is there. We have yet to determine how much it enhances our observation, documentation, assessment, and curriculum design.

The new media present us with new ethical, professional, and personal issues, in the form of new twists on concerns about confidentiality, questions regarding access to data, and the question of who takes responsibility for the storage and later dissemination or destruction of the records. Whether or not "outside" professionals such as consultants should have access to recordings has not been established; the boundaries need to be drawn. When personal information is recorded, risks always arise regarding its inappropriate use—what are the ethical criteria associated with these technologies?

This chapter has discussed the types and potential uses of various technologies. It is hoped that readers will want to practise using the various means of recording available to them and to develop their own strategies for their use with or for children in their care. Financial considerations may limit their incorporation into all programs; some schools and child-care programs have found ways of overcoming this through budgeting for specific funds, applying for grants, or using their own hardware. We are in the very earliest stages of using these technologies to record children's behaviour. Many educators use cameras for portraiture only rather than activity. We have yet to develop ways of making technologies fit our purpose, or to actually design or alter existing technologies to meet our needs as observers. Finding effective means of recording, of sifting through large quantities of material, and of analyzing the data so produced will be an ongoing challenge.

Key Terms

confidentiality

context

environment

ethical issues

life book

media technique

narrative observation

naturalness

objectivity

portfolio

recording (technological)

sign language

spontaneous play

subjective

Weblinks

http://electronicportfolios.com
Information on constructing and developing electronic portfolios.

www.geocities.com/Athens/Olympus/7123/camera.html
Tips for using digital cameras in the classroom.

Observation Sample

This photographic record could be put in a photo album or in the child's portfolio. The comments provide a context to explain the significance of the picture.

In what ways might you use photographs to document the behaviour of children in a preschool program?

Name: <u>Ashley (second from right)</u>   Age: <u>5 years, 7 months</u>

Date: <u>May 27, 2004</u>

Others represented: <u>(from left) Kayleigh, Elizabeth, Lashonda</u>

Situation: <u>On the bus on the way to an outing at the Museum of Science</u>

Comments: Ashley tends to be a loner. Her home life is unsettled (her parents were recently divorced and her grandmother, whom she is very close to, is quite ill), and this seems to have contributed to her reluctance to form close relationships with the other children. Elizabeth, who lives next door to Ashley, sometimes invites Ashley to be part of her group. Perhaps because she was excited about the trip, Ashley let herself be drawn into the fun with the other girls on the bus, as seen in this photo. Observation of Ashley's interests may help her teachers find other activities to draw her into social interactions with other children.

Observer: <u>   Josh</u>

Portfolios

When carefully structured, portfolios display the range of a child's work. Above all they integrate instruction and assessment.

Samuel J. Meisels (1993)

Teachers are moving to performance and portfolio assessment because they are seeking information about the child's development and learning in all domains and content areas. They want a longitudinal portrait of the child and documentation of the change, rather than assessment of a limited range of skills at a particular time.

Sue C. Wortham (1998)

When children take the lead in selecting the contents for their portfolio, their interests become vested and their motivation to learn more intrinsic.

Margaret B. Puckett (1994)

Portfolios document a child's development for the benefit of both educators and the family. A visual presentation of a child's portfolio can help parents understand the assessment, especially if they speak English as a second language.

Features of Portfolios

DEFINITION: Portfolio

A **portfolio** is a record-keeping device in which observations, health and social information, test results, work samples, and other significant information about an individual child are stored. The system enables educators to keep records over a period of time, add items as necessary, evaluate the child's performance, evolve plans to meet the child's needs, and review progress.

While the child study is undertaken primarily to support a student's learning, the portfolio is done to help a practising teacher find out more about the child, for the child's benefit. In spite of this difference, they have many features in common.

Performance assessment, authentic assessment, and portfolios

Performance assessment is a simple and straightforward practice, with a philosophy behind it that needs to be understood. Performance assessment depends on the child's demonstrating or performing something that shows her understanding of it. It is a way to "show what you know" through demonstration. This way the educator can appreciate the knowledge, skills, and dispositions (attitudes) that the child has gained. Rather than being tested on that knowledge in a more formal way, the child shows her ability as she goes about her day playing and learning. The teacher's task is to document these performances in a way that is meaningful. This may involve observing and recording, videotaping, or keeping product samples.

Performance assessment is a form of **authentic assessment**. The assessment is authentic (or genuine) because it occurs naturally and without stress as part of everyday experience. An educator applies authentic assessment appropriately when the child's learning experience is also authentic, when the child is self-directed and the process of her learning is considered more important than its products or test results. When developmentally appropriate practice lies at the core of curriculum design, then developmentally appropriate assessment must be aligned with it.

Authentic assessment can take many different forms depending on what the educator thinks is genuine. It is in the interest of the children, families, and the educators to agree on the child's learning experiences and the way those will be assessed. If the educators and parents are comfortable with a philosophy and practice that is developmentally and culturally appropriate to that child, they will want to keep within that philosophy to measure how well the children are performing.

Some educators use the term *performance assessment*; the teachers of older children probably use it more often. They may work with the children to develop ways to show what they know. However, the broader term of *authentic assessment* is used within childcare and early-years education. It includes all the informal data-collection methods discussed in this book, and especially **portfolio assessment**.

Using portfolios as an assessment approach offers an even broader view of the child and her abilities because it looks beyond separate observations and bits and pieces of information. Portfolios offer a **holistic**, or all-round, understanding of the child's development within the context of "who she is." The portfolio itself becomes an assessment after the data have been gathered. The adults, and the children themselves—if they are mature enough—reflect on the materials and analyze the learning behind them. This should lead to education and developmental decision-making that benefits the child.

Why some educators are moving to strengthen authentic assessment

There is a movement in education that values standardized tests and considers them preferable to portfolio assessment, or to authentic assessment generally. Proponents believe standardized tests offer comparisons at a program level and support healthy competition between children. These supporters think that standardized measures will increase performance levels, improve accountability, and offer a fair way of measuring performance.

This is not true. As Sacks states in Standardized Minds (2000), "Evidence strongly suggests that standardized testing flies in the face of recent advances in our understanding of how people learn to think and reason. Repeatedly, in the research conducted over the past few years, especially in the grade school arena (K–12), one finds evidence that traditional tests reinforce passive rote learning of facts and formulas, quite contrary to the critical thinking skills many educators now believe schools should be encouraging." Although Sacks confines his remarks to the school system, there is no reason to think that the narrow approach of standardized testing is any less abhorrent for younger children!

Later in his book Sacks recommends an approach to assessment that counters the problems entrenched in standardized measurement: authentic assessment. Many educators and researchers support authentic ways of assessing learning. Among them is Gardner, who offers insights into the multiple ways of being smart—the Multiple Intelligences theory. Chard and Katz have researched Italy's **Reggio Emilia's** documentation process, which is a living monument to authentic learning and documentation.

It is well known that education in Finland is of a high calibre. Finland is one of several countries that lead in exemplary practice in both child-care and education. Pedagogy there binds together learning and assessment, both of which are integral to successful authentic assessment practice. Finland's approach incorporates assessment in a way that complements the authentic learning that occurs in the classroom. Many countries—especially Finland—demonstrate and profess a confidence in authentic assessment that is solid and that emphasizes a new look at the ecological context of development and overall learning.

Authentic assessment is often seen as a reaction to the biases and difficulties embedded in more "traditional" approaches, or what we think of as formal assessment. However, authentic assessment existed long before the testing movement or examination boards. Skills or knowledge acquired in school or everyday life were "tested" when the learner had to demonstrate her new competence—this was in fact authentic assessment! An apprentice carpenter demonstrates his success by his cabinet-making, house-building, or creating sample objects that highlight his skills. Traditionally, a child's reading ability was monitored by a demonstration—reading a story. More complex learning might require more detailed observations, demonstrations, and perhaps conversation with the learner about any underlying concepts or theories. Mathematical problems, scientific experiments, or even philosophical ideas were assessed using methods that fitted the kind of learning. These might include examining the products of the learner's work, listening to debates between learners, evaluating learners' pieces of writing, reviewing presentations or demonstrations, and observing the candidates in action. Educators used, authentically, whatever method allowed their learners to show what they knew or demonstrate the skills they had acquired.

In the United States, approaches to authentic assessment vary from state to state and even within each state. The so-called reform movement and believers in back-to-basics hold that standardized testing improves standards and accountability; their stronghold is sizeable. However, there are regions where authentic-assessment practices are strong. It seems ironic that the back-to-basics followers have moved further away from the authentic assessment that occurred before educators meddled in it with pseudo-scientific testing methods.

Canadian approaches to authentic assessment vary just as much as they do in the United States, being strongest in childcare and early education. Some boards of education in Canadian provinces and territories have adopted forms of **outcome-based education (OBL)** along with **performance assessments**. Other forms of authentic assessment can be found through the education system, practices differing even within the same school. Only where there is institutional support can authentic-assessment approaches be really successful.

The term "authentic assessment" is relatively recent, coined perhaps 25 years ago. But before our present-day educators, there were Montessori, Froebel, and Steiner, among many others, who supported observational approaches to understanding how and what children learn. The actual measures taken within their philosophical approaches lean towards genuine and real-life performances.

Barrett has shifted the authentic-assessment process into a new technology-assisted generation. Companies even market trademarked portfolio systems—such as Focused Portfolios and the Work Sampling System—developed for those teachers who want a ready-to-use process for documentation. So that authentic approaches to learning and assessment are easily recognizable, names like "The Mindful School," "Total Talent Portfolios," "School-wide Enrichment Model," and "Essential Schools" are coined, denoting the kind of authenticity each represents. Each of these names is intended to conjure a vision of authenticity and exemplary practice. In another irony, the systems that these companies recommend may lead educators to impose structures that actually disallow the flexible authenticity that was their selling point!

Educators lean towards one assessment approach or another for many reasons, including

- resources
- experience and exposure to different approaches
- administrative requirements
- pressure from colleagues/peer support
- parental perspectives
- professional-development opportunities
- imitation of peers
- time
- space
- workload
- preparation/assessment schedule
- beliefs about learning
- beliefs about testing
- quality and amount of feedback from all stakeholders
- accountability within institution
- external accountability

Educators who start to develop, or continue developing, authentic assessments tend to demonstrate the following characteristics. They

- are motivated
- can articulate their beliefs about authentic learning clearly
- are independent
- are practitioners who reflect on their role as educators
- work cooperatively with parents and team members
- find time for what they think is important
- develop their own systems for managing data
- value critical thinking
- exhibit role-model dispositions they want the children to demonstrate
- facilitate the environment without dominating it

- share power effectively
- advocate authentic assessment

Educators who use authentic assessment methods do so because they

- dislike standardized tests and consider their use unfair
- regard authentic assessment as part of authentic learning
- may have had negative personal-assessment experiences themselves
- understand how children learn
- focus on children's success—perhaps by being less competitive
- recognize the damage done by labelling a child
- contextualize learning
- consider formative assessment more important than summative assessment
- want to gather information from multiple sources
- consider individual programming important
- consider conceptual, broad real-world learning central to their philosophy (rather than narrow memory-based skills)

We can appreciate that a move to portfolio assessment, or any other kind of authentic assessment, is challenging. The shift means change at the philosophical level as authentic assessment is an integral part of authentic learning.

We know that changing surface practices are unlikely to work effectively. On one level, having a mosaic of educational practices within one institution may sound desirable, as such an array might reflect the separate beliefs of each educator. However, only a cohesive approach, along with a shared philosophy of learning and assessment, can produce a community of successful learners within any place of learning, be it a school or a child-care environment. An authentic approach is vital. Each educator might follow a different authentic process, within a shared understanding system-wide about how learning should be assessed and evaluated. Likely that system would also use a portfolio process, although some teachers might favour other means of documentation that include observations and demonstrations.

The portfolio philosophy

KEY FEATURES: Portfolio

- contains a variety of observations, samples, and contextual information
- documents development over a period of time
- considers development an individual and holistic process
- analyzes and assesses development sympathetically within the individual's context
- mostly naturalistic

A portfolio is much more than a collection of information. It is an attitude and a process. While it is relatively easy to describe the potential contents of a portfolio, it is more challenging to generate enthusiasm for the concept of portfolio evaluation and record-keeping and to get each member of the team to participate in the process of data collection.

Several principles underlie the portfolio philosophy:

- The process of a child's experience is important and individual to that child.

- The most effective way to record information about a child's experience is to observe the child in a natural setting—that is, at home, in a child-care centre, or at school.

- Information about a child is most usefully supplied by parents, teachers, caregivers, and others who play a role in the child's life.

- Portfolios provide the opportunity to record data about a child's experiences and evidence of the products of his work.

- Portfolios enable the parents, teachers, and caregivers in a child's life to be involved with both the formative assessment (in process) and the summative assessment (at the end of the process) of her performance, skills, and competence, based on a valid collection of data.

- Portfolios encourage teamwork and cooperation among all those concerned in the care and growth of the child, in support of meeting his needs over the years.

- Portfolios offer the possibility of recording family health and contextual information, which puts the behavioural data into a framework.

- Portfolios encourage the child's involvement in the record-keeping process and selection of items for inclusion, a sense of responsibility and ownership for his behaviour, and a sense of control in determining the education experience in the long term.

- Portfolios are flexible in meeting the requirements of those adults caring for the child as they can contain various types of information.

- Portfolios may include input from additional professionals, as desirable; psychologists, social workers, and others may add to the portfolio to expand the information base and frequently they can validate the findings of the primary caregivers and parents.

- Portfolios encourage professional **accountability** by providing documentary evidence of evaluation processes and program-planning.

With practice, teachers and caregivers will see the value of the portfolio process. Those who say they observe all the time but do not record their observations will recognize that portfolios can help them do their jobs more effectively with the investment of only a little time and effort.

Furnished with information from a variety of sources, the teacher may be better equipped to understand children's needs and to see how their families and contexts should determine how those needs are met. Agencies that subscribe to the portfolio philosophy usually find that the practice supports close work with parents and a cooperative style of teaching. At a time when parents, boards of education, and other administrative bodies are demanding greater professional accountability, the portfolio provides good documentation of evaluation, planning, and practice.

Contents of a portfolio

CHILD DEVELOPMENT FOCUS

Portfolios may assist in observing, recording, and analyzing
- holistic development
- the process and products of development
- a child's culture and context in which she is developing
- a child's development in relation to the **norm** or goal achievement

Teachers and caregivers vary in their philosophies regarding record-keeping. The portfolio approach is flexible enough that all practitioners can adapt it to their needs.

The following list suggests the items a portfolio might contain. Those employing the system will want to choose those elements that suit them, their skills, the agency or school, and the child.

- health records (parent questionnaire, information from a physician)
- notes forwarded from previous caregiving agencies
- psychologists' reports
- social workers' notes
- photographs of special moments in the child's life
- photographs of things the child has made
- special items the child has selected
- artwork samples
- samples of the child's writing
- the child's own records-of-achievement journal
- a learning log of the child's lifetime experiences
- questionnaire responses
- **anecdotal records** (see Chapter 3)
- **running records** or **specimen records** (see Chapter 3)
- **event samplings** and **time samplings** (see Chapter 4)
- **developmental checklists** (see Chapter 5)
- contextual information (parent questionnaire, objective notes, **genogram**, **ecomap**, **life-experience flow chart**, etc.) (see Chapter 6)
- infant **charts** (see Chapter 6)
- **rating scales** (see Chapter 6)
- photographs of the child (passive or in action) (see Chapter 7)
- audiotapes of the child's language, reading, or music (see Chapter 7)
- videotapes of the child's activities (see Chapter 7)
- assessment results from **standardized tests** (see Chapter 10)

Using child studies to learn about development

A child study contains in-depth information and an analysis of one child's life and behaviour. Students frequently conduct child studies to understand more about child development. This can be a good way to get to know and understand an individual child. The study may include any of the contents of a developmental portfolio, with emphasis on an analysis of the child's development at one particular point. The study is usually more for the benefit of the student than that of the child; by carrying it out, the student develops skills in gathering data, selecting pertinent material, and analyzing all the information within a developmental framework.

Advantages

- A child study provides the opportunity to study one child in depth.
- The study reveals each aspect of the child's development in relation to that of the other children.
- Contextual information helps the observer make inferences that are more valid.
- The observer appreciates the changing process of development by gathering information over a period of time.
- A variety of observations and accumulated information can produce a more accurate picture of the child.
- The detail of analysis can surpass the detail produced by any other evaluation method.
- As a strong learning experience, a child study supports the student later in carrying out portfolio assessments in practice.

Disadvantages

- A focus on one child cannot be the basis for generalizations about all children.
- The observer's close connection with the child may mean that the inferences that observer draws are more subjective.
- The process is time-consuming and cumbersome.
- The study may not lead to any direct benefit for the child studied.
- All children in the group cannot be studied in the same depth.
- The student may make inappropriate inferences that are not challenged.
- The observer may not evaluate the large volume of material in sufficient detail to offer adequate feedback.

Using portfolios for ongoing evaluation and record-keeping

Advantages

- A portfolio provides for a comprehensive record-keeping process.
- A portfolio allows a variety of observations and information to be kept together.
- Professionals and parents can see the records and make additions.
- The record can be used at any time.

- Information is stored over a long period and can be passed on from one agency or school to the next.
- The process includes deliberate parental involvement.
- A portfolio provides for the most rigorous, thorough, and developmentally appropriate assessment because its contents are so diverse.
- Informal and formal records may be kept alongside each other, which helps identify program intentions.
- A portfolio provides for ongoing assessment. It allows for more immediate responses than some other assessment procedures.
- The system can be adapted to whatever the child's needs and abilities.
- Both the process and the product of the child's experience can be recorded.
- The child values the portfolio-assessment process, as it validates the importance of his activity.
- Keeping portfolios accommodates a wide variety of teaching and caregiving philosophies.

Disadvantages

- A portfolio requires effort to be kept up-to-date and this is time-consuming.
- A portfolio can become more of a sentimental memory box than a valid assessment tool.
- A substantial amount of file space is required.
- The focus may be deflected from the process of the child's learning to overzealous record-keeping.
- Information may be stored without having been evaluated regularly.
- The criteria for inclusion of items in the record may not be clear.
- Teachers need training in what to look for when choosing samples.
- Meetings may be required for teamwork planning.

Types of Portfolios

Baby book

Perhaps the most commonly used portfolio is the **baby book** that parents keep. Parents can use ready-prepared albums or create their own to record the significant happenings in their children's lives and to map out developmental **milestones**. Some parents may wish to maintain the book until the children reach school age, or even until the children leave home. These records might contain some of the following:

- a list of homes/accommodation where the child has lived
- a family tree
- copies of newspaper headlines on the day of his or her birth
- a lock of hair
- hand- and footprints
- lists of favourite foods, toys, etc.

- feeding and sleeping records
- caregiver information
- developmental milestones
- photographs
- religious information
- lists of gifts
- name information, record of naming ceremonies
- "firsts": words, events at daycare or school, party, steps, etc.
- artwork
- anecdotes, funny things the child said or did
- health and immunization records (dates of infectious diseases)

Some items might be included for sentimental reasons, to give the parents a concrete reminder of the child's early years. The book could also serve as a way of storing health or developmental information that may be required later.

Life book

A **life book** can be started at any stage of a child's life. It attempts to capture the individual nature of the child's own story. Initiated by a parent, guardian, social worker, adoption and fostering worker, or other child-care employee, the book can be passed on, with the child, from one person to another involved in the child's care. The child can benefit directly from such documentation. Changes, both happy and sad, should be included so that the child can reflect on her own experiences and story. Agencies may use this kind of portfolio to support mental health, particularly when the child is undergoing transitions in parenting, home, or caregiving, or other potentially traumatic changes.

A life book may contain some of the following:

- photographs of the parents/guardian
- a family tree
- pictures of significant people
- pictures of significant places/homes
- small sentimental objects
- lists of favourites: foods, games, objects
- birthday greetings
- mementoes from outings and other special occasions
- developmental charts
- health information, immunization schedules
- letters from friends and family members
- tape-recordings of people, music, etc.
- religious affiliation records, initiations
- club membership cards, friendship souvenirs
- artwork

Learning log

While a **learning log** is not in itself a full portfolio, it can form part of a solid record documenting a child's learning. Written by a teacher or, later, by the child, the log tracks the child's activity and thinking. There are two parts to this kind of log. One records the program plan, curriculum activity, or experience, and the other records how the child responded to the experience—that is, what he or she "learned." The log system requires a teacher to be diligent in record-keeping. It can provide a detailed analysis of what the child is learning. For the child who has a diagnosed **special need**, this type of record-keeping can supply data to be interpreted as part of the planning process. For teachers with large numbers of children in their care, or for whom curriculum-planning is more spontaneous, this method might not be as useful as others.

Older children capable of documenting their own experiences may keep logs, under their teachers' direction, in which they record their responses to classroom or other activities. Either the teacher or the child can maintain a more informal type of log, a **record of achievement**, an anecdotal record of skill development and achievements. The record of achievement allows for reflection and critical thinking as well as actual achievements.

Learning Log		
Date	Curriculum experience	Response

Child study

The student's assignment may require certain components or focus on particular aspects of development. Through the child study, the student appreciates the complexity of the child's context and development. As discussed earlier, the child study gives the observer the chance to study a child for the benefit of the observer's own learning rather than for the child's benefit. The student focuses on one child as objectively as possible, and to achieve a more personal view of that child's experience and development. Critics of the child-study approach say that it tends to be subjective and produces information that cannot be considered statistically significant. While this criticism may be valid to a degree, child studies can also offer educators important insights into the individuality of the developmental process.

Curriculum-based portfolio

Teachers can base their records on the formative evaluation of the children in particular curriculum areas. Formatted to record information about the curriculum experiences offered and the group and individual responses to the experiences, the curriculum portfolio documents the process of curriculum-development, an evaluation of its effectiveness, and data on which to base further planning.

	Curriculum-Based Class Portfolio		
Date	Curriculum area/activity	Group response (anecdotal record)	Individual outcomes

A teacher who is responsible for one or more particular aspects of the curriculum usually develops curriculum-based portfolios. Various choices present themselves:

- What is the purpose of the portfolio and how should it be constructed?
- Should the portfolio document the process or the products of learning?
- Is it best to follow the progress of individual children or the learning of the whole group?
- How might the portfolio develop over time?
- Who is going to collect, select, and reflect on the contents?
- What is a useful assessment cycle and appropriate time frame for collecting and analyzing the contents?
- To what extent will the children be involved with the portfolio processes of collection and reflection?

Educators who use curriculum portfolios do so to improve their delivery of the curriculum. They might focus on a content area, such as math, science, or language arts, or on a more general notion of documenting whatever learning the children demonstrate. These portfolios often become part of a teacher's own **professional portfolio**, showing clearly what he or she does best.

Professional portfolios

Society increasingly demands that educators be accountable in all aspects of their roles. At the same time teachers want to monitor their own professional and personal development, evaluate their performance, and determine future directions for themselves. The professional portfolio provides teachers with an open-ended tool to

- document the learning of the children for whom they are responsible;
- include observations and samples of the children's work while linking the curriculum and program goals;
- record pertinent information associated with their own teaching and learning experiences;
- store memorabilia associated with teaching, such as thank-you cards, letters of appreciation from parents, and other items such as photographs and newsletters that represent their time with a group of children;
- keep letters of reference, certificates, grade reports, and professional-development attendance sheets;
- write a personal-philosophy statement;
- evaluate the delivery of the program;
- comment on each artifact included in the portfolio; and
- demonstrate the achievement of a professional standard, licensing standard, program outcomes, and other professional benchmarks.

The process of portfolio development is often considered an enlightening professional development activity. Through the refinement of collecting the materials, careful performance-evaluation, and forward planning, the teacher becomes a more **reflective practitioner**. This person plans carefully, reflects regularly, is sensitive to feedback, adapts to people and circumstances as they change, and furthers his or her professional career at the same time.

Learning-assessment portfolio

Either a teacher or a child, as he matures and moves into adolescence, can keep an individual learning-assessment portfolio to detail the child's own learning. This kind of portfolio documents general experiences as well as more formal learning situations. Experience is described in terms of the **competencies** the child has achieved as a result of that experience. These **learning outcomes** are then analyzed to establish what the experience has enabled the child to do.

Teachers and learners at all stages of their education find the learning-assessment portfolio a useful device. The process of recording and examining experiences forces the individual to really learn and to evaluate that learning.

An early childhood educator may wish to log a child's experiences day by day and evaluate the effectiveness of the program by determining and recording her newly acquired competence. This requires practice in recording behavioural information, but once having mastered it the educator ensures that the portfolio tracks the child's learning.

With help, older children can log their own experiences and what they have learned from them. Identifying what has been learned helps the child consolidate what he has learned.

More mature children may want to explore their experiences to express their learning outcomes in terms of acquired competencies. Learning to evaluate their own experiences and determine their skills will equip them eventually to gain credit and access to college and university programs, and may prove useful one day in job evaluations too. This idea is gaining more and more acceptance in education. To start this process in early childhood settings will help the child who is growing up in the currently changing education and work environments.

Program-documentation portfolio

The idea behind program documentation is to record the evolution of learning of a group of children. This is a key part of the **project approach** that centres on project-based learning (see Chard 1999). The **Reggio Emilia** philosophy uses this kind of documentation, which values the work of the group of children as well as the activity of each individual child. The documentation supports "learning made visible," a term describing the photographic and narrative descriptions that are included as part of the recorded process of learning. The documentation also allows families to become more involved with their children's education, supplies educators with a tool for reflection, and at the same time encourages children to think critically about what they have been doing. This reflective process is known as **metacognition** (thinking about thinking) and it is crucial to complex project development.

The Plowden Report shaped the programs of British infant schools (for 4/5– and 7/8-year-old children) in the 1960s and 1970s using a similar project approach. While the British infant-school tradition of project-focused learning and assessment has continued in some schools, the push to school reform and the required National Curriculum have spoiled what was working successfully. The Reggio Emilia approach has taken project-learning and documentation to new levels of success—ones that many educators are trying to replicate in their North American classrooms and child-care centres. The interest in Reggio Emilia may reflect the need for educators and children to be motivated and engaged in learning and assessment in ways that the current systems of direct instruction and standardized tests do not make possible. Howard Gardner and others from the Harvard Graduate School of Education have undertaken Project Zero, a research project that explores how people learn and work together in groups by observing the work in Reggio Emilia, Italy. The findings of their study are presented in a new book, *Making Learning Visible*, which examines how to keep records in the context of individual and group learning.

Another form of assessment based on documentation has been developed that seamlessly blends together curriculum and assessment. Well-prepared early childhood educators employ the "YMCA Playing to Learn" curriculum with young children in appropriately designed environments. The philosophy behind it is somewhat eclectic, being informed by Froebel in the 1890s, Vygotsky from the 1960s, Yardley and Erikson in the 1970s, Suzuki, Gardner, Katz, and several other 1980s and 1990s educators. More current, up-to-date neuroscientific findings are also reflected in this curriculum approach. It emphasizes play as the means of learning, incorporating curriculum and assessment into the program simultaneously by means of thorough documentation. As with the Reggio Emilia approach, YMCA Playing to Learn promotes displaying, as well as documenting, children's work—their play—so that play is honoured, shared, and reflected on. The documentation process contains the following elements:

- anecdotes based on day-to-day observations
- ongoing developmental review
- representative samples of children's work
- photographic and audio-records of the processes and products of children's learning
- notes from colleagues who also teach the child
- notes from conversations with parents and, on occasion, other professionals

(Source: With permission from Children's Services, YMCA of Greater Toronto. YMCA Playing to Learn: A YMCA Guide to Quality Care and Education of Young Children [Susanne T. Eden and Lorrie Huggins], 2001.

The Playing to Learn Curriculum specifies how to align curriculum and assessment. As well as providing an assessment of interacting groups of children, it serves as a comprehensive mechanism for overall program review with direction for supporting individual children. The variety and complexity of the documentation allows for a fuller review of what is really happening within the program than most other types of portfolio. Thus armed, educators can make informed decisions about implementing the play-based curriculum as well as what and where to focus their attention. These educators are prepared to deliver the curriculum and to make assessments founded on refined professional skills.

Digital/Electronic Portfolios

In the course of Chapter 7's discussion of how technology can support observation and assessment through various media, there was mention of the use of digital portfolios. They add a new dimension to how portfolio documentation, assessment and curriculum-planning can work together.

As already pointed out, Finland has a reputation for progressive and successful education practice; that country shares the same reputation regarding digital-portfolio development. Their model offers a great deal to those who live and practise in other parts of the world. Marja Kankaanranta of the University of Jyväskylä has led a recent study, publishing the research as a text, *Developing Digital Portfolios for Childhood Education* (2002). She and her colleagues adopted an ecological model as the philosophical premise for portfolio development. Mindful of Bronfenbrenner's model of **ecological systems** (see Chapters 2 and 6), the ecological model explains the different social systems within which each child functions, and the portfolio ensures that these are represented through both data-collection and assessment processes. The concept here incorporates technology-enriched learning environments that actually shape learning; the information ecology prompts an evolution in the chains of interdependence. (As the technology is adopted it alters the way we communicate and what we communicate.) The project clearly advocates an ethical use of technology because of its potential power.

In practical terms this model of digital portfolio follows the processes by which we learn. Technology heightens that learning for both educators and children. It encourages reflection and metacognition. This raises the portfolio process above basic data collection and storage. The digital portfolio becomes part of the learning process rather than an add-on assessment function. A real challenge for the project lies in the ethical considerations associated with digitizing information—the practicalities of collecting, sifting, and storing information. The ethical issues have become more important regarding limited access to data, excluding identifiable personal material, to what extent the technology should shape the process, who shares responsibility for controlling the contents of the portfolio, and the ongoing concern that, however detailed those contents, they can never adequately reveal the identity of the learner. We can learn from Finland's experience and employ the technology, taking advantage of some preliminary discussion about these issues. But after all this, many educators may consider acquiring the computer skills and accessing the hardware their primary concern!

The Purpose of the Portfolio

Before starting any kind of portfolio, the educator must have a clear vision or intention. Because there are so many different types, contents, selection processes, and assessment protocols, everyone involved with the portfolio must understand its concept and agree on its focus.

Some of the main reasons for developing portfolios in childcare and education are to

- document a child's development
- record key features of a child's learning
- store relevant formal documents
- demonstrate a child's abilities
- reveal the interactions between children
- collate children's artwork and work samples
- identify children's special needs
- document for purposes of accountability
- show the program's success
- record stages of curriculum delivery
- help student teachers understand children's development
- assess developmental progress
- evaluate the children's learning outcomes
- provide opportunity for teacher reflection
- encourage children's reflection and self-evaluation
- communicate with parents
- design curriculum and guidance strategies
- evaluate the program's effectiveness at meeting children's needs

Most teachers will incorporate some, but not all, of these potential purposes in their use of portfolios. In any case they need to articulate which of these purposes they are considering. Most teachers will keep their intentions broad, more in keeping with open-ended portfolio assessments, while some will state particular portfolio goals.

Portfolio Entries

Health records

Health information should be updated regularly. A child's health history is an ongoing, changing record that needs additions as new health and growth information becomes available. This type of data will help you know the child better, and also enable you to respond to her needs. Health conditions affect a child's development and are therefore an important part of her portfolio. A child health-information questionnaire is best completed with the parent at an interview. Students should ask only those questions that help them understand the child's development. (See page 278 for a sample showing how to frame health questions.) Use an additional updating sheet to make more entries as needed. Because of the strong correlation among growth, health, and development, it may be a good idea to include measurements as the child grows. (Chapter 6 suggests prepared formats for height, weight, immunization, feeding, and sleeping charts. A sample health questionnaire can be found on pages 279–280).

TAKING A SPECIAL LOOK: Prenatal and neonatal conditions

Some babies are born with fetal alcohol syndrome (FAS) or other prenatal and neonatal conditions caused by the mothers' exposure to alcohol, illegal or prescription drugs, or other chemicals. Teachers and caregivers working directly with such children may observe particular behaviours. Very young babies may be underweight, breathe poorly, and even suffer from withdrawal. More lasting effects may include diminished intelligence, learning disabilities, and problems in social adaptation.

Increasing numbers of children contract HIV from their mothers. Parents may decide to keep this information to themselves, fearing that their children will be excluded from agencies or schools, or cut off socially. While caregivers may observe behavioural or appearance changes that might indicate illness, they cannot diagnose these symptoms or any other diseases themselves. They must always follow "universal precautions" to ensure that infections of any type are not spread.

Menu plans should be provided for parents to review, and known allergies must be catered to. Adults must also observe and record any significant behavioural changes.

Contextual information

A working portfolio makes much more sense and is likely to be interpreted more accurately if it contains some **contextual information**. You might make some of the entries according to observation; you will probably have to rely on parental input for a large amount of background information. An initial interview in the child's home can help forge links between home and the agency you represent. There is a fine line between asking for information that is pertinent and asking questions that seem to be none of your business. Conduct these interviews as an informal chat rather than a long question-and-answer-type questionnaire process.

"Why do you want to know that?" is a fairly typical and reasonable question. If you can explain why the information is helpful to you before you ask any questions, the parents' response is more likely to be favourable. Parents can decline to offer information. You must respect this decision.

Child Health Information Questionnaire

Please take time to complete this form. The information will help us know your child better and respond appropriately to his/her needs.

Today's date: _____

Recorded by: _____

Family information

1. Child's name: _____
                                 (first)   (last)
   "Pet" name, nickname: _____

2. Child's address: _____
   _____
   _____
   Home telephone number: (___) _____

3. Mother's name: _____
   Mother's home telephone number: _____
   Mother's home address (if different from above): _____
   _____
   Other contact during day: _____
   phone: _____
   fax: _____

4. Father's name: _____
   Father's home telephone number: _____
   Father's home address (if different from above): _____
   _____
   Other contact during day: _____
   phone: _____
   fax: _____

5. Child's sex (male or female): _____

6. Child's year of birth: _____
                            month   day   year
   Age (years/months): _____

7. Other family members living at the child's address (names and ages of children): _____

_____

8. Previous child-care agencies/schools attended: _____

_____

_____

Birth history

9. Child's weight at birth: _____

10. Length of pregnancy (premature/full term, # of months): _____

11. Were there any complications with the pregnancy or birth? If so, what? _____

_____

12. Did your child have any medical problems at or soon after birth? If so, what? _____

_____

13. Family physician's name: _____

Family physician's address: _____

_____

Family physician's phone number: _____

14. Pediatrician's name: _____

Pediatrician's address: _____

_____

Pediatrician's phone number: _____

15. Dentist's name: _____

Dentist's address: _____

_____

Dentist's phone number: _____

Health status

16. Please give a complete history of your child's immunization schedule (this may need to be verified by your doctor).

Immunization type   Date given

_____   _____

_____   _____

_____   _____

17. What infectious diseases has your child ever suffered from? (Circle Yes or No and add date if Yes.)

measles   Yes   No   Date: _____
rheumatic fever   Yes   No   Date: _____
chicken pox   Yes   No   Date: _____
pneumonia   Yes   No   Date: _____
mumps   Yes   No   Date: _____
meningitis   Yes   No   Date: _____
whooping cough   Yes   No   Date: _____
others: _____ Date: _____
        _____ Date: _____

18. Has your child suffered any repeated infections? (cold, flu, tonsillitis, etc.) _____
_____
_____

19. Has your child ever received treatment in a hospital emergency room? If so, why? _____
_____
_____

20. Has your child ever been admitted to hospital as an in-patient? If so, why? _____
_____
_____

21. Does your child take any medication on a regular basis? If so, what? _____
_____
_____

22. Please offer any information about your child's health check-ups. Has your child recently been evaluated by any of the following? (Circle Yes or No and add result if Yes.)

dentist   Yes   No   Result: _____
eye doctor   Yes   No   Result: _____
hearing specialist   Yes   No   Result: _____
pediatrician   Yes   No   Result: _____
other specialist   Yes   No   Result: _____

23. Does your child have any known allergies?   Yes   No
To what? _____
Severity of reaction: _____

24. (a) Does your child have problems with any of the following? (Circle Yes or No and describe if Yes.)

asthma	Yes	No	Describe: _____
hayfever	Yes	No	Describe: _____
skin sensitivity	Yes	No	Describe: _____
reaction to the sun	Yes	No	Describe: _____
warts	Yes	No	Describe: _____
dairy products	Yes	No	Describe: _____
constipation	Yes	No	Describe: _____
easy bruising	Yes	No	Describe: _____
concentration	Yes	No	Describe: _____
mood swings	Yes	No	Describe: _____
sleep	Yes	No	Describe: _____
spasms, twitches, tics	Yes	No	Describe: _____
habits	Yes	No	Describe: _____

other _____

(b) Are there any genetic diseases in the family? _____

25. Does your child behave in any way that concerns you? If so, what? _____

_____

26. Has your child ever been exposed to any significant traumatic event? (witnessed violence, divorce in family, moving home, death of relative, etc.)   Yes   No

Describe: _____

27. Does your child play in a way that you would expect?   Yes   No

Describe: _____

28. Do you have any concerns about your child's speech, communication, or understanding? If so, what?

_____

29. What is your child's height? _____

weight? _____

shoe size? _____

30. Describe your child's feeding/eating patterns. (number of meals, snacks, types of food/milk/formula, attitude to eating) _____

_____

Health Update

Name: _____ Age/D.O.B.: _____ Today's date: _____

New immunizations (cross-reference to immunization record card):

Immunization type   Date given

_____   _____

_____   _____

Recent health conditions: _____

Medication: _____

Physician's reports (attach if appropriate): _____

Updates on growth information (also plot data on growth chart)

height: _____

weight: _____

shoe size: _____

Identified health needs: _____

The following background information form may help you know what to ask. Review the questions ahead of time. You may have to modify areas according to legal requirements, your understanding of the need to ask the questions, and the parents' comfort level. The parents are not to complete the questionnaire directly, although they must be asked for input and allowed access to what has been recorded. It is more useful to use the questions as a basis for discussion. When you record data, gain permission from the parents to do so beforehand. Most jurisdictions have freedom-of-information and privacy provisions of which you should be aware, as your information-gathering processes must comply with such legislation. (The sample background information form on page 281 uses appropriate questions.)

A full set of contextual information may also include a sociological survey of the child's home neighbourhood.

Background Information

Recorded by: _____   Date: _____

1. Child's name: _____
                         last   first   middle   pet name

2. Current age: _____ D.O.B.: _____

3. Child's appearance: height: _____
    weight: _____eye colour: _____
    skin colour, birth marks, texture: _____
    identifying features: _____
    hair colour, style, condition:_____

4. What does the family see to be their nationality, race, citizenship, ethnic origin? (In some jurisdictions, this question may need to be altered or omitted.) _____

5. What is (are) the language(s) spoken in the home? _____

6. Family composition (mention all those living at the same address and their relationship): _____
    _____

7. Extended family: _____
    _____

8. Mother's occupation, if employed: _____
    Mother's hobbies/interests: _____

    Father's occupation, if employed: _____
    Father's hobbies/interests: _____

    Guardian (if not mother or father): _____
    Guardian's occupation, if employed: _____

    Is the child fostered, adopted, or in the care of adults who are not the child's parents? _____

9. Abilities/disabilities observable in nuclear family: _____
    _____

10. Accommodations/residence type: _____
    # bedrooms: _____   # bathrooms: _____   # people living in home: _____
    living space: _____

11. Pets/animals living in home: _____

12. Locality of residence (urban/rural, industrial, residential, etc.): _____

13. Play space available to child: _____

14. Availability of playthings/books: _____

15. Child-care/educational/recreational programs where the child is registered: _____

    _____

16. Transportation access (bus, train, car, etc.): _____

17. Who are the significant adults in the child's life? _____

18. Does the family require welfare, social insurance, grants, etc.? _____

19. What changes in the family have occurred since the birth of this child? _____

    _____

20. Does the family practice a particular religion? _____

21. Can family members trace their family tree? _____

22. What is the parenting style? _____

23. What kind of lifestyle does the family enjoy? _____

24. Are there particular mealtimes/bedtimes or other rituals? _____

25. Does the family express or demonstrate particular attitudes, values, or beliefs? _____

    _____

Changing Circumstances – Portfolio Update

Child's name: _____   Date: _____

Age: _____   D.O.B.: _____

Entry made by : _____

Nature of change (move home, divorce, unemployment, etc.): _____

Identified need of the child: _____

Observations

Observations are an essential part of the portfolio. They are the core to which you add the other components. You will choose your observational methods on the basis of the developmental information they can reveal. You will have to exercise a variety of styles, repeating some. Refer to the chapters on different methods of observation to help you with your choices.

Unless you focus on what a child can do and observe his behaviour in a natural setting, you will not be able to make adequate evaluations. The central part of the portfolio will be observations from both home and the care agency or school. Those written by the professionals require **objectivity** and detail; parents' contributions should be valued even if they are not written in the format and language of the teacher or in a completely objective fashion.

Not all your written observations will, or could, be included in the portfolio; you will be selecting from that material. Choose the observations that offer the most up-to-date or significant developmental information.

You can make copies of blank observation forms available for parents to complete. Some may be more comfortable with giving you oral anecdotes of what they have seen. Record them on a parent sheet if that works best.

A parent's spontaneous comments may not always be the best record. A mother may tell you about her child's reaction to catching his parents in an intimate moment or may tell you how exasperated she is about her child's irritating habit of nose-picking. These comments may not be appropriate to keep in a formal record. On the other hand, you might see the validity of including accounts of how the child first slept through the night, rejected breast-feeding, or became more cooperative in play with his cousins. These professional decisions are based on understanding what is significant.

Parental input

On busy days, we sometimes think that we provide the most significant influences in a child's life. This is not true; parents are the centre of the child's world, and our task is to support them. Parents can help us ensure the children's happy development by providing them with information about their children. They know their children well and are almost always in a better position to decide what is best. We may find it difficult to accept parents' opinions when their values differ from our own, but we must maintain a professional respect for their perspective on their task.

In addition to any forms, questionnaires, and reports filled out during or after communication with parents, it is useful to keep a log of meetings with parents, as a summary of dates, permissions granted, and topics discussed. A sample parent-meeting log can be found on pages 282–283.

If parents have been part of the portfolio process for a while, they might give you information about how a guidance strategy is working, how they are implementing a learning plan, or what they have learned from a health professional or psychologist.

A teacher-parent journal can aid both parties in communication. Some notes may focus on practical requests like "Please drop off more diapers," while a more analytical approach might include thoughtful comments about the child's mood, interests, or development. This record book can be included in the portfolio and would provide an interesting picture of changes in the child's development.

Records from previous agencies

You will be fortunate if earlier assessments, health records, and reports have been transferred to your agency. Treat the material with respect while being cautious about believing everything you read. You will be tempted to think that the records are accurate and objective, but without some verification of the findings, avoid making any programming decisions based on them.

Legal requirements govern the transfer of this kind of information, and they vary according to the jurisdiction. Be aware of the legalities and policies that pertain to you, whether they are by-laws, municipal guidelines, board-of-education policies, procedures agreed to by agencies, or local practices.

The contents of the record may prompt useful questions for you to ask the parents; they may wish to see the record themselves and offer opinions on the contents. Their rights may include the option of removing items or including more items or commenting on the information.

Use the records as a base for some informal observations as the child settles into her new environment. Records can be obsolete by the time they are passed on. You may note considerable development and life-experience changes in the time between the child's leaving one agency and starting at another.

Some supervisors limit access to children's histories because they do not want to colour the attitudes of the teachers directly responsible for the children. Teachers are trained to be objective and professional and to be aware of inappropriate influences. Usually they should evaluate for themselves the content of the records they receive.

Professional reports

Assessment records, reports, suggestions, and plans from professionals contributing to a child's health, education, and well-being may be included in the portfolio. When the caregiving agency requests a report from a specialist, the consent of the parents is usually required. Parents may also seek a specialist's help directly. The report that results from such intervention may be unavailable to you, as caregiver or student, for personal reasons that you may never know. These reasons may have nothing to do with mistrust, although you might feel that you could help the child and the parents better if you had as much information as possible.

In some situations, your input may be crucial to the assessment process. Even if you agree to offer input, you will not necessarily receive feedback.

If assessment results do not reinforce what you have already observed, neither perspective may be "wrong"; you may simply be evaluating the child from a different perspective. Your observations are carried out in a naturalistic setting, so they are more likely to represent what the child can do every day. When test results indicate a level of achievement below that which you have observed, the test was likely inappropriate or presented in a way that induced stress in the child or elicited unexpected responses from him. However, if the results duplicate your findings, you can consider your inferences more likely to be valid. Keep in mind that you could both be wrong! Ideally, the team will work together, the parents will be involved, and you will agree on the outcomes.

Some child-care facilities and schools have access to resource teachers and assistants. **Resource teachers** have specialized training to provide physical assistance, learning activities, emotional and social support, and other aids to children with special needs in mainstream settings. Assistants are sometimes hired specifically to work with one or two particular children with diagnosed special needs; usually, however, they provide general support to the overall program.

Artwork can be included in a portfolio to demonstrate a child's skills, emotions, and perceptions. The child may also choose a favourite piece of work as a personal contribution to the portfolio.

Products of learning and experience

Observations may enable you to glimpse the process of a child's learning, and examples of the products confirm achievements. In keeping products, such as artwork and writing samples, you still value the process by which they were made. Concrete examples of the child's end products can help the professional appreciate the particular stage of the child's development.

While you must remain cautious about making invalid, unsupported inferences, representative samples of a child's works can help you evaluate her progress. With knowledge of the sequence of drawing skills and representation of the child's world in art, you can make pertinent comments about the child's feelings, skill level, and perception. You can analyze writing and math work on a similar basis. By looking at what the child can do, you can attempt to appreciate her conceptual understandings and discern her **construction of knowledge**.

Selecting items for the portfolio can be difficult when the child creates a large volume of products. You may be tempted to select "the best" according to your personal responses. More significant is the most typical of the child's work at this time.

Media recordings

Photographs, video- and audio-recordings, and other **media techniques** help you gather information for the portfolio. With them, you can put together a more comprehensive collection of items than you could using only traditional observation techniques.

Video- and audio-recordings of the child supplement the portfolio by adding details about his activity and language that are often superior to a narrative record. Remember that recordings, of themselves, are not interpretive unless a teacher narrates them or analyzes them in detail after the event. (Review Chapter 7 to help you employ media techniques.)

We are accustomed to using photographs for identification and record-keeping. Keeping a loaded camera near the children's activity will help you be ready to "snap" the children in action. A variety of action and posed pictures make useful additions to the portfolio and bring it to life for readers.

Inclusions made by the child

A child feels a greater sense of involvement in and ownership of the education process when she has some control over the input to her own record. In choosing pieces for inclusion, the child can identify items of particular significance. If the item is too precious to be stored in the portfolio, perhaps you could photograph it and include the photograph instead.

As the child develops she will be able to take a more active role in selecting samples. She will also reflect on her work, evaluate it, and, with help, be able to plan for future success.

Assembling a Portfolio

Since you are aiming here at building and encouraging a team approach, in which the parents and the child-care practitioners work together, it may be a good idea to decide collectively on the system to be used for record-keeping.

Organizing the contents for storage

You will decide how to keep the portfolios depending on the space you have available for them. File folders are most commonly used. However, they can be too small to accommodate large pieces of artwork. To get around this problem, you might take photographs of the artwork—instead of including flaking paint and unstuck macaroni! Box files can be expensive and may not give you the kind of privacy and storage space you need. A local manufacturer might be able to let you have boxes—shirt boxes or others of that size can work well. Pizza boxes (if clean) may be another possibility. You could also put items into ring binders in chronological order for each child and remove them as necessary. Consider accordion files as well, which provide sections for organizing items by type. Whatever method you use, be aware that this kind of record-keeping requires space that is both accessible and secure.

Keep the portfolio in good order. Label it on the outside, and label each item inside clearly and date it. Develop a system to ensure that you remember to make additions.

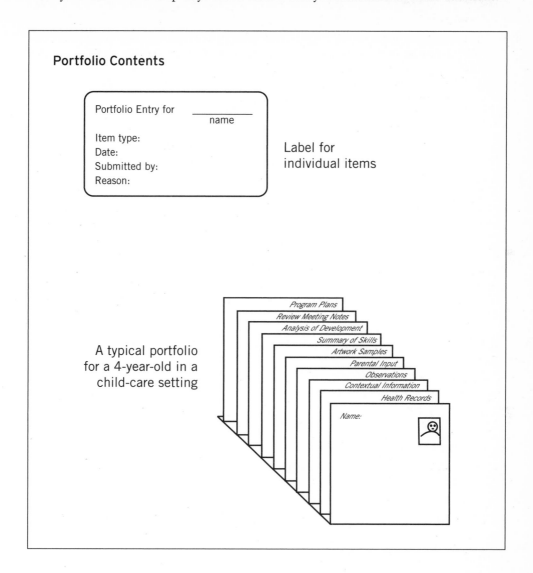

Portfolio Contents

Portfolio Entry for _____
name

Item type:
Date:
Submitted by:
Reason:

Label for individual items

A typical portfolio for a 4-year-old in a child-care setting

Program Plans
Review Meeting Notes
Analysis of Development
Summary of Skills
Artwork Samples
Parental Input
Observations
Contextual Information
Health Records

Name:

Choice of contents

What you put into the portfolio will depend on your philosophy and why you are keeping the records. Your team might like to discuss the following considerations to help decide on those contents:

- the purpose of each type of record
- the space available
- who will keep the portfolio up to date

- who will have access to the portfolio
- how the data can be analyzed
- the cost of keeping the system
- the philosophy of the agency (Child-centred programs may have fewer standardized tests; some may focus on the process of learning and accentuate observations; others may want you to include more products.)
- privacy and confidentiality
- the time available to collect and process information
- the attitude of staff and parents

Rubrics

Rubrics are a set of assessment criteria that specify the learning that constitutes a particular level. Educators frequently use them in authentic assessment instead of grades, or, occasionally, to determine a grade (by adding numerical values to each criterion) when an educational institution demands grades as part of its reporting processes. Rather than being assigned a grade, the learners work to fulfill the criteria set, and know they will be assessed according to the predetermined specifics. Younger children will be unable to understand the criteria unless they are presented in picture form, but you can still use a rubric to measure their performance. Rubrics allow for subtleties in learning and require the assessor to indicate the level of a performance as well as whether or not the child demonstrated the skill or knowledge. Where rubrics are linked with grades they can overcome some of the limitations of grading; they can provide clear reasons why the performance merited the grade. In a learning-outcome model you can develop the rubric with the outcomes in mind and so produce a picture, over time, of a child's progress towards achieving specific outcomes.

In portfolio assessment there are several ways to use rubrics:

- to provide a mechanism for evaluating the creation of the portfolio itself
- to offer feedback on any part of the portfolio and to help in the selection of the child's "best work"
- to offer a clear benchmark for what constitutes success
- to assist in developing curriculum or program plans in response to the rubric's evaluation
- to offer a step-by-step sequence of skill development from basic to mastery level

Portfolio Assessment

After gathering all this material, we still have to make sense of it. Some teachers have criticized the use of portfolios for evaluation as glorified **work sampling** rather than real assessment. However, a thorough assessment of a well-kept portfolio leads to a real understanding of the child. The following steps outline the process of careful **portfolio assessment**:

1. **Sort, date, and label all items:** Without a good labelling system, the portfolio will be just a confusing collection of information.

2. **Organize the contents:** Items can be organized by date or by types of data. Add a contents page to show what is included and how it is ordered.

3. **Write an introduction:** Explain the process you have used to create the portfolio. Ensure that you show you are celebrating an individual!

4. **Summarize the material:** Probably the best way to summarize is to scan the current material and categorize skill developments according to developmental domain. A **summary** can help the assessor determine how well the child is reaching any learning outcomes, expectations, or profile of learning. At this stage, sort objectively; do not explain. (See the sample portfolio summary on pages 284–285.)

5. **Make inferences about the child's skills:** Using clear statements, write an **analysis** of the child's development. Your **inferences** might be based on

   • applying theoretical models to explain a behaviour, skill, or performance

   • matching the child's performance against an acceptable **norm of development** to see where the child is in relation to a specific age or stage (avoiding inappropriate judgments)

   • determining a pattern or cause of behaviour

   Validate or support all your inferences using reasoned arguments and citing reliable sources. Be sure to refer to all sources correctly. (A sample portfolio analysis can be found on pages 286–293.)

6. **Write a portfolio review report for the parents and for your records:** Restate your inferences in a way that avoids jargon and that helps parents appreciate what you are trying to say. (See a sample report on page 294.)

7. **Present the parents with the portfolio:** Most parents are anxious to be part of the assessment process. Be prepared to adjust any inferences in your portfolio-review report according to their perceptions. If the child is old enough to appreciate the portfolio collection process, she should be part of the process. At this time, the teachers, parents, child, and other concerned parties (such as social workers or grandparents) can develop an **action plan**.

8. **Design an individual program plan (IPP) or individual education plan (IEP):** Create an IPP or IEP according to the skills that you see emerging. If you have documented the child's learning in all developmental domains, you will be better prepared to design activities that support all domains for him. For children with special needs, you may have to design a plan that contains developmental or incremental stages. (Sample program plans can be found on pages 35 and 38–39.)

9. **Continue the portfolio collection and observations for future in-process assessment.**

Portfolio Review Meeting Report

Child's name: _____   Date: _____

Age/D.O.B.: _____   Meeting called by: _____

Those present: _____

Intention of meeting: _____
_____

Review of recent additions to portfolio: _____
_____

Changed context, social or family circumstances: _____
_____

Developmental summary given by: _____

Summary details: _____

Cognition: _____
_____

Personality: _____
_____

Language and communication: _____
_____

Emotional development: _____
_____

Physical development: _____
_____

Social skills: _____
_____

Curriculum implications: _____
_____

Program plan/strategies: _____
_____

New directions in portfolio use

Emerging trends in portfolio documentation parallel advances in technology and developments in thinking about how children learn. Another force is also evident: the move to greater **accountability** blended with efforts to reform education. Historically, opinions about the form and function of education change constantly and regular patterns emerge over time. The current education models challenge educators, who may have to bridge existing and new practices. This is certainly true regarding portfolio use. Often educators who are child-centred in their approach and who implement developmentally appropriate practice have difficulty documenting children's learning in ways that conform to the reporting requirements of their current administrations. Some may abandon what they know is good practice and move to a teacher-directed approach to "cover" the curriculum and to satisfy the need to teach to the test. There are better ways of using portfolios to track the children's learning as it occurs and match it to the standards, outcomes, and other curriculum requirements. If we trust in appropriate practices rather than rote-learning, we must be consistent in aligning our assessment methods with our practice. Little compromise is necessary because the children will be successful in a broader sense than they can be in any narrower reform approach. If standardized testing is demanded, incorporate it along with the authentic assessment that fits with authentic learning. Used this way it may confirm the effectiveness of developmentally appropriate practice. As a consequence of these shifts in education we may see early childhood educators using portfolios more and more to

- document the process of learning through display as well as through storage
- assess performance using benchmarks that the education system provides
- record projects undertaken by groups of children
- design, implement, and record the group's progress in single curriculum areas as they align with curriculum outcomes
- monitor the effect of a technological tool, such as digital portfolios, on the process of learning
- support the developmental needs of individual children who have special needs
- involve the children more in the portfolio process from an early age—seeing portfolios as a means for learning as well as a process of assessment

Summary

Portfolio assessment is founded on a philosophy of education, and it is more than a mere collection of observations and other materials. Behind portfolio practice lies a set of beliefs about how learning occurs and how it can be measured. Those who use portfolios tend to focus on a child's individual patterns of development and the importance of child-directed experience, and they see learning and assessment as bound together into a whole. On the one hand, portfolios can provide an alternative to education practices based on content-focused curricula and testing-based assessment. On the other hand, portfolios can offer a holistic and authentic way of documenting an individual's, or group's, learning while monitoring the progress of either or both. Educators need to commit themselves to the philosophy of portfolio assessment so that it can succeed.

Portfolios can take many forms. Even a parent's baby book constitutes a portfolio. Typically the term refers to a systematic documentation of a child's behaviour and learning. Observations and other materials are usually gathered to gain insight into the individual's motivations, interests, stages of development, and other signs of progress. The portfolio would also include some form of analysis of the materials that it contains, and these insights would lead to recommending some course of action, curriculum, or intervention.

Many educators adapt the portfolio process to accommodate their own circumstances and philosophy of practice. While most portfolios would contain a selection of observations, such as running records, anecdotal records, checklists, or rating scales, what each educator seeks—and which child behaviours are to be recorded—remains within the educator's control. Some teachers may need to document the children's achievement of specific competencies. This kind of outcome-based education approach offers educators considerable flexibility. With the portfolio method, educators can record children's specific attainments, or document any other interesting activities that might occur.

The portfolio can also include a wide variety of materials that offers glimpses into the individual child's context—family information, health data, and items connected with that person's culture and social background. This interesting information affects other parts of the portfolio and helps the educator and other team members get to know the child better and see his behaviour within that context. Samples of the child's work or creativity along with photographs and video-recordings can help round out the portfolio. Thus parents can be actively involved in the child's education through a living document. In time the children themselves can choose to contribute what they consider important; the process becomes a collaborative one.

Without some form of analysis the portfolio remains little more than a collection of materials of some sentimental value. The educators, family members, and other team participants must review these collected observations and materials and make some valid inferences about the child's progress from them. Use of the portfolio makes assessment less of a surprise to everyone as all have participated in its development. The analysis usually flows naturally to recommendations and curriculum ideas. As a cycle of collecting data, analyzing it, and developing program plans, the portfolio is never completed. Ideally the portfolio follows the child through the education system and provides a useful tracking of her challenges and progress.

The variety of portfolios has broadened, as has the technology available to educators and parents in building them. Some agencies and schools are successfully creating and using digital or electronic versions. Others combine both an electronic part and a work-sample part in their portfolios. Whatever you eventually choose, consider what resources are available to you before you establish a portfolio process.

Heated debates about approaches to education have tended to produce educators who are either for or against the portfolio approach. Those who have not yet had the opportunity to see a complete and successful portfolio system might try a modified form of portfolio. They may be persuaded to expand the scope of their portfolio process over time.

Key Terms

analysis
anecdotal record
authentic assessment
baby book
chart
checklist
child study
competency
contextual information
digital portfolios
ecomap
event sampling
formative assessment
genogram
holistic
individual education plan (IEP)
individual program plan (IPP)
inference
learning log
life book
life-experience flow chart

media technique
metacognition
objectivity
observation
performance assessment
portfolio
portfolio assessment
professional portfolio
project approach
rating scale
record of achievement
reflective practitioner
Reggio Emilia
rubric
running record
specimen record
standardized test
summary
summative assessment
time sampling

Weblinks

http://tiger.coe.missouri.edu/~vlib/glenn.michelle's.stuff/GLEN3MIC.HTM
Information about authentic assessment, various methods of assessing, and commonly used terminology.

www.newassessment.org/public/assessments/AndMore/FocusedPortfolio.cfm
Key features and components of a good portfolio that may be created by educators or parents.

http://ericeece.org/reggio.html
Information and resources related to the approach to early childhood education developed in the preschools of Reggio Emilia, Italy.

www.odyssey.on.ca/~elaine.coxon/rubrics.htm
Forms of assessment and evaluation as well as links to online rubric and checklist-creation sites.

Observation Sample

It is important for caregivers to ask health questions that will help them provide consistent care and assess children's development, and not to ask questions that are unnecessary or that infringe on the family's privacy. The process shown here will help students frame questions appropriate to their purposes.

Do you agree with the student's rationale for asking the two questions she has developed? What other questions might you ask the parents of an infant in your care?

FRAMING THE QUESTIONS FOR A HEALTH QUESTIONNAIRE

Student's name: Aaron **Date:** September 16, 2003

Component: Routines

Significance: I need to know the child's daily routines in order to help in the transition from home to group care. According to <u>Infants and Toddlers</u>, routines give the infant or toddler a sense of security. The infant learns to trust repetition and lack of change. Although the child may not <u>think</u> about the implemented routines, she or he <u>feels</u> the security of the familiar activities. Many daily routines nurture physical health, particularly those related to cleanliness, eating, and sleeping. Perhaps one of the most recognized and important routines is the child's need for rest and relaxation (in accordance with what is practiced at home). Infants follow their own individual rest schedules, which should be somewhat consistent with home. Opportunities for rest and relaxation, for example, are part of the development and individual needs of children. Therefore, I need to know the child's "normal" routines to fulfill the child's needs and optimize her or his well-being.

Questions I will ask:
1. Describe your child's sleeping patterns.
2. Does your child sleep with any security items? If yes, please specify.

Source: Wilson, L.C., Douville-Watson, L., & Watson, M.A. (1995). <u>Infants and Toddlers: Curriculum and Teaching</u> (3rd ed.). Albany, NY: Delmar.

Observation Sample

This health questionnaire was completed by interviewing the child's mother. The information will help the caregivers provide appropriate care, ease the transition from home to daycare, and assess the child's development.

How might you determine the appropriateness of questions? How might you alter some of these questions if you thought the parent might be uncomfortable answering them?

---

1 of 2

Health Questionnaire

Child's name: _Katie_   Date: _October 29/04_

Age/D.O.B.: _June 2/02_   Recorder: _Tanya_

BIRTH HISTORY

1. At birth, what was your child's length? _20.5 in._ and weight? _7 lb 11 oz_

2. What was the length of your pregnancy? _42 weeks_

3. Please describe any complications: _She was not positioned properly; her head was facing the wrong way at delivery._

4. What was the child's state of health at birth (jaundice)? _Born with Trachea Malacia (premature windpipe)-closing of windpipe. The cartilage in her windpipe wasn't formed, very soft. Her airway would close when she cried or fed._

5. Please describe your child's health after birth: _She was ill a lot, breathing complications. In and out of the hospital for her first year. She is much better now._

DEVELOPMENTAL PATTERNS

6. Do you think your child's growth is fairly steady?   (YES)   NO

7. What is your child's approximate weight now? _36 lb_

BEHAVIORAL PATTERNS

8. Do you consider your child to be outgoing?   (YES)   NO   SOMETIMES

9. Do you consider your child to be shy?   YES   NO   (SOMETIMES)

10. Are there people or objects that comfort your child when s/he's upset? _Mom, Elmo blanket, and her babies (dolls)_

DAILY ROUTINES

11. Does your child generally enjoy mealtime?   (YES)   NO

12. Does your child have any diet restrictions? (cultural, religious, food allergy or sensitivity)   YES   (NO)
    Although I do not allow her to have pop and chocolate (very rare)

13. Please describe an average day on the weekend for your child. Please include when s/he wakes up, feeding, sleeping, and play times until s/he goes to bed in the evening. _8-9 wake up, wash, change diaper, brush hair, teeth. 9:30 breakfast. 10-12 play, watch TV, go outside, on swings, games, neighbors come over. Use potty. 12:30 eat lunch, clean up. 1-5 have snacks, use potty, go visiting at Grandma's, stay home and play, clean together, out for walks. 5:30-6:00 help get dinner prepared. 6:00 dinner._

6:30-7:00 brush teeth, use potty, bedtime story. 7:30 bed.

HEALTH STATUS

14. Do any family members have known allergies or chronic conditions?　　**YES**　　NO
    If YES, what: _____ Allergies _____

15. Has your child had any allergic reactions? (environmental, food, animals, or medications)　**YES**　NO
    Please explain which allergen and the severity: _____ Grass, hayfever-aggravates asthma _____

16. Has your child ever been to a medical specialist?　　**YES**　　NO
    If YES, what was the ailment? _____ Asthma and premature windpipe _____

17. Does your child take medication on a regular basis?　　**YES**　　NO
    If YES, which medication(s)? _____ Vanceril (for asthma) _____

18. Please describe your child's general health. (e.g., recurrent ear infections, skin conditions, colds)
    _____ Health has improved over last few months; she does seem to catch colds quite
    often. _____

19. Is your child ill on a fairly regular basis?　　YES　**NO**

20. Which infectious diseases has your child had?

Mumps	YES	**NO**
Whooping cough	YES	**NO**
Measles	YES	**NO**
Chicken pox	YES	**NO**
Meningitis	YES	**NO**
Pneumonia	YES	**NO**

IMMUNIZATION RECORD

21. Please list your child's immunization schedule:

IMMUNIZATION TYPE	DATE RECEIVED	ANY REACTIONS
DPT	August 2/02	-
DPT	October 25/02	-
DPT	January 30/03	-
MM Rubella	approx. 12 months old	-
DPT	January 24/04	-

Observation Sample

These questions were put together by an ECE student to gather contextual information about a child. Rather than ask the parents to fill out a formal questionnaire, the student met with the child's mother to learn about the family through informal conversation.

Background Information

Recorded by: *Simon* Date: *November 7, 2003*

Method of recording: *Interview with mother*

Child's name: *Robert* Pet name: *Robbie*

What is the composition of your family? (# of adults/children) *Four adults and one child (Robbie). He lives with mom, dad, uncle, maternal grandma and grandpa. Grandpa works in the Middle East, and he sometimes lives there.*

What links do you have with your extended family? (aunts, grandparents, etc.) *We are all very close. Robbie usually meets with his paternal grandparents, aunts, and uncles every weekend.*

Are there any special activities that your family enjoys doing together? *Birthday parties, picnics, Christmas, Thanksgiving dinner, and we usually have a Halloween party at the house.*

What kind of home do you have? *We live in a condominium townhouse with a small yard shared with neighbors.*

Do you see yourself as belonging to any particular cultural, religious, national, or ethnic background or heritage? *We are a mix: Catholic, Islamic, and Trinidadian. Robbie goes to a Catholic church.*

What languages are spoken in your home? *Creole, French, and English.*

Is there any special information about your family? (e.g., particular talents, family experiences, interests, special needs, home moves, or stories) *We are all interested in sports. I play soccer in the Ontario Soccer Association. His uncle is a soccer player too.*

Do you work outside the home? *No. I used to work at Consumers Gas as a clerk.*

What are your current child-care arrangements? *Robbie attends the child-care centre at Centennial College, where I am taking classes.*

What were your previous arrangements for child care? *My grandma used to take care of him – that is, his great-grandma.*

Do you have pets in your home? If so, what? *No, we used to have a cat, but when the baby was born we got rid of it.*

In your family, do you have special words for things? (e.g., toilet = pee-pee) *In my family, we are used to calling the toilet a "potty."*

What do you hope for your child when s/he grows up? *To have a heart, be able to make good decisions, enjoy life to the fullest and all it has to offer. But most of all, to have an education, so that he will become somebody in the world. It might be hard, but I don't want him to give up ever!*

Observation Sample

This log is a simple record of all meetings and discussions with a child's parents. Such a record provides a quick summary of which permissions have been requested, which questionnaires have been completed, and what other discussions have taken place.

What other purposes might a parent-meeting log serve? How might you encourage a reluctant parent to become involved in portfolio assessment of his or her child?

Parent Meeting Log for Portfolio

Child's name: Jean-Paul   **Student's name:** Cara

February 6, 2004: First formal approach to Jean-Paul's parents, Mr. and Mrs. Legore, re: observation of their son. Approached with the approval of toddler room supervisor, Christy. Introductions are made and I immediately describe the purpose of my observation. I receive written consent for the event sampling, informing them that further consent forms will be forthcoming for future observations. I now have to start recording.

February 21, 2004: Meet with the parents to discuss Jean-Paul's general routine as recorded in the format of a daily log. At this meeting, I inform Mrs. Legore of Jean-Paul's impressive oral skills and attempts at autonomous activity. We do discuss, however, Jean-Paul's tendency to become very agitated when a child takes his toy or a situation does not coincide with his immediate need for gratification. It is decided that the best way to deal with this typical behaviour is to encourage verbal expression of Jean-Paul's thoughts and feelings, needs and wants. This is not inconceivable given Jean-Paul's strong oral skills.

March 13, 2004: Approach Mr. and Mrs. Legore in the morning to acquire permission to complete remaining elements of the portfolio assignment. I present two permission forms to be checked and validated--one to perform general observation for the purpose of a checklist observation, the second to take photographs of the child as a component of the portfolio. Permission is granted on both counts. Mr. Legore is also informed that a brief meeting will be needed for the purpose of acquiring contextual information. We agree to conduct this meeting the same day--March 13, 2004--at approximately 5:00 p.m., when Mr. Legore arrives back at the child-care to pick up Jean-Paul.

Later that day, Mr. Legore arrives back at the child-care and we conduct a short 10–15 minute meeting to fill out the contextual questionnaire. The interview is done in a direct, no-nonsense manner in order to keep the meeting short and to the point; both Jean-Paul and his older sister are waiting for Mr. Legore and me to finish in order to return home. At the end of our interview, I inform Mr. Legore that a similar meeting will

---

have to be conducted for the purpose of obtaining information on Jean-Paul's medical history. We agree to set next Friday afternoon--March 21, 2004--as a tentative date for the next meeting to take place. I also receive verbal permission from Mr. Legore to obtain photocopies of Jean-Paul's immunization record from the centre; we agree that this will save time at our future meeting.

March 21, 2004: Mr. Legore arrives at the end of the day to inform me that he cannot meet at this time due to car problems. I ask him if next Thursday afternoon--March 27, 2004--would be an acceptable time for rescheduling. He agrees, and the meeting is temporarily postponed.

March 27, 2004: Mr. Legore arrives shortly after 5:00 p.m., and we immediately sit down in the office to commence the meeting. Once again, we are both motivated to conduct the interview quickly; the children are waiting for their father and it is the beginning of Easter weekend. The questioning is fairly routine and Mr. Legore shows no reservations about answering the questions that I choose to ask. We get into an interesting discussion about blood type and why it is not a required component of child-care health questionnaires, nor a subject even mentioned in the Day Nurseries Act. The interview goes well. I opt to omit certain contextual details from my questioning in order to focus more on the child's health and to keep the meeting moving along at a good pace.

Observation Sample

This summary of skills was prepared as part of a portfolio assessment. The skills are categorized by domain, but they are not explained and no inferences are drawn.

What other developmental criteria or categories might be added to this summary—information that could be drawn from most running records, video-recordings, and time sampling?

SUMMARY OF SKILLS   1 of 2

Child's name: Kirsten   Recorder: Damian
Age/D.O.B.: 19 months   Date: June 4, 2003

Drawn from the following samples: running record, video recording, time
sampling

<u>Appearance</u>
-girl
-dark brown hair
-ears pierced
-fair-skinned
-teeth in upper and lower front

<u>Posture</u>
-stands erect at water table with legs apart
-sits on carpet with back straight and legs extended in front

<u>Mobility</u>
-walks without assistance
-toddles quickly

<u>Physical Skills</u>
Gross motor:
-sitting
-walking/toddling

Fine motor:
-palmar grasp (picking up cup)
-pincer grasp (pinching sponges)
-eye-hand coordination (pouring water out of cup into bin)

<u>Language/Communication</u>
-puts words and sounds together
-squeals (apparently when excited)
-uses one word to signify whole thoughts
-"mine," "frog"

<u>Sensory Explorations</u>
-dips hands in water and moves them around
-creates splashes by raising hands in air and forcefully lowering them
 into water
-collects water in cup and then slowly pours it out
-feels sponges with her hands

<u>Demonstration of Cognitive Function</u>
-demonstrates understanding of function of a cup
-fills cup with water and then pours it out
-names objects: "frog"
-responds to experiences with some facial movement (smiling)

<u>Demonstration of Emotions</u>
-periodically squeals and laughs
-smiles while splashing water
-appears satisfied with her accomplishment
-screams and then hits another child
-at this time, apparently unwilling to share or cooperate

<u>Social Interaction</u>
-appears to be quite independent
-engages in solitary play at water table
-engages in associative play with three other children when playing with
 float

Observation Sample

This portfolio analysis provides a developmental profile of the child. Based on a variety of observations, including narrative recordings (see running record, pp. 116–118), charts, media recordings, and parental input, the student draws inferences about the child's development. The inferences are supported with theories and norms, which are detailed in the list of references.

How might the content of this analysis be shared with parents who have limited English language skills?

PORTFOLIO ANALYSIS

Child's name: Mandy   Observer: Daisy
Age: 25 months   Date: December 2, 2003

The components of Mandy's portfolio were gathered from September 1998 to the present (December 2, 1998). She has reached some significant developmental milestones during this observation period, including the transition from emerging expressive language skills to acquisition of new vocabulary and quickly developing expressive language capabilities. The following analysis gives an overview of Mandy's developmental progress, skills, and behaviours in the following domains: physical, language and communication, emotional, social, cognitive, and temperament/personality.

Physical Development

Mandy's large muscle control appears good and is at a developmental level expected for a 2-year-old. As the checklist (for 2- and 3-year-olds) indicates, she has mastered the large motor skills identified as typical for a 2-year-old (walks alone, bends over and picks up toy without falling over, seats self in chair, walks up and down stairs with assistance) (Allen & Marotz, 1994, pp. 165-166). In fact, Mandy has shown competence in some physical skills identified as normal for 3-year-olds (runs well in forward direction, jumps in place with two feet together, throws ball, kicks ball forward) (Allen & Marotz, 1994, 165-166). The photographs of Mandy in the playground-- running, walking, climbing into and out of riding toys and on and off tricycles--also offer evidence that she is coordinated and able to use her body competently to participate in chosen physical activities. The running record observation offers many examples of Mandy's large muscle coordination, including use of a variety of riding toys, climbing stairs with ease, and climbing up the slide from the bottom.

Her small muscle control is also typical for most 2-year-olds. The checklist indicates that Mandy has mastered use of a spoon; taking off her coat, socks, and shoes; holding and drinking from a cup; turning pages in a book; placing rings on a stick; and placing pegs in a pegboard. One area requiring more practice is the zipping and unzipping of zippers. The only zippers Mandy has experience with are on her coats, and they are smaller than a "large practice zipper." Props in the environment to offer practice would be helpful here.

During the matching game identified in the anecdotal record (October 28), there was evidence that Mandy preferred to use large muscles rather than small muscles. Instead of using her hands and eyes to match the pictures, she chose to stand on the matching picture. This may simply mean that she found the game more fun this way, but may also be an indication that she is more comfortable using her body in this way. While she displays no difficulty with small motor activities undertaken, it may be that, while her visual acuity is maturing, she is more comfortable using larger muscles rather than hand/eye ("How Language Develops").

Language and Communication

Mandy's receptive language skills are excellent. She seems to understand what is said to her and is beginning to express herself verbally using sentences with correct grammatical structure (e.g., "I want to go outside"). The checklist indicates that she has mastered the language skills normal for a 2-year-old and has advanced in many areas to a 3-year-old level. During the anecdotal record done November 5, Mandy's mother was able to communicate to her that she had to leave and go to work. Mandy accepted this immediately and responded accordingly by saying good-bye and leaving her mother to join the group.

Evidence of good expressive language skills is apparent in the anecdotal record done November 19. Mandy was able to ask the caregiver what she was doing, and responded in a manner that showed understanding ("Can I help?"). She understood the question, "What colour is this?" and responded correctly. Between the ages of 30 and 36 months, it is normal for toddlers to label objects (Wilson, Douville-Watson, & Watson, 1995, p. 348); answer questions appropriately (Allen & Marotz, 1994, p. 93); use pronouns and prepositions (Barrett et al, 1995, p. 235); and say many intelligible words (Sheridan, 1975). Mandy's language skills demonstrate all of these competencies, indicating a mastery of language and communication skills beyond expectations for a 2-year-old.

Mandy uses correct words, but sometimes mispronounces them. On the audiotape, she refers to the "sound" on the tape as "tound" and "yellow" as "lellow." As her muscle control matures and Mandy is exposed to appropriate modelling of the proper pronunciation, her next step in development will be to correctly pronounce vowel and consonant sounds. It is normal for children in the age range of 18 to 36 months to simplify the pronunciation of words they find difficult: "All of these implications show that your child is actively learning the sound patterns of language" (Skarakis-Doyle, 1988a).

The contextual questionnaire completed by Mandy's mother identifies language skills as "good for her age." She records that conflicts with Mandy are generally handled via verbal communication, and that this usually works. The same applies when Mandy reacts to new situations. These are also strong indicators that Mandy's language and communication abilities exceed the norm.

Emotional Development

Mandy appears to be well-adjusted emotionally to her routine at daycare. The daily log chart indicates that she moves through routines and transitions well, and that she is able to anticipate what is coming next in her day (e.g., she finds her cot after lunch, and knows that after nap she needs to find her shoes and put them on). She displays a cheerful disposition consistently, exploring her environment and engaging caregivers with confidence. According to Allen and Marotz (1994), "the 2-year-old gradually begins to function more ably and amiably" (p. 78). The event sampling based on observations done October 8 and 15 indicates that Mandy displays autonomous behaviours as they relate to her self-help skills. She consistently tries to do things for herself, but does not hesitate to ask for help when she needs it: "Erikson has pointed to the struggle for autonomy as the big issue in the toddler's life. Autonomy means self-determination, independence. It is the ability to decide for oneself what one is going to do. Autonomy means, 'Me do it!' It means, 'no!'" ("Foundations"). Mandy is often heard saying both of these phrases; however, avoiding direct commands successfully avoids power struggles when caregivers need Mandy to move through a transition (e.g., leaving a play activity to prepare for lunch).

Another issue in toddlerhood affecting Mandy's emotional development is toilet training. Her mother has started leaving Mandy's diaper off at home and has asked for consistency at day care. The event sampling indicates that Mandy's attempts at toileting are positively supported and that she does not seem to be experiencing any stress in relation to this new routine. She accepts it as part of her day; however, this is a new skill. Sensitive and positive encouragement is very important to keep her from feeling that she is being pressured. Positive reinforcement (big fuss when successful!) results in pride-like behaviour on Mandy's part.

Separation is an issue in toddlerhood, and Mandy appears to have successfully achieved the ability to separate from her parents. The anecdotal record done November 5 is evidence that she has formed a positive attachment and trusting relationship with her mother. This enables her to separate, knowing her mother is going to work and will return later. Wilson, Douville-Watson, and Watson (1995) suggest that "becoming a separate psychological being is one of the most complicated tasks a toddler has to face. During the two years starting from birth, the child establishes a very strong attachment to the mother" (p. 302). The more secure this relationship has been prior to 2, the easier the separation process.

Greenspan's (1985) theory of emotional development indicates that, by 24 months of age, children should be encouraged to express their feelings as emotional ideas rather than just act them out. Mandy is very successful at this and often chooses to play in the dramatic play area with dolls, dress-up clothes, toys, and materials from other parts of the room. She is also able to create images in her mind, pretending to be "mommy" while she cuddles a doll (Greenspan, 1985). Her excellent language skills enable her to express her role in play and to use items symbolically.

Mandy's ability to make independent choices throughout the day and her even, cheerful disposition are indicators that her emotional development is healthy for a 2-year-old. She is now entering Erikson's stage of initiative versus guilt, reflecting the "beginning of guilt-like behaviour, pride-like behaviour and shame-like behaviour" (Barrett et al., 1995, p. 262). Her level of emotional development at 2 puts her on good footing to face this next phase of emotional development positively.

Social Development

Mandy is happy to play alongside the other children, engaging most often in parallel play. The running record observation and photographs give evidence that she likes to watch what others are doing, or likes to play alongside them. Her play behaviour in the playground as she walks along with the children playing with the wagon is evidence of onlooker play. The daily log chart identifies pretend and symbolic play activity in which Mandy participates in solitary play or plays parallel to other children. While she may engage other children in play briefly, she prefers to play her own game. According to Barrett et al. (1995), Mildred Parten identified six categories of social play. Mandy's play activity best fits Parten's second, third, and fourth levels--solitary, onlooker, and parallel, respectively: "The second level in Parten's hierarchy, solitary play, involves a child playing independently and making no effort to interact with anyone else. The next level, onlooker play, occurs when a child watches other children play. At the fourth level, parallel play, a child plays in similar ways as another child with similar toys but does not interact with the other child" (Barrett et al., 1995, p. 326). The running record observation gives evidence of both solitary and onlooker play. The daily log chart gives evidence that Mandy, while engaged in pretend play, was playing alongside other children in dramatic play, but participating in her own activity.

Mandy likes to play with a variety of materials while in day care. Her mother identifies her favorite activities at home as "playing with dolls, reading, riding her bike, and helping mom with cleaning or laundry." Likewise, at daycare, Mandy engages in a variety of play activities throughout the day. Her ability to move between different activities contributes to her ability to practice social skills with caregivers and other children in the room: "When toddlers play together, they talk to one another, and this gives them a chance to practice both their language and social skills" (Barrett et al., 1995, p. 238).

The checklist indicates that Mandy imitates adult behaviour in play, as seen in her play behaviours identified in the daily log chart and by her mom in the health report. Although she is egocentric (see the incident in the running record where she is upset that another child is using the slide at the playground), Mandy's language skills contribute greatly to her ability to communicate with caregivers and other children. She is aware of her peers throughout the day; she screams with the other toddlers at the playground in response to their screaming. Still participating in her own play, she does not hesitate to "join the fun" with the others.

Mandy's social development is within the norm for a 2-year-old. She enjoys dressing up, imitates family activities, likes to be around other children, but tends to observe, sometimes imitating their actions (screaming), and explores everything, including other children. She is independent, but able to approach caregivers when she feels the need (Allen & Marotz, 1994, p. 83). In a photograph of Mandy in the playground, she is motioning that she would like to be picked up; the running record shows that she approached a caregiver for a cuddle.

Cognitive Development

Mandy loves to explore her environment and tries most materials and activities in it. When something new is introduced, she is eager to see what it is and make a decision about her level of participation. She prefers activities that do not involve "getting her hands dirty." As a result, a variety of sensory experiences must be available so that she gets the stimulation she needs as well as opportunities for creative expression through creative art activities.

Mandy's ability to expand symbolic thinking skills contributes greatly to her language development. Her ability to represent things with other things (e.g., she brings a toy car to the dramatic play center and uses it as a bus to take us to the store; she uses a large box in the room as a slide) indicates that she is moving into the first substage of Piaget's preoperational stage, called "preconceptual." For example, Mandy is able to keep track of time by understanding what is coming next (e.g., "We are going to eat lunch and then it is time for a nap"; understanding the routine, she knows that she is to go to her cot after lunch). She is beginning to classify and label objects (matching game, mittens and hats) and has some understanding of quantity (more, gone), number (more), space (up, down, behind, under, over), and time (soon, now). Wilson, Douville-Watson, and Watson (1995) identify these concepts as typical for Mandy's age.

Mandy's love of books positively contributes to her cognitive and language development. She is exposed to a variety of topics and information, facilitating her learning about the world around her. She loves to manipulate linking blocks, and enjoys making things out of them. For example, she loves to make a hat out of star linking blocks--linking them in a circle and putting them on her head!

Mandy also displays "deferred imitation" in her play activities. For example, during water play in which soap was added to make bubbles, Mandy went to the kitchen center and brought out some dishes. She identified her activity, "Washing dishes!"--clearly representing imitation of washing dishes at home. The developmental checklist used for this analysis identifies imitation of adult behaviours as within the norm for a 2-year-old.

Mandy's physical development is a factor in her cognitive development: "Toddlers learn with their whole bodies, not just their heads. They learn more through their hands than they do through their ears. They learn by doing, not only by just thinking. They learn by touching, mouthing, and trying out, not by being told" (Gonzalez-Mena, 1986). The use of her whole body rather than just her hands during the matching game is an example of physical development contributing to a cognitive learning experience.

Emotional development also contributes to cognitive learning. Mandy's trust in and comfort with her environment enable her to explore and therefore experience with confidence. This greatly facilitates her learning; she can make choices and find activities that have meaning for her. The major accomplishments of toddlerhood include "growing independence . . . self-help skills such as dressing, feeding, washing and toileting. . . . Learning to use the toilet, like all the other self-help skills, is a physical feat, as well as an intellectual and emotional one" (Gonzalez-Mena, 1986).

Temperament/Personality

The health questionnaire identifies Mandy as "sometimes shy, sometimes outgoing, friendly, cautious, and easygoing." The daily log chart indicates that Mandy is cheerful, adapted to routines, and most often in a positive mood. Her activity level is high. She moves easily from one activity to another and is eager to explore new materials in the environment. While Mandy approaches new situations with confidence, it is important to allow her to join the experience at her own pace. She will often watch for a few minutes before joining in.

Transitions pose little problem for Mandy. She listens to instructions and is usually eager to please when asked to do something. Her continuing need for independence should be fostered by caregivers. Mandy responds best when given choices that ultimately encourage the desired behaviour, rather than when direct demands are made.

Mandy's cheerful disposition and positive interactions with caregivers and peers can always be depended on. She loves to engage caregivers in her games, especially pretend play, and is able to extend the play experience as it progresses. A dress-up activity turned into a major cleaning out of the dress-up bench--trying on new outfits throughout the activity! Her mother is quite right about Mandy's friendliness. As she matures, pro-social and helping skills are emerging, and her ready smile makes her a positive influence on everyone in the room.

The Whole Child

Mandy's development in all domains meets the norms for her age (2 years) and in some areas exceeds normative expectations. While this analysis looks at each domain separately, it is important to note that development remains integrated in toddlerhood. Balance is needed to facilitate development: "Overemphasis in one area or limited involvement in another may create unnecessary stress or it may delay development for the child" (Wilson, Douville-Watson, & Watson, 1995, p. 35).

The fact that Mandy was born eight weeks prematurely (see health report) does not seem to have delayed her development in any area. Her physical stature is small (she weighs about 21 lb.--the average identified in Allen and Marotz (1994) is 26 to 32 lb.); however, her physical capabilities fall within the norm. Two-year-olds typically weigh about four times their birth weight; this puts Mandy right on the norm (birth weight was 5 lb. 2 oz.). She is emotionally able to take risks. Her natural curiosity encourages lots of exploration in her environment; this is significantly facilitated by her physical competence, which also contributes greatly to her feelings of confidence.

Mandy's excellent language skills are also critical to her overall development. She can express her needs and desires verbally, understand simple directions and questions posed by caregivers, assert her independence positively, understand the meaning of symbols facilitating symbolic representation and pretend play activities, and expand her knowledge of the world around her via verbal expression and receptive language.

Overall, Mandy is a normal toddler, actively exploring her world, eagerly trying new things, all the while asserting her independence. Her egocentricity is beginning to give way as emerging pro-social skills are observed. She is liked by her peers and rarely gets into power struggles with other toddlers. Her sunny disposition makes her a positive influence in the toddler room.

References Used

Allen, K.E., & Marotz, L.R. (1994). *Development profiles: Pre-birth through eight* (2nd ed.). Albany, NY: Delmar.

Barrett, K.C., et al. (1995). *Child development.* Westerville, OH: Glencoe.

Biracree, T, & Biracree, N. (1989). *The parents' book of facts: Child development from birth to age five.* New York: Facts on File.

Brazelton, T.B. (1992). *Touchpoints: Your child's emotional and behavioral development.* Reading, MA: Addison-Wesley.

Foundations: Observation and development [Handout, course CY-106]. Toronto: Centennial College.

Gonzalez-Mena, Janet. (1986, November). Toddlers: What to expect. *Young Children.*

Greenspan, S.I., & Greenspan, N.T. (1985). *First feelings: Milestones in the emotional development of your baby and child.* New York: Viking.

How language develops and what you can do [Handout, Toddler Development]. Toronto: Centennial College.

Intellectual development. (1995). *Readings Package,* 8b iv. Toronto: Centennial College.

McCaie, L. [Supervising teacher, Child-Care Center]. Personal conversations.

Outline of expected ages and stages in the development of spoken language. (1995). *Readings Package,* 8b vii. Toronto: Centennial College.

Sheridan M.D. (1975). *The developmental progress of infants and young children* (3rd ed.). London: Her Majesty's Stationery Office.

Skarakis-Doyle, Elizabeth. (1988a). Language development. Tuscon, AZ: Communication Skill Builders.

Skarakis-Doyle, Elizabeth. (1988b). Speech development. Tuscon, AZ: Communication Skill Builders

Weir, M. [Mandy's mother]. Personal interviews.

Wilson, L.C., Douville-Watson, L., & Watson, M.A. (1995). *Infants and toddlers: Curriculum and teaching* (3rd ed.). Albany, NY: Delmar.

Observation Sample

This report, presented to the parents at the time of a portfolio-review meeting, briefly outlines the contents of the portfolio, the child's developmental profile, and new program plans. It summarizes the inferences made in the portfolio analysis, stating them clearly and concisely for the benefit of the parents.

What curriculum plan could you develop from this report?

PORTFOLIO REVIEW MEETING REPORT

Child's name: Jill   **Date:** November 21, 2003
D.O.B./age: Nov. 22, 2002/1 year old   **Meeting called by:** Art (ECE student)
Those present: Art, Adam and Dulcie (parents), and Tina (teacher)
Intention of meeting: To review portfolio

Review of recent additions to portfolio: Photographs, art work, and summaries
Changed context, social, or family circumstances: None
Development summary given by: Art

Summary details: Observations (time sampling, checklist, and running record), health report, ecological systems, family tree, videotapes, baby book from parents, daily logs

Cognition: Jill understands the use of many everyday objects. She understands simple directions and has an understanding of object permanence.

Personality: Jill is striving for independence right now and is starting to enjoy doing things on her own, such as eating. She has demonstrated curiosity in new experiences.

Language and communication: Jill babbles typically for a child her age. She also has demonstrated the beginning of her vocabulary by saying "hello." Jill is always able to convey her needs, whether it's by reaching up toward what she wants or by falling down when she does not want to move.

Emotional development: Jill shows no fear of strangers or of being hurt by her actions, which is typical for an infant of her age. She also has demonstrated consistently her wants and needs.

Physical development: Jill's physical development is consistent with a child of her age; however, she does need some encouragement in the area of stair climbing. Her gross motor skills are very advanced and her fine motor skills are also extremely good for her age; she grasps and passes items from one hand to the other.

Social skills: Jill is egocentric, which is quite usual at this age. She seems to enjoy the company of other adults and is not afraid to approach them and ask to be held.

Curriculum implications: Activities are being planned to help Jill in her social skills such as playing beside other children in parallel play. Also there are activities to help her stair-climbing motor skills.

Program plan strategies: Activities involving more pro-social, self-help skills and social interaction will benefit Jill at this time and should be offered to her throughout the day.

Observation Sample

This is an example of the YMCA Playing to Learn curriculum and assessment documentation.

Compare and contrast it with the traditional assessment process and typical observation methodologies.

Purses and Bags

The infants were very curious about the large paper bag that I brought in and left in the middle of the playroom floor. Simryn and Claire were the first to venture over to see what was inside the bag. Megan and Conor were not far behind. Claire stuck her head inside the bag and pulled out a blue purse, which she carried over to the climber to investigate. Simryn felt that the black backpack went better with her ensemble. She put the straps around her neck and off she went. Conor could not decide what item to choose and after examining them thoroughly, he selected a white purse that he then draped over his body. Megan chose the black shiny purse and the red gift bag. All of the children moved about the room with their new acquisitions, opening and closing them, filling them with blocks and small toys, dumping them out and repeating the actions. The purses and bags remained in the classroom for two weeks, and the children never grew tired of them. They seemed to find new and different ways of playing with them every day.

Note: This was such a good example of functional, imitative play. They were not exactly role-playing, but they did engage in pretend activities. It was interesting to see how their choices reflected other aspects of their personalities. It was also interesting to see how many other aspects of development came into their investigations. Simryn, for example, discovered that her feet and legs fit inside the big white shopping bag.

Measuring Outcomes

chapter 9

Whether students learn something well is more important than when they learn it.

Waterloo County Board of Education (1993)

From the perspective of educators, learner outcomes are a discrete expression of a philosophy of education.

Gayle Mindes, Harold Ireton, and Carol Mardell-Czudnowski (1996)

Significant outcomes focus on the "big picture" instead of discrete facts, rote memorization, or decontextualized bits of information.

Kay Burke (1994)

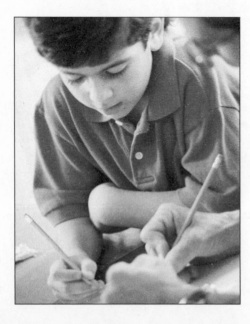

Outcome-based education assesses a child's mastery of specified learning outcomes based on knowledge, skills, and dispositions.

Focus Questions

1. Why are there such wide differences of opinion about the philosophy of outcome-based education (OBE)?

2. What might you observe in a school or other agency that might lead you to think that OBE was being practised?

3. What makes OBE approaches to assessment the same as or different from any other assessment approach?

Learning Outcomes

- Learners will assess the measurability of learning outcomes.
- Learners will develop ways of observing and documenting the achievement of learning outcomes.

Features of Outcome-Based Education

Outcome-based education (OBE) can take a variety of forms. It tends to focus on the following principles:

1. All people can learn.
2. The outcomes of education should be stated.
3. Curricula should be designed to ensure that the outcomes are achievable.
4. Outcomes are measurable and observable.
5. This approach to education will help society solve its problems.

Some forms of OBE emphasize self-directed learning as an essential component of the philosophy, although OBE specifies neither exactly how learning occurs nor what the content of the curriculum should be. How learning should occur, how it should be stated as outcomes, and how that learning can be measured are issues open to a variety of interpretations. Since, however, the philosophy of OBE usually implies that individuals construct their own meaning from experience, the underlying practice of OBE is typically based on cognitive learning theory and constructivism.

Because OBE is part of an evolving philosophy of education, it may not always be clearly identified. Specific elements may appear as part of a stated OBE approach, may be merged with other education philosophies, or may exist without any relation to OBE.

Terminology used in outcome-based education and linked philosophies

The philosophy of outcome-based education, rooted in the behaviourism of Bloom (1956), developed by Tyler (1965) and his work on educational objectives, and Spady's

(1977) articulation of **exit outcomes**, has at its core a belief in transformational education empowered by social action. Although highly controversial, elements of OBE are evident in many of today's education practices. They may be identified in a number of differing ways and associated with OBE to varying extents as they are blended with other education philosophies. Here are some of the terms related to OBE (these terms are sometimes labelled by their acronyms—which is particularly confusing because some share the same acronym):

- Outcome-Based Education (OBE)
- Outcome-Based Learning (OBL)
- Problem-Based Learning (PBL) or (PL)
- Mastery Learning (ML)
- Project-based Learning (PL)
- Active Learning
- Performance-Based Learning (PBL)
- Standards-based Learning (SL)

These terms are not the same in philosophy, though they share some characteristics associated with a focus on the end products or exit standards of the education process (or the learning process itself), rather than focus on a subject-oriented perspective. The more recent developments in the sphere of OBE incorporate elements of **constructivism**, which are based on newer understandings about how children learn. Interestingly, some outcome measures incorporate Gardener's **multiple intelligences** theory (1993) and applications of up-to-date brain research. For clarity this chapter deals with OBE in its most obvious form.

Observable components of OBE

The following elements will help you recognize OBE environments:

- Mission statements address how all children can learn, and their goals include issues of social justice.
- The curriculum is framed in terms of learning outcomes.
- Learning is identified in areas of knowledge, skill, and **dispositions** (attitudes).
- Programs offer an integrated and/or thematic curriculum.
- Child-directed learning is emphasized.
- Rote-learning is eliminated.
- Children are encouraged to learn from each other.
- The assessment criteria are the learning outcomes.
- Assessment is ongoing and focuses on success.
- Assessment involves work sampling and student conferences.
- Dispositions such as being cooperative, being open to teamwork, and being empathetic and pro-social are valued.

- Social studies are a high priority in the curriculum.
- Teachers act as motivators and facilitators.
- Teachers work in teams.
- Computers are used for teaching and for portfolio record-keeping.
- Collectivism is the norm for teachers and children.
- Age groups are mixed.
- Children are promoted to the next grade whatever their assessment results.
- Children with special needs are integrated into the class or room.
- Parents are considered partners.
- Social interventions may be offered to those "in need."
- The school may be called a "community of learners."

The purposes of outcomes

The intention behind the articulation of outcomes, whether they are program outcomes, child development outcomes, standards or individual learning outcomes is to make improvements in some way. Each of these is associated with **social reform**. Some outcomes make individual improvements the priority while others focus more on collective improvement. Both are interconnected. Social reform can be seen from different perspectives:

- individual development and learning
- family development and improvement
- societal development and improvement
- global development and improvement

When assessing outcomes, bear in mind that supporting the individual child is a small part of supporting the whole. OBE targets social reform by supporting learning and development at the individual level.

Accountability is another purpose of outcome measurement. Assessment of each individual can contribute to the larger picture of the successful performance of a program, school, locality, or society. Typically some budgetary considerations associated with accountability measures can be controversial.

OBE assessment

DEFINITION: Outcome-based education assessment

Outcome-based education (OBE) assessment measures an individual's demonstrated competence against specified learning outcomes.

The outcome-based education approach to assessment usually employs alternative assessment techniques—naturalistic observations, role-performance demonstrations, and work samplings—rather than traditional testing to summarize the acquisition of knowledge, skills, and dispositions (or attitudes) as they relate to certain criteria called **learning outcomes**.

The OBE curriculum is delivered and outcomes are assessed differently according to the individual philosophy of the school or agency and the practices of the local school boards and administrations. The OBE approach is found in school settings most often, although child-care centres may articulate and assess their own outcomes.

Learning outcomes

DEFINITION: Learning outcome

A **learning outcome** is a broad statement that establishes the knowledge, skill, and disposition that a child will acquire through experience or from an education program.

Each learning outcome should be measurable, achievable, and observable. A child's **role performance**, or demonstration of **competency**, is evaluated for

- **knowledge:** the information that the child must demonstrate that he or she knows;
- **skill:** the action that the child must perform (often demonstrating the knowledge); and
- **disposition:** the manner in which the skill is performed, or the demonstrated value.

Learning outcomes are usually written in broad general terms. For example, the outcome "uses patterns and relationships of the fundamental concepts found in mathematics" implies a particular understanding of mathematics and focuses on general rather than specific skills.

The three aspects may not always be stated implicitly in the outcome. Some learning outcomes may state only a skill while implying the knowledge needed to demonstrate that skill. For example, the outcome "communicates ideas in complete sentences" states a skill and also implies that the individual has knowledge of the language. Learning outcomes may exclude dispositions because they are not measurable. For example, the outcome "attends to orally presented stories and poems" requires the demonstration only of attention, not of enthusiasm.

Most learning outcomes specify performance criteria. For example, the outcome "uses a variety of construction materials to build three-dimensional models" requires the understanding of the properties of construction materials, the concept of three-dimensional models, and the connection between these two concepts through the demonstration of a specific skill.

Sometimes learning outcomes are articulated at differing levels of performance on a **rating scale**, such as the following (used by the York Region Board of Education in Ontario).

1. beginning to work toward mastery
2. demonstration of mastery not yet consistent
3. consistent demonstration of mastery at grade level
4. demonstrating performance beyond expectations

Levels could also be described as

a. skill demonstrated
b. skill emerging
c. skill not yet demonstrated

In some cases, levels of performance may be indicated according to the way the learning outcome is stated. The outcome statement may be made more complex when the type of skill demonstration is also specified. The following examples show the conditions of performance in brackets:

1. identifies characteristics of mammals living on land (by drawing and labelling diagrams)
2. compares and contrasts characteristics of mammals living on land (by discussing the characteristics in essay form)
3. analyzes the characteristics of mammals living on land to hypothesize possible processes of adaptation (by conducting literature and scientific research and documenting the results)

These learning outcomes indicate the levels of critical thought required for their demonstration. The least challenging might be number 1, the most challenging number 3. The conditions for demonstration may be assumed to follow the same sequence of difficulty for many people. However, for some children, drawing might in fact be more challenging than writing an essay or conducting research.

Learning outcomes may be derived from **standards**. These standards may be broken down into performance criteria that are listed within the learning outcome.

- **standard:** The learner will gain self-help skills that enable him or her to be self-sufficient in modern society.

- **learning outcome:** The learner will demonstrate a range of self-help skills that enable him or her to function independently in order to earn a living, live independently, access resources, feed and clothe herself or himself, and become mobile within the local community.

Learning outcomes and education objectives Learning outcomes may appear to be similar to the **objectives** that are articulated as part of the process toward achieving education goals, and some people use the terms "outcomes" and "objectives" interchangeably. Although both are statements of learning that are measurable and reflect the intentions of the educator, there are some significant differences between them:

Learning outcomes	Education objectives
• use broad statements of learning	• use more specific statements of learning
• refer to end products	• refer to a step toward a stated goal
• focus on integrated learning	• focus on separate "pieces" of learning
• are rooted in OBE philosophy	• are rooted in behaviouristic philosophy
• do not relate to a time frame for learning	• typically have a specified time frame
• do not indicate the curriculum content	• may emanate from a set curriculum
• do not imply how the learning will occur	• may imply a process of learning
• include skills and dispositions	• focus on knowledge and skills
• may imply knowledge base	
• are written so that they are measurable, achievable, and observable at the end of an experience or education program	• are written so that the discrete pieces of learning can be assessed during a formal course of learning
• can fit with authentic assessment processes	• usually require more traditional methods of assessment

Expressing curriculum as learning outcomes The following excerpt from a Grade 2 music curriculum shows how the curriculum can be expressed as learning outcomes. These particular outcomes focus on knowledge rather than specific skills. The references to the children's aesthetic sense show how dispositions can be included in outcomes.

Music: Critical Thinking

By the end of Grade 2, students will

- express their response to music from a variety of cultures and historical periods (e.g., "Largo al factotum della città" from The Barber of Seville by Rossini, "Lunatic Menu" by Ippu Do)

- communicate their thoughts and feelings about the music they hear, using language and a variety of art forms and media (e.g., create a dance, dramatize a song)

- recognize that mood can be created through music (e.g., in a work such as Carnival of the Animals by [Camille] Saint-Saëns)

- explain, using basic musical terminology, their preference for specific songs or pieces of music

- recognize and explain the effects of different musical choices (e.g., slow music that is loud can be dramatic or ceremonial whereas slow music that is soft can suggest thoughtfulness)

Source: Ontario Ministry of Education and Training, The Arts: The Ontario Curriculum, Grades 1-8 (1998).

The OBE controversy

It is impossible to include a chapter about measuring learning outcomes without returning to OBE as a controversial philosophy of education. Those who disagree with the approach offer such strong philosophical and political criticisms as

- OBE is an exercise in social engineering.
- OBE contradicts some religious beliefs.
- OBE manipulates personal values and attitudes.
- OBE is a move away from content-based education.
- OBE reduces the family's role in the child's nurturance and education.
- OBE diminishes education standards.
- OBE represents a move from individualism to collectivism.

Many people may have a problem with only one or two components of OBE or may be uncomfortable about some local practices related to OBE. Others may be skeptical about what they perceive as "New Age" practices, without determining their source or appreciating the interconnected nature or real goals of OBE philosophy. Teachers may be concerned that some OBE practices are not labelled as such or that the origins of OBE are unclear.

Proponents of the purer forms of OBE believe that, if implemented thoroughly by teachers who are well aligned with its principles, OBE offers an opportunity for broad-based and far-reaching education improvement. They see OBE's potential to have significant social impact, enabling those who have been traditionally disadvantaged to be more successful and to make a more positive contribution to society by being more productive. They believe that a more equitable society is possible if the education process in general, and the educators in particular, facilitate the acquisition of relevant knowledge, allow for the development of needed skills, and reflect dispositions compatible with social justice. These elements are the basis of the child's learning outcomes, according to OBE.

Using outcome-based assessment

Those on each side of the debate perceive the advantages and disadvantages of OBE assessment differently. The following lists outline some of the most common arguments for and against the system.

Advantages

- Learning outcomes are articulated criteria for assessment.
- Assessment of learning outcomes addresses knowledge and skills.
- Dispositions can be evaluated.
- Values are stated rather than assumed.
- Assessment methods can be flexible.
- Learning outcomes are comprehensive.
- OBE assessment is congruent with OBE curriculum.
- All can understand the learning outcomes.

- Learning-outcome measurement is fair and applied equitably.
- OBE and OBE assessment are catalysts for social transformation.
- OBE and OBE assessment are congruent with other types of school reform.
- OBE assessment can incorporate other types of assessment.
- OBE assessment is simple and straightforward.
- OBE assessment ensures that learning can be measured.

Disadvantages

- Learning outcomes themselves must be assessed for their appropriateness.
- Knowledge components may be implied rather than stated.
- Many educators are concerned about assessing values and attitudes.
- The values stated may not be acceptable to everyone.
- Assessment methods may be subjective.
- Some learning outcomes are limited to certain subject areas and are not open to interrelated learning.
- If OBE philosophy is considered disagreeable, then OBE assessment is also not acceptable.
- Some learning outcomes are open to interpretation.
- The criteria for learning outcomes are no fairer nor more equitable than any other articulated criteria.
- OBE and OBE assessment have the potential to manipulate social systems and beliefs.
- Although education reform might be necessary, disagreement exists about the nature of OBE.
- OBE assessment may neglect significant developmental assessment.
- OBE assessment assumes that learning occurs only when outcomes are taught or assessed; it does not assess learning that is not included in the stated outcomes.

Measuring Outcomes

Measurement methods

The simplest way to assess learning outcomes is to list them and check off when or whether the child has achieved them. However, the child's performance may not be assessed very accurately. This method offers little evidence of how the child achieved that learning outcome. The assessment might be improved if the list had a rating scale attached, but this in itself would not increase objectivity or offer details about the child's performance. If a list or rating scale included observational evidence and used **work sampling** as evidence, the outcomes could be evaluated more meaningfully.

An alternative approach might be to make naturalistic **observations** and, from these recorded data, complete a checklist or rating scale of the expected outcomes. If this method were supplemented by work sampling, the assessment might be more appropriate and reliable. A sample list of learning outcomes with observational evidence can be found on page 312; a sample list with both observational evidence and a rating scale can be found on page 313.

A **rubric** is a scoring system that identifies the criteria for assessing a piece of work or the achievement of a learning outcome. Rubrics can be used as either a template for expectations or as a grading grid. This method might offer more refined assessment, in which the results would only be as good as the rubric was valid. Using prepared rubrics that have been tested for reliability and validity may contradict the philosophy of OBE, because they are likely to produce results that categorize student performances or even grade them, which might appear to encourage inappropriate competition. Rubrics are associated with OBE and they are frequently used in a variety of authentic assessment methods. (See Chapter 8 to explore the use of rubrics.)

Many advocates of OBE, as well as proponents of philosophies of **developmentally appropriate** practice (DAP), think that grades are unhelpful when measuring the competence of young children. Counterproductive to the aim of enabling OBE assessment to be more developmentally appropriate, some educators who want children to be successful in assessment try to "teach" outcomes rather than see them as the products of children's activity. Measuring the outcomes of a process of education should not mean abandoning DAP. If the outcomes are appropriate, then the appropriate experience will enable children to achieve them. In the Canadian Child Care Federation journal *Interaction* Shipley (2002) argues vehemently for play as the core of the child's curriculum: "Now, more than ever before, play-based early childhood education guided by developmentally appropriate learning outcomes is the answer to many of the educational and economic challenges we face."

Both **normative assessments** and **criterion-referenced assessments** may pose problems for OBE advocates. Norms could be considered contrary to the philosophy of continual advancement and may be thought potentially detrimental for cultural reasons, or minority groups might be seen as disadvantaged or underrepresented in the normative profile. Any criterion other than the learning outcomes themselves may well be considered incompatible with OBE. OBE systems may use developmental profiles such as **checklists** as part of their assessment processes, a practice which does not fit with OBE in a pure form.

Self-evaluation may be part of the assessment process even for very young children. Some institutions encourage this practice and ask preschool and kindergarten children to comment on their work and play and to select items of their "best work" as portfolio samples. Older children can be provided with methods for more careful reflection, which may involve using happy and sad faces, devising a visual rating scale, recording their verbal comments, or, as they become literate, writing their own reflections. Personal **learning logs** and reaction papers may also encourage self-assessment.

On occasion, educators may use **peer evaluation**. Children are frequently subjective in their reactions; their evaluation of another child's work may be based more on whether they like that child than on a true evaluation of that child's work. When asked to comment on another child's drawing, a child might be influenced by whether or not the drawing represents an object. If peer evaluation is used carefully as part of the learning process, it can have some merit—for example, in highlighting the teacher's own biases—but it must be undertaken with great sensitivity.

Here is a summary of some possible measurement methods:

Use the learning outcomes as a checklist for each child.

Use a list of learning outcomes and add a rating scale for each child.

Use the learning outcomes as a checklist with observational evidence for each learning outcome.

Use the learning outcomes as a rating scale with observational evidence for each learning outcome.

Use the learning outcomes as a checklist with observational evidence and work samples for each learning outcome.

Use the learning outcomes as a rating scale with observational evidence and work samples for each learning outcome.

Record naturalistic observations (**running records** and **anecdotal records**) and, on the basis of these data, check off learning outcomes on a checklist or rate them on a rating scale.

Record naturalistic observations, check off learning outcomes on a checklist, and use a variety of forms of evidence (photographs, videotapes, and so on) to support your findings.

Use prepared learning-outcome documentation portfolios.

Design customized-portfolio or other assessment processes on paper or in computerized record-keeping systems.

You can supplement any of the above methods with screenings, standardized tests, or developmental checklists, although these do not measure the learning outcomes directly. In addition, you might include the child's self-evaluation, peer evaluations, and parental observations in the process.

Thinking About School

Name: _____

How I feel about school   ☺   😐   ☹

How I feel about my friends   ☺   😐   ☹

How I feel about reading   ☺   😐   ☹

How I feel about math   ☺   😐   ☹

How I feel about art   ☺   😐   ☹

My favorite activity is _____

I don't like _____

I am going to get better at _____

This self-evaluation form for Grade 2 students allows children to reflect on their own performance and interests.

Levels of OBE assessment

There are three levels of OBE assessment, reflecting varying degrees of complexity and frequency of information-gathering. The lists below show the common assessment documents used at each level; the asterisked (*) items would be used only for elementary-grade children, not for those in preschool or kindergarten.

Basic-level OBE assessment

- learning outcome checklist

At the basic level, the checklist is usually completed on a weekly or monthly basis. Assessment reports are sent home twice a semester.

Intermediate-level OBE assessment

- as above and...
- running-record observations
- anecdotal-record observations
- learning-outcome **inventory**
- checklist and observational evidence
- art samples
- work samples*
- photographs of learning-outcome performances
- prepared learning-outcome portfolios
- parent conference reports

At the intermediate level, information is gathered on a fairly frequent basis, and assessments done when they are needed or at least every month. The curriculum may be shaped as a result of whole-class assessments.

Advanced-level OBE assessment

- as above and...
- video sequences of performances
- contextual information
- health data
- parental observations
- self-chosen work samples
- self-evaluations*
- student conference reports*

At the advanced level, information is gathered and sorted on an ongoing basis. Assessments are made regularly, every two or three weeks, with parents and children participating. In this model, the curriculum is adapted to fit individual learning needs as those needs become apparent.

Evaluating learning outcomes as assessment criteria

Learning outcomes need to be measurable, achievable, and observable. Only when these conditions are met can outcomes be used as the criteria for assessment. Teachers should evaluate the outcomes before they are used for any form of assessment.

Use the following checklist to evaluate learning outcomes as assessment criteria. The answer to each question should be "Yes."

1. Are the learning outcomes up to date?
2. Were the learning outcomes developed in accordance with the community's agreement?
3. Are the learning outcomes relevant to the local community?
4. Are the learning outcomes consistent with prevailing and minority religious perspectives?
5. Are the learning outcomes consistent with the range of political thought expressed in the community?
6. Do the learning outcomes allow for demonstrations of various forms of learning styles, varying cultural experiences, and individuality?
7. Are the learning outcomes developmentally reasonable expectations?
8. Are there separate learning outcomes developed for children with special needs within the institution?
9. Are the core learning outcomes based on typical maturational levels for the age/stage of the child?
10. Are the learning outcomes progressive from level to level?
11. Are the learning outcomes achievable within the given time constraints?
12. Are all subject areas represented in the learning outcomes?
13. Is there an equal distribution of learning outcomes among subject areas?
14. Is the curriculum geared to providing the opportunity to acquire the knowledge required in the learning outcomes?
15. Is the curriculum geared to providing the opportunity to acquire the skills required in the learning outcomes?
16. Can all children experience some success?
17. Are there learning supports in place to achieve the learning outcomes?
18. Are the learning outcomes stated in understandable language and not open to interpretation?
19. Are the learning outcomes broad enough to allow for contexts of demonstration to change?
20. Is the listing of the learning outcomes comprehensive in all subject areas?
21. Does the set of learning outcomes reflect the philosophy of the institution?
22. Is the set of learning outcomes consistent with the curriculum-delivery model?
23. Do all the teachers and parents (and children, where appropriate) understand the learning outcomes?
24. Can the school provide extra supports for those experiencing difficulties in achieving the learning outcomes?

25. Is there opportunity for children to progress beyond the learning outcomes?

26. Is there a regular process for refining and updating the learning outcomes?

27. Is there a process to ensure that the learning outcomes are measured appropriately?

28. Is there a confidential process to assess achievement of the learning outcomes?

29. Is there a process to ensure program accountability?

30. Is there regular in-service training for teachers in OBE and assessment?

Responding to measured outcomes

It might seem that the teacher's job is done when a child's learning has been assessed. In fact, this is only one part of the learning cycle. Assessment should lead to action. The next step is to evaluate the effectiveness of the program and to determine whether the program is meeting the learning needs of some, or all, of the children. One or more of the following responses may be appropriate:

- **Individualize the program.** If some children are not successful, determine why and address the issues. For example, a child may speak English as a second language, be socially isolated, have joined the group late, or be under stress. Children who have not been learning well do not necessarily lack potential, but they may require more appropriate learning conditions. Observe individual performance carefully; children with unusual personalities or different learning styles may be more successful than you first thought.

- **Fill in the gaps.** Teachers may address the outcomes that the children have not yet fully achieved by providing activities, experiences, or program content to bridge the gap.

- **Continue the program.** Many teachers decide to keep their responsive programs running as long as they believe that the programs support the idea that development cannot be hurried.

- **Continue with the current plan but lengthen the time frame.** Allowing more time is consistent with OBE; however, changing the time frame may be impossible since classes and grades are usually structured on an annual cycle.

- **Continue evaluating.** Some children acquire learning rapidly (and unexpectedly).

- **Have the child repeat the program.** Repeating a level fits with the idea that some people take longer than others to achieve the same outcomes; however, lack of promotion may have counterproductive social and emotional implications.

- **Offer an intensification of the program.** Special help may be offered within the classroom. Some children need direct "teaching," while others are more self-directed. Children with special needs and disabilities may require resource teachers or assistants to help them.

- **Offer extra help outside the classroom.** Some children need one-on-one help to attain certain skills. People may dislike special treatment and argue against withdrawing a child from the class, but the real problem arises from labelling the child (which can be a self-fulfilling prophecy).

Outcomes as part of program design

There tend to be three levels of outcomes in many outcome-based systems. We have focused on the child and therefore targeted learning outcomes. Additional outcomes are integral to the outcome-based philosophy, including course and **program outcomes**. Course outcomes are not part of the early childhood approach, but program outcomes may be articulated for both child-care and education programs. These tend to be broader statements that indicate the direction the program should be taking. They should reflect the philosophy of the program, be developmentally appropriate, be achievable, and allow for measurement of their success. Learning outcomes, course outcomes (if used), and program outcomes need to be stated congruently. To ensure effective curriculum-planning there will be clear **curriculum alignment**—an appropriate connection between the levels of outcome.

Summary

Although they are controversial, outcome-based education (OBE) and other related approaches to education that focus on products and exit levels have become popular in many education settings. Learning outcomes are an integral part of the outcome-based approach. They state the broad achievements that are expected of the children at each stage of the program. They usually include the knowledge, skills, and dispositions that are central to the outcome. Although learning outcomes do not specify how they are to be achieved, they are usually incorporated within a philosophy that honours how to learn rather than what to learn. The far-reaching intention behind outcome-based education is to act as a tool for social reform; the process focuses on improving the condition of both the individual and society in general.

Some observable components of OBE might point to the philosophy of the program, whereas many variations of the approach could lead to confusion. Assessing each child's achievement of the outcomes themselves can take several forms. The educator may find naturalistic observation methods most suitable; some use levels of mastery of each outcome in the form of a rating scale or a rubric. While there are numerous links between outcomes and objectives in education, the outcome tends to be a broader statement that excludes discrete facts. Objectives of a program tend to be more knowledge-based whereas outcomes tend to be performance-based, and include the integration of knowledge, skills, and attitudes or dispositions. As with other approaches to education, proponents and opponents can be vehement in their beliefs about OBE and associated philosophies and practices. As the differing levels of OBE are not always obvious; the observer should take careful note of the characteristics of a program to appreciate its underlying values and philosophy, as well as the congruence between curriculum and assessment practices.

Key Terms

accountability

active learning

anecdotal record

behaviourism

checklist

competency

constructivism

criterion-referenced assessment

developmentally appropriate

disposition

exit outcomes

inventory

knowledge

learning log

learning outcome

mastery

mastery learning (ML)

normative assessment

objectives

observation

outcome-based education (OBE)

outcome-based learning (OBL)

peer evaluation

performance-based learning (PBL)

rating scale

role performance

rubric

running record

self-evaluation

skill

social reform

standard

standards-based learning (SL)

work sampling

Weblinks

www.ed.gov/databases/ERIC_Digests/ed377512.html
Essential elements of outcome-based education.

www.hrdc-drhc.gc.ca/sp-ps/arb-dgra/publications/research/abr-96-4e.shtml
This Human Resource Development Canada (HRDC) site feature an article favouring outcome-based education.

www.ctf-fce.ca/e/what/other/assessment/high-stakes.htm
The Canadian Teachers Federation (CTF) site discusses the future of education in Canada and how the testing of children is driving the education system.

Observation Sample

This excerpt from an assessment shows how observational evidence can be used to measure a child's achievement.

How effective is this documentation in relating Ben's activity to the stated outcomes?

Learning Outcomes in the Arts: Grade 3

Child's name: ___Ben_____ Recorder: ___Rhonda_____

Age/D.O.B.: ___8 years, 5 months_____ Date: ___January 16, 2004_____

By the end of Grade 3, students will

Outcome	Observation	Achievement
Understand that many aspects of a work of art contribute to its effect	Ben liked the kinetic art at the gallery and tried to copy it using coat hangers and ping-pong balls. Ben noticed the use of white, blue, and gray in a Monet print.	Ben is alert to these ideas but needs more experience of variety.
Understand that each of the arts requires specific skills	Ben was unsuccessful at his first attempts at making a mobile. Ben acknowledged the difficulty of building a model boat that another student brought in.	Ben is very aware of these skills and has made some efforts to increase his repertoire.
Use the right terms in discussing ideas and techniques in works of art, as well as their own artistic ideas	Ben mentioned several techniques when he discussed painting, collage, and model making.	Ben has the interest as well as the terminology.
Understand that the arts of different cultures have similarities as well as differences	Ben received our work on Native art positively. He suggested that the simple lines in the drawings were bold and quite like cartoons telling a story.	Ben's appreciation of art is impressive, and he has sensitivity to the different art forms and links to culture.
Understand that technology can be used in creating works of art	Ben uses CorelDraw to create images. Ben noticed the large metal modern sculptures outside the bank towers. He said, "They must be pretty well built so they don't fall down on people."	Yes.
Be aware that certain aspects of works of art, such as rhythm and balance, have a wider appreciation in daily life	Ben responds to music and likes strong beats and clear lyrics, which he says are like some of the pictures we have discussed in class.	Ben's attitude is open; he needs time and experience.

Source: Adapted from Ontario Ministry of Education and Training, *The Common Curriculum, Grades 1–9* (1993).

Observation Sample

This excerpt from a child's assessment shows how a rating scale and observational evidence can be used to measure the learning outcomes.

To what extent do the numerical progress ratings contribute to this assessment of performance?

Learning Outcomes: Kindergarten

Child's name: _Anjana_   Recorder: _Carolee_

Age/D.O.B.: _5 years, 2 months_   Date: _February 2-25, 2004_

Time in kindergarten: _4 1/2 months in senior kindergarten_

Context: _informal observations in classroom and outdoors_

Key: 5 = achieved outcome; 4 = emerging skill; 3 = attempts performance;
           2 = engaged but not ready; 1 = not yet engaged in performance

What children will know and be able to do at the end of kindergarten:

Culminating performance	Progress	Observation/inference
8. Children will demonstrate basic understanding of the concepts of time, quantity, shape, distance, speed, space, seasons, size, weight, floating and sinking, sorting, matching, seriating, mass, and other core ideas using appropriate descriptive language.	3	- some understanding may be limited by language - uses language associated with all math concepts (except mass and floating--no experience yet) - explores properties of materials and uses them appropriately - counts to 25+ by rote and counts objects correctly to 6 - sorts items according to one characteristic - seriates 3 items correctly - matches items by where they belong
9. Children will identify similarities and differences between objects.	4	- points out similarities between items using colour labels - ? limited by language to describe differences
10. Children will represent their understanding of the world through a variety of creative media.	4	- uses painting to express ideas enjoys working with clay but does not make obvious representations
11. Children will estimate what will happen in basic situations.	3+	- guessed "what would happen if . . ." (some correct answers)
12. Children will memorize short poems, songs, and rhymes.	4	- joins in with songs and rhymes - recites sounds (meaning?)
13. Children will retell an event, describe objects, and identify the key features in a story.	2	- language limitations but will point to images representing key ideas in a story
14. Children will count items accurately up to ten and continue counting in sequence up to twenty.	5	- as in #8 above
15. Children will demonstrate their understanding of cause and effect in basic situations.	3	- repeats actions that create a response - demonstrates some logic in guessing some relationships

---

Screening
and Assessment

chapter **10**

Our society has embraced the formal testing mode to an excessive degree.

Howard Gardner (1993)

The basis of screening is the comparison of the baby's level of development with that of an average baby of the same chronological age; it follows that a thorough knowledge of the "average" or "normal" is essential.

Ronald S. Illingworth (1990)

Tests have an impact on equity. Research has shown that tests are biased against certain minority groups and the poor.

Nova Scotia NDP Caucus (2001)

Assessment of a child's performance in every developmental domain is more authentic if it is done in a naturalistic way.

Features of Screening and Assessment Tools

CHILD DEVELOPMENT FOCUS

Screenings and assessments may
- identify a child with a specific need
- confirm or contradict naturalistic observation
- provide detailed developmental profiling
- suggest developmental supports
- imply readiness for a specific program

Screening

DEFINITION: Screening

Screening is a process of reviewing and evaluating specific behaviours or characteristics of individuals across a population or group in order to identify those who are in need of a more thorough assessment or specific support.

Screening procedures usually involve the use of **standardized tests** in assessing a large population of children in a brief, relatively inexpensive manner. They are usually carried out by medical professionals, psychologists, or diagnosticians. Child-care workers and teachers use informal screening techniques to identify children whose development is in some way atypical.

Early identification of a health concern or developmental challenge can make a significant difference to the child's later progress. **Early intervention** programs may be available either through resource teachers at the school or agency, school administration, or through external consultants.

Screenings for young children may focus on identifying any one of the following:

- health or medical issue
- growth
- motor skill
- learning disability
- language acquisition
- hearing
- vision
- other specific developmental concern

The screening process is intended to identify only those children who need intervention, support, or monitoring. The screening itself does not diagnose a condition, indicate the type of intervention necessary, or prescribe a particular response. The screening is important because it identifies children who are somehow vulnerable or in need, who might not otherwise be noticed.

The screening involves a kind of test or assessment focused specifically on the one particular behaviour or indicator being looked for. Frequently the screening tool is called an "instrument." This is a professional term; a **screening instrument** is simply the test that is conducted.

KEY FEATURES: Screening tools

- use standardized procedures to evaluate the health or development of a large number of children
- identify children in a special category of need
- are usually nonparticipatory
- are usually applied in a testing location

TAKING A SPECIAL LOOK: Screening for disabilities

One reason to observe children is to ensure that they are supported in every way possible. Beyond observing children's development, educators must use screening to determine whether the children have any specific conditions, syndromes, chronic illnesses, or other exceptionalities. The need for ongoing observation and assessment continues after a child has been screened; subsequent open-ended observation may reveal other concerns not identified by a tool aimed at screening for one or two specific conditions.

Assessment

The assessment process may take many forms, including informal observation, standardized tests, teacher appraisal, developmental **checklists**, parental observations, **self-evaluation**, medical diagnosis, or any combination of these or other methods. A variety of professionals such as health professionals, psychologists, social workers, teachers, caregivers, early childhood specialists, and parents may carry out these assessments; the most effective process involves a team.

Medical and psychological professionals have developed standardized tests as tools to help them assess particular aspects of children's health, growth, or development. Sometimes these tests are carried out separately from other assessments, but they are usually more helpful when conducted in a more thorough, contextualized, and holistic manner. The results of any one test tell us about the child in only a single specific regard, rather than offer a full story about the person, his family, motivations, interests, and other domains of health and development.

Assessments may focus on one domain or on multiple aspects of a child's performance. Assessments may use one standardized test or several forms of information-gathering. Assessments should be carried out to benefit the child, but in practice this does not always happen. Administrators may use assessments to exclude a child from a program, just as they might use the outcome of the test to include a child.

Here are some of the most frequently used types of assessments of young children that employ standardized tools, or instruments:

- language
- reading/decoding
- kindergarten readiness
- fine and gross motor skills/self-help skills
- social behaviour
- information-processing/intelligence/cognitive/problem-solving
- personality/style indicators
- learning disabilities
- school grade-performance tests
- admissions tests (even for preschool)
- drawing skills

KEY FEATURES: Standardized assessment tools

- review the behaviour of a child in a specified developmental domain

- measure performance with reference to a norm or specified criterion

- are considered valid and reliable

- may require trained skills for administration

- are sometimes administered in a testing location

Evaluating standardized tests

Even if your early childhood philosophy emphasizes evaluation through naturalistic observation, you will need to recognize the strengths and weaknesses of standardized tests and be able to evaluate the data they provide. The trend has been to use a wide variety of standardized tests to determine **readiness**, **skill acquisition**, developmental stages, learning disabilities, and so on. Acknowledge why some teachers think tests are desirable and useful; you do not have to agree with the approach or follow the trend if you think you can gain the information more easily, naturally, effectively, and cheaply by other means.

Underlying the belief in standardized testing is a philosophy that values some or all of the following ideas:

- A test can measure what it purports to measure.
- A child's behaviour can be evaluated by comparison with an expected **norm** or stage.
- A test situation can elicit objective information.
- The outcome of a test is a predictor of later development.
- Children evaluated to determine deficits in development can benefit from improved programming.
- Teachers and other professionals can determine behavioural goals and learning on the child's behalf.
- Test data can improve an agency's **accountability**.
- Evaluation of published information regarding the **reliability** and **validity** of tests can filter out possible bias or inaccuracies.
- Testing procedures benefit rather than harm curriculum-development.
- Teachers, caregivers, and parents can interpret test results accurately and successfully.

Professionals often use tests to aid their work, in the belief that tests will offer them more **objectivity** than other sources of information. Considering the way in which the data are collected, it is doubtful whether the results can be objective. Children may not perform the same way in a "test" situation that they would in their natural surroundings. Some tests are administered by someone other than the regular caregiver; in that case the child might be affected by the strangeness of the test or the tester. Without appreciating a child's regularly displayed behavioural patterns, you can tell little about her overall progress. With little understanding of her family background, current issues in her life, or what is normal for this child, you have limited scope for effective evaluation.

Comparisons with norms derived from a general population may provide few points of reference as, even if accurate, those norms will tell you little about what to do if a concern is identified. Particularly worrisome is the undetected cultural **bias** of many well-used standardized tests. For example, in some cultures, children do not learn self-help skills early in life because they are fed, clothed, and toileted longer. This does not mean that they will not develop "normally." Results that reflect acquired skills may not give you more than a quick "snapshot" of children's current development—in themselves, such comparisons do not help determine appropriate curricula.

If a test has a well-founded theoretical basis, it may indicate the stage through which a child might progress next. When the child will develop particular skills is as much a matter of **maturation** as the child's response to the adult's strategy. All that the child needs is the construction of an appropriate learning environment and responsiveness to his adaptations to that environment. A test would serve little purpose.

A key issue in evaluating a test is to determine exactly what it does measure. The name of the test or elements of it does not necessarily indicate the test's content, so you cannot be assured that it actually tests what it is meant to test. For example, an IQ test may not test intelligence but problem-solving, which is only one component of IQ. Consider the readiness test; it may evaluate a set of skills that the test designer believes are important in determining a child's readiness for, say, kindergarten. In fact, it may reflect skill acquisition in some areas, but not all; these tests commonly leave out social skills.

Before administering a test, teachers and other professionals should consider the appropriateness of that test for children with varying language and cultural heritages, ages, personalities, interests, motivations, powers of concentration, and so on. There are so many possible built-in biases, such as skill assessment in one developmental domain that depends on expressive language, which may not be the area tested. Test items may rely on a child's familiarity with particular domestic items unknown to him because of his culture. Questions may rely too heavily on logical thought, which may be an unfavourable approach for a creative mind. A child's self-esteem may be evaluated as "poor" because the test did not allow for different emotional responses.

Administrators and teachers who wish to test children to prove their own effectiveness work on the premise that quality programming can be measured in the short term. Significant data are provided only if the "before" and "after" are measured, and then only

TAKING A SPECIAL LOOK: Referrals

Observing children can lead us to recognize that further assessment of them is necessary. Some situations require professional skills beyond our scope or from a different discipline. While the parents should initiate contact with any specialists, teachers or caregivers may prompt the parents to do so by sharing observations. For example, Kerry's teacher observed that Kerry was not responding to questions, was easily distracted at story time, and would sometimes make comments out of context. She shared her observations with Kerry's mother, who took Kerry to an audiologist. Tests showed that Kerry's hearing was slightly impaired, and she was fitted with a hearing aid.

if the data are viewed in terms of stages of growth rather than adherence to timeliness. There are many other, more successful ways of determining quality programming. Why not spend the time with the children and the money on the learning environment itself?

Standardized tests as part of authentic assessment

If teachers and caregivers use standardized tests instead of employing ongoing naturalistic observation, they will miss much of "who the child is." However, there can be a real place for standardized tests and their results in a child's **portfolio**. A test may confirm what the teachers have observed naturalistically, in which case they can feel sure that their perceptions are correct. Or the assessment might highlight something that they were unable to detect using everyday techniques. In this case, they might respond in a variety of ways, perhaps questioning the test's outcome, checking its findings in other ways, or seeking another professional opinion.

The amount of formal assessment material in an average portfolio is likely to be very modest. For some children, there might be a greater need to consult professionals who use standardized testing. Children who might be more likely to need formal assessments include those who

- exhibit behaviours that are difficult to interpret
- have socially disruptive or adaptive difficulties
- suffer chronic health conditions that influence their developmental patterns
- have long-term, serious, or terminal illnesses
- were born prematurely or with low birth weight and continue to have growth or developmental difficulties
- are diagnosed by professionals as having particular conditions or syndromes
- are born into families with genetically inherited conditions
- appear to be developing at a slower rate than expected
- demonstrate particular gifts or talents
- demonstrate discontinuity in their developmental patterns
- regress in their development without obvious reason
- have been brain-injured
- communicate with difficulty or fail to make attachments
- show particular difficulty in paying attention
- experience traumatic events or changes in their lives
- are somehow "at risk"
- have been physically, emotionally, or sexually abused
- show unusual ways of processing information
- have sensory deficits
- face mobility challenges

As you can see from the list above, there are many reasons why a child may not perform as expected. Parents, caregivers, and teachers are the people who frequently advocate for a child and his need to be understood whatever his background, life experience, or potential. They may see that not only does the use of the standardized test itself present the possibility of damage, but that, when the assessment is conducted without a full appreciation of the whole child within his family and social context, the potential for the assessment to actually harm the child is immense.

Interpreting assessment results

Some medical assessments and psychological evaluations look as if they are written in a foreign language! In a way they are, because they use professional jargon. The most obvious way of understanding what they say is to ask the person who wrote the report to explain them or to ask for a summary of the findings. While it can be helpful to understand some frequently used terms, many reports refer to syndromes, conditions, and assessment results that even those working in the field would have to look up.

Most important for the adults working directly with the child are the recommendations, interventions, and program plans that they will have to implement. These must be very clear; in some cases, parents, caregivers, and teachers will have to acquire certain skills in order to help the child. Ask lots of questions and offer input into the ongoing assessment process by recording plenty of observations of the child while you are involved in the program.

Response to assessment results

Educators and parents who have been part of the assessment team from the beginning of the process will understand better the subject of the test or tests. An assessment should lead to a program of action to be effective. Educators and families can work as partners to support the child. Ideally, when able and mature enough, the child will be a part of the team as well as being at the centre of attention!

An assessment is usually carried out for a particular reason. This reason should be recalled when interpreting the results. Action should be based primarily on the reason for conducting the assessment in the first place. However, sometimes unexpected results may materialize, and responses may have to be developed accordingly. Some such responses include

- planning special activities at home
- referral to medical specialists
- referral to **psychological services**
- access to **assistive devices**
- referral for targeted **therapy**
- adding assistants in school or childcare
- access to early-intervention programs
- development of individual program plans (IPPs) within the child-care or school setting
- referral to special schools or programs
- seeking the assistance of **resource teachers**

Always plan ahead for the cycle of assessment. Interventions must be evaluated for their own effectiveness. If the intervention proves to be effective, it should be continued. Financial constraints may mean limited access to services. Those in the most need don't always manage to gain access to the necessary services. Local and political advocacy are usually essential to ensure that every child's needs are met.

Psychologists and doctors may be the people trained to conduct a standardized test, though they are not always the only people who can respond to the child's needs as these come to light through the assessment process. Parents, caregivers, and teachers can frequently provide a bridge from the stark assessment to the child's day-to-day life. They are most likely to know what kind of intervention might succeed, once they understand the assessment results. For this reason teamwork is essential, as are honesty and openness.

Individual program plans (IPPs) or **individual education plans (IEPs)** may be developed on the basis of standardized tests. Ensure that the test is only one mode of assessment, as it alone may not offer a broad enough picture. The IPP or IEP will usually focus on particular skills that need support and suggest activities that address these skills; the plans will further indicate how these activities might be designed, who will be responsible for carrying them out, and how their success will be measured.

Assessments should trigger action, review, and further assessment. In this way progress can be monitored effectively. The first assessment establishes a baseline that enables the assessor, parents, and professionals to follow the progression or regression that results. Ideally, the cycle should be regular but not as frequent as monthly; conducting a re-assessment every six months, or yearly, may often be appropriate depending on the age of the child and the nature of the challenge. Developing new IPPs or IEPs more regularly can provide a structure to propel the action. When the child achieves the aim of each plan, or when a certain amount of time has elapsed without the child's demonstrating success, the assessment team can develop a new plan.

Using standardized tests

Advantages

- Psychologists usually design and administer standardized tests.
- Tests provide uniformity of administration.
- Tests give a quantifiable score.
- The tool will have been tested for validity.
- Repeated use may increase reliability.
- A wide choice of tests is available.
- Standardized tests offer specific information to parents, teachers, and psychologists.
- Tests may be administered to an individual or a group.
- Tests identify what the child can do.
- Tests may support other informal assessment.
- Tests may identify potential concerns.
- The results may help indicate appropriate curriculum or activity plans.
- The results may be available quickly.

Disadvantages

- Adults unknown to the child may carry out standardized tests.
- The child may not respond well to a testing situation.
- Contextual information may not be available.
- Scores may be open to inappropriate interpretation.
- Norms may not consider cultural or language diversity.
- Users of tests are not always aware of concerns about validity.
- Reliability within one group does not mean intercultural reliability.
- Users may not have access to an appropriate range of tests.
- Standardized tests are expensive to buy and administer.
- Training may be needed to administer the tests.
- Test scores should not be used alone to determine evaluation and to construct a program for the child.
- Time taken in testing and test preparation might be better used for the child's play or learning.
- Tests may focus on what the child cannot do.
- Skills not identified on a test will not be evaluated.
- The child may be able to demonstrate the skill in a nontesting situation.
- A lack of evidence of skill mastery may be incorrectly interpreted as an inability to perform a task.
- Tests may provide insufficient evidence on which to base program-planning.
- Most tools lack flexibility.
- Tests may not be based on current teaching principles.
- Some assessment/screening tools are not designed for diagnosis but are frequently accepted as such.
- The outcome may result in inappropriate labelling.
- Screening and assessment tools may be seen as interchangeable (though their purposes are quite different).
- Parents seldom have an opportunity to supply their own input or observation.
- Tests may be used by teachers as a "quick" method of evaluation rather than naturalistic observation, which is time-consuming and more effective.

Opposing views regarding standardized tests

Not all standardized tests are used for curriculum-planning or to develop strategies to assist those children who are in any category of special need; some standardized tests are conducted so that programs can be compared with others at a local or even national level. Those who oppose these notions of **accountability**, such as Kohn, are adamant that "accountability usually turns out to be a code for tighter control over what happens in the classrooms by people who are not in the classrooms, a danger that has approximately the same effect on learning that a noose has on breathing" (2002). In contrast, Ontario's "Expanded Testing Program" claims that "a standardized approach to education, including a rigorous new curriculum and regular testing, makes it possible to compare results among schools or among school boards. This helps to identify areas that need improvement and target resources accordingly" (*Report to Ontario Taxpayers, Fall 2001*). One perspective considers accountability measures essential and considers standardized tests the best way of ensuring clear results and improving standards as the tests proceed. The opposing perspective considers standardized testing an intrusion into the classroom that limits the children's breadth of learning, leads to inappropriate education decisions, and provides little useful data, especially among diverse populations.

By having established standards in their own educational institutions, administrators wish to measure which students are reaching those standards and which are not; this trend is increasing across Canada, the United States, and Europe. In practice these administrators are not necessarily trying to concentrate attention on those children who "fail"; they usually aim to establish a statistical measure of achievement for reasons of program or school accountability. The question of who sets the official standards fuels further debate, as do the content and level of those standards.

The use of standardized tests as assessment methods with individual children is just as controversial. Arguments abound about the relative usefulness of screening populations of children. Some claim that screenings create an expense that society cannot afford, given the low numbers of children who are identified with special needs. Others insist that some screenings are essential because they identify particular children who should receive early interventions; waiting until those children exhibit more evident signs and symptoms means those children sometimes receive intervention too late to be effective. While some students test well, others are intimidated, overwhelmed, have not had the learning opportunities to succeed, or are being tested in a second language. Assessors should bear this in mind.

Individual assessments of children may also cause concern if those assessments are carried out in ways contrary to authentic assessment or are conducted without factoring in adequate contextual information. Various issues come to the fore: cost, bias, appropriateness, focus, fairness, test anxiety, and what is to be done as the result of the assessment. Employing standardized tests, whether evaluated as valid and reliable or not, guarantees heated debate. Rather than considering this a superficial concern, educators must understand that dichotomous values that are part of differing philosophies and political persuasions lie at the heart of these issues.

Choosing a Test

If you appreciate the concerns regarding testing, you may not wish to use a standardized test at all. But if you do use one, the following criteria will help you choose one that best fits your purpose.

1. **Determine your own role in the testing procedure.** Will you receive the test results as a teacher, supervisor, administrator, parent, or child-care worker? You will want information that is useful to your role and presented in a way you can easily understand and interpret. The role of tester may be appropriate for you if the test you choose fits your qualifications and experience. If you need to find a tester, factor this into your decision-making. Consider the possibility of taking training to administer a test.

2. **Identify your reason for wanting a test carried out.** Do you want very specific information about one child, screening for all children in your care, or an assessment system to be used over a period of time? Evaluate the tests available to you to see if they can provide the screening or assessment data you wish. Are you sure a test measures what you want it to measure?

3. **Determine the type of assessment you need.** Are you focusing on health, development, or development of a particular skill? You will have to find a test that contains the criteria for evaluation that fit your needs.

4. **Ensure that the test covers the age and developmental stage levels you need.** Are you choosing a test because the title sounds correct, while the span of developmental stages is insufficient? To re-use a test over a period of time, ensure it will include a wide developmental range.

5. **Check that the test will produce information in each of the developmental domains or skills you are seeking.** Are you sure that these domains or skill areas are sufficiently detailed to give information about the quality as well as the presence of the behaviours you want to test?

6. **Review the test material for objectivity, use by others, and published critiques.** Have you read only the information produced by the writers and publishers of the test material, or have you checked it out more thoroughly? Look at test validity, reliability, and usefulness.

7. **Find out if the test can be obtained easily and how much it costs.** Do you have a budget that allows for the testing you want? Many procedures require updating or the use of duplicate forms that have to be purchased after you obtain the initial kit. Pieces of the testing equipment may also be lost, so check that you can replace them easily. Some have copyright prohibitions that prevent your copying the evaluation forms. A few tests may require computer access for scoring; ensure that your hardware and software are compatible. Most of the recognized tests and inventories require verification of your professional qualifications before you can buy the materials.

8. **Evaluate the test items for possible bias (cultural, sex, or language).** Will the test be appropriate for the particular children you have? Consider test items to ensure that they are not faulty in their expectation of Eurocentric responses or a strong dependence on English language skills. If there are such items as a doll in the assessment kit, could you change the type of doll to match the ethnicity of the child to be tested? Check for any built-in biases that might be relevant in tasks such as sequencing a storyline or identifying similarities or differences that children from various cultural backgrounds might perceive differently.

9. **Consider the test's ability to give you results that are easily understood.** Can you interpret the statistical information and understand the terminology of the test's results? You will waste money in buying testing procedures that are probably quite valid in themselves yet produce scores or outcomes that the teacher cannot use. This type of information may lead to impressive record-keeping, but be of very little help in program-planning.

10. **Think about how you will use the test results.** Will you use them for screening or across the group for evaluation? What will you do when you identify a child in need of further assessment or an individual program plan? Work out whether you can make the necessary responses. What will you do with the information on the progress of each child?

If you use a test with caution and understand its limitations, it can help you be more sensitive to a child's needs and modify the learning or social environment for his benefit. If it enables you to work with your colleagues and the child's parents more effectively, you may have chosen an ideal method of testing. You might also have collated better information through informal observation and achieved your intentions more effectively and inexpensively by using a parent-involved naturalistic assessment.

The most effective assessments are **portfolio assessments** that involve a variety of information-gathering techniques. This ideal form of evaluation includes a careful selection of observations of the child's spontaneous play and social learning activities, some interpretive checklists of skill development, any necessary screening or test results, examples of the child's art, evidence of academic skills in the child's products, photographs of the child's activities or constructions, video-recordings of play, audio-recordings of language and music, and any other samples that reflect the child's processes and products of learning. These elements can produce a more accurate, broader contextual picture of the whole child. The perceptive teacher can select the methods most pertinent to her own skills, time, budget, and team of colleagues, as well as to the context, the degree of parental involvement, and the child's stage of development.

Summary

The more educators know about standardized tests, the better. Some significant issues surround the use of assessment methods—specifically that, although considered valid and reliable, these tests may not provide a holistic picture of the child tested. The mere mention of standardized tests can inflame some informed adults with passion. Some believe that they offer accountability and raise education standards. Others think that they absorb precious learning time and are drenched in biases that lead to inappropriate and unfair education decision-making.

Screening instruments can help identify children who are particularly vulnerable or in need of some kind of intervention. Screenings are quick and efficient tools that do not provide a whole understanding of the child or indicate what should be done to respond to any identified need. While assessments can be broad-based and thorough, use of a standardized test rarely provides adequate information for educators or parents to act on. When standardized assessment tools are used the educator is wise to collect other data as well, including observations, to offer a rounder understanding of the child who is the subject of the assessment. Supporting the standardized test with authentic assessment processes will provide a more useful set of information. These observations and other documentation can confirm or contradict the findings of the standardized test.

Responding to the outcome of assessments is necessary; otherwise, the whole process is a waste of time. Parents and educators who, it is hoped, have been part of the assessment team, can ensure an assessment cycle that evaluates any intervention for its effectiveness, develops individual program plans (IPPs), observes and documents progress or regression, devises alternative or additional strategies to support the child, and ensures the conducting of further assessments at appropriate intervals.

accountability

assessment

assessment cycle

assessment instrument

assistive devices

bias

checklist

developmentally appropriate

early intervention

individual education plan (IEP)

individual program plan (IPP)

objectivity

portfolio

portfolio assessment

psychological services

readiness test

reliability

resource teacher

screening

screening instrument

self-evaluation

skill acquisition

standardized test

standards therapy

validity

Weblinks

www.ecewebguide.com/assessme.html
Resource for those involved in the assessment of young children.

www.naeyc.org/resources/position_statements/pstestin.htm
This National Association for the Education of Young Children (NAEYC) site features the position paper "Standardized Testing of Young Children."

www.ldac-taac.ca
This Learning Disabilities Association of Canada (LDAC) site outlines in-depth assessment strategies for children with suspected learning disabilities.

Environmental Observation and Evaluation

chapter **11**

*In quality ECD [Early Childhood Development] environments, caregivers with educa-
tion in child development use their skills of observation to plan appropriate experiences.*

Karen Chandler (2003)

*A well-planned environment will be safe and healthful, will meet the needs
of both children and adults, will facilitate classroom management,
will enhance the process of learning through play, and will support
the implementation of program goals and objectives.*

Carol E. Catron and Jan Allen (1993)

*In observing a program it is important to remember that no program can ever be
perfect, and that a given day will never be repeated.*

Carol H. Schlank and Barbara Metzger (1989)

Outdoor play spaces need
careful design. Their safety
depends on satisfactory
equipment, careful use of
space, good supervision,
developmental appropriateness, and suitable use.

The Child's Environment

What is an environment?

The child's **environment** involves every aspect of her surroundings and experience. These include her family, housing, geographic location, economic status, social relationships, space, resources, and other relatively concrete circumstances. There are other aspects of her context that are less easily observed. These environmental factors include the values, attitudes, and beliefs of those around her, her culture, religion, perceptions of safety, and other less easily documented experiences and exposures. In this chapter we consider the individual child's environment as well as the environment of groups of children.

Do we have control over the environment?

Educators, parents, and caregivers can control some of the elements of the environment. Others are the responsibility of community agencies. These things determine the overall health of the community. It could be argued that some environmental conditions fall outside everyone's control. But even the climate can be influenced by human beings!

Which environment is good for children?

What specifics you consider most important in an environment depend on your own values and priorities. For example, some people think the qualities of the learning environment are most important. If you ask many parents what they look for in a good environment, their first priority will likely be safety. So the criteria for a good environment depend on what adults value most highly—social competence, independence, intellectual functioning, or other aspects of human development. At the most basic level, the environmental conditions necessary for survival include:

- clean drinking water
- an adequate food supply
- appropriate shelter and housing
- good air quality
- safety and protection from harm
- sufficient space
- access to social services
- a positive standard of living (absence of poverty)
- a health service that meets individual and community health needs
- access to appropriate education

All of the things mentioned above serve to meet children's **basic needs**. As informed adults we need to be aware of children's needs and advocate for the high-quality provision of these elements for all children. While we know, of course, that meeting these needs is essential, meeting them alone is not enough for healthy child development. It is essential to provide for individual **psychological needs**, which support a child's sense of self and allow the child to become a fully functioning human being. The adult's responsibility is to provide for

- physical contact
- nurturance
- consistency of relationships
- encouragement and the conditions for experiencing success
- conditions for individuation (enabling the child to become a separate person)
- facilitating the emergence of the child's sense of "self" and his "categorical self" (the child knows who he is and his individual characteristics)
- support to become independent
- opportunity to acquire social skills and to function within a group
- validation of the child's experience of emotions
- support to recover from difficult situations
- the development of social emotions (empathy, altruism, etc.)
- self-respect and respect for others
- building resilience to imperfect relationships and environments

These conditions for psychological health and well-being can be met only through human relationships. As these constitute a core part of the child's experience, we will consider them as parts of the child's environment, even more significant than other, more tangible elements.

Why observe environments?

Behaviour cannot be understood outside its context. We must observe the elements of a child's environment in order to appreciate the behaviour we observe. Environmental conditions influence children's functioning, learning, and well-being, so we need to observe them in relation to how children behave. Of course there is often an indirect connection between what a child does and the environmental conditions that might have shaped that behaviour. We should also consider the child's previous experience; more than the immediate environment has influenced that child's behaviour. This is something over which we may have little input and which we should avoid judging. We can exercise some influence over the child's present and future only.

What is the adult's responsibility for the children's environment?

The challenge for the adult who takes responsibility for children's environments is to

1. seek out information that leads to designing and implementing exemplary environments for young children
2. function as though she or he is part of the child's environment
3. recognize that the child experiences environments over time (past, current, and future)—not only in one snapshot moment
4. educate community partners about relevant environmental concerns (if necessary) and build a common vision for improving the children's environment with colleagues, parents, and other stakeholders
5. observe the environment critically and improve elements of it that are within our control or influence
6. advocate for the environmental conditions necessary for healthy children's development
7. consider the influences of both the physical environment and the psychological environment on the behaviour of individual children and groups of children
8. determine possible links between children's behaviour and their environments, individually and collectively
9. regularly document relevant information relating to aspects of the environment, having conducted an **environmental scan** (an environmental evaluation based on specified criteria)
10. implement an **action plan** aimed at improving that environment

Although observation is only one of a number of responsibilities for the adult, without it there can be no useful program evaluation or improvement.

What is the difference between the environment and the curriculum?

In early childhood practice the two terms are closely associated. The **curriculum** is the planned part of the child's experience. It usually involves stating what content the child is to learn, or the outcomes or achievements that each child is expected to make through a program's delivery. It may include directions as to the content—of what is to be learned and how it is to be learned (or taught)—and the outcomes, or end product of the learning process. The curriculum is usually written in a document that directs educators on what to do. All curriculum documents are based on beliefs about how children develop and learn; some state these beliefs, others do not. The curriculum is delivered within an environment—one that is shaped, in part, by any curriculum being delivered. But the child's experience is much larger than the curriculum, depending on existing physical conditions, general environment, and emotional climate. Much of this experience is other than what the curriculum or teacher intended and is called the **hidden curriculum**. This includes all the values and beliefs of the institution, staff, and parents that become apparent in the way the children are treated and how decisions are made concerning them. The hidden curriculum can influence the children as much as the actual curriculum does.

So the environment is everything that happens to the child, what is demonstrated by adult actions and the concrete surroundings that she experiences. The curriculum is the part of that experience that is planned.

Is there a difference between programs and environments? The terms are often used together

The program that is offered is the delivery of the curriculum itself, and it includes other unintended experiences as well. The environment includes every aspect of the child's experience. There is a big overlap between the terms. **Program evaluation** and **environmental evaluation** tend to mean different things. Evaluation of the program is a broad process that looks at how the curriculum is delivered and how effective it is at reaching its goals. An evaluation of the environment can include these things but usually focuses on a few specific aspects of the child's experience.

How do I develop a rationale for observing?

We need to be focused when we are gathering data about a program. Before we start to observe we need to know why we have decided to observe the environment. There are many reasons for **environmental observation**. Knowing what to look for is particularly important, but casual observation may reveal information that lies outside the criteria but is still relevant. Some of your reasons for observing the children's environment might include

- helping to understand a child's family context (home life), cultural background, ethnicity, and sociological perspectives, to demonstrate appropriate sensitivity and accommodations

- helping to understand a child's behaviour and its causes and providing appropriate guidance

- helping to appreciate a child's conception of the world and so to support the child's learning

- helping to understand a child's level of social competence and to therefore provide appropriate experiences and support to improve the social environment

- helping to plan new experiences based on the success or failure of previously planned learning environments

- facilitating a better routine for the day, using space effectively, minimizing safety risks, and promoting health and healthful practices
- supporting a child's emotional development through improvement of the organization of groups, space, and time
- determining a child's interests by identifying his interaction with the environment
- maximizing the adults' interactions to enrich the children's language environment and nurturance
- identifying the influence of climate, temperature, colour, space, and atmosphere on individual or group behaviour
- helping to appreciate the hidden curriculum regarding attitudes, beliefs, and practices that affect the atmosphere, self-esteem, and success
- fulfilling a regular process of program-evaluation and -upgrading
- ascertaining that a balanced curriculum is being offered and ensuring that the children's interests and development shape program-planning

How do we observe the environment?

There are many ways. We could adopt any of the following perspectives: scientific, environmental health, personal safety, ethnological, statistical, professional development for teachers, and so on. While each of these is relevant, this book focuses on aspects of quality in environments for children and considering the **climate** of the environment. **Quality** childcare and education are the foundation for positive practice; recent research lays out its criteria.

In looking at environments we consider

- specific aspects of the environment (such as quality criteria),
- the children's behaviour within that environment, and
- adult-child relationships.

We may also consider

- the children's previous experiences, and
- how the children behave after exposure to the program.

What constitutes good-quality programming? What am I looking for?

We can find the conditions for quality in many diverse programs. Rather than stipulate exactly what a quality program should look like, we can apply the numerous quality characteristics to programs offered in many different ways. Audrey Curtis, the president of OMEP (Organization Mondiale pour l'Education Préscolaire, the international organization for Early Childhood Education), suggests that some educators are concerned about suggesting that there is any one way of providing quality care and education. She says that there should not be a "universal decontextualized child" but that "good practice does not exist in a vacuum, it is part of a complex situation in which cultural values and assumptions also play a part as well as an understanding of child development" (2000).

In her speech to OMEP in 2000, Curtis suggests four ways of determining quality, each of which must "acknowledge a diversity of circumstances and a diversity of perspectives and values." Quality services for children include indicators that relate

1. directly to the children and curriculum content,
2. to the staff,
3. to the family and community, and
4. to cost analysis and program quality.

The values underlying delivery of the service for children will shape the way a program is delivered. Following the same curriculum, or even a similar philosophy statement, does not ensure the same program delivery. Also, each child's experiences within a program will differ, and what the educators and parents think about the program will also vary. Experience is always individual.

There are several useful ways of looking at quality environments. In her *Five perspectives on quality in early childhood programs*, Lillian Katz (1993) suggests several useful ways of looking at quality early childhood programs:

1. The top-down perspective (which includes setting characteristics and measurable features of the program)
2. The bottom-up perspective (considering the child's experience of the program)
3. The outside-inside perspective (parent-teacher relationships)
4. The inside perspective (colleague relationships, staff-parent relationships, and relationships with a sponsoring agency)

We can also look at the quality of a program by measuring the climate of the place, which overlaps with the model cited above. This measure is usually found in school practice rather than child-care, and it has something to offer both settings. The climate is a more subjective measure of experience of those involved with an institution both inside and outside the community. It concerns what people think about the service that institution provides, how they feel about it, whether or not they feel comfortable or safe within it, how they value it, and other dimensions of their experience of it. To describe this measure as subjective does not mean this perspective is unimportant; the way people feel about an institution or service affects how it will be used and how well participants will benefit from it.

Measuring a climate usually means conducting interviews and focus groups, sending out questionnaires, and compiling observations of those participating in the program. The challenge comes in analyzing the data that are produced in order to determine themes. Determining the climate of a program delivered to young children is very difficult because it involves asking the children directly what they think. Asking parents about their children's responses to the program and observing the children as they are involved in it can be most helpful.

Deciding what constitutes quality care can be challenge enough for most of us; the question of why society should be concerned and support such care is another issue entirely. More than educators and parents are concerned about quality child-care. It can have benefits for society. According to *The Benefits and Costs of Good Child Care:*

The Economic Rationale for Public Investment in Young Children (Cleveland & Krashinsky 1998), quality care has long-lasting effects: "The future of our society absolutely requires good care for young children. Can we afford to spend the money for good child care? If we want an equitable and economically effective society, we cannot afford not to."

CHILD DEVELOPMENT FOCUS

Environmental observation and evaluation may

- lead to physically or personally safer environments

- allow for better use of space for all activities

- maximize learning opportunities

- increase inclusion of all children

- improve adult-child relationships

Are observing the environment and measuring the environment the same thing?

Observation can contribute to evaluation, but observation and evaluation are not the same thing. Just as we observe children in ways that contribute to our assessment of their behaviour, so we observe programs that offer data for a program-evaluation process. Multiple observations, as well as other ways of gathering information, add to our collection of adequate data to evaluate a program's effectiveness.

How many data are necessary for a meaningful environmental evaluation?

Both educators and parents can form impressions of an environment based on very little information. We need to ensure that we do not judge a climate, or a whole environment, too quickly or superficially. Here are a few misconceptions born of too little communication or only surface observation:

- Cheri visited a preschool program and was impressed by the depiction of children from different cultures on the walls. She thought that this must mean that the program accepted children from different cultures openly. When she took a morning off work to observe the program in action, she noticed that at circle time the educator called on only the white children to answer questions. This one incident too might have offered her an incomplete picture of the program's practice. She needed to observe other parts of the program.

- Looking for a program's guidance strategies, as directed by her college teacher, a student educator watched a resource teacher directing a child's play. When she came back to the college, she said that she thought that the program wasn't very child-centred;

after all, she had watched an adult assist a child's play when the student believed the teacher "should" have let the play be spontaneous. Another student educator told her that this was a child with a disability who needed one-on-one assistance with understanding the steps needed to complete a task. The two student educators saw the same thing, but one sought more information when she questioned a part of the program that might have defined the quality of play experiences.

- Seeing three children in the toddler program sitting on potties or the toilet in a row made one visitor think that the program didn't respect the children or give them personal space. What constitutes good practice is determined by culture as well as research. Whether or not these children were being respected and whether the environment was one to offer them private space were debatable.

The more information an observer gathers, the better. Using a variety of types of observation and recordings, with other information-gathering tools, provides a better overall picture of any program.

Are there different levels of quality in early childhood environments?

Yes, there are many different levels of quality, whatever yardstick you are using for measurement. Most programs for children demonstrate an acceptable standard, but not all do. Some offer environments that satisfy some children's needs, and others offer environments that meet the needs of the children's families. Each program has its own strengths and weaknesses.

Many researchers take a global view of quality programming based on the goal of ensuring that the child's basic needs and psychological needs are met. Some environments may meet these needs while other environments surpass them. By observing different environments, the learner sees how very different programs can appear to be successful, even according to the same criteria.

When you develop the criteria necessary for your environmental observation, keep each separate criterion in mind. Understand that the characteristics that you observe that are associated with those criteria may be at a high or a low level. Consider selecting a method of observation that includes a rating scale to document this.

Are indicators of quality the same for childcare, schools, and other children's programs?

Educators in all settings share some ideas about what constitutes quality. That said, the bodies of research tend to look at the broad environmental needs of all children or the specific environmental needs of children in either child-care or education settings. Both sectors may learn something from each other's research. Clearly educators emphasize the learning environment, although they differ in their articulation of what that actually means. The child-care environment provides both child-care and education (within a differing philosophy, some may say), so their emphasis is different.

If a kindergarten-aged child is in a half-day program at school and he spends the other half day at a child-care centre, should the environments be the same? Should they offer the same indicators of quality? Maybe they should be observed using the same quality criteria, because the child's needs may remain the same. However, the programs' goals differ, and what constitutes a quality environment therefore changes with them. This is a challenging issue that has not been resolved!

We might also think that a set of quality indicators might tell us what constitutes a good school. The OSSTF/FEESO (Ontario Secondary School Teachers' Federation/La Fédération des enseignantes-enseignats des écoles secondaires de l'Ontario) lays out a broad view of what makes a "Good School" in public education in their AMPA House Paper (the annual meeting of the Provincial Assembly of the OSSTF) (2001):

1. universality—access for all
2. comprehensiveness—opportunity for all
3. proficiency—achievement for all
4. accountability—value for all

The document then discusses how each of these goals could be measured. The four principles do not in themselves offer specific criteria for measurement: they constitute expansive characteristics that might form the structure for more specific, measurable criteria. The organization shows its intentions clearly and states its values: whether or not these principles could be applied outside the settings for which they were developed is uncertain because they depend on specific underlying beliefs.

Those involved in early and later childhood education have conducted research that influences today's thinking about quality environments for children. Lawrence Lezotte (1991) has been particularly influential. His "Seven Correlates of Effective Schools" are central in his work:

1. safe and orderly environment
2. clear and focused mission
3. climate of high expectations of success
4. opportunity to learn and student time on task
5. frequent monitoring of student progress
6. positive home-school relations
7. strong instructional leadership

No one is likely to take immediate offence at Lezotte's leading indicators for effective schools. At the same time it should be pointed out that these indicators, too, imply certain beliefs about the goals of education. Together they denote a "reform" perspective and exclude other indicators that some educators might value just as highly. In applying any measuring yardstick educators demonstrate that they are considering some indicators and eliminating others. So selecting the criteria is of enormous importance. Lezotte's criteria are not necessarily "wrong"; however, they are value-laden.

The Vista School District, Newfoundland & Labrador, has developed a school-evaluation tool that others can adopt. It studies 40 criteria statements built around five dimensions of school life:

1. the learning experience
2. school leadership

3. school climate and culture

4. school/community relationships

5. the teaching environment

To ensure that each of these is measurable the district has developed a criteria statement linking each of the goals to one of the five dimensions. In the form of a chart to be completed using questionnaires, focus groups, personal interviews, observation, and group discussion, the internal team documents what has been done, how well it has been achieved, and then evaluates what these results tell them. The process is logical and detailed and produces the results each school needs. The evaluation also contributes to the province's efforts to make its child-care and education system accountable. (For details, go to **www.K12.nf.ca/vista/schooldevelopment/internalcriteriaas.html**.)

These notions of "good schools" and effective learning environments may have some application to child-care settings. Close examination points to the fact that early childhood educators working in child-care and teachers working in schools may have different philosophies or may think that they are offering entirely different services. This distinction is of considerable importance because it highlights the differing emphases possible in measuring the environment. North American early childhood practice tends to separate the functions of nurturance and education to the possible detriment of the children. Agreement about what is good practice, how children's needs are best met, what constitutes an optimal environment to support healthy child development, and what services families need may be a long way off. We can make learning from other countries that have developed services to fit both children's and families' needs a high priority, instead of trying to meet those needs through existing education institutions.

On what basis are quality indicators and criteria for positive climates developed?

As we have discussed, we reach decisions about what constitutes quality from

- our own positive and negative experiences
- our individual and collective values and beliefs
- research into the links between environmental indicators and children's outcomes
- what we want for our children
- current issues in child-care and education

Who should decide what is a quality early-childhood environment?

All the stakeholders in programs for young children should participate in determining the specific criteria for developing positive early-childhood environments, for evaluating those environments, and for making changes as necessary. These people include

- parents
- community members

- educators and paraprofessionals
- directors, supervisors, and principals
- the children (when they are able to participate)
- the program's administration, owners, and government departments
- key informants (such as university faculty and community experts)

Only when these people share a common vision can they also share an understanding of how those environments should be funded, supported, evaluated, and explained, and how the parents and educators will work together to improve the children's overall experience.

So where do I begin observing the environment?

At first it may seem simple to observe the environment, but you may find it more complicated than it looks! You will need to

1. determine your reason for observing and recording
2. develop criteria that demonstrate the characteristic you are seeking
3. create a format to document the information
4. observe and document what you see in relation to each criterion

If you have taken these four steps you will have documented useful data that you can analyze in keeping with your reason for observing the environment in the first place.

How do I use the observational material to evaluate the environment?

When you have collected your data, you may want to sort the information, especially if it has become overwhelming. Themes may emerge when you review the information, or even as you collect it. You may find the following steps useful in moving towards a plan of action:

1. Sort data according to themes.
2. Present main themes—paper, charts, and diagrams can be helpful.
3. Review data for strengths.
4. Suggest strategies to build on those strengths.
5. Review data for weaknesses or gaps.
6. Develop strategies to address these negative aspects.
7. Create an overall plan for change.
8. Formulate a timeline for implementation of plan.
9. Communicate plan to all stakeholders.
10. Ensure a regular cycle for environmental evaluation.

Environments: Details of the Children's Contexts

KEY FEATURES: Environmental observation

- involves observing and recording data on how items in the environment are being used

- identifies all components of the child's environment, including the hidden curriculum

- includes observing children's behaviours related to any of these components

- is usually naturalistic

What to look for in the child's environment

Anytime and anywhere are the times and places to observe a child's environment. If you observed a child's context only in formal times of organized learning in a planned environment, you would miss most of the child's experiences.

You might gather much of the information regarding that context directly from the parents. Some parents might, quite fairly, resent your request for this information. Some initial interviews for childcare are held in the child's home—if this is the case, avoid the clipboard-checking-off approach, as this can seem clinical and off-putting to parents. Seek the information through more natural conversation about the child's home situation, while being open about recording some of the bits of information that the parents reveal. Be sure to record the sources of the information.

Here are some things you might look for that constitute the "environment" in a broad sense:

Home and family

- **nuclear family**—composition and size
- siblings, birth order
- health, abilities and disabilities of family members
- location of extended family
- changes in family composition, moves
- nonfamily adults or children in the child's home
- religious or cultural heritage and practices
- mother's role and guidance
- father's role and guidance
- sibling(s)' or others' roles in caregiving and guidance
- day-care or school enrolment and attendance
- memberships
- play space, play materials
- books and toys available
- TV, VCR, video games
- employment of parent(s), hours of work
- finances
- accommodation (rent or own)

- number of rooms (privacy or shared)
- clothing availability
- laundry facilities
- kitchen, food-preparation equipment
- temperature, indoor climate
- practical needs met or not met

- safety of environment
- outdoor space
- transportation, access, mobility
- need for social work, therapy, or other support
- family concerns

Sociological and geographic context

- nation and city of residence
- urban, suburban, or rural location
- accommodations (rent or own)
- type of neighbourhood
- population density
- building types, age, and history
- transportation, mobility
- shopping amenities
- local industry
- community services and buildings
- banks, finances, economy, taxation, benefits
- cultural mix of local population
- play spaces

- schools
- provision of childcare
- community concerns
- religious buildings and practices
- health services
- restaurants, cafés, fast-food outlets
- social organizations
- communications
- climate
- prevalence of disease
- demographic changes
- employment
- social services

Child-care agency/school

- type of establishment
- number and organization of staff, full-time or part-time schedules, supply staff
- funding and budget
- age ranges, hours open, size of group or classes, ratios
- catchment area
- staff qualifications, union membership, sex of staff, representation of ethnic groups
- indoor space and organization
- interior design of space
- philosophy as reflected in design
- stated philosophy
- variety of activities (name them)

- washrooms—access, independence level for child
- routines—meals, sleep, etc.
- food preparation and snacks
- policies, procedures, meetings, communications
- guidance strategies
- exterior space and equipment
- emergency plans
- safety precautions indoors and outdoors, first aid
- transportation
- availability of parking
- resources, space, and access
- involvement by parents, available parent education

- involvement with community—trips, within centre
- relationships between staff and children
- types of programs offered
- expendable resources—paint, paper, soap, etc.
- temperature and humidity
- hygienic practices
- provision when child is sick
- staff liaison with child's home

- entry or acclimatizing plan for new children
- accommodation for children with special needs
- cultural or ethnic mix of those enrolled
- referrals to other services if and when required
- personal belongings, storage
- structure, flexibility, expectations

Recording information about the child's environment

Looking at the world with the eyes of a child is one of the most effective ways to really see a child's environment. Recording the context involves much more than checking off the presence or absence of an element of that environment on a list. Compare the checklist and the narrative in the following excerpt from a family context.

Family Context

A. Checklist	Yes	No
Child has own room		✓
Child has personal storage space in bedroom	✓	
Child has appropriate toys	✓	
Child owns books	✓	

B. Narrative

Sian lives in a downtown third-floor apartment with her mother and two older sisters, with whom she shares a small bedroom. The apartment offers space for Sian to play between the kitchen and living room where Mom can watch over her. The three girls go to the library with their father alternate Saturday mornings when he has custody. The shared arrangement with the father is amicable, according to Mom, who said she liked to have a little time to herself when the girls are out. When they returned to sleep at home on Saturday night, I observed Mom playing with Sian. Her toys are not all new but seem to challenge Sian without causing her much frustration. . . .

As you can see, the **narrative observation** offers much more detail and background than the Yes/No approach of a **checklist**. While open to greater interpretation, the narrative description also provides pertinent information that explains the content of the checklist. Neither is incorrect, but each presents a different version of the situation.

Checklists can be handy when you want to record lots of information quickly, and they serve as a reminder to look for particular criteria. The narrative takes much longer and is more open-ended, so it can include what the observer thinks pertinent.

Rating scales can also be helpful in recording the degree to which an attribute or characteristic is present. Both checklists and rating scales require that the observer make inferences while collecting that data.

Open-Ended Checklist

14. small wheel toys, cars, trucks   yes/no/not applicable

    comment/description _____

    _____

15. carpentry/sewing/cooking equipment   yes/no/not applicable

    comment/description _____

    _____

16. child-sized furniture   yes/no/not applicable

    comment/description _____

    _____

17. outdoor play equipment   yes/no/not applicable

    comment/description _____

    _____

You can make visual representations of the environment using photographs, video-recordings, and **mappings**. Any of these can add usefully to checklists or narratives, and they offer a record of the context that may be quicker, more detailed, and longer lasting. Recording the environment in one of these ways enables you as observer or evaluator to consider the depiction away from the site or after the context has changed.

You can also use acetates designed for overhead projection for floor plans and over-lay them to compare the use of space. Alternatively, you can draw a blank floor plan and photocopy it so that you can plan room arrangements.

Features of Environmental Evaluation

DEFINITION: Environmental evaluation

Environmental evaluation involves consideration of all the planned and unplanned aspects of a child's surroundings to ascertain their appropriateness or quality.

- evaluates any or all components of the environment against the stated philosophy of care and education

- determines the effectiveness of any or all components of the environment for safety, inclusion, nurturance, learning potential, or other criteria

- develops plans to improve environmental conditions in line with program goals

- is usually naturalistic

Examples of environmental measurement

The narrative or checklist approach to observation can provide a relatively unbiased account of a child's environment. This account is desirable for understanding what constitutes the child's context, though it does not offer direct evaluative information from which a social worker might decide on some form of intervention, a caregiver might decide on compensatory measures, or an educator might identify contextual barriers to learning. Assessing the child's environment requires a much deeper understanding of all the component parts of the child's experience and how they interact. Base a **qualitative evaluation** of any environment on a clear understanding of the philosophy underlying the construction and use of that environment. For example, you would find it difficult to assess a curriculum for **anti-bias** if you did not subscribe to the concept of anti-bias education.

The simplest evaluation format is the checklist. The items must be clear, focused, and as complete as the writer can make them. A more open-ended checklist may have space for including "add-on" items. You can attach a rating scale to the list of environmental criteria, allowing for a more qualitative response than simply a presence or absence or a "good" or "bad" answer.

Checklist for Quality Inclusive Education

I.1.c **Visual displays reflect equity in representation.**   F   O   S

I.1.c.16. Do I display photographs and pictures of children involved in a variety of activities? e.g.,

- girls in nontraditional activities
- boys in nontraditional activities
- children with varying abilities engaged in active play

Examples:

	F	O	S

I.1.c.17. Do I balance displays of children in special, traditional clothes in appropriate situations (e.g., celebrations) with displays of children in their everyday clothes? ☐ ☐ ☐

Examples:

I.1.c.18. Do I use visual displays that represent diversity?

	F	O	S
• varying physical, visual, and sensory abilities	☐	☐	☐
• varying ages	☐	☐	☐
• varying appearances	☐	☐	☐
• different beliefs	☐	☐	☐
• multicultural backgrounds	☐	☐	☐
• different family compositions	☐	☐	☐
• females and males	☐	☐	☐
• multiracial backgrounds	☐	☐	☐

Examples:

F = frequently   O = occasionally   S = seldom

Source: Rachel Langford et al., <u>Checklist for Quality Inclusive Education: A Self-Assessment Tool and Manual for Early Childhood Settings</u>. Alberta Association for Young Children (1997).

Standardized checklists prepared by an authority are checked for **validity** and **reliability** and reflect a particular philosophy. The best known, most reliable, and most user-friendly environment rating scales are Harms and Clifford's *Early Childhood Environment Rating Scale* (1998) and Harms, Cryer, and Clifford's *Infant/Toddler Environment Rating Scale* (1989). You can use another rating scale Harms and Clifford have developed, the *Family Day Care Rating Scale* (1989), for evaluating home-based childcare.

Use these scales in a variety of early childhood settings; a wide variety of professionals, including teachers and assistants, can administer them. Each rates an item on a scale of 1 to 7 and allows space for comments. Each of the major categories is divided into several components, with clearly identified criteria for grading. Completing them is straightforward, and good results depend on general early-childhood training and familiarity with some terminology. You can gather checklist and rating scale results from both parents and professionals. If the criteria are clear, the perspectives of both parties may offer insight; frequently the outcomes will be similar.

FAMILY DAY CARE RATING SCALE

Name of lead caregiver *Roberta Poole*

No. of caregivers present

Most children attending at one time 5

Number of children present today 5

Ages of children enrolled (youngest to oldest in months) *9 mos.* to *40 mos.*

Name of rater *Pam Eckerd*

Position of rater *Resource and referral trainer*

Date *June 29, 2003*

SPACE AND FURNISHINGS FOR CARE AND LEARNING

1. Furnishings for routine care and learning
1 2 3 ④ 5 6 7
Children kneel on chairs—not adapted for their size.

2. Furnishings for relaxation and comfort
1 2 3 4 ⑤ 6 7

3. Child-related display
1 2 ③ 4 5 6 7

4. Indoor space arrangement
1 2 ③ 4 5 6 7
Space safe and adequate.

5. Active physical play
1 2 3 4 ⑤ 6 7
Fenced outdoor area. Uses activity records indoors on rainy days.

6. Space to be alone
a. infants/toddlers
1 ② 3 4 5 6 7
Doesn't interest frequently enough.

b. 2 years and older
1 2 3 4 ⑤ 6 7
Private space used for older children's games.

Total Space and Furnishings (Items 1–6)
27

BASIC CARE

7. Arriving/leaving
1 2 3 4 5 6 ⑦

8. Meals/snacks
1 2 3 4 ⑤ 6 7

9. Nap/rest
1 2 3 4 ⑤ 6 7

10. Diapering/toileting
① 2 3 4 5 6 7
Doesn't wash hands after each child.

11. Personal grooming
1 ② 3 4 5 6 7
Children's hands not washed before eating.

12. Health
1 2 3 ④ 5 6 7
Not careful about preventing spread of germs; no set rules for giving medicines to children.

13. Safety
1 2 ③ 4 5 6 7

Total Basic Care (Items 7–13)
27

Teachers College Press

Quality Control: A Manual for Self-Evaluation of a Day Care Agency (Campbell 1987) offers a format for assessment covering all the functions of a child-care centre. Supervisors and daycare operators may find this a useful overview of a centre's general effectiveness. It may not offer enough detail to help educators examine the learning environment in a specific area. The steps for program evaluation, however, are clear and can be applied even when used with other evaluation systems. Another strength of the evaluation is that it incorporates parental input. Based on a rating scale attached to "Standards of Performance Statements," parents score components such as administration, facilities, staffing, admissions, and the program.

Measurement of the home and family environment has long intrigued many researchers, who have suspected a link between characteristics of families and IQ or achievement. Caldwell (1979) devised a measure of the environment called the HOME inventory—*Home Observation for Measurement of the Environment*. The evaluator scores a series of Yes/No questions, makes observations and interviews the parent about a typical day in the family, interactions with the child, and the material environment. The original intention was to see whether the *Home* inventory scores and the children's IQs were correlated, which they were. Replication of these studies has highlighted the importance of some of the components of the inventory, while we do not understand all the reasons for the correlations. The studies agree that features of children's home environments do have an impact on their performance, competence, or IQs. While the inventory was designed for research purposes, it could be used for evaluation of individual families. What to do with the results is less certain; only a relevant professional's identification of a clear dysfunction can justify any intervention in a family's lifestyle and interaction.

In 2000 the University of Guelph's Centre for Families, Work and Well-Being in Ontario published "You Bet I Care—Caring and Learning Environments: Quality in Child Care Centres Across Canada" (Goelman et al.). This important project links quality care with program characteristics, teaching-staff wages and working conditions, and teaching-staff characteristics and attitudes. The low levels of provision of care cited—in more than 7 percent of the programs investigated—and the poor levels of care found for infants and toddlers are of particular note. The findings present a powerful argument for delivering quality programs and for early childhood educators' pushing for better work conditions.

> The Canada-wide studies examine the wages, working conditions and best practices in child-care centres, and the overall quality of care in child-care centres and in family child-care homes. Findings from the first study detail the human resource challenges of a workforce that is chronically underpaid and undervalued. The latter two quality of care studies found that it is the norm for children to be cared for by warm and responsive adults in settings that protect their health and safety, but that there is significant room to improve on the third dimension of quality—the provision of activities that support and stimulate children's development (*You Bet I Care*, 1998).

The "You Bet I Care" study applied a variety of measures of quality including the Early Childhood Environment Rating Scale–Revised (ECERS-R). Its findings cannot be questioned. Other evaluation tools might have produced other outcomes; the results depend on the benchmark of quality used. While this was not a comparative study, we have to wonder how well other countries are faring in the delivery of quality programs when we look at the findings.

We frequently run into difficulties when we compare quality by using different indicators. The United Nations Special Session on Children (UNICEF) (2000) recently suggested a model for making such comparisons in education: "A new way forward in defining the issue of quality education is to view it through a broader lens, involving at least five dimensions: what learners bring, content, processes, environments, and outcomes." Experts agree on the "critical importance of education quality to genuine learning and human development and reviewed best practices." Representatives of a wide group of countries have developed a plan for the World Declaration on the Survival, Protection and Development of Children as part of the World Summit for Children. It calls for each country to establish appropriate mechanisms for the regular and timely collection, analysis and publication of data to monitor relevant social indicators relating to children's well-being. Over the last ten years, UNICEF and its partners have helped establish international agreement on a common set of indicators by which to measure progress.

Not all countries have signed the Convention on the Rights of the Child and, unfortunately non-participating countries can lack support for their children's needs and the power to advocate for change with other countries outside the Convention.

The Canadian Institute of Child Health published its findings on Children's Developmental Health in 2001. In its section on early environments and developmental health, supported by the NLSCY (National Longitudinal Survey of Children and Youth) study (Brink & McKeller 2000), it discusses the impact of neuroscience on children's development. The study suggests that

> the developing brain is an environmental organ that is influenced by the social and physical environments of children. During the earliest period of development—from conception to entry into the public school system—children live in families, neighbourhoods, and early childhood settings (such as child-care, preschool, playgroups and kindergarten). Societal environments influence developmental health directly and indirectly through their impact on immediate environments. (p. 19)

This study throws even greater weight behind the push to observe and measure the quality of children's environments and to refine which indicators of quality are most important. Schwartz and Chance (1999) raise another issue in the Canadian Child Care Federation's *Research Connections Canada 2: Supporting Children and Families*. They underscore the link between the environment and health from a protective stance rather than from the usual educator's perspective, an approach that highlights exposure to dangerous chemicals, climate change, and the need for air and water quality assessment. The 1998 Declaration of the Environment Leaders of the Eight [the G8] on Children's Environmental Health discusses associated health problems and provides a framework for domestic, bilateral, and international efforts to improve protections of children's environmental health. We must keep these broad-based environmental issues in mind as we work to ensure the quality of our own programs and environments. Global and local views of the environment are equally important.

At the beginning of this chapter we discussed the basic and psychological needs of the child. UNICEF is endeavouring to support these and educators are trying to refine them. The real heart of quality environments for children lies in providing for all those needs.

A short section follows that discusses further what constitutes good environments for young children.

Appropriate environments

"Appropriate practice" is a phrase commonly used in child-care circles, though its meaning varies. The National Association for the Education of Young Children (NAEYC), the American organization that has identified the components of **developmentally appropriate** practice, endorses a holistic and child-centred approach as its philosophy. Based on research into the determinants of quality programs, the NAEYC publication *Developmentally Appropriate Practice in Early Childhood Programs Serving Children from Birth Through Age 8* (Bredekamp 1997) serves as a manual of good practice. You can use it to evaluate an existing program or to help develop provisions from scratch. The age-stage integrated components of appropriate and inappropriate practice cover goals, ratios, and teacher qualifications as well as specific developmental practice. If you use each item with a rating scale, putting appropriate practice at one end and inappropriate practice at the other, the charts become an evaluative tool. The items can be used to focus discussions with parents or staff and to support a more structured environmental evaluation.

Integrated Components of Appropriate and Inappropriate Practice for 3- to 5-year-old Children

Appropriate Practices

- Teachers observe and interact with individuals and small groups in all contexts (including teacher-planned and child-chosen learning experiences) to maximize their knowledge of what children can do and what each child is capable of doing with and without coaching, scaffolding, or other supportive assistance. To help children acquire new skills or understanding, teachers select from a range of strategies, such as asking questions, offering cues or suggestions, demonstrating a skill, adding more complex materials or ideas to a situation, and providing an opportunity for collaborating with peers.

Inappropriate Practices

- Teachers are uninvolved in children's play, exploration, and activities, viewing their role as merely one of supervision. Teachers fail to take an active role in promoting children's learning, assuming that children will develop skills and knowledge on their own without adult assistance.

- Children do much paper-and-pencil seatwork in which there are only right or wrong answers. Thus teachers have little idea about the process of children's problem-solving or their specific areas of difficulty and competence. As a result, teachers do not know how to help children who do not understand and are frustrated or how to further challenge children who get the problem "right."

Appropriate Practices

- Teachers stimulate and support children's engagement in play and child-chosen activities. Teachers extend the child's thinking and learning within these child-initiated activities by posing problems, asking questions, making suggestions, adding complexity to tasks, and providing information, materials, and assistance as needed to enable a child to consolidate learning and to move to the next level of functioning.

- Teachers provide many opportunities for children to plan, think about, reflect on, and revisit their own experiences. Teachers engage children in discussion and representation activities (such as dictating, writing, drawing, or modelling in clay), which help children refine their own concepts and understanding and help the teacher understand what children know and think; for example, teachers use children's own hypotheses about how the world works to engage them in problem-solving and experimentation.

- Teachers provide many opportunities for children to learn to work collaboratively with others and to construct social knowledge as well as develop social skills, such as cooperating, helping, negotiating, and talking with other people to solve problems. Teachers foster the development of social skills and group problem-solving at all times through modelling, coaching, grouping, and other strategies.

Inappropriate Practices

- Teachers do not help children make good use of choice time. Teachers rarely intervene when children do the same things over and over or become disruptive. Rather than assisting children in developing decision-making skills, teachers overuse time-out or use punishment to control disruptive children.

- During children's play and choice activities, teachers assume passive roles, contributing little or nothing to children's play and learning.

- Teachers expect children to respond with one right answer most of the time. Teachers treat children's naive hypotheses as simply wrong answers rather than clues to how they think. Not realizing how much learning young children are capable of, teachers do not engage them in dialogues in which they take children's ideas seriously, nor do they encourage children to express ideas through other (nonverbal) modes of representation.

- Feeling pressured to cover the curriculum and believing that returning to the same topic or experience is a waste of time, teachers present a topic only once and fail to provide the revisiting opportunities that make possible fuller, more refined understanding.

- Underestimating children's intellectual abilities, teachers do not provide the time and support for children to develop concepts and skills.

- Children are expected to work individually at desks or tables most of the time. Typically teachers give directions to the total group, with few opportunities for meaningful social interaction with other children.

- Teachers rarely use children's social relationships as a vehicle to address learning goals. Teaching strategies are not designed to support children's social competence.

Source: Sue Bredekamp, Developmentally Appropriate Practice in Early Childhood Programs Serving Children from Birth Through Age 8 (1997).

A program can be observed and evaluated by turning performance objectives into questions. Schlank and Metzger (1989) have developed an easy-to-use, open-ended tool that uses a minimum of jargon. While the questions could be answered with Yes or No, they are likely to provoke some explanation. This type of evaluation allows for parental input and is clear in its philosophy because each component starts with a statement of intention.

Learning (physical)

It is important for young children to gain awareness of their bodies and to develop their physical capabilities. They may need help to feel okay about their differences in size, appearance, strength, and agility.

Is there opportunity for active physical play?

Does the caregiver encourage children to become involved in physical activities?

Is there large equipment such as a climber, large boxes, or a rocking boat for large muscle development? Is there adequate space indoors or outside for physical activity?

Are there activities to help children develop an awareness of their bodies in space? For example, are there activities such as walking on a line, moving to music, and jumping in place?

Are there materials such as blunt scissors, pegboards, and puzzles for the development of small muscle coordination?

Source: Carol H. Schlank and Barbara Metzger, A Room Full of Children (1989).

Devising Your Own Environmental Observation or Evaluation Tool

Informal methods

A list of environmental components may suit your own observation purposes. Serving as a reminder of things to look for, it may help refine your perceptions. As you form the list, you will probably become aware of the philosophy behind the criteria; the fact that you include an item means that it is important to your belief system. You might want to explore the philosophy further to ensure that the listing is complete and organized. As you work, you may decide to limit your task and narrow your focus more precisely. You might also want to structure it under separate headings to make the parts more manageable. As the list evolves, you might phrase the items throughout more consistently as questions with a Yes/No reply or as statements to be graded. Trial use of the checklist or rating scale will probably reveal some gaps and items that need to be restated. This kind of tool can be useful as it fits the setting well; remember that it may not be as inclusive or objective as other tested tools, or it may not be valid or reliable if applied elsewhere.

Structured methods

An effective tool records or measures what it intends to measure. To devise such a tool for environmental observation or evaluation, work through the following process:

1. Identify the need for evaluation.
2. Specify the area(s) to be observed or evaluated.
3. State the goals of the project and the philosophy underpinning the tool.
4. Seek team or committee support.
5. Assign the roles and responsibilities of team members.
6. Clarify the process through which the tool is to be devised.
7. Agree on a timeline.
8. Arrange for a trial of the tool.

The methods for devising a tool may include any or all of the following activities, separately or simultaneously and in any sequence:

- researching existing tools
- reviewing stated philosophies
- evaluating the environment by using different tools
- brainstorming ideas
- surveying parents, professionals, and /or the community to determine opinions and needs
- revising tools used previously
- identifying component parts of "environment"—that is, stating your criteria
- editing
- conducting trial runs with items used as checklists, rating scales, or open-ended criteria
- clarifying grading criteria

Working through a structured method in devising a tool makes that tool more likely to fit the need, to reflect a common philosophy, and to be more detailed and inclusive than a checklist informally put together. It will probably find wider acceptance and be more reliable in its use.

As fashions in education come and go and research constantly supplies us with new information, you will probably find your existing observation and evaluation tools less effective than you would wish. You must continue to update, change, and recreate your tools. You will also find the qualitative methods most likely need modification because the purely observational approaches make fewer inferences and are more open.

Caregivers, parents, and educators most frequently review the health and safety, quality, appropriateness, and effectiveness of the children's environment. You do not have to keep these categories if other concepts are more suitable. Each major category can have many component parts that you will need to identify. Where your evaluation is based on an interpretation of observed information, you will have to clarify the specifics. For example, you would have to define "high family involvement," "low ratio," or "type of accommodations for special needs" more precisely. A qualitative observation or evaluation relies on the recorder's consistent and clearly defined use of his or her terms.

Philosophy Statement and Indicators

We believe that . . .

Children's development needs to be observed, understood, and supported for it to occur at an optimum level. Objective recording of ongoing observational information guides decision-making in all elements of our work with children.

In our lab schools, the indicators that this is being practiced are as follows:

Indicators	Yes	No	Examples of practice
1. Children are observed daily and written notation made.			
2. Observed information reflects the whole child and does not only focus on problem areas or difficulties.			
3. Daily observations are used as a basis for program planning and are obviously reflected in activity plans, room arrangement, schedule, etc.			
4. Developmental assessments are completed biannually and shared with parents in formal meetings.			
5. Ongoing observations of children are shared with parents through daily interactions and written notation.			
6. The opportunity is provided, and parents are encouraged, to share their observations about their child.			
7. Ongoing observations of children are shared with other staff in a professional manner to facilitate problem solving and program adjustments to better respond to children's needs.			
8. Students' assignments requiring the collection of observational information are welcomed and supported.			

Source: Centennial College Early Childhood Education Programs and Child Care Centres, <u>Philosophy Check-In</u> (1998).

Indicators of appropriate environments for young children

The following lists feature broad components that warrant consideration when observing, evaluating, or planning group-care environments. You may have to itemize specific criteria according to your own needs and settings. When you have defined these components, you can then use them in the form of a checklist, as the criteria for a rating scale, as the basis for a narrative description, as the focus of group discussion, or as a starting point for plans to create or modify an agency. The items are set out in no particular order of priority.

Environmental Evaluation

Rating scale:

5 = exemplary performance: maintains high standard
4 = good performance: exceeds minimum standard
3 = adequate performance: meets minimum standard
2 = below adequate performance: falls short of minimum standard
1 = poor performance: fails to meet minimum standard

Indicator	Observation	Identification of need	Rating

This chart can be used to evaluate environmental indicators. Depending on the school or agency, the standard against which performance is measured may be determined by the province or state, by a local board, or by the agency or school itself.

General indicators of a quality environment

- clearly stated philosophy based on researched indicators of quality
- small group size
- low ratios
- demonstration that individual children's needs are being met
- appropriate and stimulating learning environment
- developmental appropriateness of design, activity, and guidance
- high degree of staff training
- high level of parental involvement and partnership
- positive quality of interactions with children
- effective teamwork with parents and professionals
- low staff turnover

- positive communications among staff
- optimal safety, health, and nutrition
- regular program evaluation

Inclusion

- clearly stated anti-bias policy and practice
- welcome and **inclusion** of all children whatever their race, appearance, class, ethnicity, ability, sex, origin, religion, or beliefs
- high level of staff training in **diversity**, anti-bias education, and acceptance of diverse lifestyles
- avoidance of superficiality, **tokenism**, **stereotypes**, and **touristic approaches**
- presentation of cultural and ethnic variety in music, images, scripts, artifacts, food
- sensitivity to range of family backgrounds
- accommodations made for children's differing needs and abilities
- resources available for children with **special needs**
- support of first languages and cultural heritages
- developmentally and individually appropriate activities and experience
- activities in which children of all abilities can participate and cooperate

Every area of the curriculum can be assessed for its inclusion. The effectiveness of an anti-bias curriculum can be measured by environmental checklists and observation of the children within the setting.

- large-group and small-group activities that allow children to participate at their own levels
- range of activities and playthings to allow independence while also providing challenges to children of varying abilities
- active encouragement of community involvement in program
- effective communication and partnership with parents
- knowledgeable and sensitive communication with all children, demonstration of respect to all
- avoidance of labelling
- access to support resources to aid inclusion
- ongoing evaluation of all books, images, toys, playthings, and materials for their appropriateness
- policies and practices that address racism, prejudice, judgmental behaviours, and exclusion
- effective communication with parents and involvement of families
- acknowledgement of a wide variety of parenting styles and child-rearing practices

TAKING A SPECIAL LOOK: Inclusion and integration

In recent years, the **integration** of children with special needs into mainstream care and education has become an important trend. This practice produces a more natural environment for all children and an acceptance of diversity. However, child-care agencies and schools that advocate integration face challenges in terms of time, equipment, support, and expertise. These issues need to be resolved before inclusion and integration become feasible in many mainstream settings.

Physical well-being
- good **hygienic practices** that control spread of infection
- policies, practices, and protective measures for physical and emotional safety
- minimizing of inappropriate stressors
- clearly stated policies and procedures for health, safety, and nutrition
- provision of first aid
- demonstration that children's physical and emotional needs are being met
- adequate kitchen equipment, food storage, preparation, and serving of food
- nutritious and healthful snacks and meals
- adequate space and opportunity for physical play
- positive **role models**
- resources and support available to parents on health-related issues

- provision for sick children
- adequacy of toileting and washroom
- protection from extreme weather conditions
- health education for children
- regular program evaluations and review
- environment constructed for children's safe use and healthy development
- routine safety checks
- supervision adequate for children's well-being
- maintenance of a safe environment
- children encouraged to take risks within safe boundaries
- provision for rest, sleep, and quiet
- high level of cleaning, sanitizing, and sterilizing appropriate to building, furniture, and materials
- monitoring pollution
- appropriate waste management
- reporting to parents of changes in behaviour, health conditions, and general development
- effective communication with parents
- maintenance of appropriate temperature, humidity, and air quality
- confidential and complete health records
- adequate clean-water supply
- community health resources accessed
- adequate training and professional development of all staff in matters of health, safety, nutrition, and first aid
- compliance with local, provincial or state, and federal legislation and regulations
- sensitive consideration of parental wishes
- accident and serious-occurrence records
- documentation and sensitive handling of allergies and medical conditions
- regular and continuous observations of children's health and behaviour
- early identification of behavioural changes and indicators of concern
- children's positive attitudes to well-being demonstrated
- appropriate storage of materials
- accommodations for specific abilities and disabilities
- separation of areas for different purposes
- maintenance of caregivers' health and management of stress

Nurturance

- small group size
- low child-to-adult ratio

- personal space for belongings
- acceptance of individual styles and behavioural patterns
- opportunities for personal attachments
- children's demonstrating enjoyment, fun, and enthusiasm
- sensitivity, responsiveness, and attunement to individual children
- positive role models that demonstrate the range of human feelings
- opportunity for play activity with peers
- consistency of caregivers
- flexibility of routines and patterns to meet individual needs
- stability of family and home circumstances
- positive approaches to changes in accommodation, caregiving, and parenting
- positive communications between parents and caregivers
- maintenance of stable, consistent program
- opportunity for family involvement in the program
- design of agency for contrasts to suit children's moods and temperaments
- acceptance of cooperative and solitary activity
- play encouraged as therapeutic activity
- observation and monitoring of the program's emotional climate, with adaptations as necessary
- demonstration that feelings are acknowledged and allowed
- encouragement of emotional expression
- open exploration of reality and fantasy
- positive communication with children about feelings, changes, crises
- encouragement and modelling of empathy
- encouragement of objects that link home and agency
- support to develop children's strategies to cope with strong feelings
- acceptance of diversity in action and voice
- practical indications of support for children's self-identity
- opportunity for children's self-categorization and self-discovery
- support for positive body-image awareness
- fostering of creative thinking and success
- demonstration of support regarding separations and reunions
- catering to needs for privacy and quiet
- clear indication of the parameters of behaviour and the consequences for noncompliance
- opportunity for the children to make choices
- open-ended activities that avoid correct or incorrect responses or winners and losers
- process-focused activity

- authentic praise and encouragement
- support of adults for each other
- common nurturing philosophy among caregivers

Learning

- design meets children's needs
- child-sized furniture and materials
- opportunity for children to make choices
- self-direction allowed
- spontaneous play valued
- focus on process of activity
- freedom of movement enabled
- developmentally appropriate programming
- observation of children to help determine their needs and programs
- opportunity for experimentation and discovery
- sensitivity to the child's stage of understanding
- space organized for movement flow
- children's leads followed
- adult enthusiasm demonstrated for children's efforts
- activity extended (but not directed) by adults
- curriculum evolved from children's interests
- activities that allow for success and minimize failures
- communication of ideas encouraged
- open-ended and evolving program
- stimulation of children in all developmental areas
- focus on hands-on activity and participatory learning
- avoidance of limiting structure and rigid timetabling
- family contribution and participation encouraged
- children's natural curiosity encouraged
- imitative, fantasy, and sociodramatic play provided
- language supplied to help children classify and conceptualize new experiences
- adult interactions that help children focus on learning
- knowledge extended from the base of the child's current understanding
- language, print, symbols, and literature promoted
- sensory exploration promoted
- strategies to overcome challenges offered
- role models and support of moral understanding provided
- clear direction regarding expectations and behaviour

- program changes made at differing pace according to needs
- wide range of traditional and nontraditional curriculum components
- children's range of feelings acknowledged
- interactive learning and construction of knowledge
- children's understanding of similarities and differences encouraged
- sensitivity to different needs of members of the group demonstrated
- plans for individual and collective needs
- therapeutic or compensatory care
- programming responsive to changing needs
- well-trained staff share a philosophy of how children learn
- cooperation and communication with parents
- regular evaluation of program
- regular observation of children
- learning planned from what is known to what is unknown
- open-ended activities and materials that encourage creativity
- curriculum that sets appropriate and achievable challenges
- higher-order thinking promoted
- success encouraged and errors treated as learning experiences
- skills development monitored
- program justified in measurable ways
- community resources used and dialogue maintained with community representative
- compliance with all regulatory bodies

Responding to an Environmental Evaluation

Earlier in this chapter we reviewed the stages of environmental evaluation. Here we discuss issues arising out of that process.

We move toward better planning and programming by carrying out an environmental evaluation. Before we attempt to change things, however, we need general agreement among the team members that change is necessary. Change can be unsettling and can make people feel that they have failed at their jobs; team members may need some time and encouragement before they are ready to adapt their program or ways of doing things. In some circumstances, administrators or even legislated requirements drive change, and it may be necessary to move forward without complete agreement. Working out an efficient and effective process of change is most likely to produce a successful outcome. If the team agrees on the process at the start, and all the parties have an opportunity to participate, people are more likely to "buy into" the need to make changes.

What to change

Like any other kind of evaluation, evaluating the environment may tell us what the problem is, but will not usually tell us how to fix the problem. Review your evaluation outcome and do some collective problem-solving to determine how to address each issue. Some issues may be related, so one solution may address several problems.

Remember that not everything is within your power or scope to change. You may be unable to improve your budget or change the staffing situation overnight! You might want to filter your results according to what you all consider possible. Some of the more flexible people involved may prefer to take a look at whatever needs changing, however challenging it may appear. As a group, you might choose to be undaunted by some obvious limitations. The bigger issues, those concerning philosophical issues or values, are harder to address. If you must look at these big issues, do so, but accept that they demand effort and heart-searching.

List the things that need to be changed, with or without reference to the relative difficulty of achieving those changes. Examine the list to see if the items are superficial and cosmetic or whether they signal a more profound problem. Your evaluation may show several unconnected items, or they may be clustered in a particular area. Scattered items are more likely to be bits and pieces that can be "fixed" quickly. A group of related things can highlight a need for philosophical reflection or a deeper evaluation of the program's achievement or direction. Of course, your bits and pieces may actually relate to deeper issues as well; check for any connection.

You may need to set priorities in your activities according to the time, money, and professional-development opportunities available.

Taking action

After reviewing and discussing the data comes action, preferably with a timeline and specific responsibilities assigned. Keep timelines realistic; bear in mind that a transition period might be harder to deal with than the actual change will be when fully implemented. The scale of the change also makes a difference to how the change should be accomplished. If you need to move some furniture, few people may resist the change. On the other hand, if the change requires a review of policies regarding inclusion, equity, and anti-bias, you might need to plan for a lengthy discussion of those topics.

Depending on the urgency of the issue, the possibility of making changes speedily, and the need for complex negotiation, you will want to create an action plan. Here using a prepared format can be helpful. A sample action plan can be found on page 366.

The process of evaluation and change needs to be a cycle rather than a one-time experience. If you evaluate your environment regularly, you will find the process of change becomes easier. Individual responsibility for evaluation is commendable, yet programs for young children are usually of higher quality if regular evaluation is a mandated requirement. This process requires a budget, encouragement, time, and staff training.

Every element of the environment should be evaluated regularly. An inclusive environment will provide books and other materials suitable for children of varying abilities, and will represent cultural diversity in its materials and displays.

Summary

The environment is something we can easily take for granted, although it shapes the experiences that we offer children and our interactions with everyone. For very young children the environment is an integral part of their curriculum; it is their experience. What we can afford financially is only part of what determines the quality of that environment. As parents and educators we hold values that determine how that environment is shaped as well. While there are many aspects to any environment, for purposes of improvement the details are as important as the general overview. Adults bear the responsibility for monitoring every aspect of the child's environment and for taking steps to bring every element to the highest level. At the least, we must do everything we can to make every aspect of the child's experience the best possible.

At the global level we face ecological issues that need to be addressed to ensure that current and future generations have good-quality air, water, and a generally good living environment. This chapter looks at the environment at the micro level, the level within the control of the adults in the lives of the children under their care.

In appreciating a child's basic needs, educators have a baseline of what is considered vital within the child-care centre or classroom. Safety measures are essential; we need to evaluate these regularly while the details will vary according to the particular setting, materials, and objects being used. Psychological needs may be more difficult to determine, but also must be met. How adults behave within that environment is just as important as the walls, physical amenities and objects.

Several bodies of research help inform us through their environmental observation and evaluation. Some base their findings on notions of what constitutes quality environments. We can agree on common elements within most environments for children. From such research, environmental rating scales have been developed for use in childcare. Other studies highlight characteristics of environments in which children are found to be successful. Some of these measures are both valid and reliable. We must take care in selecting a tool that conforms to the philosophy of the school or centre where it is to be used.

In designing an evaluation tool to monitor and improve a particular environment, we are wise to base it on research that focuses on "quality." This will mean including such aspects of the programs as adult-child ratios, space, safety and health issues. We must consider translating what each element of quality means in a particular place, which can be as difficult as it is worthwhile. Consider adding or eliminating items according to the goals or philosophy of the program. Well-being, nurturance, the learning environment, and the program's approach to inclusion are each elements of a quality environment that we need to evaluate.

Action Plan to Improve the Environment

Agency: _____   Date: _____

Recorder: _____   Date of environmental evaluation: _____

Context: _____

Concern (from evaluation)	Action to be taken	Time line	Responsibility

---

Key Terms

action plan

anti-bias

basic needs

checklist

child-centred

climate

compensatory care

context

curriculum

developmentally appropriate

diversity

ecological psychology

environment

environmental evaluation

environmental observation

environmental scan

hidden curriculum

hygienic practices

inclusion

inference

integration

mapping

narrative observation

nuclear family

nurturance

objectivity

program evaluation

psychological needs

qualitative evaluation

quality environments

rating scale

reliability

role model

routine

special needs

spontaneous play

stereotype

therapeutic care

tokenism

touristic approach

validity

Weblinks

www.cafcc.on.ca/choose.htm
The Co-ordinated Access for Child Care (CAFCC) site provides families with information and tools that will help them choose appropriate quality childcare.

www.safety-council.org
The Canada Safety Council serves as a credible, reliable resource for safety information, education, and awareness in all aspects of Canadian life.

www.wstcoast.org
The West Coast Child Care Resource Centre site is "committed to contributing to healthy communities by supporting families, promoting equality for children, and strengthening and enhancing quality child care."

Observation Sample

This environmental observation provides comments on various health issues. These observations could be used to evaluate the environment and to suggest changes and improvements.

What could this type of recording tell the educator about its centre's health programs? What other criteria might be added?

Environmental Observation: Health

Observer's name: *James* Date: *December 9-12, 2003*

Setting: *Unionville Child Care Centre (a centre for 60 children, birth to school age)*

Number of children: *14* Number of adults: *2*

Ages: *3 years, 3 months, to 5 years, 7 months*

Space available: *L-shaped room. One end used for gross motor activities, sleep, and meals.*

Purpose of observation: *To evaluate the environment for its part in supporting the children's healthy development*

Criteria	Observations
1. Good hygienic practices	*regular hand washing, disinfecting using a bleach solution*
2. Positive role model	*teachers follow proper practice*
3. Nutritious snacks/meals	*bananas, oranges, apples for snack; meal plans appear appropriate*
4. Protection for extreme weather	*2 sets of clothes are stored (spring/winter)*
5. Effective communication with parents	*parent board, reports, and communication logs*
6. Health education	*posters, art supplies, talking*
7. Toileting/washroom adequate	*2 washrooms (1 large, 1 small)*
8. Parent reports	*separate reports for everyone*
9. First aid provision	*box/kit in each room, large in office*
10. Parental wishes adhered to	*notes taken in communication log and passed on if necessary*
11. Separation of areas for different purposes	*reading area, blocks, floor toys, table toys*
12. Appropriate storage	*large cupboard in each room labelled and cleaned regularly*
13. Accommodations for abilities and disabilities	*minimal stairs, lots of space for gross motor, etc.*
14. Accident and serious occurrence records kept	*each child has a file, book of "serious occurrences" shown to parents*
15. Maintenance and stress for caregivers	*separate/comfortable room for breaks and quiet time*
16. Demonstrated positive attitudes to well-being	*talk about vitamins in oranges, milk, etc., hand washing*
17. Documentation and sensitive handling of allergies and medical conditions	*lists in every room for every child and separate larger one in individual rooms*

Observation Sample

This action plan begins with concerns raised by an environmental evaluation. It outlines how the issues will be addressed and provides a time line and a list of specific responsibilities for each team member.

What else do you need to know to make this plan work?

Action Plan to Improve the Environment

Agency: Yellowknife Centre   Date: June 1, 2003

Recorder: Julie   Date of environmental evaluation: May 22-27, 2003

Context: The ministry suggested that we do a program review because we have had our new supervisor for a year. We used criteria from Martin, *Take a Look*.

Concern	Action to be taken	Time line	Responsibility
Supervision because of safety concern around swings in preschool play space	- Children not allowed to play on swings until a new barrier is erected	Urgent (today)	**JD** will announce to staff that the swings are not to be used until a barrier is put up. **JD** will contact plant operations and request building of barrier. **JD** will inform staff when swings can be used again.
A wider depiction of culture in books, pictures, and play-things	- New pictures to be collected and made into puzzles - New toys to be purchased	Soon (this week) Also long term	**KC** will order new posters from NAEYC. **JD** will ask all staff to collect pictures for use in materials. **JD** will set aside money in next year's budget for dolls and new books.
Staff training in guidance strategies for toddlers	- Investigate budget - Investigate external facilita-tors/workshops - Investigate internal work-shop/resources	Medium term	**JD** will seek funding. **KC** will review literature to find professional development opportuni-ties. **DD** will make contact with possible facilitator. **RC** will bring in guidance video to be viewed on lunch breaks.
Improve observation and record-keeping	- Create new port-folio system	Medium term (by end of October)	**JD** will seek funding and review fundraising possi-bilities. **DD** will develop a plan for communicating port-folio philosophy to parents. **LR** will see if she can find a box system (from pizza boxes). **JD** will organize a series of evening meetings for **group** to plan process.

Glossary of Key Terms

accountability the process of demonstrating the success, and usually financial effectiveness, of a program or intervention

action plan a plan for change developed as the result of an environmental assessment

action research a branch of qualitative research involving observation, documentation, and analysis conducted while maintaining responsibility for a group or class of children

active learning the experience of performing actions on an aspect of the environment that leads to acquiring knowledge, skills, or attitudes; spontaneous play and discovery provide the opportunity for active learning.

analysis a process of gaining an understanding of recorded observational data through the study of the component parts of those data, making inferences, and validating them

anecdotal record a short narrative account of a child's activity

antecedent event the event that occurred just before the example of the sample behaviour

anti-bias active opposition to negative or inappropriate attitudes towards or pre-judgment of groups of people, practices, or things

assessment measurement of an individual's performance or development, which may be based on observations, tests, or the person's products

assessment cycle the sequence of observation, data collection, analysis, and planning that is an ongoing part of assessment

assessment instrument the tool or mechanism used for assessment (see **assessment**)

assistive devices any mechanical or supportive aid that enables an individual to function better

assumption a reaction to a behaviour that accepts as true an approach that has not been considered objectively or analytically

attachment the process of making an affectional bond or emotional connection with another individual

authentic assessment assessment of learning that focuses on performance of skill or knowledge in a manner within an appropriate context; naturalistic, developmentally appropriate, and culturally sensitive evaluation of children using observation and other informal methods of data collection

baby book a book or album used for recording information about a child, often used by parents

bar chart a graph that represents observational material as bars of varying heights along an axis

baseline observation the overview of a child's health and developmental status used as a measure for later comparison (of the same child)

basic needs the conditions required to sustain life; conditions that allow a human being to survive

behaviour the actions and reactions of an individual; that is, anything a person does, whether deliberate or not

behaviourism a school of psychology that involves the objective study of responses of animals or human beings; behaviourism views learning as formed from the outside, by the external environment

behaviour modification a technique that attempts to change, stop, or modify a demonstrated behaviour

bias a known or unknown perspective or point of view the personal or philosophical values, attitudes, or beliefs of which influence objectivity

biological clock the force of an individual's program of maturing that is determined by the nature of the individual or organism and by genetic inheritance; one of three forces that drive human development through the life cycle

causality a supposed connection between events that indicates what brought about one or more of those events

cephalo-caudal principle a principle of development that states that bodily control typically starts with the head and proceeds down

chart a prepared format or map on which observed information is recorded according to specified criteria

checklist a listing of skills or other behaviours used as a guide for recording the presence or absence of each behaviour

checkmarks the marks used on a checklist (✓) to indicate the presence of a behaviour

child-centred a philosophy of childcare and education that emphasizes the importance of the child's need to direct his or her own activity, to make play choices spontaneously, and to learn at a self-determined level

child development the dynamic process of change and progression that enables each child to become increasingly independent, knowledgeable, skilled, and self-sufficient

child study a collection of information about a child, gathered by a student, researcher, or teacher over a period of time, that may be used for record-keeping, research, evaluation, or program-planning

climate (school) the way people think about, feel, and experience an educational institution, or an aspect of that institution; this involves internal and external stakeholders

cognition the process of knowing, thinking, and understanding

compensatory care nurturance or education that addresses negative experiences or deprivations

competency what an individual is able to do or perform; the component part of a learning outcome that is measurable and observable

confidentiality the principle of privacy behind the practice of storing information securely so that its disclosure is made only to those considered appropriate

consequent event the event that occurred immediately after the example of the sampled behaviour

construction of knowledge the creation of meaning through personal experience; the child constructs knowledge by experimenting and building "schemes" of understanding.

constructivism a school of thought that considers learning a process of adaptation and that believes that individuals create their own meaning of the world through experience

context the circumstances, situations, or background in which an observation is recorded

contextual information family, social, cultural, medical, geographic, economic, or other information about the background of the child that enables a teacher or another stakeholder in the child's life to have some insight into the factors affecting the child's health, growth, or development

criterion-referenced assessment assessment based on specific and clearly articulated criteria, designed to measure the specific skills and knowledge of an individual

cue an indication or communication given by a child that an adult "reads." A cue may consciously or unconsciously communicate a need or desire and may be conveyed through facial expressions, gestures, or changes in posture.

cultural diversity individuals from varying linguistic, ethnic, or religious backgrounds within the same group

curriculum the child's whole experience; usually refers to the teacher's or caregiver's provision for the child's developmental needs

curriculum alignment the connection between individual learning outcomes, course outcomes, and program outcomes; the degree to which each relates to the others

data the observational facts from which inferences can be drawn or the information that the analysis produces

developmental diversity individuals with varying levels of ability within the same group

developmental sequence the series of observable stages of progression

developmentally appropriate the way in which a program or procedure suits an individual's stage of progress and personal needs

developmental psychology the school of study that focuses on the individual's progressive change, explaining how that adaptation occurs within a cognitive framework

diary record a recording made on a regular, usually daily, basis

disposition the attitude or value demonstrated in the performance of a role

diversity a wide range of various abilities, appearance, ethnicity, sex, culture, belief, religion, or place of origin

duration the length of time a behaviour is observed

early intervention a plan to try to avoid potential challenges in a child's development or relationships, or if difficulty is already diagnosed a plan to support the child's development

ecological psychology the social science concerned with connections between the individual and his or her environment

ecological systems model a model that explains the components of the environment that influence an individual's life and development (for example, Bronfenbrenner's model)

ecomap   a diagram representing an individual's environment and his or her relation to the elements of that environment, including people, activities, and organizations

emerging skill   a learned behaviour at a starting or incipient stage

emotion   a feeling or, in observable terms, a change in arousal patterns

emotional intelligence   a term coined by Goleman to describe an ability to understand and use an individual pattern of responses to personal advancement

empirical evidence   information gathered through careful observation or experimentation

environment   an individual's surroundings, including places, objects, and people

environmental evaluation   a consideration of all the planned and unplanned aspects of a child's surroundings to ascertain their appropriateness or quality

environmental observation   observation of the use of a child's surroundings, including those elements that are designed and implemented deliberately and those parts that occur without planning

environmental scan   a review of a program, setting, or aspect of that setting using predetermined criteria

ethical issues/ethics   concerns relating to moral beliefs and professional conduct

event   an example of a selected category of behaviour

event sampling   a method of observation in which occurrences of a preselected category of behaviour are recorded

evidence   observed information—what was seen in respect of specified criteria

exceptional child   a child whose development is not typical (atypical) of those of a similar age; the child's development may be less advanced, uneven, or gifted

exit outcomes   the required learning gained by the end of a course or program of instruction

family tree   a diagram representing a person's ancestry

fine motor skills   learned behaviours involving the small muscles of the body

forced choice scale   a rating scale that requires the observer to judge the degree to which a characteristic or quality is evident

formative assessment   an ongoing assessment, in process, designed to indicate a child's educational

progression from the identified skill level or to enable the educator to set learning goals for the child

frequency   the pattern or number of occurrences of a specified behaviour

functional assessment   behavioural observation and analysis that seek to identify a challenging or "problem" behaviour, determine its purpose, and develop alternative ways of behaving that are more acceptable

genogram   a diagram representing a family structure, which may include historical and observational information about its style and functioning

graphic scale   a rating scale designed to record judgments of characteristics or qualities on a continuum according to predetermined word categories

gross motor skills   learned behaviours involving the large muscles of the body

hidden curriculum   elements of the child's experience that are affected by the unstated attitudes and beliefs of the responsible adult

hygienic practices   all behaviours that promote cleanliness, sanitary conditions, or the sterilization of bodies, materials, furniture, buildings, or other aspects of the environment

inclusion   the practice of ensuring that all children are treated equally and given equitable support in their development, regardless of their ability, ethnicity, sex, or beliefs

individual education plan (IEP)   an individual plan of goals and objectives, tailored to a child's needs

individual program plan (IPP)   a curriculum, activity, task, or education plan designed for an individual child

inference   a deduction made from observational data

input/outcome-planning model   curriculum-planning based on observed information as well as designated requirements, such as competencies

integration   the practice of including children with special needs in mainstream care and education

interpretive graphic representation   visual presentation of information analyzed from data previously collected

inventory   a complete and comprehensive listing of skills, competencies, or specific requirements

irreducible needs   a term used by Brazelton and Greenspan and others to refer to the physical, social, and emotional needs of every individual without which he or she cannot develop adequately

knowledge   what is to be known; may be articulated at levels varying from identification to comprehension to analysis and synthesis

language   a complex means of communication that requires the acquisition of both a vocabulary and the rules governing the structure of communication

learning log   a record-keeping device used to document the objective description of experiences and the child's response to the experiences

learning outcome   a complex role performance requiring knowledge and skill; an outcome may also specify the disposition of the performance

life book   a book used to record significant people and experiences in a child's life over a period of time; often used by social workers and adoption-agency workers

life-experience flow chart   a diagram representing the series of key experiences in an individual's life

map or mapping   a diagram or map of an area where children are observed, used to record their movements or evaluate the program

mastery   the highest level of learning or competence that indicates the integration of knowledge, skills, and attitudes

mastery learning (ML)   the process that leads to the achievement of the highest (see **mastery**) level of learning; based on the idea that all people, given sufficient time and support, can succeed.

maturation   the innate aspects of human growth and development, or the observable and measurable characteristics of stages of growth and development

media technique   any method of recording or storing observational data that is achieved by mechanical, electronic, or technical means

metacognition   the process of thinking about thinking; being aware of one's own thinking processes

milestones   observable steps or stages during the process of human development

morality   an intellectual understanding of right and wrong and a social understanding of the consequent social responsibilities; morality may be rooted in religious or cultural beliefs

multiple intelligences   the theory, developed by Gardner, that people have different ways of being "smart" or different forms of intelligence, including spatial, logical/mathematical, linguistic, bodily/kinesthetic, musical, interpersonal, and intrapersonal

narrative observation   a sequentially written, detailed description of a child's actions

naturalistic   without interference, or as nature would determine

naturalness   the behaviour of individuals without interference or influence

negative behaviour   a behaviour judged to be undesirable, inappropriate, or socially unacceptable

neural plasticity   the brain's ability to "sculpt," adapt or "wire itself" in response to experience, injury, or maturation (which is functional change but not clearly observable change, although it may influence behaviour)

neuroscience   the discovery of the structure and functions of the brain and central nervous system

nonparticipant observation   the observation of an individual or a group by a person who is not interacting with that individual or group

norm   an average level of demonstrated behaviours, skills, results, or measurements determined from statistically significant populations

normal patterns   the expected sequence of development of the individual; what is expected may come from personal experience of children or, more reliably, from a statistically significant sample of a population

normative assessment   assessment based on researched norms of behaviour or performance; the norms are stated as average levels of performance and may be expressed as percentiles

norm-referenced assessment   the process of interpreting data according to an accepted range of performance (usually age-related)

nuclear family   immediately related individuals who reside together

numerical scale   a rating scale that requires the observer to quantify the degree to which a characteristic or quality is evident

nurturance   the whole care and experience of the child that fosters development

objectives   the behaviours that are considered necessary to achieve a set goal or aim

objectivity   the quality of an approach that is undistorted, impartial, unbiased, analytical, and reliable

observation   the informal or formal perception of behaviour of an individual or group of people, or the perceptions gained from looking at an environment or object

observation chart   a prepared chart with sections used for categorizing and recording behaviour at the time it is observed or soon after

observation scale   a measurement of characteristics, showing the degree to which a characteristic is present

operational definition   a working, usable description of the behaviour to be sampled

outcome-based education (OBE)   a philosophy of education that structures curriculum and assessment on learning outcomes

outcome-based learning (OBL)   a philosophy of learning that structures curriculum and assessment on learning outcomes

participant observation   the observation of an individual or a group by a person who is interacting with that individual or group at the same time

pattern of development   the sequence of skill acquisition in each developmental area or domain

peer evaluation   the assessment of a performance made by members of the same group

perception   receiving information through any one, or any combination of, the senses and processing it to deduce meaning

performance assessment   a form of authentic assessment that requires a demonstration or performance of specified knowledge or skills

performance-based learning (PBL)   learning based on action and culminating in a demonstration that indicates the integration of new knowledge and skills

personal narrative   the reflective writings of a person that tell his or her own story or an element of his or her own experience

personality   an individual's personal characteristics including temperament, patterns of behaviour, awareness of self, and ability to meet challenges

phenomenology   a philosophy that studies personal experiences from the point of view of the subject rather than that of the "objective" world; also, the systematic study of conscious experience, the study of the experience of a person re-created as a new experience by another person

physical development   an individual's growth and acquisition of gross and fine motor skills and sensory acuity

pictorial representation   any form of recording or interpretation that displays collected data in visual form

pie chart   a circular diagram that represents "slices" of a circle to depict proportions or percentages

play pattern   the recurring sequences of activity that a child directs

portfolio   a collection of information about a child's development gathered over time, used by teachers for assessment and record-keeping

portfolio assessment   the process of observing, recording, and gathering contextual information about a child in order to evaluate his or her performance, support development, and create an appropriate curriculum

positive behaviour   a behaviour judged desirable, appropriate, or socially acceptable

problem-based learning (PBL or PL)   gaining new skills and knowledge from solving real-life challenges; term used interchangeably with **project-based learning**

process (of learning)   the steps taken to create, make, discover, or learn

product   the object that is evidence of a process of learning; products may become work samples that demonstrate learning and progress

professional portfolio   a collection of materials, reflections, and evaluations of performance that represent the personal and/or professional development of an educator or other professional

professionalism   the appropriate and ethical way of behaving that is appropriate for trained, skilled, and practising workers as they perform their roles

program evaluation   the collection of information, review, and analysis of data regarding each aspect of an educational or caregiving environment, using predetermined criteria, conducted to improve service delivery

program outcomes   the intended achievements at the end of a program, course, or intervention; often used as the yardstick or measure of success for each participant (these are usually broad statements incorporating required knowledge, skills, and dispositions)

progress or progression   improvement in learning or development

project approach   an approach to learning that centres on children's learning and results from a child-directed central project (this is a broader concept than themes of learning)

project-based learning (PL)   curriculum based on major projects that thread through different subject areas and address all domains of development; term used interchangeably with **problem-based learning**

pro-social skills   performance of behaviours that are considered positive that supports a desired morality

proximo-distal principle   a principle of development that states that bodily control typically starts at the centre of the body and proceeds to the extremities

psychoanalytic (theory)   the set of ideas developed by Freud that comprise a psychology leading to treatment or understanding of human development

psychological clock   the force of an individual's quest to meet his or her own needs; one of the three forces that drive human development through the life cycle

psychological needs   the conditions and relationships required for social and emotional development

psychological service   any support system, either privately or publicly funded, that assesses individuals and provides them with therapy or other interventions for their emotional and social health, well-being, and development

psychosocial development   the eight-stage theory of development proposed by Erikson that explains human behaviour with reference to the "self" and others, and the crises that a person needs to address in order to progress

qualitative   pertains to research that is concerned with (the quality of) human experience

qualitative evaluation   the measurement that involves the kind and degree of developmental change

quality environments (school or child-care centres) those settings that demonstrate agreed indicators of good care and education; the environment includes all aspects of the physical and human surroundings

quantitative (research)   research concerned with numerical data collection

rating scale   a predetermined list of behavioural characteristics that is accompanied by a numerical, semantic, or other grading system

readiness test   a test designed to evaluate the individual's cognitive functioning in order to determine his or her potential success in a program at a "higher" level

record of achievement   a record kept by the teacher or learner (child) that logs anecdotal notes regarding the learner's skill development and achievements

recording (technological)   mechanical, electronic, or technical methods of recording information

reflective practice   the regular cycle of reviewing one's effectiveness as educator in a program; reflection may consider any aspect of the curriculum, environment, relationships, or other elements of practice and one's own role within it

reflective practitioner   an approach to the role of educator (or other professional) that involves frequent sensitive evaluation, review of practice, personal qualities, and effectiveness

Reggio Emilia   a region in Italy; in early childhood education an Italian approach to education that involves the whole community, is driven by the children, recognizes the different channels (or voices) of the children, and documents the process and products of learning to "make learning visible"

regression   the loss of skills or learning

reinforcement   the process of supporting a behaviour by offering an inducement or encouragement

reliability   the degree to which a method can be consistent; the degree to which scores for a test or measurement tool remain constant, consistent, or reliable

representational   a presentation (often visual) that shows data collection, sorting of information, or theoretical ideas

research methods   the methods of inquiry, including qualitative and quantitative approaches, used to answer a question, prove an hypothesis, or explore a topic; a scientific method of research requires the use of standard methods of inquiry and that questions be formed appropriately and that the process of data management and analysis be documented

resilient   the ability to withstand poor conditions, environments and/or relationships without undue harm

resource teacher   a specially prepared teacher who works with children diagnosed with medical, developmental, or learning needs

role model   a demonstration of the behaviours associated with a particular task, employment, or responsibility

role performance   the demonstration of the skill of a learning outcome; may imply knowledge of certain information and demonstration of a specific disposition

routine   a planned or responsive sequence of activity

rubric   a set of criteria used to measure the level of performance indicating learning; an assessment tool (most often used instead of grading) that specifies the requirements of a performance, presentation, or product that demonstrates that learning has taken place

running record   a sequential written account of a child's behaviour that employs rich description and detail

sampling   an observation in which examples of behaviour are recorded as they occur or behaviours are recorded as they are demonstrated at previously decided intervals

scaffolding a term coined by Bruner to describe the adult's role in assisting the child in learning

scale a way of measuring information that uses lists of behaviours or other items and rates them according to predetermined values

screening a process of reviewing and evaluating specific behaviours or individuals' characteristics across a population or group to identify those who need a more thorough assessment or specific support

screening instrument the tool or mechanism used for **screening** (see above)

self-evaluation the process of evaluating one's own performance or creation of a product, involving comparison with a norm, measurement against specified criteria, or a general reflection on one's own process of learning

semantic differential scale a rating scale designed to record judgments of characteristics or qualities on a continuum, listing pairs of opposites

sensitive period a time in the developmental process when an individual is susceptible to particular kinds of influence

sensory acuity the degree to which the senses perceive information accurately or in detail

sequential model a diagram representing a curriculum plan to design learning based on the breakdown of a competency into a series of stages

severity the degree to which a behaviour has been observed—that is, "irritability" might be described as mild, moderate, or severe (which involves making a judgment)

sexual development the domain of development concerned with identification by sexes and roles, physical growth and maturation, emotional and social competence, and reproductive capability

sign language a set of hand signals to communicate, used by hearing-disabled people, such as American Sign Language (ASL)

skill a learned behaviour that can be observed and measured

skill acquisition the process of gaining new behaviours or of modifying or refining existing skills

social clock the force of society's and the family's expectations; one of the three forces that drive human development through the life cycle

social interaction the process of communicating, sharing, playing, or otherwise interacting with another individual

social map a representation of social relationships by means of a diagram

social play play activity involving others, whether seen or unseen

social reform the process of improving the experience, opportunity, and standard of living of individuals and groups in society

sociogram a diagram representing the social relationships of those within a peer group

sociometry the study of social interactions using pictorial representations to record data

special needs the necessities required to support the health and development of a child whose development is atypical in one domain or more

specimen record an extremely detailed, sequential narrative recording of an observation of one child made as the behaviours are observed; frequently uses coding devices to ensure that the particulars are accurate and complete

spirituality an approach to experience that may involve personal reflections, a connection with a power outside the self, or an appreciation of the significance of people and things; may relate directly to religious or philosophical beliefs about our existence

spontaneous play the naturally occurring, unstructured activity of the child, which the child directs

standard a broad statement of achievement that is accepted as a requirement at a specified level

standardized test a valid and reliable tool for evaluation that specifies the method of administration, content, and scoring

standards-based learning (SL) experience or curriculum that leads to gaining pre-set levels of learning, and measuring achievement against that predetermined level of learning

stereotype a description or image of individuals or groups that depicts them according to clichés, or exaggerated or erroneous criteria, without regard for actual characteristics or individual differences

subjective distorted, partial, biased, lacking in analysis, or unreliable

summary a categorization of the essential parts of an observation, listing and organizing the behaviours observed

summative assessment the total outcome of a range of assessment procedures or the total result of a particular evaluation tool

tally a system of marks used to count the observed behaviour

temperament an individual's typical style of response to experiences and situations

theoretical perspective the viewpoint of a person, process, or organization

theory-bound the beliefs implicit in a process

therapeutic care nurturance, education, or special measures that attempt to address negative or missing experiences or trauma

therapy any support or intervention that provides the individual with the resources to manage more effectively

time sampling an observation method in which random or previously chosen behaviours are recorded at pre-set time periods

tokenism the practice of exceptional favour, based on negative prejudice, to "prove" one's fairness

topic-planning planning for children based on predesignated areas of learning

touristic approach the practice of presenting cultural differences and places of origin in a superficial holiday, festival, or vacation style

tracking a diagram or map of an area where a child is to be observed, onto which the child's movement is recorded; may be used to identify interests, mobility, concentration span, or interactions

validate to ensure that the inferences made from observational data are supported or confirmed by one or more reliable authorities

validity the degree to which a test or observation tool measures what it purports to measure

webbing model a planning model that relates all curriculum areas through a single topic or focus

whole child a concept of the child that sees all domains of development as interacting, the child being more than the sum of the domains

work sample any product of a child's art, creativity, work, or other evidence of learning

work sampling a teacher's, parent's, or child's choice of work intended to demonstrate a particular competency

zone of proximal development a phrase coined by Vygotsky that refers to the supposed gap between what the child can do in an independent manner now and what the child can do in a supported way

Bibliography

Adamson, L.B. (1996). *Communication development during infancy*. Boulder, CO: Westview.

Ainsworth, M.D. (1972). Individual differences in the development of attachment behaviors. *Merrill Palmer Quarterly* 18.

Allen, K.E., & L.R. Marotz. (1994). *Developmental profiles: Pre-birth through eight* (2nd ed.). Albany, NY: Delmar.

————. (2003). *Developmental profiles: Pre-birth through twelve* (4th ed.). Albany, NY: Delmar.

Allen, K.E., et al. (1998). *Exceptional children: Inclusion in early childhood programs*. Scarborough, ON: ITP Nelson.

Arena, J. (1989). *How to write an I.E.P.* Novato, CA: Academic Therapy Publications.

Bandura, A. (1977). *Social learning theory*. Englewood Cliffs, NJ: Prentice Hall.

Barna, Ed. (2002, Winter). High noon for high stakes: Alfie Kohn at Middlebury College. *Paths of Learning*.

Barrett, K.C., et al. (1995). *Child development*. Westerville, OH: Glencoe.

Beaty, J.J. (1996). *Preschool appropriate practices* (2nd ed.). Fort Worth, TX: Harcourt Brace Jovanovich.

————. (1998). *Observing development of the young child* (4th ed.). Upper Saddle River, NJ: Prentice Hall.

Bentzen, W. (1993). *Seeing young children: A guide to observing and recording behavior* (2nd ed.). Albany, NY: Delmar.

Bergen, D. (1994). Authentic performance assessments. *Educational Leadership* 70(2).

Bergen, D., & J. Coscia. (2001). *Brain research and childhood education: Implications for educators*. Olney, MD: Association for Childhood Education International.

Berk, L.E. (1994). *Infants, children, and adolescents*. Needham Heights, MA: Allyn & Bacon.

Bertrand, J. (2001). *Summary of research findings on children's developmental health*. Ottawa, ON: Canadian Child Care Federation.

Best, J.W., & J.V. Kahn. (1989). *Research in Education* (6th ed.). Englewood Cliffs, NJ: Prentice Hall.

Biracree, T., & N. Biracree. (1989). *The parents' book of facts: Child development from birth to age five*. New York: Facts on File.

Bloom, B. (1956). *Taxonomy of educational objectives: The classification of educational goals. Handbook 1: The cognitive domain*. New York: Longmans Green.

Boehm, A.E., & R.A. Weinberg. (1987). *The classroom observer: Developing observation skills in early childhood settings*. New York: Teachers College Press.

Bowen, M. (1978). *Family therapy in clinical practice*. New York: Aronson.

Bowlby, J. (1965). *Child care and the growth of love*. Harmondsworth, England: Penguin.

Brazelton, T.B. (1992). *Touchpoints: Your child's emotional and behavioural development*. Reading, MA: Addison-Wesley.

Brazelton, T.B., & S.I. Greenspan. (2000). *The irreducible needs of children: What every child must have to grow, learn and flourish*. Cambridge, MA: Perseus Publishing.

Bredekamp, S. (ed.). (1997). *Developmentally appropriate practice in early childhood programs serving children from birth through age 8* (rev. ed.). Washington, DC: National Association for the Education of Young Children.

Bredekamp, S., & T. Rosegrant. (eds.). (1992). *Reaching potentials: Appropriate curriculum and assessment for young children* (Vol. 1). Washington, DC: National Association for the Education of Young Children.

————. (eds.). (1995). *Reaching potentials: Transforming early childhood curriculum and assessment* (Vol. 2). Washington, DC: National Association for the Education of Young Children.

Brian, J., & M. Martin. (1986). *Child care and health for nursery nurses*. Chester Springs, PA: Dufour.

Bronfenbrenner, U. (1979). *The ecology of human development: Experiments by nature and design*. Cambridge, MA: Harvard University Press.

Brown, J.L. (1995). *Observing dimensions of learning in classrooms and schools*. Alexandria, VA: Association for Supervision and Curriculum Development.

Bruner, J.S. (1966). *Toward a theory of instruction*. Cambridge, MA: Harvard University Press.

Burke, K. (1994). *How to assess authentic learning*. Palatine, IL: IRI/Skylight Training and Publishing.

Burke, K., R. Fogarty, & S. Belgrad. (1994). *The mindful school: The portfolio connection*. Arlington Heights, IL: IRI/Skylight Training & Publishing.

Bushweller, K. (1995). The high-tech portfolio. *The Executive Educator* 17(1), 19–22.

Caldwell, B.M., & R.H. Bradley. (1979). *Home observation for measurement of the environment*. Little Rock, AR: University of Arkansas Press.

Campbell, S.D. (1987). *Quality control: A manual for self-evaluation of a day care agency*. Ottawa: Health and Welfare Canada.

Canadian Child Care Federation. (1995). *Towards excellence in ECCE training programs: A self-assessment guide*. Ottawa: Canadian Child Care Federation.

Canadian Day Care Advocacy Association. (1992). *Caregiver behaviours and program characteristics associated with quality care*. Ottawa: Canadian Day Care Advocacy Association.

Canadian Paediatric Society. (1992). *Well beings: A guide to promote the physical health, safety and emotional well-being of children in child care centres and family day care homes*. Ottawa: Canadian Paediatric Society.

Catron, C.E., & J. Allen. (eds.). (1993). *Early childhood curriculum*. New York: Merrill Publishing.

Centennial College Early Childhood Education Programs and Child Care Centres. (1998). *Philosophy check-in*. Toronto: Centennial College.

Center for Effective Collaboration and Practice. *Functional Behavioral Assessment*. CECP "mini-web" at **cecp.air.org/fba/default.htm**

Chandler, K. (2003). *Administering for quality*. Toronto: Pearson Education Canada.

Chard, S.C. (1999, Spring). From themes to projects. *Early Childhood Research & Practice* (Vol. 1, No. 1) and at **ecrp.uiuc.edu/v1n/chard.html**

Chess, S., & A. Thomas. (1996). *Temperament: Theory and practice*. New York: Brunner/Mazel.

Choate, J.S., et al. (1995). *Curriculum-based assessment and programming* (3rd ed.). Needham Heights, MA: Allyn & Bacon.

Chud, G., & R. Fahlman. (1985). *Early childhood education for a multicultural society*. Vancouver, BC: Western Education Development Group.

Clemmons, J., D. Cooper, & L. Lasse. (1996). *Portfolios in the classroom*. Jefferson City, MO: Scholastic.

Cleveland, G., & M. Krashinsky. (1998). *The benefits and costs of good child care: The economic rationale for public investment in young children*. Toronto: Childcare Resource and Research Unit, University of Toronto.

Cohen, D., & V. Stern. (1978). *Observing and recording the behavior of young children*. New York: Teachers College Press.

Creswell, J.W. (1998). *Qualitative inquiry and research design: Choosing among five traditions*. Thousand Oaks, CA: Sage Publications.

Curtis, A. (2000). *Indicators of quality in early childhood education and care programmes*. Speech by World President, OMEP. **www.worldbank.org/children/nino/basico/Curtis.htm**

Department of Health, Great Britain. (1988). *Protecting children: A guide for social workers undertaking a comprehensive assessment*. London: Her Majesty's Stationery Office.

Dewey, J. (1963; orig. ed. 1938). *Education and experience*. New York: Collier.

Dodge, D.T., C. Heroman, & L.J. Colker. (2001). *The Creative Curriculum® Developmental Continuum Assessment Toolkit for Ages 3–5*. Washington, DC: Teaching Strategies.

Doherty-Derkowski, G. (1994). *Quality matters: Excellence in early childhood programs*. Don Mills, ON: Addison-Wesley.

Elkind, D. (1988). *The hurried child: growing up too fast too soon* (rev.). Reading, MA: Addison-Wesley.

———. (1994). *A sympathetic understanding of the child: Birth to sixteen*. (3rd ed.). Boston: Allyn & Bacon.

Elliott, B. (1995). *Measure of success*. Toronto: Association for Early Childhood Educators, Ontario.

Ely, M., et al. (1991). *Doing qualitative research: Circles within circles*. London: The Falmer Press.

Engel, B.S. (1990). *An approach to assessment in early literacy*. In C. Kamii (ed.), *Achievement testing in the early grades: The games grown-ups play*. Washington, DC: National Association for the Education of Young Children.

Erikson, E.H. (1963). *Childhood and society* (2nd ed.). New York: Norton.

———. (1994). *Identity and the life cycle*. New York: Norton.

Farr, R., & B. Tone. (1994). *Portfolio and performance assessment: Helping students evaluate their progress as readers and writers*. Fort Worth, TX: Harcourt Brace.

Franklin, J. (2002, Spring). Assessing assessment: Are alternative methods making the grade? *ASCD Curriculum Update*.

Friendly, M. (1994). *Child care policy in Canada: Putting the pieces together*. Don Mills, ON: Addison-Wesley.

Froebel, F. (1974; orig. ed. 1826). *The education of man*. Clifton, NJ: A.M. Kelley.

Gardner, H. (1993). *Multiple intelligences: The theory in practice*. New York: Basic Books.

Gardner, H., et al. (2001). *Making children visible: Children as individual and group learners*. Reggio Children/USA.

Garmezy, N., & M. Rutter. (eds.). (1983). *Stress, coping and development in children*. New York: McGraw-Hill.

Glaser, R. (1963). Instructional technology and the measurement of learning outcomes: Some questions. *American Psychologist* 18, 519–21.

Goelman, H., et al. (2000). *You bet I care! Caring and learning environments: Quality in child care centres across Canada*. Guelph, ON: Centre for Families, Work and Well-Being, University of Guelph.

Goleman, D. (1997). *Emotional intelligence*. New York: Bantam.

Gonzalez-Mena, Janet. (1986, November). Toddlers: What to expect. *Young children*. Washington, DC: NAEYC.

Goodrich, H. (1996/97). Understanding rubrics. *Educational Leadership* 54(4), 14–17.

Goodwin, W.L., & L.A. Driscoll. (1980). *Handbook for measurement and evaluation in early childhood education*. San Francisco: Jossey-Bass.

Grant, J.M., B. Heffler, & K. Mereweather. (1995). *Student-led conferences: Using portfolios to share learning with parents*. Markham, ON: Pembroke Publishers.

Greenspan, S.I., & N.T. Greenspan. (1985). *First feelings: Milestones in the emotional development of your baby and child*. New York: Viking.

———. (1985). *First feelings: Milestones in the emotional development of your baby and child from birth to age 4*. New York: Viking.

Hall, G.S. (n.d.). The content of children's minds on entering school. *Pedagogical Seminary*.

Harms, T., & R.M. Clifford. (1990). *Family day care rating scale*. New York: Teachers College Press.

———. (1998). *Early childhood environment rating scale*. New York: Teachers College Press.

Harms, T., Cryer, D., & R.M. Clifford. (1990). *Infant/toddler environment rating scale*. New York: Teachers College Press.

Harrington, H.L., et al. (1997). *Observing, documenting, and assessing learning: The Work Sampling System for teacher educators*. Ann Arbor, MI: Rebus.

Harrow, A.J. (1972). *A taxonomy of the psychomotor domain: A guide for developing behavioral objectives*. New York: D. McKay.

Havard, L.A. (1995). *Outcome based education through the school system*. New York: Norton.

Health and Welfare Canada. (1980). *Children with special needs in daycare*. Ottawa: Health and Welfare Canada.

Hedgecoe, J. (1992). *Complete guide to video: The ultimate manual of video techniques and equipment*. Toronto: Stoddart.

Herman, J.L., et al. (1992). *A practical guide to alternative assessment*. Alexandria, VA: Association for Supervision and Curriculum Development.

Hews, J., Massing, C., & L. Singh. (1995). *Many ways to grow: Responding to cultural diversity in early childhood settings*. Edmonton, AB: Alberta Association for Young Children.

Hills, T.W. (1992). *Reaching potentials through appropriate assessment*. In S. Bredekamp & T. Rosegrant (eds.), pp. 43–63.

Hornby, G. (1977). *Photographing baby and child*. New York: Crown Publishers.

Illingworth, R.S. (1990). *Basic developmental screening, 0–5 years* (5th ed.). Oxford: Blackwell Scientific Publications.

Ireton, H. (1995). *Teacher's observation guide*. Minneapolis, MN: Behavioral Science Systems.

———. (1997). *Assessment: Appreciating children's development using parents' and teachers' observations*.

EarlyChildhood.com [On-line]. Discount School Supply. Available: **http://www.earlychildhood.com/articles/asmntobs.html**

Irwin, D.M., & M.M. Bushnell. (1980). *Observational strategies for child study*. New York: Holt, Rinehart, and Winston.

Jablon, J., et al. (1994a). *Work Sampling System omnibus guidelines: Kindergarten through fifth grade* (Vol. 2, 3rd ed.). Ann Arbor, MI: Rebus.

———. (1994b). *Work Sampling System omnibus guidelines: Preschool through third grade* (Vol. 1, 3rd ed.). Ann Arbor, MI: Rebus.

Kankaanranta, M. (2002). *Developing digital portfolios for childhood education*. Jyväskylä, Finland: University of Jyväskylä Institute for Educational Research.

Katz, L.G. (1993). *Five perspectives on quality in early childhood programs*. ERIC/EECE, available at **ericeece.org/pubs/books/fivepers.html**

———. (1993). *Multiple perspectives on the quality of early childhood programs*. ERIC/EECE Digest EDO-PS-93-2 and at **ericeece.org/pubs/digests/1993/lk-mul93.html**

Katz, L.G., & S.C. Chard. (1996). *The contribution of documentation to the quality of early childhood education*. ERIC/EECE Digest EDO-PS-96-2 and at **ericps.ed.uiuc.edu/eece/pubs/digests/1996/lkchar96.html**

———. (1989). *Engaging children's minds*. Norwood, NJ: Ablex Publishing.

Katz, L.G., & B. Cesarone (eds). (1994). *Reflections on the Reggio Emilia approach*. Urbana, IL: ERIC/EECE.

King, J.A., & K.M. Evans (1991, October). Can we achieve outcome-based education? *Educational Leadership*.

Klaus, M.H., J.H. Kennell, & P.H. Klaus (1995). *Bonding: Building the foundations of secure attachment and independence*. Reading, MA: Addison-Wesley.

Krathwohl, M.B. (1964). *Taxonomy of educational objectives: The classification of educational goals. Handbook 2: The affective domain*. New York: McKay.

Langford, R., et al. (1997). *Checklist for quality inclusive education: A self-assessment tool and manual for early childhood settings*. Barrie, ON: Early Childhood Resource Teacher Network of Ontario.

Leavitt, R.L., & B.K. Eheart. (1991, July). Assessment in early childhood programs. *Young Children*.

Lewington, J., & G. Orpwood. (1993). *Overdue assignment: Taking responsibility for Canada's schools*. Toronto: John Wiley.

Lewis, R. (1993). *Learn to make videos in a weekend*. New York: Alfred A. Knopf.

Lezotte, L.W. (1991). *Correlates of effective schools: The first and second generation*. Okemos, MI: Effective School Products Ltd.

Linder, T.W. (1990). *Transdisciplinary play-based assessment: A functional approach to working with young children*. Baltimore, MD: P.H. Brookes.

Locke, J. (1989; orig. ed. 1963). *Some thoughts concerning education*. New York: Oxford University Press.

Lorenz, K. (1937). Imprinting. *The Auk* 54, 245–73.

McCain, M.N., & J.F. Mustard. (1999). *Early years study: Reversing the real brain drain. Final report*. Toronto: Canadian Institute for Advanced Research.

McCullough, V.E. (1992). *Testing and your child: What you should know about 150 of the most common educational and psychological tests*. New York: Plume.

McGoldrick, M., & R. Gerson. (1985). *Genograms in family assessment*. New York: Norton.

Mager, R.F. (1962). *Preparing instructional objectives*. Belmont, CA: Lake Publishing.

Martin, S. (1988). Your child study: A new approach. *Nursery World*.

Meisels, S.J. (1992). *Early screening inventory revised*. Ann Arbor, MI: Rebus.

———. (1993). Remaking classroom assessment with the Work Sampling System. *Young Children*.

———. (2002). *Performance assessment*. Teacher Resource Center, Scholastic Inc., at **teacher.scholastic.com/professional/assessment/perfassess.htm**

———. (1996–97). Using work sampling in authentic assessments. *Educational Leadership* 54(4).

Meisels, S.J., & D. Steele. (1991). *The early childhood portfolio collection process*. Ann Arbor, MI: Center for Human Growth and Development, University of Michigan.

Meisels, S.J., et al. (1998). *The work sampling system*. Toronto: Pearson Early Learning.

Mindes, G., H. Ireton, & C. Mardell-Czudnowski. (1996). *Assessing young children*. Albany, NY: Delmar.

Montessori, M. (1963; orig. ed. 1913). *Montessori training course*. Ann Arbor, MI: Ann Arbor Press.

Morris, D. (1995). *Illustrated babywatching*. London: Ebury Press.

National Association for the Education of Young Children. (1988). *Healthy young children: A manual for programs*. Washington, DC: National Association for the Education of Young Children.

Nicolson, S., & S.G. Shipstead. (1998). *Through the looking glass: Observations in the early childhood classroom* (2nd ed.). Upper Saddle River, NJ: Prentice Hall.

Niguidula, D. (1997). Picturing performance with digital portfolios. *Educational Leadership* 55(3).

North York Board of Education. (1992). *Beginnings: The early years*. North York, ON.

Nova Scotia NDP Caucus. (2001). *Public education: Limitations and successes of the past, visions for the future*. Halifax, NS: Nova Scotia NDP Caucus, at **www.ndpcaucus.ns.ca**

O'Neil, J. (1995). Future of OBE is up in the air. *Education Update* 37.

Government of Ontario. (2001). *Report to Ontario's taxpayers, fall 2001*. Toronto.

Ontario Ministry of Education and Training. (1998). *The arts: The Ontario curriculum, grades 1–8*. Toronto: Publications Ontario.

Ontario Secondary School Teachers Federation. (2001). *What makes a good school?* AMPA 2001 House Paper, at **www.osstf.on.ca/www/abosstf/ampa01/goodschools/whatmakesgoodschool.html**

PACER Center. (1994). *What is a functional assessment?* Parent Advocacy Coalition for Educational Rights, at **www.pacer.org/parent/function.htm**

Parten, M.B. (1932–33). Social participation among pre-school children. *Journal of Abnormal and Social Psychology*.

Pastor, E., & E. Kerns. (1997). A digital snapshot of an early childhood classroom. *Educational Leadership* 55(3).

Pestalozzi, J.H. (1906). *A father's diary*. New York: Appleton.

———. (1894). *How Gertrude teaches her children*. (L.E. Holland & F.C. Turner, trs.). London: Swan Sonnenschein.

Phillips, D.A. (ed.) (1991). *Quality in child care: What does research tell us?* Washington, DC: National Association for the Education of Young Children.

Piaget, J. (1929). *The child's conception of the world*. (J. & A. Tomlinson, trs.). New York: Harcourt Brace.

———. (1954). *The child's construction of reality*. (M. Cook, tr.). London: Routledge & Kegan Paul.

Picciotto, L.P. (1996). *Student-led parent conferences*. New York: Scholastic Professional.

Pimento, B., & D. Kernested. (1996). *Healthy foundations in child care*. Toronto: Nelson.

Pinder, R. (1987, September). Not so modern methods. *Nursery World*.

Popham, W.J. (1998). *Classroom assessment: What teachers need to know* (2nd ed.). Boston, MA: Allyn & Bacon.

Preyer, W. (1973; orig. ed. 1888). *Mind of the child*. New York: Arno Press.

Puckett, M.B. (1994). *Authentic assessment of the young child: Celebrating development and learning*. New York: Macmillan.

Purcell, J.H., & J.S. Renzulli. (1998). *Total talent portfolio: A systematic plan to identify and nurture gifts and talents*. Mansfield, CT: Creative Learning Press Inc.

Purkey, W.W. (1999). *Creating safe schools through invitational education*. ERIC Clearinghouse and at **www.ed.gov/databases/ERIC_Digests/ed435946.html**

Quilliam, S. (1994). *Child watching: A parent's guide to children's body language*. London: Ward Lock.

Robertson, J., & J. Robertson. (1967–71). *Young children in brief separation* (Videocassette series). London: Tavistock Institute of Human Relations.

Rose, V. (1985, November). Detecting problems with growth development charts. *Nursery World*.

Sacks, P. (2000). *Standardized minds: The high price of America's testing culture and what we can do to change it*. Cambridge, MA: Perseus Books.

Sax, G. (1997). *Principles of educational and psychological measurement and evaluation* (4th ed.). Belmont, CA: Wadsworth.

Schermann, Ada. (1990). Learning. In I. Doxey (ed.), *Child care and education: Canadian dimensions*. Scarborough, ON: Nelson.

Schlank, C.H., & B. Metzger. (1989). *A room full of children: How to observe and evaluate a preschool program*. New York: Rochester Association for Young Children.

Schwartz, S. & G. Chance. (1999). Why focus on children? Environmental contaminants and the special susceptibility of children. In *Research Connections Canada 2: Supporting children and families*. Ottawa, ON: Canadian Child Care Federation.

Shepard, L.A. (1994). The challenges of assessing young children appropriately. *Phi Delta Kappan* 76(3), 206–12.

Sheridan, M.D. (rev. and updated by M. Frost & A. Sharma). (1997). *From birth to five years: Children's developmental progress*. London: Routledge.

———. (1975). *The developmental progress of infants and young children* (3rd ed.). London: Her Majesty's Stationery Office.

Shinn, M.W. (1975; orig. ed. 1900). *The biography of a baby*. New York: Arno Press.

Shipley, D. (1994). Learning outcomes: Another bandwagon or a strategic instrument of reform? *Educational Strategies* 1(4), 3.

———. (1997, Spring). Play—for development and for achieving learning outcomes. *Interaction*. Ottawa, ON: Canadian Child Care Federation.

Shore, R. (1997). *Rethinking the brain: New insights into early development*. New York: Families and Work Institute.

Simpson, E. (1972). *The classification of educational objectives in the psychomotor domain*. Washington, DC: Prentice Hall.

Southern Early Childhood Association. (n.d.) *Early childhood assessment* (Special series of reprints from *Dimensions of Early Childhood*). Little Rock, AR: SECA.

Spady, W. (1977). Competency-based education: A bandwagon in search of a definition. *Educational Researcher* 6 (1), 9–14.

Spitz, R.A. (1965). *The first year of life: A psychoanalytic study of normal and deviant development of object relations*. New York: International Universities Press.

Steiner, R. (1982; orig. ed. 1924). *The roots of education*. London: Rudolf Steiner Press.

Steinhauer, P.D. (1996). *The primary needs of children: A blueprint for effective health promotion at the community level*. Working paper for the Promotion/Prevention Task Force, Sparrow Lake Alliance, Toronto.

Sunseri, R. (1994). *Outcome-based education: Understanding the truth about education reform*. Sisters, OR: Multnomah Books.

Tindal, G.A., & D.B. Marston. (1990). *Classroom-based assessment: evaluating instructional outcomes*. Columbus, OH: Merrill Publishing.

Toronto Observation Project. (1980). *Observing children through their formative years*. Toronto: Board of Education for the City of Toronto.

Tufte, E. (2001). *The visual display of quantitative information* (2nd ed.). Cheshire, CT: Graphics Press.

Tyler, L.E. (1965). *The psychology of human differences* (3rd ed.). New York: Appleton-Century-Crofts.

Van Manen, M. (1990). *Researching lived experience: Human science for an action sensitive pedagogy*. London, ON: The Althouse Press.

Vista School District. (2002). Critical Assessment Worksheet. Vista School District, Newfoundland & Labrador, at **www.k12.nf.ca/vista/schooldevelopment/internalcriteriaas.html**

Vygotsky, L.S. (1978). *Mind in society: The development of psychological processes*. Cambridge, MA: Harvard University Press.

Waterloo County Board of Education. (1993). *Invitations to literacy learning*. Waterloo, ON.

Watson, J.B. (1930). *Behaviorism*. Chicago: University of Chicago Press.

Weitzman, E. (1992). *Learning language and loving it: A guide to promoting children's social and language development in early childhood settings*. Toronto: Hanen Centre.

Whitbread, N. (1972). *The evolution of the nursery-infant school: A history of infant and nursery education in Britain, 1800–1970*. London: Routledge & Kegan Paul.

Wiggins, G. (1996/97). Practice what we preach in designing authentic assessments. *Educational Leadership* 54(4).

Wilson, L.C., L. Douville-Watson, & M.A. Watson. (1995). *Infants and toddlers: Curriculum and teaching* (3rd ed.). Albany, NY: Delmar.

Wortham, S.C. (1992). *Childhood, 1892–1992*. Wheaton, MD: Association for Childhood Education International.

———. (1996). *The integrated classroom: The assessment–curriculum link in early childhood education*. Englewood Cliffs, NJ: Merrill Publishing.

———, A. Barbour, & B. Desjean-Perrotta. (1998). *Portfolio assessment: A handbook for preschool and elementary educators*. Olney, MD: Association for Childhood Education International.

YMCA. (Susanne T. Eden and Lorrie Huggins). (2001). *YMCA Playing to Learn: A guide to quality care and education of young children: A YMCA guide to quality care and education of young children*. Toronto: YMCA of Greater Toronto.

Zitterkopf, R. (1994). A fundamentalist's defense of OBE. *Educational Leadership* 51(6).

Index